EARLY REVIEWS

Kirkus Reviews writes:

"Historians will find a trove of useful data on everyone associated with the Company, along with appendices reprinting important documents, charters, and Dudley's evocative letter describing the deaths and hardships endured by colonists. Cotton's prose is lucid and workmanlike, and he includes raucous anecdotes—Harvard's first professor was prosecuted for beating students with a cudgel, and his wife accused of feeding them hasty pudding adulterated with goat dung—as well as piquant biographical sketches like The transformative love [John] Cotton experienced in marriage filled his sermons with connubial and oral images full of sexual innuendo."

Eve LaPlante, author of "American Jezebel" writes: "A gap in our shared knowledge has recently been filled by Barry Arthur Cotton in his book, A Tale of Two Bostons."

A TALE OF TWO BOSTONS

A TALE OF TWO BOSTONS
EMERGENCE OF THE BOSTON MEN

BARRY ARTHUR COTTON

scéalta
sinsear
HERITAGE PRESS

A TALE OF TWO BOSTONS
The Emergence of the Boston Men
© 2025 by Barry Arthur Cotton

All rights reserved.

No part of this book may be reproduced, stored in a retrieval system, or transmitted in any form or by any means—electronic, mechanical, photocopying, recording, or otherwise—without the prior written permission of the publisher.

Published under the imprint Scéalta Sinsear Heritage Press
Austin, Texas, USA
https://bacotton.online/

Hardcover ISBN: 978-1-953317-02-5
Paperback ISBN: 978-1-953317-01-8
eBook ISBN: 978-1-953317-00-1
Library of Congress Control Number: 2025923673

Library of Congress Cataloging-in-Publication Data
Cotton, Barry Arthur, 1947–
A Tale of Two Bostons : the emergence of the Boston Men
Barry Arthur Cotton.
pages cm. — (New England Origins ; volume 1)
Includes bibliographical references and index.
ISBN 978-1-953317-02-5 (hardcover)
ISBN 978-1-953317-01-8(paperback)
ISBN 978-1-953317-00-1 (ebook)

I. Title. II. Series: New England Origins ; v. 1.
Printed in Peterborough - Cambridgeshire - UK
First Edition

1. Massachusetts—History—Colonial period, ca. 1600–1775.
2. Boston (Mass.)—History—Colonial period.
3. Puritans—Massachusetts—History.
4. Massachusetts Bay Company—History.
5. Boston (Lincolnshire, England)—History.
6. United States—History—Colonial period, ca. 1600–1775.

All original illustrations created by the author and/or photos taken by the author are protected under copyright and may not be reproduced or distributed without explicit permission. Other visual materials, including historical photographs, paintings, engravings, and lithographs—are believed to be in the public domain in their country of origin, where copyright terms have expired (typically the life of the artist plus 70–100 years or fewer). As applicable, the author has made every effort to use images:

- Published before January 1, 1925, and/or
- Registered before January 1, 1925 with the U.S. Copyright Office, and
- Free of known copyright restrictions in the United States.

Some images in this volume were generated or enhanced using AI-assisted tools using public domain artworks, seed portraits, and visual research in 16th- and 17th-century costume, painting, and print culture. These works are intended as historically inspired reconstructions or visualizations and are not intended to infringe upon any existing rights. Photographic reproductions of public domain paintings and prints, when not themselves creative reinterpretations, are not considered original works and are typically not subject to copyright. Every reasonable effort has been made to identify and contact any rights holders of visual material.

If you are a rights holder and believe a copyright has been inadvertently infringed, please contact the author via the following website: https://bacotton.online/contact/

*This series is dedicated to
the inhabitants of Bostons: Old & New.
And to the memory of John & Judy Cammack,
who welcomed me to old Boston with open arms.
Their love of history for both Bostons inspired
me to tell the story of the Two Bostons.*

CONTENTS

Forword by Eve LaPlante	xiii
Author's Preface	xvii
Acknowledgments	xix

THE BOSTON MEN

Prologue	3
Boston's Vicar	13
Boston's Congregation	23
Puritanism & Calvinism	27
The 1626 Forced Loan	37
Clinton Earls of Lincoln	49
Clinton Marriages	61
Planters & Adventurers	75
City on a Hill	91

THE MASSACHUSETTS BAY COMPANY

FOUNDING FACTORS

Political Strife	123
Religious Strife	143
Family Ties	153
School Ties	179

FOUNDING FACTIONS

Colonial Masterminds	183
Godly Allies	187
Dorchester Remnants	191
London Tradesmen	195

FOUNDING STORY

Timeline	201
Membership	211
Royal Charter	243

APPENDICIES

Boston Men's Motives	255
Tudor Origins of Massachusetts	259
Dudley's Letter to the Countess of Lincoln	269
Charter of the Great Council for New England	289
Grants under the Great Council for New England	313
Petition of Right	357
Massachusetts Bay Company Royal Charter	367
Cambridge Agreement	391
Humble Request	395
James I & Witchcraft	399
James I - Published Works	403
Thomas Knyvett & the Gunpowder Plot	407
Notes	411
Bibliography	449
Index	467
Timeline	489
About the Author	505
The New England Origins Series	507

FORWARD

by Eve LaPlante

Few Americans have heard of the English city of Boston or its foundational role in American history. This gap in our shared knowledge has recently been filled by Barry Arthur Cotton in his book, *A Tale of Two Bostons,* an in-depth account of a group of Englishmen who banded together 400 years ago to found a company based on principles that are now bedrocks of the American identity. The early American immigrants brought to life in this book are not only the ancestors of millions of contemporary Americans but also important figures in our nation's history.

More than 150 years before the American Revolution, these English immigrants were deeply suspicious of taxation without representation, and willing to make petitions to and file grievances against their rulers. In the 1620s, when the English king imposed on them a forced loan, imprisoning those who did not pay, these men joined together in support of a Petition of Right stating that taxation required the consent of parliament. Through clever collaboration with members of Parliament, they obtained a royal charter to establish a "new plantation" called Massachusetts Bay Colony. A year later, they crossed the Atlantic to create a new kind of government and society in New England, which evolved into modern democracy.

Cotton's book explores the roots of aspects of our nation's political spirit and dispels some of our nation's origin myths. It counters the conventional belief that John Winthrop was the sole central figure in establishing the Massachusetts Bay Colony by demonstrating the crucial roles played by Simon Bradstreet, Isaac Johnson, Richard Bellingham and many others from Lincolnshire, England.

The book convincingly downplays the role of religious persecution in founding New England and describes both Plymouth Colony and Massachusetts Bay Colony as for-profit enterprises. "Despite the commonly held view that America was founded by those fleeing religious persecution," Cotton writes, "the Massachusetts Bay Company was established as a for-profit enterprise. The Mayflower story better fits a religious persecution scenario, but it, too, was established as a for-profit enterprise. Of the Mayflower's 102 passengers, only 37 were pilgrim separatists." Most were adventurers, merchants, entrepreneurs, and their families and servants.

A Tale of Two Bostons is refreshingly factual, referencing more than 230 sources, 70 of them primary. Based on Cotton's many years of research in England and New England, it presents personal and sometimes intimate details of important political and historical events. Cotton reveals the ways in which Lord Saye & Sele manipulated the writing of the royal charter, and the central role played by one of King James I's homosexual lovers, the Duke of Buckingham, in our nation's founding. Cotton explains how the Earl of Lincoln's circle of friends fueled investment in the Massachusetts Bay Company, and the importance of a Cambridge University friendship (between Isaac Johnson and William Blaxton) in the settlers' decision to locate their main town on the peninsula that became Boston, Massachusetts. The book's appendices include all the primary documents described in the narrative, including James I's 1620 charter to the Council for New England "to make several plantations in the Parts of America," the 1628 Petition of Right, and the 1629 Royal Charter of the Massachusetts Bay Company, which the king soon revoked but never got back.

As a biographer of important figures in colonial America, I have known Barry for more than two decades, during which we have worked together on both sides of the Atlantic to increase public awareness of seventeenth-century New England.

FORWORD BY EVE LAPLANTE

Barry and I met in 2003 at a meeting of the Partnership of Historic Bostons, a non-profit partnership between people in Boston, Massachusetts, and Boston, Lincolnshire, England, aimed at highlighting the histories of the two Bostons and filling the gap in American historical memory for the 150 years between the founding of colonial Boston and the Revolution. In addition to sharing a commitment to promoting public understanding of our founders, Barry and I are distant cousins through our mutual ancestor, the influential Puritan minister John Cotton.

John Cotton is a central character in this book and in my biography of another ancestor, *American Jezebel: The Uncommon Life of Anne Hutchinson, the Woman who Defied the Puritans* (HarperCollins, 2004, 2005). Although not as well known today as his grandson Cotton Mather, John Cotton was the seventeenth-century equivalent of a rock star. A spell-binding preacher who kept his congregation in Boston, Lincolnshire, England, on its feet for hours several times a week, he preached Puritanism for two decades during which most of his Puritan colleagues were arrested, tried, and silenced by the Church of England. The Reverend Cotton was so good at evading church censure that he could explain away the nonconformity of his congregation even when it entailed smashing statues and stained-glass windows in St. Botolph's Church, as it did in 1621. Not until 1633, when a new, deeply anti-Puritan Archbishop of Canterbury issued a warrant for his arrest and sent soldiers to Boston to bring him to London to be tried, did John Cotton go into hiding and, disguised as a tradesman, sail to the New World, where his parishioners named the new Boston in his honor.

In 2019, Barry Cotton and I were both invited to Boston, Lincolnshire, England, a market town on the North Sea about five hours north of London by car, to speak at a history symposium, *From the Stump to the Statue of Liberty*. (The Stump is the nickname of St. Botolph's Church.)

FOREWORD BY EVE LAPLANTE

At the symposium, chaired by the BBC presenter Dr. Jonathan Foyle and attended by more than 200 people, Barry introduced the people described in this book, while I spoke about Anne Hutchinson and *American Jezebel*. Barry and I both contributed chapters to *BOSTON: the Small Town with a Big Story* (Chris Cook, 2019, 2023), a collaborative work of history about Boston, Lincolnshire, England, that was launched that day and is now in its second edition.

My other writing on American history includes the Massachusetts Book Award-winning *Salem Witch Judge: The Life and Repentance of Samuel Sewall* (HarperCollins, 2007, 2008), *Marmee & Louisa: The Untold Story of Louisa May Alcott and Her Mother* (Simon & Schuster, 2012, 2013), *My Heart is Boundless: Writings of Abigail May Alcott* (Free Press, 2012), *Who Needs a Statue?* (Tilbury House, 2024), and many essays and articles.

Now, as our nation commemorates its 250th birthday and the city of Boston, Massachusetts, approaches its 400th, this book is especially timely. The growing hunger to understand our nation's past is demonstrated again and again, as when 20,000 people visited Boston for the 250th anniversary of the Boston Tea Party, and even more gathered to view the PBS documentary, "The American Revolution." We seek answers to questions such as: Who created our democracy, and how? Where did our notions of liberty and freedom arise, and how did they evolve?

A Tale of Two Bostons addresses these and other important questions.

AUTHOR'S PREFACE

My historical narrative journey began in 2002 when I first visited Boston, Lincolnshire, England, where my 7th great-grandfather, the Rev. John Cotton, lived from 1612 to 1633. During an Evensong Service at St. Botolph's Church, a chance encounter with the curate led to a meeting with Boston's former mayor, Judy Cammack. Later that year, I met up with Judy and her husband, John, in Boston, USA, and was invited to join the *Partnership of Historic Bostons*. Through the *Partnership*, I met several accomplished authors, including Eve LaPlante, Robert Allison, and Francis Bremer, whose works inspired me to delve more deeply into the life of John Cotton. While researching Cotton's life, I came across ten men from Boston, Lincolnshire, who banded together in 1627 to form a venture that evolved into the Massachusetts Bay Company. Upon discovering their story had never been told, I knew I had to document it. My decision to self-publish stemmed from the advice I received after winning the 2017 *Writers League of Texas Manuscript Contest for Nonfiction*. My prize was admission to the *WLT Agents & Editors Conference* and meeting the judge the nonfiction contest. Despite liking my work, I was told that finding a publisher would difficult since 17th-century history was a small niche market. So I decided to 'handcraft' my books using *Vellum Press* and attempting to master graphic design. My first venture is a series titled *New England Origins*, focusing on 17th-century Anglo-American history with illustrations and quotes from 212 primary sources and 226 secondary sources that document a compelling story, told in the four books detailed at the end of *A Tale of Two Bostons* in:

THE NEW ENGLAND ORIGINS SERIES

ACKNOWLEDGMENTS

I would like to thank all those in both Bostons whose warm hospitality has supported me for 25 years.

First of all, my deep appreciation to Eve LaPlante for graciously writing the forward to my book and for her dedication to the history of the two Bostons.

Gratitude to Dr. Sarah Bendall, Archive and Library Fellow at Emmanuel College, Cambridge University for hosting me on a tour of Emmanuel College and showing me John Cotton's signature in the college archives in April 2005.

To those in Boston, Lincolnshire gratitude to the co-founders of the Partnership of the Historic Bostons, Mayor Judy Cammack and her husband John and their family for hosting me on numerous occasions and to the Boston Mayors I have met since.

Gratitude to St. Botolph's Church (The Stump) and former Vicar; Robin Whitehead, Polly Wilkinson and Allison Fairman.

Gratitude to Boston Borough Councilors Richard and Alison Austin and to everyone at Blackfriars, the Guildhall and Fydell House, and Boston's historian, Neil Wright, former chair of the Society for Lincolnshire History and Archaeology.

To those in Boston, Massachusetts, I want to thank the co-founder of the Partnership of the Historic Bostons, Will Holton, president emeritus, former professor of sociology at Northeastern University. To Rose Doherty, president emerita of the Partnership, fellow of the Massachusetts Historical Society, and member of the Colonial Society of Massachusetts. (*Rose graciously reviewed my parts of my book.*)

To Stephen Kenney, PhD from Boston University and director of the Commonwealth Museum of Massachusetts. And to Stephen Busby, Charles Butts, and the memory of Ralph Buonopane and Miriam Butts.

I would also like to thank those academics and authors who have helped and inspired me.

To Robert Allison, President of the Colonial Society of Massachusetts and professor of the history at Suffolk University who also teaches the history of Boston at Harvard Extension School.

To Francis Bremer, Professor Emeritus and former Chair of the History Department at Millersville University, who has published numerous books dealing with puritanism in Old and New England.

To David Hall, Professor Emeritus at the Harvard Divinity School, who introduced me to Doug Winiarski, who is writing a book about my 5th great grandfather, Josiah Cotton.

To Doug Winiarski, Professor of Religious & American Studies at the University of Richmond, who kindly reviewed the first draft of my book and provided me with valuable feedback.

Gratitude to the former pastor of the First Church in Boston, Stephen Kendrick, and the First Church for their ongoing support of the Partnership of Historic Bostons.

In memory of John Winthrop Sears (1930–2014), former member of the Massachusetts House of Representatives and sheriff of Suffolk County, Rhodes Scholar and graduate of Harvard University, who advocated that: *"Boston UK is the mother of Boston USA"*

And finally, to Fred Meyer, Board Member of the Partnership of Historic Bostons, who—when I first presented the story of two Bostons in 2006—encouraged me by saying:

"Only you can tell this story! You have to publish it!"

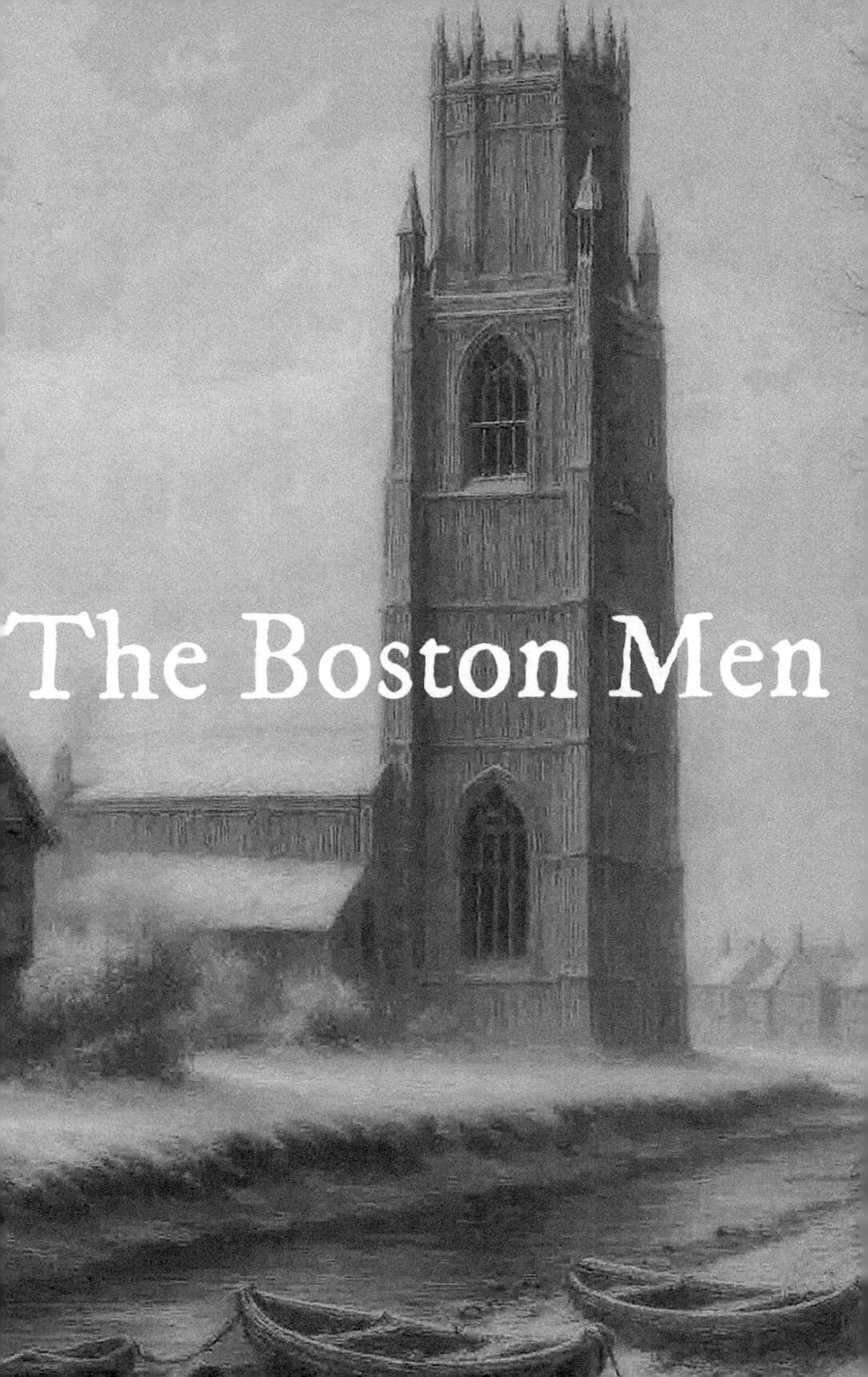
The Boston Men

PROLOGUE

Book One of the New England Origins Series tells the little known story of how a group of men from Boston, Lincolnshire, England, united in response to Stuart tyranny to form the Massachusetts Bay Company. Political strife following James I's ascension to the throne and his insistence on the divine right the king fostered resentment among Parliamentarians—particularly in Lincolnshire, where the Forced Loan Charles I imposed in 1626 was seen as a violation of their rights as Englishmen. Religious tensions—fueled by Archbishop Laud's High Church reforms and the persecution of dissenters—further galvanized opposition to church and crown. The Boston Men emerged defiant, opposed Stuart tyranny, were arrested and imprisoned. When released, they networked with Cambridge-educated clergy, like John Cotton and John Preston, and noble peers in the House of Lords like Lord Saye & Sele and the Earl of Warwick, to transcend class and regional boundaries by uniting nobles, MPs, gentry, and tradesmen against the tyranny that ended in civil war and regicide. Doing so they formed a transatlantic alliance rooted in shared political and religious ideals that planted the seeds of dissent that gave birth to the USA a century and a half later.

PROLOGUE

During what is known as the *Great Migration*, 20,000 individuals migrated from England to New England from the 1620 departure of the *Mayflower* to the 1640 opening of England's Long Parliament.[1]

- 90% of this migration occurred after 1630 in response to the founding of the Massachusetts Bay Colony.[2]
- 80% occurred after 1633 in response to William Laud's elevation to Archbishop and his religious persecutions.[3]

The Massachusetts Bay Company anchored at Salem in 1630.

Despite the importance of the *Great Migration* to American history, Cambridge-trained historian David Cressy argues that it is largely irrelevant to most British historians and had a minimal impact on the history of England.

> *The movement of people across the Atlantic has naturally commanded more attention in American than in English history. The thousands who sailed to New England in the 1630s, forming what Americans know as 'the great migration,' represented less than half of one percent of the population of England.*
>
> *Indifference to American affairs has, to a large extent, been transferred to modern British historians. It is rare that one finds references to America, New England, or Massachusetts in the indexes of modern texts and monographs about Stuart England.*[4]

PROLOGUE

Yet in 1887, eminent Anglo-American historian Pishey Thompson wrote,

> There was probably no town in England that sent forth so many of its best citizens to the great work of colonizing America as this of Boston.[5]

"*The great work of colonizing America,*" to which Pishey Thomson refers, came about after men from Boston, Lincolnshire, were imprisoned in 1626 for defying the forced loan imposed by Charles I.

Discontent with the Stuarts began when Elizabeth I died without an heir, and James VI of Scotland assumed England's throne as James I. Never before in England's history had a Scot occupied its throne.

James married his daughter, Elizabeth Stuart, to Frederick V, the Elector Palatine, in February 1613.[6] Five years later, Frederick invaded Bohemia, deposed Ferdinand II, the Holy Roman Emperor, and ignited the *Thirty Years' War*.

As a result, England's Parliament was forced to support James Stuart's son-in-law in the most destructive war in European history.[7]

The *Thirty Years' War* drained England's treasury and proved disastrous to James' son, Charles, who by any means was not well suited for the throne and never would have been king if it were not for the death of his older brother, Henry, in 1612.[8]

Elizabeth Stuart of the Palatine

Charles stood a mere five feet four inches tall, was physically frail, and had a severe stutter.[9]

PROLOGUE

James I with Charles I (left) & Frederick V, Elector Palatine & Elizabeth (right)

In 1626, Charles suspended Parliament to block the impeachment of his late father's homosexual lover, the Duke of Buckingham.

Doing so, Charles forfeited an opportunity to secure funds to support his uncle, Christian IV of Denmark, in the *Thirty Years' War*.[10] Months later, Christian IV was defeated at the *Battle of Lutter*. In response, Charles imposed a forced loan on England to support Denmark and assured the Danish ambassador that[11]

> *he would render his uncle every assistance, even at the risk of his own crown and hazarding his life.*[12]

As a result, over twenty years of unprecedented political and religious strife followed that culminated in civil war, the abolition of the monarchy, and the only regicide in England's history—the beheading of Charles I.

PROLOGUE

The Lincolnshire Fens

Though the town of Boston enjoyed relative autonomy isolated in the Lincolnshire fens, this autonomy ended when its residents galvanized in opposition to the king's attempt to extort money from them. The *Boston Men* who resisted the Forced Loan were imprisoned rather than submit to the crown's tyranny.

Once released, they encouraged like-minded individuals to join a venture to colonize New England. In 1628, they obtained the *Rosewell Gran*t that enabled the formation of the New England Company, which emerged a year later as the *Massachusetts Bay Company*.

In 1630, the Massachusetts Bay Company invited Rev. John Cotton to preach a farewell sermon as two hundred and ten individuals departed England for Massachusetts. Twenty-one of the fleet's passengers were members of Cotton's Boston congregation.

The fleet consisted of eleven ships that set sail from Southampton on April 8th, 1630, and anchored at Salem, Massachusetts, between June 12th and July 6th, 1630.[13]

As Archbishop Abbot lay on his deathbed in 1633, William Laud, then Bishop of London, issued a warrant for John Cotton to appear before the *Star Chamber*.[14]

PROLOGUE

To avoid being prosecuted, Cotton fled England for Massachusetts with fifty-two of his parishioners. Edward Hutchinson and his family from Alford, twenty-five miles northwest of Boston, joined him.

The following year, Anne Hutchinson and thirty-two individuals from Alford followed Cotton to Massachusetts.

Seventeen individuals from Boston joined Hutchinson, including the Earl of Lincoln's sister, Lady Susan, her husband, John Humfrey, and Richard Bellingham, who later served as a ten-term governor of Massachusetts.

Ten Massachusetts Bay Company founding members were among the first to migrate from Boston, Lincolnshire.

Four of the ten (*Bradstreet, Bellingham, Dudley, and Leveret*) were repeatedly elected and reelected governor or deputy governor for the fifty-seven years that the Massachusetts Bay Company existed.[15]

BOSTON MEN	Governor	Dep Gov	Assistant	Total
Bradstreet	8	0	48	56
Bellingham	10	13	19	42
Dudley	4	13	6	23
Leverett	6	2	8	16
Pelham	0	0	8	8
Coddington	0	0	7	7
Hough	0	0	1	1
Johnson	0	0	1	1
Total Years	28	28	98	154

Given that most people are unaware that Boston, England, even exists, it is little wonder that its role in helping found New England has yet to be fully recognized on either side of the Atlantic.

LINCOLNSHIRE'S GREAT MIGRATION 1620 - 1640

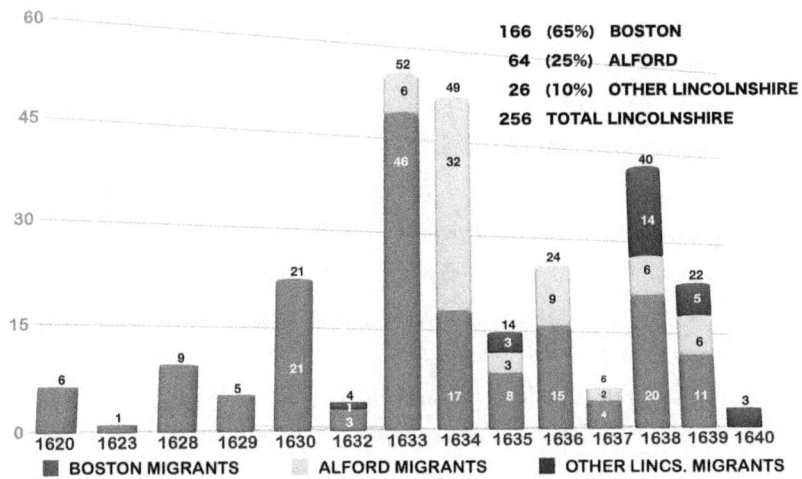

During the *Great Migration,* ninety percent (90%) of migrants from Lincolnshire came from two towns: Boston (65%) and Alford (25%).[16]

Forty percent (40%) of this migration occurred during 1633 & 1634.

Despite their having served the Massachusetts Bay Company for its entire existence, an internet search of the *Boston Men* yields no results, and a search of the Massachusetts Bay Company fails any mention the *Boston Men.*

Rose-Troup is one of the few authors to mention the *Boston Men.* Her motive, however, seems to have been to denigrate their role in founding the Massachusetts Bay Company.

> The Boston Men, who may be identified with the Earl of Lincoln's family or with John Cotton's church, had not become fully-fledged Adventurers before 2 March 1629.[17] In view of this fact, we are astounded by the statement made by Dudley in these words, "About the year 1627 some friends being together in Lincolnshire, fell into some discourse about New England and the planting of the Gospel there; and after some deliberations, we imparted our reasons by

letters and messages to some in London and the West Country where it was likewise deliberately thought upon, and at length with the often negotiation so ripened that in the year 1628, we procured a patent." *He (Dudley) then proceeds to claim that* "We sent out Endecott to begin a plantation with those we had sent from Dorchester." *It can only be described as preposterous that he should claim that those in Lincolnshire had introduced the religious element, ascribing the honour and glory to his friends. Yet these upstart Lincolnshire men claimed all the glory attaching to the task at least four years earlier, and it was not until after the favorable report of Endecott that their spirits began to be awakened to the consideration of personal emigration to a colony already established and promising to prove successful.*[18]

In a review of Rose-Troup's work, Stewart Mitchell concluded that her acrimonious rejection of the *Boston Men* stemmed from an obsession with proving that Rev. John White "*laid the cornerstone of the Massachusetts Bay Colony.*"[19]

By contrast, historian Michael Winship says,

> *The Massachusetts Bay Company emerged out of agitation against the Forced Loan in Lincolnshire. This agitation has been called* 'one of the most effective protests against Crown policy in the entire pre-Civil War period.'[20] *The Earl of Lincoln, Theophilus Clinton, active in the organization of the Massachusetts Bay Company, spearheaded the protest.*[21] *His confederates included the ministers-to-be of Salem and Boston, Samuel Skelton and John Cotton, and future Massachusetts assistants Atherton Hough, Isaac Johnson (the earl's son-in-law), William Coddington, Richard Bellingham, and John Humfrey, along with future Massachusetts governor Thomas Dudley, who was Lincoln's steward.*[22]

PROLOGUE

Despite Rose-Troup's refusal to recognize the *Boston Men's* role in establishing the Massachusetts Bay Company, she did acknowledge that the company's early records have often been misinterpreted, and its early history remains largely unexplored.

> *The early history of the Massachusetts Bay Company has never fully been elucidated. The few records remaining have frequently been misinterpreted, causing confusion so that the course of events is not clearly understood.*[23]

In his *History of Grants Under the Great Council for New England,* S.F. Haven states that the Earl of Warwick and Ferdinando Gorges, who headed the Council for New England, are primarily responsible for this confusion.

> (They) *conducted their affairs in a confused manner from the beginning, and the grants they made were so inaccurately described and interfered so much with each other as to occasion difficulties and controversies, some of which are not yet ended.*[24]

Over one hundred and fifty years have passed since Samuel Haven presented these findings to the Massachusetts Historical Society, and it has been nearly one hundred years since Frances Rose-Troup published *The Massachusetts Bay Company and Its Predecessors.*

What follows is a meticulously researched story of two Bostons and the *Boston Men:*

- who were imprisoned for opposing the 1626 *Forced Loan,*
- who established the Massachusetts Bay Company, and
- who manipulated a Royal Patent to ensure their autonomy in New England.

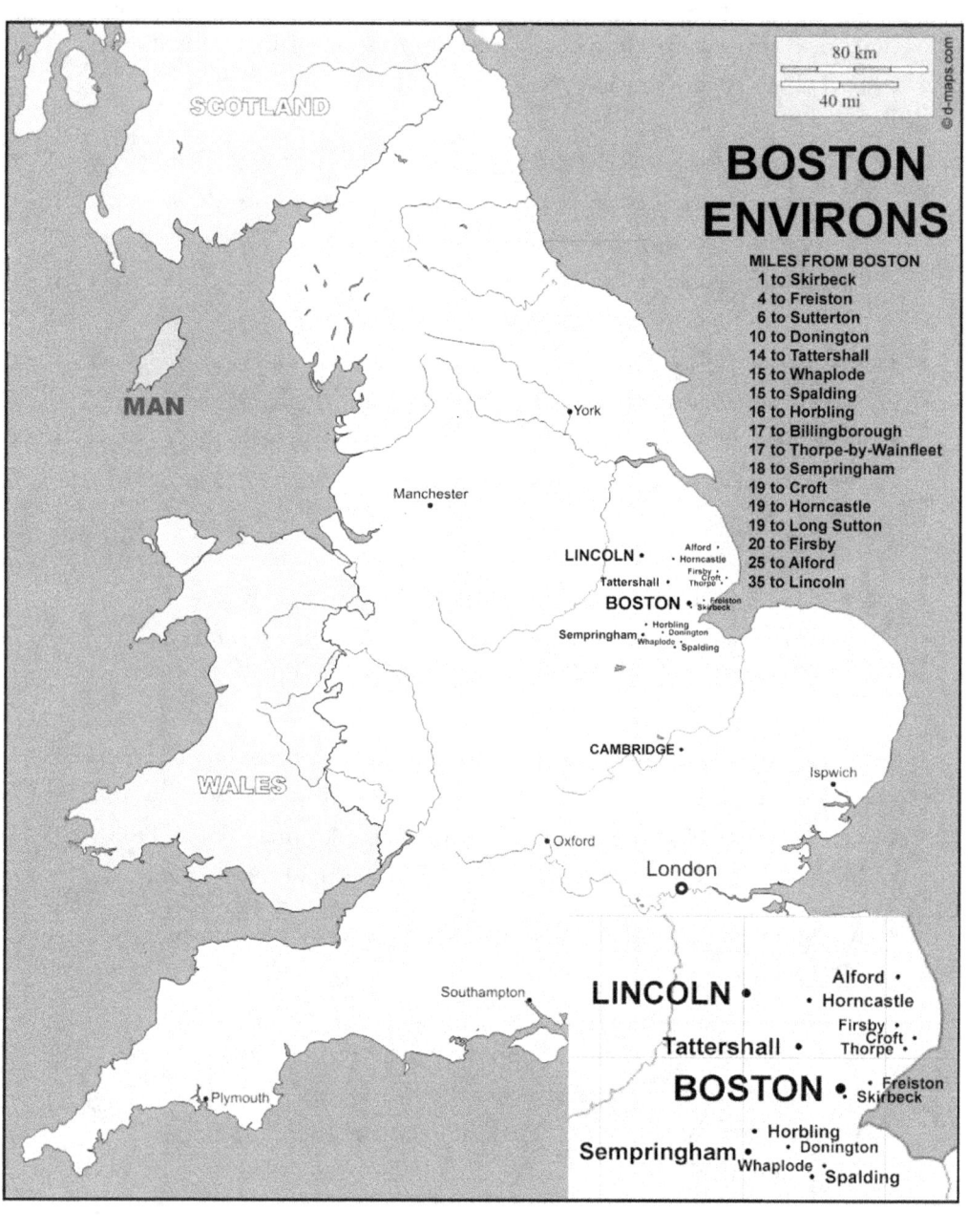

BOSTON'S VICAR

John Cotton

When the Borough of Boston elected John Cotton to head their parish in July 1612, they had no way of knowing that to become their new vicar, Cotton's life would be turned completely upside down.

From the heights of Cambridge's academe, where mastery of Greek, Latin, and Hebrew drew praise, Cotton moved deep in the fens of Lincolnshire to head a congregation of farmers and tradesmen incapable of appreciating his linguistic acumen.

Years later, Cotton expressed remorse over the intellectual conceit he suffered upon first arriving in Boston.

A TALE OF TWO BOSTONS

It is a wonder to see, when Scholars are admitted into the Ministry in their young times, how they despise the People, think themselves unmet to condescend to Peasants, but they will rather exercise their Gifts in the University.[1]

The Parish of Boston was formally established in 1486 when the Benedictine Convent of St. Mary at York was named Boston's advowson.[2]

In 1545, Boston was granted a charter and became its own advowson after Henry VIII established the Church of England and dissolved the monasteries. Thereafter, Boston became responsible for selecting and funding its own vicar.[3]

Boston Borough records show that on April 6th, 1612, *Mr. Thomas Wooll, the now vicar of Boston, shall now forthwith be ffreely presented to the Parsonage of Skirbeck.*

The Bishop of Lincoln pressured Wooll to step down for refusing to conform to Archbishop John Whitgift's *Three Articles*.[4]

Rather than surrender his livelihood, Wooll agreed to move to St. Nicholas Church in nearby Skirbeck, and Benjamin Alexander, the mayor's chaplain, *yielded up his place and is chosen vicar.*[5]

Alexander resigned one month later, and Thomas Wooll was asked to head a delegation to Cambridge to identify candidates to replace him as vicar.[6]

In preparation, Wooll contacted two Cambridge worthies, Paul Baynes and Richard Sibbes, to identify potential candidates.

Once at Cambridge, the delegation experienced difficulty from an upstart within their ranks named Peter Baron. Although Baron had been duly elected to Boston's Borough Council in 1609, the other aldermen did not receive him well.[7]

In addition to being French and an Arminian,[8] Baron insisted on being esteemed to the point where, in August 1609, Lord Burghley, the Earl of Exeter, who was a mentor of Baron's father, interceded on his behalf by writing to the mayor of Boston.[9]

> *There are (as I hear) some few of the Aldermen far inferior to the Said Doctor Baron who refuse to give him place. I have there upon thought good hereby to write and advise you that your brethren the Aldermen would avoid further discontentment that he may hold his place in your town and if there is any opposition against him, I pray you send me their names that further action maybe taken to redress them.*[10]

As a result of Burghley's letter, a year later, in 1610, Peter Baron was elected mayor. Though he was no longer mayor in 1612, he was one of four Boston assemblymen assigned to accompany Wooll to Cambridge to select a new vicar.

At the time, the town of Boston was at odds with William Barlow, the Bishop of Lincoln, who viewed the people of Boston as *a factious people who were imbued with the puritan spirit.*[11]

Barlow's opinion was likely influenced by the conflict between Baron's Arminianism and Boston's historical bias toward Calvinism.

Given his strong Arminian views, Peter Baron opposed John Cotton being nominated as Boston's next vicar. Later, Cotton recalled:

> *When I was first called to Boston in Lincolnshire, so it was that Mr. Baron, son of Dr. Baron (the divinity reader of Cambridge, who in his lectures there, first broached that which was then called Lutheranism, since Arminianism.) ... though he were a physitian by profession, (and of good skill in that art,) yet he spent the greatest strength of his studies in clearing and promoting the Arminian tenets.*[12]

Despite Peter Baron's desire for an Arminian vicar, Wooll relied heavily on the recommendations of Paul Baynes and Richard Sibbes, who endorsed Cotton as Boston's next vicar.

The delegation returned with this recommendation, and Cotton was elected Boston's new vicar at the next meeting of the Borough Council on July 5th, 1612.[13]

The Bishop of Lincoln, however, refused to approve of the election.[14]

> *He (Cotton) found some obstruction from the Bishop of the Diocese, which was B. Barlow, who told him he was a young man, and unfit to be over such a factious people.*
>
> *Mr. Cotton, being ingenuous, and undervaluing himself, thought so too and was purposing to return to College again.*[15]

Cotton appears to have accepted Barlow's rejection, as he lacked any pastoral experience and had yet to perform a single baptism, marriage, or funeral.

The training Cotton received at Cambridge University was academic, and though he was renowned for his sermons, Cotton's Cambridge audience was one of the most erudite in England. By contrast, Boston's congregation consisted mainly of farmers and tradesmen, few of whom could read or write.

Undeterred by Bishop Barlow's refusal to endorse Cotton, the Borough of Boston gained his approval by bribing his right-hand man, Simon Biby, aka *Simon & Bribery*.[16]

> *Some of Mr. Cotton's Boston friends, understanding that one Simon Biby was to be spoken with, which was near the Bishop, they presently charmed him; and so the business went on smooth, and Mr. Cotton was a learned man with the Bishop, and he was admitted into the place, after their manner in those days.*[17]

Boston Corporation Minutes state that Cotton occupied the town vicarage as the town's chosen vicar on July 13th, 1612.

> At this assemby the presentatcion to the Vicaridge of Boston is sealed & delivered unto Mr John Cotton Maister of Arts lately chosen viccar of this Burrough.[18]

An amusing but mistaken anecdotal account of Cotton's selection as vicar appears in Cotton Mather's *Magnalia Christi Americana*.[19]

> At this time the mayor of the town, with a more corrupt party, having procured another scholar from Cambridge, more agreeable to them, would needs have him preach before Mr. Cotton: but the church-warden pretending to more of influence upon their ecclesiastical matters, overruled it. However, when the matter came to a vote, amongst those to whom the right of election did charter belong, there was an equi-vote for Mr. Cotton and that other person; only the mayor, who had the casting vote, by strange mistake, pricked for Mr. Cotton. When the mayor saw his mistake, a new vote was urged and granted; wherein it again proved an equi-vote; but the mayor most unaccountably mistook again, as he did before. Extremely displeased hereat, he pressed for a third vote; but the rest would not consent unto it; so the election of upon Mr. Cotton, by the involuntary cast of that very hand which has most opposed it.[20]

By the summer of 1612, John Cotton was twenty-seven years old and perhaps the most distinguished fellow at Cambridge University. Although his life had not been cloistered, he had limited experience outside the university. Cambridge's academic year had regimented Cotton's daily routine for fourteen years. Although he agreed to become Boston's vicar, Cotton was ambivalent as to whether it was the right decision. He had yet to complete his Bachelor of Divinity and knew nothing of Boston or its people.

The prospect of becoming Boston's vicar was as life-altering as entering Cambridge University when he was thirteen. To date, the only real decision he had faced was to transfer from Trinity College to Emmanuel College in 1604 to complete his Master's Degree.[21]

Yet, Cotton knew that if he did not accept Boston's offer, he would violate the trust of his mentors, Richard Sibbes and Paul Baynes, who likely reminded him of Emmanuel College's *De Mora Statute* that required graduates to head a church upon completion of their Bachelor of Divinity Degree.[22]

Although the Borough of Boston made it clear that they sought a Cambridge Divinity Degree graduate who was married, Cotton was single.

As a result, his mentor, Paul Baynes, cajoled Cotton to marry.

> *Settled now at Boston, his dear friend, holy Mr. Bayns, recommended unto him a pious gentlewoman, one Mrs. Elizabeth Horrocks, the sister of Mr. James Horrocks, a famous minister in Lancashire, to become his consort in a married estate.*[23]

Having spent fourteen years at Cambridge, Cotton had to abandon the life of a scholar to marry and become Boston's vicar.

Much to his surprise, however, Cotton later acknowledged that marriage was the seminal moment that marked his rebirth into conjugal bliss.

Early in 1613, Cotton refurbished Boston's vicarage in preparation for married life. In recognition of his efforts, the Boston assembly awarded him a gratuity of twenty pounds.

> *...having been at great chardge with the reparyreing of the vicardidge and being now to take his Degree of Batcheller of Divinity.*[24]

To complete his Bachelor of Divinity Degree, Cotton devoted himself to finishing his thesis in Latin.

However, he was interrupted when the Boston assembly requested Cotton's help to find a headmaster for the Boston Grammar School.

Cotton contacted a student he had tutored at Emmanuel College named BarJonas Dove.[25] Dove matriculated as a sizar in 1609 and was due to receive his bachelor's degree on July 2nd—the same commencement that Cotton was to receive his divinity degree.[26]

The Boston Assembly accepted Cotton's recommendation and elected BarJonas Dove, the schoolmaster of the Free Grammar School of Boston, on July 23, 1613.

> *BarJonas Dove was elected & chose to be schoolmaster of the ffree grammar school of Boston in room & place of Mr John Blackborne late school master there who hath surendred & yieled up his said place of schoole mastershippe.*[27]

Shortly thereafter, two prominent local families requested Cotton's help in placing their sons at Cambridge University.

Cotton again stopped working on his thesis to help facilitate the entry of Anthony Tuckney and Samuel Whiting to Emmanuel College.[28]

Both men cultivated lifelong relationships with Cotton, and both happened to be cousins of his second wife, Sarah Hawkred.[29]

When Cotton fled England for Massachusetts in 1633, Tuckney replaced him as Boston's vicar, and Samuel Whiting later joined Cotton in New England, where he authored the first published account of Cotton's life.[30]

The last week of June 1613, Cotton traveled from Boston to Cambridge to present and defend his Bachelor of Divinity thesis at Emmanuel College.

Cotton's thesis was a *Concio ad Clerum* (Discourse to the Clergy) on Matthew, Chapter 5, Verse 13:

> You are the salt of the earth: but if the salt has lost its savor, how shall it be salted? It is thereafter good for nothing, but to be cast out, and to be trodden under foot of men.[31]

Samuel Whiting wrote of Cotton's thesis presentation and defense.

> In handling of which, both the matter and the rhetorical strains, elegancy of phrase, and sweet and grave pronunciation, rendered him yet more famous in the University. And so did his answering of the Divinity Act in the Schools, though he had a very nimble opponent, Mr. William Chappel by name, who disputed with him.[32]

Chappell was a Fellow at Christ's College and widely acknowledged as the greatest disputant at Cambridge.[33] He was also known as a zealous enemy of Calvinism. Norton says that Cotton performed so well *that in Cambridge, the name of Mr. Cotton was much set by.*[34]

On Tuesday, July 2, 1613, Cotton was awarded his Bachelor of Divinity at Emmanuel College in Cambridge.[35]

The following day, Wednesday, July 3rd, Elizabeth Horrocks and John Cotton were wed at Holy Trinity Church in Balsham, ten miles southwest of Cambridge.[36] Though both were twenty-eight and married late in life, the two were well-matched.

> Here was another Puritan whose marriage had provided him the clearest taste of God's love. Being joined in matrimony to Elizabeth Horrocks, he knew himself simultaneously espoused to Christ. She represented the Beloved to him in such a way that she almost become the bridegroom to his bride. Perhaps more than another Puritan preacher, John Cotton understood his self-identity as a minister to be molded by his role as Christ's bride.[37]

Despite having been *born again* before moving to Boston, Cotton was reborn again through marriage to Elizabeth Horrocks and later proclaimed, *God made that day, a day of double marriage to me!*[38]

> *The crucial erotic constraints that Cotton and other puritans sought, the sharp divisions they drew between spiritual-erotic and libidinal-erotic, indicate not a fear of sexuality but of sexuality unbounded by spirituality.*[39]

The transformative love Cotton experienced in marriage filled his sermons with *connubial and oral images full of sexual innuendo.*[40]

Through his marriage, Cotton's religiosity embraced sexuality. His sermon on *The Song of Songs* likened *the lips of the sensual bride* receiving *the kiss of the Beloved* to that of receiving the revelation of Christ's love.[41]

Cotton described his ministry as *the breasts of Christ from whom the faithful suckle the milk of the Word.*[42] This same metaphor is reflected in the title of his well-known catechism,

> *Milk for Babes Drawn Out of the Breasts of Both Testaments-Chiefly for the Spiritual Nourishment of Boston Babes in Either England.*[43]

This catechism remained in print for over two hundred years in editions of *The New England Primer*—the primary grammar textbook used in America from 1640 to 1850.[44]

With a devoted partner at his side, Cotton's transition from academic to pastoral life was made easy. The Boston community was quick to embrace his wife, and she them.

Elizabeth Horrocks moved to Boston from an area of Lancashire west of Manchester that is home to Wigan, Winstanley, Bolton, and Horrocks Fold.[45]

Her father, Christopher Horrocks, was a fuller from Bolton-le-Moors.[46] Elizabeth's uncle, Alexander Horrocks,[47] was vicar of Deane Parish in nearby Bolton and graduated from Christ's College, Cambridge, with a Master of Arts degree in 1608.[48] While a student at Christ's College, one of his tutors was Paul Baynes.[49] As a result, it is more plausible that Elizabeth Horrocks was introduced to Paul Baynes by her uncle Alexander than by *Mr. James Horrocks, a famous minister in Lancashire,* as Cotton Mather contends in *Magnalia Christi Americana*.[50]

Elizabeth Horrocks had two siblings—Cecily and Thomas.[51] Thomas Horrocks was admitted as a sizar at St. John's College, Cambridge University, in April 1631 and earned his M.A. degree in 1638. In December 1650, he was the executor of his uncle Alexander's Will.[52]

Cecily Horrocks married Gilbert Winstanley of Wigan in September 1595.[53] The two had eight daughters and four sons. In 1627, their daughter, Ellen Winstanley, moved to Boston to live with her aunt Elizabeth.[54] At the time, John Angier, an Emmanuel College graduate, was living and being tutored in the Cotton home.

The following year, in April 1628, John Cotton conducted vows for Ellen Winstanley and John Angier, and a year later, he baptized their son, John Jr.[55] In July 1647, John Angier Jr. entered Cotton's alma mater, Emmanuel College, Cambridge.[56] Due to poor grades, he dropped out and sailed to Boston, Massachusetts, where he married Hannah Aspinwall, the daughter of William Aspinwall, in 1652.[57]

John Angier Jr., his wife, Hannah, and their child moved in with the Cotton family. With Cotton's help, Angier enrolled at Harvard College.[58] Cotton's *Will and Last Testament*, dated September 30, 1652, mentioned Angier, his wife, and child as follows,

> To my cosigne John Angier, with his wife and child (who now live in my house) ye sume of 10£, over and above what moneyes I have laid out for him formerly.[59]

BOSTON'S CONGREGATION

Although Cotton lacked pastoral experience before moving to Boston, during his first year as vicar, he conducted over 60 baptisms, 30 marriages, and 100 burials. Over the next twenty years, he averaged 100 baptisms, 35 marriages, and 120 burials annually.[1]

Being present at his congregation's most significant life events enabled Cotton to integrate intimately with the Boston community. One of the first pastoral duties he performed was the August 1612 baptism of an infant named John Leverett.[2] Three months later, Cotton conducted the burial of the infant.[3] In 1613, a month after his July marriage, Cotton baptized an infant named Jane Leverett—only to preside at her burial the following day.[4]

Both infants were the children of Thomas Leverett and his wife, Anne Fitche.[5] The Leverets married in Boston on October 29, 1610. Thomas Leverett apprenticed with a *"Mr. Anderson"* before becoming a freeman of Boston in 1619. He served as both coroner and alderman of the Borough of Boston and later became a founding member of the Massachusetts Bay Company.[6]

All in all, Cotton baptized thirteen Leverett children, though only three survived to accompany their parents to Massachusetts with Cotton in 1633.[7]

The eldest of the three, John Leverett, later served six terms as Governor of the Massachusetts Bay Colony; his son, John Leverett Jr., served as President of Harvard College from 1708 to 1724.[8]

In October 1613, the Corporation of Boston again sought Cotton's help in overseeing the Boston Grammar School. Earlier in June, he had recommended BarJonas Dove to fill the position of School Master; now, he is asked to approve the selection of a new school usher.[9]

The Boston Grammar School had been endowed by Queen Mary in 1555 and was established for boys who were *bonâ fide* inhabitants of Boston to provide them with instruction in Greek, Latin, French, German, mathematics, and a *sound English education* for fifteen shillings per quarter.

The town required that the master and usher of the school be *graduates of one of the Universities of Cambridge, Oxford, or Durham and members of the Established Church*.[10] As reflected in the minutes of the Corporation of Boston on October 12th, 1613:

> Mr Doctor Baron, Mr Cotton, Mr Ingoldsbye & Mr Wooll or any three of them are appoynted to make triall whether Mr. Hummaby be a fitting & sufficient man to exercise the place of the Usher of the Grammar school within this Borroughe & to confeere with him to know whether he will conforme him selfe to teach after such rules as Mr Dove the cheife Schoolmaster doth.[11]

Helping oversee the Boston Grammar School gave Cotton valuable experience as he established North America's first public school in Boston, Massachusetts, in 1635.

In November 1613, John Cotton conducted wedding vows for Mary Hawkred and Thomas Coney.[12]

By doing so, he united the two Boston families that, over time, became the most prominent in his life.

Mary Hawkred was the daughter of Anthony Hawkred, a prosperous Boston merchant who served as alderman and mayor of Boston. At the time, Mary Hawkred was seventeen. Thomas Coney was twenty-three and a steward of the Borough of Boston and was then filling in as town clerk, while the regularly appointed town clerk, Sir Thomas Middlecott, served a one-year term as mayor.[13]

A decade later, Cotton again conducted marriage vows for the Hawkreds and Coneys when John Coney and Elizabeth Hawkred wed in 1624.[14]

Two generations later, their grandson, John Coney, achieved fame in New England as Boston's leading gold and silversmith. He passed his craft on to a young French Huguenot apprentice named Apollos Rivoire, who, in turn, passed it on to his son, Paul Revere.[15]

Cotton first officiated for the Hawkred family on December 27, 1612 at the burial of their infant son, William.[16] Anthony, his wife, Isabel, and his three daughters, Mary, age sixteen; Sarah, age eleven; and Elizabeth, age seven, attended the burial.

Also in attendance was Hawkred's thirteen-year-old ward, Anthony Tuckney, whose father's Will requested,

> *I desire my godbrother, Mr. Anthony Hawkred, take upon him the education & guardianship of my son.*[17]

Anthony Tuckney was a half-nephew of Hawkred's wife, Isabel. Soon after Cotton moved to Boston, the Hawkred Family solicited help placing young Tuckney at Emmanuel College, Cambridge.

Tragedy struck the Hawkred family in June 1614, when its matriarch, Isabel Hawkred, died soon after giving birth.[18] Cotton baptized their new son, John, and ten days later, buried his mother, Isabel.[19]

A few months later, Cotton baptized Samuel Coney, the firstborn son of Thomas and Mary Coney. Fifteen years later, Cotton facilitated Samuel's matriculation to Emmanuel College, Cambridge.[20]

That same year, in 1614, Thomas Coney was permanently appointed town clerk and remained Boston's town clerk until he resigned in 1647.[21] In March 1629, Coney attended a Massachusetts Bay Company meeting and presented the interest of ten *Boston Men,* who wanted to invest in the company.

Thomas Coney was Cotton's chief contact with the Boston Borough Council and paid Cotton his monthly stipend. Boston Borough records reflect that John Cotton struggled to make ends meet, and in 1614, the Borough Council voted an increase to his annual stipend to £100.

> *Wheras Mr Cotton the Viccar being a Worthye man and well deserving both for his learning & life & his meinteinance of the Viccaridge very small & twoe litte to meinteine him it is thefore agreed that he shall have for the ffurther augmentacon of his liveiry the somme of £20 payed him yearlye dureing the pleasure of this house at ffowre tearmes of the yeare by eaven porcons the ffirst payemt therof to beginn the 24th of June next yearlye out of the ereccon landes parte wherof was hertofore ymployed towardes the Meintenance of a preacher to assiste the Viccar.*[22]

Having officiated at Hawkred baptisms, marriages, and burials for nearly two decades, Cotton eventually married into the Hawkred family in 1632, after his beloved first wife, Elizabeth, died from a virulent form of malaria—known locally as *fen fever* or *tertian ague.*[23]

PURITANISM & CALVINISM

Over time, Cotton's prominence grew, and new parishioners were attracted to St. Botolph's Church in Boston.

> *The thirty-year-old minister whose tastes had been shaped almost exclusively by the academy, whose habit of mind was cautious observation and hesitancy before decision, whose character was shy and patient.[1] His hospitality did exceed all that I ever heard of, his heart and door were ever open to receive all that feared God.[2]*

By 1615, Cotton came to the attention of Richard Neile, the newly appointed Bishop of Lincoln, who sent officials to evaluate his growing popularity.[3] Neile's representatives reported Cotton was:

> *A young man not past some 7 or 8 years Mstr of arts; but, by report a man of great gravity and sanctity of life, a man of rare parts for his learning, eloquent and well spoken ... not only with his parishioners at Boston but with all the Ministery and men of account...willing to submit their judgements to him, in any point of controversie as though he were some extraordinary Paraclete yt could not erre.[4]*

The Bishop's representatives noted, "*there were as many sleepers as wakers, scare any man but sometimes was forced to winke and nod,*" as Cotton's morning sermons lasted six hours and afternoon five. They also reported that Cotton's sermons were *poysned with some errour or other*. As a result, he was sanctioned for non-conformity.[5]

In Cotton's defense, Thomas Leverett swore before the diocesan court in Lincoln that Cotton was a *conformable man* and enabled him to return to the pulpit.

Though Leverett swore to Cotton's being *conformable*, in reality, Cotton feigned conformity and was a Puritan.

The term Puritan was coined in a pejorative sense to brand *extremist* all those who desired to purify the church of all Roman Catholic influence and tradition.

Puritans viewed the remnants of Catholicism, such as music, stained glass, religious images, surplices, and anointed priests, as obstacles to communion with God and interpreted scripture literally. Puritans revered the Old Testament equally with the New.

Puritans were ardent Calvinists and considered themselves *the godly* in the Calvinist sense of being *saints eternally elect*.[6]

Puritans loved sermons, and sermons played an essential role in their worship.

For the Crown, Puritanism's most alarming aspect was its insistence on being free from intervention by the Church of England and its hierarchy of bishops.[7]

During Cotton's early years at Cambridge, he focused on academics to the exclusion of religion. Although students were required to attend daily chapel, Cotton avoided any entanglement in religion until early 1602, when he was required to attend a sermon by William Perkins, head lecturer at St. Andrew the Great.[8]

Perkins was renowned as *the prince of puritan theologians and the most eagerly read.*[9] His works outsold those of John Calvin and all other Puritan writers combined.

Despite Perkins's renown, Cotton was so troubled by his sermon that he rejoiced when Perkins died in October 1602 at forty-four of complications from kidney stones.[10]

Cotton Mather wrote of the incident:

> *When he heard the bell toll for the funeral of Mr. Perkins, his mind secretly rejoiced in his deliverance from that ministry by which his conscience had been so oft beleaguered.*[11]

John Norton's memoir of Cotton also documented his reaction to Perkins' death:

> *The motions and stirring of his heart which then were... suppressed... thinking that if he should trouble himself with matters of religion, according to the light he had received, it would be a hindrance to him in his studies, which then he had addicted himself unto... hearing the bell toll for Mr. Perkins who then lay dying, he was secretly glad in his heart, that he should now be rid of him who had laid siege to and beleaguer'd his heart.*[12]

Like many in 17th Century England who lived in the angst of being damned under Calvin's tenant of *unconditional election*, Cotton seems to have struggled with the possibility of being predestined to damnation.[13]

The Church of England's position on predestination, authored by Archbishop John Whitgift in the Lambeth Articles of 1595, affirmed the Calvinist view that we are preordained to eternal damnation or eternal salvation.[14]

> Between 1560 and 1625, the doctrine of predestination was accepted without question by virtually all of the most influential clergymen in England, puritan and nonpartisan alike.[15]

A few months before Cotton was selected Boston's vicar, Samuel Clarke relates how Richard Sibbes helped resolve Cotton's struggle, as *God had been pleased to convert him.*[16]

> *Hearing Dr. Sibs (then Mr. Sibs) preaching a Sermon about Regeneration...Mr. Cotton saw his own condition fully discovered, which (through Gods mercy) did drive him to a stand, as plainly seeing himself, destitute of true Grace, all his false hopes, and grounds now failing him: and so he lay for a long time, in an uncomfortable despairing way. Thus he continued till it pleased God to let in a word of Faith into his heart, and to cause him to look unto Christ for his healing, which word also was dispensed unto him by the same Doctor Sibs, which begat in him a singular, and constant love to the said Doctor, of whom he was also answerably beloved.*[17]

Cotton Mather relates Cotton's conversion:

> *Mr. Cotton became now very sensible of his own miserable condition before God... that after no less than three year's... the grace of God made him a thoroughly renewed Christian, and filled him with a sacred joy, which accompanied him to the fulness of joy forever. For this cause, as persons truly converted unto God have a mighty and lasting affection for the instruments of their conversion; thus Mr. Cotton's veneration for Dr. Sibs was after this very particular and perpetual: and it caused him to have the picture of the great man in that part of his house where he might oftenest look upon it.*[18]

Not long after Cotton's conversion, John Preston attended one of Cotton's sermons and, in turn, was converted.

> *The famous Dr. Preston, then a fellow of Queen's College in Cambridge, and one of great note in the university, came to hear Mr. Cotton.*
>
> *Before the sermon was ended, he found himself pierced at heart—his heart within him was now struck with such resentments of his own interior state before the God of heaven, that he could have no peace in his soul, till with a wounded soul he had repaired unto Mr. Cotton; from whom he received those further assistances, wherein he became a spiritual father to one of the greatest men of his age.*[19]

In light of Calvinism's tenets, conversion surpassed ordination in importance for Preston, Cotton, Sibbes, and Baynes. Their mutual affirmation of election to sainthood *reinforced each individual's conviction of his election and sustained their advocacy of Calvinist principles.*[20]

Thus, Baynes, Sibbes, Cotton, and Preston formed a successive line of spiritual kinship or *godly mafia* by which *Paul Baynes begat Richard Sibbes, who with William Perkins, begat John Cotton, who begat John Preston, who begat Thomas Shepard, and so on.*[21]

> *Knit together by the thread of grace and a legacy of shared experiences, members of this communion formed a network of friends who were determined to maintain their unity as they labored together to advance the reform cause. Brought together by shared doctrines or temperament, the puritans of early Stuart England formed a fellowship of faith that set them apart from their peers.*[22]

Cotton's conversion by Sibbes and his shift to Sibbes' plain evangelical preaching were affirmed when John Preston knocked on Cotton's door to tell him how his sermon had converted him and enabled *God to speak effectually unto his heart.*[23]

Before his conversion, Preston *thought it below him to be a minister and held the study of Divinity to be a kind of honest silliness.*[24]

Preston matriculated as a sizar to King's College, Cambridge, in 1604 to study music, medicine, and astronomy. In 1606, he transferred to Queen's College, Cambridge, and was appointed a Fellow in 1608. With Cotton's help, he was converted in 1612.[25]

Once converted, Preston embraced Cotton as a friend for life and sent him *near fledgling students for finishing.*[26] Preston regularly visited Cotton in Boston and often preached at St. Andrew's Church in Sempringham, where the Earl of Lincoln's family befriended him.

In particular, Lady Elizabeth, wife of the 3rd Earl of Lincoln, regarded Preston highly and asked him to mentor her son, Theophilus, to prepare for his accession to the 4th Earl of Lincoln.

Preston was reputed to be *the greatest pupil monger in England* and easily facilitated Theophilus Clinton's entry to Cambridge.[27]

Simon Bradstreet, rector of St. Andrew's Church in Horbling, also befriended Preston, who, with Cotton's help, arranged for his son's entry to Emmanuel College, Cambridge. While at Emmanuel College, Preston recommended young Bradstreet to the Earl of Warwick as a tutor for his son.

In 1621, Preston came to the attention of James I's homosexual lover, the Duke of Buckingham, who was both feared and despised by Puritans in Parliament.[28]

Sir Ralph Freeman suggested that Buckingham's popularity with Puritans in Parliament might improve were he to befriend Preston.[29]

As a result, Buckingham charmed Preston in hopes of gaining Puritan support in Parliament. Under Buckingham's patronage, Preston was elevated to unparalleled status.[30]

Over the next two years, Preston was appointed Prince Charles' chaplain, succeeded John Donne as preacher at Lincoln's Inn, and replaced Laurence Chaderton as Master of Emmanuel College, Cambridge University.[31]

Ultimately, a Royal Decree granted Preston a Doctor of Divinity Degree to accompany Sir Arthur Chichester to Cologne, hoping to negotiate a truce in the Thirty Years' War.[32]

After James I died in 1625, Preston and Calvinists in the House of Commons attempted to formalize the results of a Calvinist Synod held in the Dutch Republic at Dort.[33]

Although James supported the 1619 Dort Decrees, the topic had become sensitive due to his son and successor, Charles I's Arminian leanings.

Future Archbishop William Laud lobbied Buckingham to persuade Charles to oppose the Dort Decrees. Calvinists in the House of Commons countered by censuring Richard Montagu for his Arminian work, *Appello Caesarem,* which attacked the Calvinist tenets of predestination and the perseverance of the saints.[34]

In an affront to Calvinists in Parliament, Charles ignored the censure and appointed Montagu one of his chaplains.

He then commissioned five leading Bishops to advise him on resolving the Montagu issue. The five concluded that Montagu's work conformed to the doctrine of the Church of England.

Although most bishops in the Church of England were Calvinists, William Laud presided over a group of Arminian clerics at the coronation of Charles I in February 1626.

Soon after Charles I's coronation, Laud opened Parliament by attacking Calvinists in the House of Commons.

In response, Lord Saye and the Earl of Warwick rallied Puritan support to exploit the Crown's desire to champion Protestantism in Europe by lobbying Buckingham to persuade Charles to condemn Montagu's writings and accept the results of the Dort Synod.

Preston　　　Buckingham　　　Warwick　　　Saye & Sele

When their overtures were again ignored, Warwick demanded that Buckingham redress the issue. In response, Buckingham organized the York House Conference at his residence on February 11, 1626. The Conference opened with Buckingham having stated:

> *Some private speeches had lately passed between my Lord of Warwick and him concerning sundry matters that were said to be erroneous and dangerous in Mr. Montagu's works.*[35]

Despite Buckingham having curried favor with Preston to gain Puritan support in Parliament, he also befriended William Laud and made him his chaplain.

At the York House Conference, Laud's Arminianism was pitted against Preston's Calvinism. By playing both sides against the middle, Buckingham ultimately alienated Preston and the Calvinists in Parliament, whom he had hoped to win over.

Once relations with Buckingham soured, Preston revitalized the *Feoffees for Impropriations* and encouraged Calvinist tradesmen to buy parish livings to install clerics sympathetic to the Puritan cause.[36]

Lord Saye and the Earl of Warwick supported the *Feoffees for Impropriations*.[37] Twelve feoffees were selected based on their experience and representation in the Puritan community—or, as one hostile commentator put it:

> *Four clergymen to persuade men's consciences, four lawyers to draw all conveyances, and four citizens who commanded rich coffers.*[38]

Richard Sibbes, the preacher of Gray's Inn, was the most influential of the twelve feoffees. Six of the twelve feoffees later joined the Massachusetts Bay Company.[39]

- John Davenport, a cleric at St. Stephen's Church in London
- Samuel Browne, a lawyer at Lincoln's Inn from Essex
- John '*Century*' White, a London lawyer at Lincoln's Inn
- Francis Bridges, a saltier from Surrey
- Richard Davis, a vintner from London
- George Harwood, a haberdasher from London

Lord Saye followed the *Feoffees for Impropriations* through his close ties with Sibbes and Davenport. Subsequently, he organized opposition to the aristocratic control of the East India Company by shifting the balance of power from a group of wealthy merchants to the company's small investors.[40]

Under Lord Saye's leadership, East India Company tradesmen and shopkeepers made the following demands:

- Replace annual meetings with quarterly ones,
- Institute quarterly accounting of finances,
- Limit governors' terms to one year.
- Implement term limits for directors, and
- Implement the ballot box at all elections.

The stakes could not have been higher for London's elite merchant class, as they controlled London's wholesale prices, which kept shopkeepers in their place.

The East India Company was an exclusive cartel that fought Lord Saye's attempt to curtail its ability to manipulate wholesale prices.[41]

Warwick and Lord Saye facilitated broad cooperation among Calvinist-leaning gentry and middle- to lower-class Puritans, including London craftsmen and shopkeepers who aspired to become merchants.

By advocating for the plight of craftsmen and shopkeepers, Lord Saye and Warwick popularized the Calvinist cause and attracted many small investors to their colonial ventures.[42]

Warwick, whose Calvinist faith justified the plunder of Spanish gold, provided funds for twenty-two parish livings to support the cause and further countered the Crown's patronage of Arminian clerics by organizing Puritan clergy to do the same.

Though Warwick supported the Puritan cause, he was known to have been a notorious privateer, though many say a pirate, whose colonial exploits were characterized by:

> *The establishment of godly communities, the plundering of Spanish trade, and a return of profits for investors.*[43]

Of all the privateering ships that sailed between 1626 and 1632, it is estimated that more than half sailed for Warwick.[44]

Warwick and his cousin, Sir Nathanial Rich,

> *played an active role—indeed a leadership role—in almost every colonial venture of the early Stuart period, including the Virginia Company.*[45]

THE 1626 FORCED LOAN

When Christian IV of Denmark, Charles I's uncle, was defeated at the Battle of Lutter in 1626, Charles imposed a *Forced Loan* on England to fund his uncle in the Thirty Years' War.

By doing so, Charles unwittingly initiated his eventual downfall.

> With tears standing in his eyes, he assured the Danish ambassador *"that he would render his uncle every assistance, even at the risk of his own crown and hazarding his life."*[1]

Although the town of Boston enjoyed relative autonomy isolated in the Lincolnshire fens, this autonomy ended when the freemen of Boston galvanized in opposition to the king's attempt to extort money from them.

The Forced Loan did not impact all English shires with equal force. Some counties complied quickly, hoping to avoid the king's displeasure. Others sank into a sullen submission born of exhaustion.

However, the loan touched something deeper than purse or pride in Lincolnshire's fenlands. In market towns tied together by kinship and trade and in parishes shaped by the preaching of ministers like John Cotton, it awakened an old instinct: that the liberties of Englishmen were not gifts from kings but inheritances from law.

Boston men had long memories. Their resistance to the king's demands did not begin with Charles. Under his father, they had already watched their world shift. They had seen Elizabeth's balance give way to James's extravagance; they had endured the imposition of Scottish favorites; they had witnessed the humiliation of beloved figures like Sir Walter Raleigh.

They knew that the Stuart idea of monarchy—rooted in divine right of the king—had been grafted onto English soil with poor understanding of its history. What the Forced Loan revealed was not just the king's need for money but his contempt for compacts between ruler and ruled.

Some of these men paid the loan grudgingly. Others refused. Those who resisted understood the stakes: refusal could mean interrogation before the Privy Council, imprisonment, or a ruinous fine. Nonetheless, a principle, once awakened, could not be silenced.

In Boston, in Sempringham, in the villages between the River Witham and the North Forty-Foot Drain, the refusal to yield to unlawful taxation became an act of conscience rather than defiance. These were not rebels by temperament. They were men who believed that freedom required both obedience and boundary—that even a king must not break faith with the law.[2]

The imprisonment of the Five Knights was watched closely in Lincolnshire. The failure of the courts to release them confirmed a truth many had begun to suspect: that neither Parliament nor the judiciary could restrain a monarch determined to rule through prerogative.

THE 1626 FORCED LOAN

In the pulpit of St. Botolph's Church, John Cotton—a preacher of rare brilliance—felt the weight of these developments. His sermons did not call for rebellion; they called for righteousness, for purity of worship, for the preservation of godly order. But the men who listened to him heard more than theology. They heard the possibility of another life, somewhere distant, where the faith of their fathers might be practiced without the shadow of royal intrusion.

By the late 1620s, a subtle transformation had begun. Men who once expected reform now spoke of flight. They followed the news of Parliament's dissolution in 1629 with a sense of finality. If the king would not consult his subjects, and if Parliament could no longer speak for them, where could they turn? The turning, in truth, had already begun. Conversations in Boston's guild halls, in manor houses near Kirton, and in the quiet rooms of Lincolnshire gentry shifted from resistance to imagination.

If England must be the king's, one man said, *let us find a place where Christ alone is sovereign.*[3]

The idea of settlement in New England did not arise suddenly. It had been germinating since the founding of Plymouth in 1620. But what had seemed improbable before the Forced Loan now became plausible. Networks of kinship and faith stretched from Boston to London, where men like Isaac Johnson, Richard Bellingham, Thomas Dudley, and John Winthrop were already contemplating the creation of a new society grounded not in the prerogative of monarchs but in the covenant of believers.

Cotton's influence—quiet, profound, and disciplined—shaped their imaginations. He had taught them that godliness required a people set apart, and that purity of worship demanded both discipline and community.

A TALE OF TWO BOSTONS

The Boston Men, as they came to be known, did not think of themselves as revolutionaries. They thought of themselves as preservers—of English liberties, of Protestant identity, of a commonwealth rooted in Scripture rather than in royal decree. Their vision was not escape but fulfillment: a restoration of what England had once been and might become again, if only distance and wilderness gave them the space to build it.

The Forced Loan was not merely a financial crisis—it was the moment when the deep fracture between king and subject became unbridgeable. The men who refused to pay, who resisted arrest, who invoked the ancient rights of Englishmen, did so not because they rejected England but because they believed England had been seized by a false principle: that a king may tax without consent, imprison without charge, and rule without counsel.

The Forced Loan had shown them something essential: a king who would rule without consent would one day rule without law. And for men raised on the memory of Elizabeth's balance, who treasured the common law, and who believed that conscience must kneel to no earthly power, such a monarch was not merely disappointing. He was dangerous.

Those men—the ones who said no when saying no carried risk—would become the nucleus of the Massachusetts Bay Company. They sought a place where they could build a community grounded not in prerogative but in covenant, not in royal decree but in mutual obligation. The seeds of New England were planted not by wanderlust but by resistance to a king who believed himself the sole author of the English constitution.

Those who resisted the *Forced Loan* were imprisoned rather than submit to the Crown's tyranny. In particular, the Earl of Lincoln resisted the Crown's oppression by distributing an inflammatory pamphlet opposing the *Forced Loan*. The pamphlet read:

> *To all English freeholders from a well-wisher of theirs calling on honest men and wise men to openly resist the loan because of the threat it offered to the liberties of the subjects and the future of parliaments.*[4]

The pamphlet argued that the *Forced Loan* was intended to:

> *Make ourselves the instrument of our own slavery by robbing the freemen of England of their liberties. All those who cared for the good of the commonwealth should oppose.*[5]

The Privy Council arraigned the Earl for expressing these views and fined him £3,000.[6] Soon after, he was ordered to appear before the *Star Chamber* and was imprisoned in the Tower of London.

Tower of London

In December 1626, Lady Bridget petitioned the Crown to grant her permission to visit her husband in the tower.

Lord of the Privy Seal, Sir John Coke, endorsed her appeal writing: *Bridget, wife of Theophilus Clinton, 4th Earl of Lincoln, prays for access to her husband in the Tower.*[7]

In 1628, Lord Saye, Lady Bridget's father, was incarcerated at the Fleet Prison for lobbying the House of Lords to support the House of Commons' *Petition of Right* stating:

> *I know of no law besides Parliament that should persuade men to give away their goods.*[8]

That same year, Charles I declared martial law.

Royal troops were billeted at Broughton Manor, Lord Saye's estate in Banbury, Oxfordshire.

As a result, nearly half the town of Banbury was consumed by flames when an unattended army cooking fire raged out of control.[9]

Broughton Manor home of Lord Saye & Sele

Boston area gentry who opposed the *Forced Loan* were arraigned and incarcerated in one of two London prisons:[10]

THE 1626 FORCED LOAN

The Fleet Prison held Sir William Armyn, Sir Thomas Darnell, William Anderson, Esq., and Alderman Edward Tilson.[11]

Fleet Prison - London

The Gate House Prison held Sir John Wray, Sir Thomas Grantham, and Sir Edward Ascough.[12]

                        vij° Marcij 1626 at Lincoln.
  The names of such Comissioners as refused to lend his ma^tie any mony in his tyme of necessytie, or to enter bond for there appearance at the Counsell bord, according to the instruccons.
  Sr John Wray Barronett
  Sr Willm Army^n Barronett
  Sr Thomas Grantham Knight
  Sir Edward Ascough
  Willm Anderson Esqr
  Willm Tharrold Esquier
  Sr Thomas Darnell
  Sr Anthony Irbie Knight refused to lend, but did enter bond for his appearance at the counsell boarde the xxiij^th of this instant March. [This entry is crossed out with a pen in the original, but is still legible.]
  Norwood.
              [Indorsed in contemporary hand]
              Loane in Lincolneshire
              Refractorie p'sons
              vij° Marcij 1626

In March 1627, Sir John Wray pleaded that he was weak and needed fresh air, so he was allowed to be confined at his country home.

Other Boston area gentry were sent to far-removed counties, where local sheriffs were assigned responsibility for them.

Grantham was sent first to Dorset and then to Kent. Armyn refused to relocate and was further detained at the Gate House Prison.[13]

During the Earl of Lincoln's incarceration in the Tower of London, Thomas Dudley and Isaac Johnson acted as intermediaries and organized opposition in Boston and the surrounding area.

As a result, the local gentry and the majority of Boston's aldermen opposed the Forced Loan.

Members of the Boston Borough Council arraigned in March 1627 for their opposition included:

- William Coddington
- Atherton Hough
- Thomas Leverett
- Edmond Jackson
- Benjamin Diconson
- Thomas Lowe
- Thomas Tooly
- John Coppyn
- William Condy
- Richard Westland
- Mayor John Whitting[14]

William Coddington, Atherton Hough, and Thomas Leverett joined the Massachusetts Bay Company in March 1629 and sailed to Massachusetts with John Cotton in 1633.[15]

THE 1626 FORCED LOAN

Att Lincoln 9 March 1626

John Whitinge, maior of Boston, beinge formerly called before his ma^{ts} Commissioners, & by them required to ayde his ma^{tie} in this way of loane, and havinge refused, was againe called before vs whose names are vnderwritten, and demanded if he still contynued in the same mynde, answered he did, And that he would not lend any mony in this kinde, And beinge told by the Commissioners that such as refused & contynued in that mynde, incurred his ma^{ts} highe displeasure; Neverthelles he still refused; And beinge required to become bounde by obligacon to his ma^{tie} in the Some of fifty pounds for his appearance before the Lordps of his ma^{ts} most hōble privie Counsell at Whitehall the xixth day of this instant, alsoe refused to be bounde.

Edward Tilson, Alderman of Boston having^e as much sayde vnto him as was sayde to the Mayor, refused to lend the Kinge so small a Some as xx^s, or to so enter bond for his appearance.

Atterton Howghe of Boston refused to lend or enter bond for his appearance, & sayde that if he suffered, he did obey.

Edmond Jackson of Boston refused to lend, or enter into bond for his appearance.

Beniamen Diconson of Boston refused to lend or enter into bond for his appearance.

Thomas Leverett of Boston refused to lend or to become bounde for his appearance.

Thomas Lowe of Boston refused to lend, or to enter into bond for his appearance.

Thomas Tooly of Boston refused to lend or to enter into bond for his appearance.

John Coppyn of Boston refused to lend ye small Some of xx^s or to enter into bond for his appearance.

Willm̄ Coddington of Boston refused to lend, or to enter into bond for his appearance.

Willm Condy of Boston refused to lend the small some of xx^s or to enter into bond for his appearance.

Richard Westland of Boston refused to lend or enter bond.

[In margin, opposite Richard] 12 in Boston refused.

Thomas Godfrey of Grantham esquier refused to lend or to become bounde for his appearance.

Christopher Hart of Tattershall refused to lend or enter into bond for his appearance; bycause he saw so many emynent men refuse.

Thomas Bedle of Tattershall refused to lend or enter into bond for his appearance.

[An entry of two lines erased, and now quite illegible, and in margin] Aveland consents by M^r Jo. Turrold of Morton esqr to pay xl^s.

John Wyncopp of Kirkby vnderwoode refused to lend, or enter into bond for his appearance.

Boston Men were charged for opposing the Forced Loan in March 1627, per the Calendar of State Papers during the Tudors & Stuarts, 1509-1714. The new year started on Lady Day, March 25th, during the 17th century. As a result, the date shows as 9 March 1626, but it is 9 March 1627, New Style.

The Privy Council sought the arrest of employees of Lincoln who encouraged opposition to the *Forced Loan*. As a result, a warrant was issued for John Hollande and Thomas Dudley in March 1627.[16] Hollande had been hired to assist Simon Bradstreet as a steward after Dudley moved to Boston.

A letter Sir Edward Heron, Sergeant-at-law for Lincolnshire, sent to Sir Henry May of the Privy Council documents efforts to apprehend Hollande and Dudley.

> *I have hearde that Mr. HOLLANDE who attended the earle of Lincolne, hath been in quest by the state; yf it be soe, I doe heare for certeine, that he was seene dyvers tymes, about a month or six weekes past upon the terras-walkes at Sempringham; but since that tyme it is privatly whispered that he is now removed to the house of one Mr. THOMAS DUDLYE, in Boston, whoe did allsoe of late tyme wayte upon the de earle; and it is very p'bable, because, Mr. HOLLANDS wyfe is observed to make often viages frome Sempringham unto Boston, and there to abide sometyme 2 or 3 dayes, sometyme a week together. Yet maye you please further to understande, that this Mr. DUDLYE beynge reported to have £300 p. an., some saye £400, refused upon our earnest request to beare 30s. towards the loane with a neyghbourh that was deeply charged as we have informed in our certificatts unto the lords of the councell, whereof I beseech your honor to direct the delyverye.*[17]

As resistance to the *Forced Loan* grew, five leading members of Parliament were jailed and submitted a *writ of habeas corpus* in opposition to the *Forced Loan*—known as the *Five Knights Case*.[18] The King's Bench refused bail for the five to avoid having to rule on their case by saying,

> *The prisoners could not be freed, as the offense was probably too dangerous for public discussion.*[19]

THE 1626 FORCED LOAN

Sir Randolph Crew, Chief Justice of the King's Bench, refused to legitimize the *Forced Loan*, so Charles I replaced him and imposed martial law throughout England.

Former Chief Justice Edward Coke, in response, issued a *Petition of Right* to Parliament to restrict the crown from seizing Englishmen's property and depriving them of their freedom without justification.[20]

By June 2nd, 1628, Charles was so desperate to support his uncle and son-in-law in the *Thirty Years' War* that he conceded to the following demands made in the *Petition of Right*.

-Sir Edward Coke, Chief Justice-

> No man hereafter be compelled to make or yield any Guift Loane Benevolence Taxe or such like Charge without comon consent by Acte of Parliament,
>
> And that none be called to make aunswere or take such Oath or to give attendance or be confined or otherwise molested or disquieted concerning the same or for refusall thereof,
>
> And that your Majestie would be pleased to remove the said Souldiers and Mariners and that your people may not be soe burthened in tyme to come,
>
> And that the aforesaid Comissions for proceeding by Martiall Lawe may be revoked and annulled.[21]

News of the king's capitulation spread rapidly, accompanied by public celebrations and church bells throughout England.[22]

CLINTON EARLS OF LINCOLN

Edward Clinton, born in 1512 became a royal ward of Henry VIII following his father's death in 1517.[1] In 1534, Clinton married Elizabeth "Bessie" Blount, mistress of Henry VIII and mother of Henry FitzRoy, Duke of Richmond. Bessie was nearly fifteen years his senior, and the match astonished many.

Though contemporary observers suggest Henry VIII encouraged the marriage, Elizabeth Blount's biographer maintains it was a love match, despite her being at least twelve years older than Clinton.[2] The Victorian historian J. A. Froude later described Bessie as *an accomplished and most interesting person, but old enough to be her boy-husband's mother.*[3]

Clinton's loyalty to the Crown during the Lincolnshire Rising of October 1536 further advanced his fortunes after he suppressed the rebellion by raising troops from his estates to stand firmly with Henry VIII at a time of widespread northern unrest.

After death of Bessie Blount in 1540, Clinton consolidated his social and economic position in Lincolnshire.[4]

Through marriage to Bessie Blount in 1534, Clinton inherited inherited the property of her first husband, Gilbert Tailboys, 1st Baron Kyme along with Tattershall Castle that Henry VIII had bestowed to Bessie.

In recognition of his years of service, the Henry VIII granted Clinton significant monastic properties confiscated during the Dissolution of the Monasteries, including Sempringham Priory, Haverholme, and Barlings Abbey—all formerly thriving religious institutions in Lincolnshire.[5]

These royal grants, combined with his earlier inheritance, made Clinton one of the most powerful and well-positioned gentry in the Lincolnshire by the early 1540s.[6]

In May 1550, Edward was appointed Lord High Admiral of the Navy and commanded England's fleet to prevent France from supplying troops to Scotland after Elizabeth I was excommunicated by the Pope in 1570. In appreciation, Elizabeth I elevated him to Earl of Lincoln.

Edward Clinton, Earl of Lincoln

Edward Clinton died on 16 January 1585 at Sempringham. He was buried in St George's Chapel, Windsor, where his alabaster monument proclaims his long and varied service. Fuller remembered him as *a Wise, Valiant and Fortunate Gentleman*.[7]

Edward's successor, Henry Clinton, the 2nd Earl of Lincoln, inherited his father's title at age forty-six in January 1585. Henry, however, was reputed to be mad having distinguished himself as the most despised peer in the House of Lords.[8]

His wickedness, misery, craft, repugnance to all humanity and perfidious mind is not amongst the heathens to be matched.[9]

In 1601, he incurred the wrath of Queen Elizabeth, who, with the Scottish ambassador, had been invited to his Chelsea home—only to be left standing after Henry fled London to escape creditors.[10]

Henry's oppressive ill-treatment of his tenants resulted in several reprimands by the Privy Council.

The *Inquisitions of Depopulation* imposed heavy fines on him in 1607 for purposely enclosing common land and depopulating the Lincolnshire village of Tattershall.[11]

> The said Earl hath taken away part of the churchyard and putt it into his mote, so that divers people were digged up, some green and lately buried, and thrown into his mote to fill it up.[12]

Tattershall Castle

In 1584, mad Henry's son, Thomas, married into a prominent Wiltshire family —the Knyvetts.[13]

Thomas Clinton's wife, Elizabeth, was the niece of Sir Thomas Knyvett, who had foiled the Gunpowder Plot in 1605 and was rewarded with a peerage.

Later, he built the first residence at the site of 10 Downing Street—the modern-day residence of the Prime Minister of Britain.[14]

In addition, Elizabeth's two sisters who married well:

- Catherine wed the younger brother of the Earl of Warwick.
- Frances married the Earl of Rutland. Their daughter, Katherine, married the Duke of Buckingham in 1620.[15]

Not long after she married into the Clinton family, Elizabeth's parents prevailed on the Privy Council to order the return of the marriage portion that her father-in-law, Henry, had pilfered.[16] He was also asked to provide *some convenient house where the young lord and lady may live with their children.*[17]

As a result, Elizabeth, her husband, Thomas, and their nine children were allowed to live at the Earl's manor at Sempringham, while Henry was forced to relocate to his castle at Tattershall, where he died deep in debt with no friends and was laid to rest on September 29, 1616.

Thomas Clinton ascended to the title of the 3rd Earl of Lincoln but died three years later, in 1619. Lady Elizabeth had borne Thomas eighteen children during their thirty-five-year marriage, nine of whom lived to adulthood. Five of Thomas' daughters inherited £2,000 as marriage portions, provided they married with their mother's consent.[18] A sixth daughter, Elizabeth, was disowned when she eloped with her father's manservant. Thomas's eldest surviving son, Theophilus, inherited his father's title and the debt his father had inherited from Mad Henry, totaling £20,000, which had to be paid within five years.[19]

Knowing her son, Theophilus, was too inexperienced to manage this debt, Lady Elizabeth sought the help of John Preston, who stopped at Sempringham whenever he visited John Cotton in Boston. Preston contacted his dear friend, Lord Saye, and together they secured the services of Thomas Dudley to steward the Earl's inheritance.[20] Dudley's biographer, Cotton Mather, recounts:

The grandfather of this present Earle was called Henry, who being a bad husband had left his heirs under great entanglements, and his son, named Thomas, had never been able to wind out of that labyrinth of debts contracted by his father, so that all the difficultys were now devolved upon Theophilus, the grandchild, who was persuaded therefore to entertain Mr. Dudley as his Steward to manage his whole estate, who though it were so involved with many great debts, amounting to near twenty thousand pounds, yet his prudent, careful & faithful management of the demesne[21] of that family, he in a few years found means to discharge all those great debts.[22]

Thomas Dudley   **Anne (Dudley) Bradstreet**

Late in 1619, Thomas Dudley, his pregnant wife, Dorothy, sons Thomas and Samuel, ages fifteen and twelve, and daughter Anne, age eight, entered the Sempringham household of Lady Elizabeth, the Dowager Countess of Lincoln, who educated Dudley's children along with her four youngest.

Dudley's daughter, Anne, benefited from having access to an education and the library at Sempringham. Later, she became America's first female poet. When Dudley's sons, Thomas and Samuel, entered university, they matriculated at Emmanuel College —no doubt through the efforts of Cotton and Preston.

Although the 4th Earl of Lincoln's estates extended over three counties, Dudley resolved his £20,000 debt by increasing rents and leasing fallow land within a few years. Dudley later reflected:

> *I found the estate of the Earl of Lincoln so much and so much in debt, which I have discharged, and have revised the rents so many hundreds per annum. God will, I trust, bless me and mine.*[23]

Mather relates that the young Earl was so impressed by Dudley that:

> *He would never, after his acquaintance with him, do any business of the moment without Mr. Dudley's counsel or advice.*[24]

Having resolved the Earl's debts, Dudley sought to establish a closer association with John Cotton, and in July 1624, he relocated his family to a rented home in Boston.[25]

Two developments made the move possible:

- The Earl spent much of his time in London attending Parliament and the Inns of Court at Gray's Inn;
- Simon Bradstreet had been hired to help Dudley two years earlier and could then easily manage the Earl's estate.[26]

Though Dudley was living in Boston, the Earl continued to require his services.

In November 1624, summoned him to London in response to a request from James I to provide a troop of three hundred horses and horsemen to support his son-in-law, Frederick V, the dispossessed Elector Palatine, in the Thirty Years' War.[27]

On his way south to London, Dudley stopped at Cambridge University to confer with John Preston.[28]

> *Towards the latter end of King James' reign, when there was a press for soldiers to go over to Germany with Count Mansfeld for the recovery of the Palatinate, when the matter was first motioned, the Earl of Lincoln, who was zealously affected toward the Protestant*

interest, was strongly inclined to have gone over with the said Earl or Count, and should have been a Colonel in the expedition, yet resolving not to go without Mr. Dudley's advice and company; and therefore he sent down to Boston, in Lincolnshire, where Mr. Dudley sojourned, to come forthwith to London, to order matters for this enterprise, and to be ready to accompany him therein. Mr. Dudley knew knot how to refuse to wait upon his lordship, yet thought it best, as well for himself as for the Earl, to take the best counsell he could, in a concern so high nature, not being unmindful of what Solomon said, with good advice make war. Therefore he resolved himself, in his passing up to London, to take Cambridge in his way, that he might advise with Dr. Preston about the design, who was a great statesman as well as a great divine, at least was conceived very well to understand the intrigues of the state in that juncture; and he altogether dissuaded Mr. Dudley, or the Earl, from having anything to do in that expedition, laying before them the grounds of his apprehensions on which he foresaw the sad events of the whole, as did really soon after come to pass.[29] Dr. Preston, by reason of his frequent intercourse with the Earl of Lincoln's family, was free to discover to Mr. Dudley all he knew, and he improved it thoroughly to take off the earl's mind from the enterprise.[30]

A history of the affair—written in 1706—recounts that Count Ernst von Mansfeldt visited London three times in 1624 to lobby James I for support of the Protestant cause in the Thirty Years' War.

As a result, James allocated six regiments (12,000 men) to the Count, along with six colonels and two troops of horses—one from the Earl of Lincoln, who reportedly would be in command.

Though the French were charged with transporting von Mansfeldt's troops and horses to Calais, the Queen of France revoked permission for him to land to avoid provoking her brother, Philip IV of Spain.[31]

A TALE OF TWO BOSTONS

Ernst von Mansfeldt   Anne, Queen of France

Mansfeldt was forced to sail with his Army into Zealand. There the soldiers lay at the Ramkins a long time in their Ships, not suffered to land.³² For the States, not dreaming of such a Body of Men, could not determine suddenly what to do with them, besides, the Inland Waters being frozen, Provisions would grow short for their own Army, much more for them.

The Ships, stuffed and pestred with Men, wanting Meat and all manner of Necessaries, such a Stench and Pestilence grew among them, that they were thrown into the Sea by multitudes; so that many Hundreds (if I may not Thousands) beaten upon Shores, had their Bowels eaten out with Dogs and Swine, to the Horror of the Beholders.

Those Bodies that drove up near those Towns where the English were, had great Pits made for them, wherein (being thrown by heaps) they were covered with Earth; but upon those Shores where they were neglected, (as they were in many parts of Holland), a great Contagion followed: and of Mansfeldt's Twelve thousand Men, scarce the Moiety³³ landed.³⁴

Although James I confined England's war effort to von Mansfeld's misguided attempt to free the Palatinate, the expedition contravened Parliament's demand that no troops be committed to the continent.

Thus, von Mansfeld's efforts were doomed once James banned him from attacking the Spanish.[35]

As a result, Dudley and Preston likely saved the Earl's life by dissuading him from joining von Mansfeldt's ill-fated expedition.

Later, Dudley again rescued the Earl after he committed a *faux pas* by failing to kneel before the Elector Palatine at court in the Hague.[36]

> *At another time, when the Earl of Lincoln (who it seems was wont to be very quick in his motions sometimes) understood that there was like to be a brave fight at the Hague, in Holland, by reason of an interview of some great princes that were then to be present.*
>
> *No body was able to direct in the expedition so well as Mr. Dudley, who on the sudden he judged could so order all matters belonging to the Earls retinue, that in two days' time they might go from the Earles Castle of Sempringham, to the Hague, in Holland, to be present at that great solemnity.*[37]
>
> *When they came there, the Earl his spirits arose to such an height that he would by no means address himself to court the Count Palatine upon the knees, although he had been crowned King of Bohemia.*
>
> *Mr. Dudley began now to think that the Earls last error was worse than his first; however, he was forced to find out the best way, he could to excuse it, which he did to the Palsgraves satisfaction.*[38]

Six years later, despite desperately needing funds to support his uncle, Christian IV of Denmark, in the Thirty Years' War, Charles suspended Parliament to thwart the impeachment of Buckingham.

Later, when he learned that his uncle had been defeated at the Battle of Lutter, Charles imposed a *forced loan* on England to obtain the needed funds and swore:

> *He would render his uncle every assistance, even at the risk of his own crown and hazarding his life.*[39]

Ironically, Charles' words proved prophetic as he lost both his crown and his life after Cromwell's Rump Parliament elected to behead him outside the Banqueting House at Whitehall.[40]

The *Forced Loan* impacted the lives of many in the Boston area, including three of Dudley's closest associates, who were central to the Massachusetts Bay Company.

- ISAAC JOHNSON - the Massachusetts Bay Company's primary investor and husband of the Earl of Lincoln's sister, Lady Arbella,
- JOHN HUMFREY - treasurer of the Dorchester Company and husband of the Earl of Lincoln's sister, Lady Susan.
- RICHARD BELLINGHAM - Boston's Town Recorder and Member of Parliament for Boston, Lincolnshire.

While the Earl was confined to the Tower of London for refusing to comply with the Forced Loan, Dudley served as his local proxy and organized resistance to it in the Boston area, unaware that events would spiral out of control and result in civil war.

In 1627, Thomas Dudley and his family were compelled to return to Sempringham after Warwick appointed Simon Bradstreet to steward the estate of his aging stepmother, Lady Frances Wray. Lady Elizabeth and Bridget welcomed Dudley's return, as they relied on him heavily during the Earl of Lincoln's imprisonment. Lady Elizabeth, in particular, had become dependent on Dudley to bridge relations with her son since he severed ties with her in 1622.

The Earl's wife, Lady Bridget, had relied heavily on Dudley during her husband's imprisonment. Later, Dudley corresponded with Lady Bridget from Massachusetts.

To Lady Bridget, Countess of Lincoln, 3 March 1631 - *Touching the plantation which wee here have begun, it fell out thus: About the yeare 1627 some friends beeing togeather in Lincolnshire, fell into some discourse about New England, and the planting of the gospell there; and after some deliberation wee imparted our reasons by letters and messages to some in London and the west country where it was likewise deliberately thought uppon, and at length with often negotiation soe ripened that in the year 1628, wee procured a patent from his Majesty for our planting.*[41]

The Earl was released from the Tower of London in March 1628.[42] Lady Bridget, the Earl's wife, died sometime before 1644. By 1647, Theophilus had remarried Elizabeth Gorges, his cousin, the daughter of his aunt, Elizabeth Clinton, and Sir Arthur Gorges.[43] Elizabeth Gorges' first husband, Robert Stanley, died in 1632. During the English Civil Wars, Theophilus was made colonel of a Foot Regiment in the Parliamentary Army. In December 1645, he became the Resident Commissioner assigned to the Scottish Army. Two years later, in 1647, Theophilus was elected Speaker of the House of Lords and, in December 1660, was made Commissioner for the Colonies.[44]

Theophilus Clinton, 4th Earl of Lincoln, died in London in 1667. His only son, Edward, predeceased him. As a result, Theophius' estate passed to his grandson (*Edward*), who died at Tattershall in 1692, thus ending the Clinton line.[45]

Cotton Mather describes the family in his Magnalia as *the best family of any nobleman then in England*.[46] Lincoln had a more intimate connection with New England settlements and must have felt a deeper interest in their success than any other noble house in England.[47]

CLINTON MARRIAGES

After the death of Thomas Clinton, 3rd Earl of Lincoln, in 1619, Lady Elizabeth, his wife, assumed responsibility for arranging their children's marriages.

The marriages she arranged for her four eldest children proved pivotal to the founding of New England.

LADY FRANCES CLINTON - 1620

Frances Clinton, the youngest of Lady Elizabeth's eligible daughters, married John Gorges, the son of Ferdinando Gorges, the so-called *Father of English Colonization in North America* in 1620.[1]

Links between the two families date back to Nicholas Gorges, a retainer of Edward Clinton, 1st Earl of Lincoln, Lord High Admiral of the Royal Navy from 1558 to 1585.[2] Gorges captained the *Swiftsure* under Clinton's command and was appointed by Clinton to represent the town of Boston in Parliament in 1584. This relationship established an early pattern of patronage that would persist across generations.

In 1597, Nicholas' nephew, Arthur Gorges, further cemented this connection through his marriage to Elizabeth Clinton, sister of Thomas Clinton, 3rd Earl of Lincoln.[3] Their daughter, Elizabeth Gorges, married her first cousin, Theophilus Clinton, 4th Earl of Lincoln, after the death of his first wife, Lady Bridget Fiennes.[4] Elizabeth was also the second cousin of Ferdinando Gorges, the father of John Gorges. As a result, the marriage between John Gorges and Frances Clinton may be understood as part of an already established alignment between the two families within a shared colonial and political framework.

Ferdinando Gorges had long patronized the Lyden Pilgrims, and his son, John Gorges's betrothal to Theophilus' sister, Frances, may have been linked to Frances' mother, Lady Elizabeth, helping secure a patent for the *Mayflower*—due in part to her husband, Thomas Clinton, 3rd Earl of Lincoln, having been among the aristocratic investors and supporters associated with the Virginia Company following its reorganization under the Second Charter of 1609.[5] Reportedly, the Countess of Lincoln secured a patent for the *Mayflower* in the guise of her male servant, John Wincop.[6]

> *By the advice of "some" friends this patent was not taken in the name of any of their own; but in the name of Mr. John Wincop (a religious gentleman then belonging to the Countess of Lincoln) who Intended to go with them. But God so disposed as he never went, nor they ever made use of this patent, which had cost them so much labour, and charge; as by the sequel will appear.*[7]

Historians are unclear why Lady Elizabeth's *Mayflower* patent was not used. Some assume that Wincop died. Others suggest that Wincop's Patent became redundant when the *First London Company* obtained a nearly identical patent granted to John Pierce. In November 1620, under the leadership of Ferdinando Gorges and the Earl of Warwick, the *Council for New England* assimilated the

CLINTON MARRIAGES

Second Virginia Company and the *First Virginia (London) Company* together with its Pierce Patent, by which the Pilgrims sailed to America.[8] In *The May-Flower and Her Log*, Azel Ames explains how Gorges and Warwick manipulated matters in their favor.

> *No one knew better than the shrewd Gorges the value of such a colony as that of the Leyden brethren would be, to plant, populate, and develop his Company's great demesne. None were more facile than himself and the buccaneering Earl of Warwick, to plan and execute the bold, but—as it proved—easy coup, by which the Pilgrim colony was to be stolen bodily, for the benefit of the Second Virginia Company and its successor, the Council for New England from the First (or London) Company under whose patent (to John Pierce) and patronage they sailed.[9]*

Second Pierce Patent granted in 1621

The Pilgrims' encounter with Lady Elizabeth and John Wincop was not their first in Boston, Lincolnshire.

Thirteen years earlier, in the autumn of 1607, a group of Pilgrims hired a ship to sail from Boston to Holland. The ship's captain betrayed them, and the Pilgrims were arrested, searched, and jailed.

William Bradford wrote of the incident:

> *There was a large company of them purposed to get passage at Boston in Lincolnshire, and for that end, had hired a ship wholly to themselves; & made agreement with the master to be ready at a certain day, and take them, and their goods in, at a convenient place, where they accordingly would all attend in readiness.*
>
> *So after long waiting, & large expences (though he kept not day with them), yet he came at length, & took them in, in the night. But when he had them, & their goods aboard; he betrayed 'them', having beforehand complotted with the Searchers, & other officers so to do.*
>
> *Who took them, and put them into open boats, & there rifled & ransacked them, searching them to their shirts for money, yea even the women furder than became modesty; and then carried them back into the town, & made them a spectacle, & wonder to the multitude; which came flocking on all sides to behold them.*
>
> *Being thus first, by the catch pole officers, rifled, & stripped of their money, books, & much other goods; they were presented to the magistrates, and messengers sent to Inform the Lords of the Council of them; and so they were committed to ward. Indeed the magistrates used them courteously, & shewed them what favour they could; but could not deliver them, till order came from the Council-table.*
>
> *But the Issue was that after a month's Imprisonment, the greatest part were dismissed, & sent to places from whence they came, but 7 of the principal were still kept in prison, and bound over to the Assizes.*[10]

THEOPHILUS CLINTON, 4th EARL OF LINCOLN - 1622

To find a match for her son, Theophilus, Lady Elizabeth relied on Thomas Dudley,[11] who, in turn, relied on John Preston, who in turn relied on his dear friend, William Fiennes, Lord Saye & Sele.[12]

It so happened that Lord Saye had a seventeen-year-old daughter named Bridget, who was an excellent marriage prospect and a distant cousin of Theophilus.[13]

Lady Bridget Fiennes

In spring 1622, Lady Elizabeth and William Fiennes, Lord Saye, blessed the match of Lady Bridget and Theophilus Clinton, 4th Earl of Lincoln.[14]

In honor of her son's marriage, Lady Elizabeth dedicated her book, *The Countess of Lincolnes Nurserie* to Lady Bridget.

The book extolled the merits of breastfeeding and was published by *John Lichfield & James Short, printers to the famous Universitie at Oxford.*

It was one of the first books ever published by a woman in England, and its dedication read: *To the Right Honourable, and approved vertuous Lady Bridget, Countesse of Lincolne.*[15]

Contrary to expectations, Lady Elizabeth's book so enraged the Earl and Lady Bridget that they severed all ties with her and moved to their Tattershall estate thirty-two miles northeast of Sempringham.[16]

By 1625, the rift between the two reached the point where Theophilus sued his mother for custody of his younger siblings, claiming that she was unfit to raise them.[17]

Through his marriage to Lady Bridget, Theophilus joined the inner circle of his father-in-law, Lord Saye, and the Earl of Warwick.

Lord Saye, the Earl of Warwick, and fifteen other peers from the House of Lords joined Theophilus's opposition to the Forced Loan.[18]

Lord Saye championed opposition to the crown. On May 24, 1628, he countered Buckingham's opposition to the *Petition of Right* and addressed the House of Lords, saying:

> *It is the due right of the subject not to be committed without cause expressed.*
>
> *The refusing to join in petition* (with the Commons) *to enjoy this right will seem strange to posterity and make us hateful to posterity if we thus degenerate from our ancestors.*
>
> *I desire my name may be recorded amongst those Lords who shall agree to join with the Commons herein for preservation of our just rights.*[19]

Lord Saye & Sele not only mentored his son-in-law, Theophilus Clinton, in the House of Lords; he was also instrumental in manipulating a Royal Charter for the Massachusetts Bay Company.

LADY ARBELLA CLINTON -1623

Although Lady Arbella lived with her mother at Sempringham, her brother's friends in London knew her to be beautiful and nubile.

A year after Arbella's brother, Theophilus, was admitted to the Inns of Court at Gray's Inn, he befriended a newly admitted Gray's Inn member named Isaac Johnson, who soon fell in love with Arbella and relocated to Sempringham to court her.[20]

Two years later, on April 5th, 1623, the Bishop of Lincoln recorded the consent of Lady Arbella's mother, Lady Elizabeth, and Isaac's grandfather, Robert Johnson, for the two to marry.[21]

> *1623 April 5 - Issack Johnson, of Sempringham, gent æt. 22, & Lady Arbella ffynes, of same, sp^r, æt. 22. His grandfather, Rob. Johnson, B.D. Archdeacon of Leicester, consents; also her mother the Countess of Lincoln. Appln. by Hen. Stafford, of Ancaster, gent.*[22]

Samuel Skelton, chaplain to the Earl and his family, likely conducted vows in a private ceremony at the Earl's Sempringham estate.[23]

Aside from Lady Arbella's immediate family, only Isaac Johnson's grandfather, Robert, and his best friend, William Blaxton, would have attended the ceremony as Isaac's father, Abraham Johnson, vehemently objected to the marriage.

> *That over-high match was not blessed...not assented to, but forbidden! They had got a clandestine marriage, never daring to own or tell their father who married them.*[24]

Isaac Johnson and William Blaxton first met in 1614 when Isaac entered Emmanuel College, Cambridge, at age thirteen. Although William Blaxton was five years older than Isaac, the two roomed together for seven years and became best friends.

Together, they completed their Bachelor's in 1618, were ordained at Peterborough in 1620, and received their Master's in 1621. The two remained steadfast friends until Isaac's untimely death in 1630.[25]

Four months after the marriage of Isaac Johnson and Lady Arbella, William Blaxton sailed to Massachusetts with Robert Gorges, the brother of Lady Francis Clinton's husband, John Gorges.

Ferdinando Gorges, then president of the *Council for New England*, granted his son, Robert Gorges, a patent for New England and named him *general governor of the country*, including Plymouth Colony.[26] Blaxton's participation in the Gorges Expedition was made possible through his friendship with Isaac Johnson and Lady Arbella's ties to the Gorges family.

Robert Gorges, accompanied by William Blaxton, one hundred twenty settlers, and two clerics, William Morrell and Samuel Maverick, set sail for New England on August 7, 1623, aboard two ships, the *Katherine* and the *Prophet Daniel*.[27] Six months later, Robert Gorges and most settlers returned to England. Blaxton, Morrell, and Maverick remained in New England.

Blaxton made his way up to the Shawmut Peninsula—later Boston—where he trapped fur, traded with the Wampanoag, planted an apple orchard, and lived like a recluse for the next five or six years. Although isolated on the Shawmut Peninsula, Blaxton kept in touch with his dear friend, Isaac Johnson.

When Robert Gorges died, he received word that John Gorges, Frances Clinton's husband, had inherited Robert's patent.[28] In 1630, several months after the Massachusetts Bay Company landed, Blaxton contacted Isaac Johnson and offered the group access to fresh water on the Shawmut Peninsula.

At the invitation of Emmanuel, contemporary and old planter, William Blackstone, he (Johnson) *led the settlement of Boston.*[29]

LADY SUSAN CLINTON -1630

Lady Susan Clinton likely met John Humfrey in the spring of 1627 when he was in Boston for the birth of his son, Johnathan, and witnessed the signing of Isaac Johnson's Will at Sempringham.

Later in 1628, after the death of his wife, Elizabeth, Humfrey returned to Sempringham to pursue an interest in Lady Susan.

One year later, in October 1629, Humfrey was elected Deputy Governor of the Massachusetts Bay Company, but relinquished the position two months later to remain in England to marry Lady Susan.

Although no marriage record exists, the two likely wed before December 9th, 1630, when, in a letter, Humfrey first addressed his brother-in-law, Isaac Johnson, as *Brother*.[30]

It was Humfrey's third marriage at thirty-four, and Lady Susan's first at twenty-seven.

Humfrey represented the Massachusetts Bay Company during his sojourn in England.

> *June 26th, 1632- Mr Humfreys this day complained to ye President & Councell for not permitting ships and passengers to pass from hence for ye Bay of Massachusetts without License first had from the President & Councell or their Deputy, they being free to goe thither, and to transport passenger by a Confirmation by his Majesty.*
>
> *Hereupon some of ye Councell desired to see the Pattent as they alleged, it preindicted former grants. Mr Humfryes answered yet the said Pattent was now in New England, and that they had oftentimes written for it to be sent hither, but as yet they had not received it.*[31]

While in England, Humfrey took advantage of the opportunity to become one of the first patentees of the *Saybrook Colony*, established in Connecticut by Lord Saye and Lord Brooke.

On April 27, 1634, Lady Susan, her husband, John Humfrey, and their daughter, Dorcas, sailed from Weymouth, England, and arrived in Boston in July. They then settled in Saugus—later named Lynn.

> John Humfrey or Humfreys, who was interested in New England from the beginning, and had been long expected, now arrived with his wife, sister of the Lady Arbella Johnson.
>
> Much was expected from his wealth and influence, and he was immediately made assistant. Lacking resolution and experiencing illluck, he played no great part. Settling in Lynn, he lost his home by fire and at length, disheartened, abandoned the country.[32]

Before abandoning New England, Humfrey exploited Warwick's desire to establish a base for his privateering exploits closer to Spanish gold routes off the coast of Nicaragua on *Providence Island*.

As shown in the *Calendar of State Papers*, Humfrey was named governor of Providence Island in 1641.

> Warwick House Minutes of Providence Island Court- March 1st Commission for Capt. Humfreys to be Governor of the island is signed.[33]

Humfrey countered the interests of the Massachusetts Bay Company by attempting to recruit colonists to accompany him to Providence Island.

This angered Governor John Winthrop, who wrote,

> Being brought low in his estate, and having many children, and being well known to the lords of Providence, and offering himself to their service, was accepted to be the next governour.
>
> Whereupon he laboured much to draw men to join with him.

> *This was looked at, both by the general court, and also by the elders, as an unwarrantable course; for though it was thought very needful to further plantation of churches in the West Indies, and all were willing to endeavour the same; yet to doe it with disparagement of this country, (for they gave out that they could not subsist here,) caused us to fear, that the Lord was not with them in this way.*[34]

As it turned out, the Spanish occupied Providence Island before Humfrey and his family were able to relocate there.

The History of Lynn suggests that, in part, the Humfrey family abandoned New England because Lady Susan was homesick.

> *It is probable likewise that his affection for his wife, whose hopes were in the land of her nativity, had some influence in determining his conduct.*
>
> *Living so far removed from the elegant circles in which she had delighted and having lost the sister who might have been the companion of her solitude (Arbella Johnson), the Lady Susan was weary of the privations of the wilderness, the howling of the wild beasts, and the uncouth manners of the savages, and had become lonely, disconsolate, and homesick.*
>
> *She, who had been the delight of her father's house and had glittered in all the pride of youth and beauty in the court of the first monarch of Europe, was now solitary and sad, separated by a wide ocean from her father's house.*[35]

On October 26, 1641, Humfrey and his wife, Lady Susan, returned to England, leaving their two daughters in the care of two male servants as they had frequently done in the past.

A TALE OF TWO BOSTONS

Lady Susan bidding farewell to her children.

Winthrop's journal states that Humfrey *much neglected his children, leaving them among...rude servants.* This ultimately resulted in the first recorded case of child sexual abuse in America's history. [36]

Minutes of the Massachusetts Bay Company documented the case.

> *Danniel Fairefeild, being a married pson, upon his owne confession, & other sufficient proofe, is found by the judgment of this court to have had canrnall knowledge of, & so, in a most vile & abominable manner, to have abused the tender body of Dorcas, the daughter of John H, Esq., one of ye then magistrates of this commonwealth, & that from time to time, for abourt her age of 7 years to about her age of 9 years, & yet hee did also, in a most uncleane & wicked manner, abuse himself upon ye body of Sara , a yonger sister of the said Dorcas, & that this wickedness was commiteted very often, & most usually by him on the Lords days & lecture days.[37] This Court therefore agreed that Danial Fairefeild shallbee severely whipped at Boston the next lecture day, & have one of his nostrils slit & then to bee seared, & kept in prison, till hee bee fit to bee sent to Salem, & then bee whipped againe, & have the other nostril slit & seared; then further hee is confined to Boston neck, so as any attempt to abuse any person as foremerly, hee shall be put to death, upon due conviction; & hee shall pay to $M^{r.\ H}$ forty pounds.*

CLINTON MARRIAGES

Jenkin Davies, for his abuseing the forenamed Dorcas was ordered to be severely whiped at Boston on a lecture day, and shalbee returned to prison till hee may bee sent to Linne, and there to be severely whiped also & from thencefourth shalbee confined to the said towne of Linne, so as if bee shall at any time go fourth of the bounds of the said towne & shalbee duly convict thereof, he shalbee put to death...further if hee shalbee duely convicted to have attempted any such wickedness (for which hee is now sentenced) upon any child after this present day, hee shalbee put to death; and hee is to pay forty pounds to M^r· for abuseing his daughter.[38] John Hudson, for abuseing the said Dorcas was ordered to be severely whiped at Boston on a lecture day, and shalbee returned to prison till hee may bee sent to Salem, & there to bee severely whipped againe; & hee shall pay unto M^r· for abuseing his daughter twenty pounds within these two years.[39] Dorcas was ordered to bee privately severly corrected by this Court, Mr. Bellingham & Increase Nowell to see it done.[40]

Humfrey sided with Cromwell when civil war broke out in England and carried the sword of state during Charles I's January 1649 trial. In July, Humfrey and Hugh Peter were appointed by Parliament to value Charles I's estate and sell everything he owned, including his priceless art collection.

Lady Susan died soon after, around 1650, and Humfrey in 1653.

While visiting Sir Henry Vane in England, Roger Williams wrote to John Winthrop to notify him of Humphry's death.

For my honourd kind friend Mr. John Winthrop at his house at Pequt in New England. From Sir Henry Vane's at Whitehall 20 Feb. 1652.

Kind Sir, Tis neere 2 in the morning, yet a line of my dearest remembrance to your loving selfe & yours, from whom I have receaved so many loving lines continually. Our old friend Col. Humphries is gone.[41]

PLANTERS & ADVENTURERS

ABOUT THE YEARE 1627 SOME FRIENDS BEEING TOGEATHER IN LINCOLNSHIRE, FELL INTO SOME DISCOURSE ABOUT NEW ENGLAND...AND AFTER SOME DELIBERATION WEE IMPARTED OUR REASONS BY LETTERS AND MESSAGES TO SOME IN LONDON AND THE WEST COUNTRY WHERE IT WAS LIKEWISE DELIBERATELY THOUGHT UPPON, AND AT LENGTH WITH OFTEN NEGOTIATION SOE RIPENED THAT IN THE YEAR 1629, WEE PROCURED A PATENT FROM HIS MAJESTY FOR OUR PLANTING.[1] Dudley's letter to Lady Bridget at Sempringham

"SOME FRIENDS BEEING TOGEATHER IN LINCOLNSHIRE" refers to a 1627 gathering in Lincolnshire organized by Thomas Dueley, Isaac Johnson, and John Humfrey to discuss the possibility of settling New England in response to the *Forced Loan*. Samuel Skelton, chaplain to the Earl of Lincoln's household, and Charles Fiennes, the Earl's younger brother, were also likely present, as both lived at the Earl's Sempringham estate. Simon Bradstreet, William Coddington, Atherton Hough, Thomas Leverett, and Boston's Borough Council members, central to founding the Massachusetts Bay Company, were also likely present.

"SOME IN LONDON" refers to the cohort of London tradesmen who supported the *Feoffees for Impropriation,* three of whom were appointed *Feoffees* and joined the Massachusetts Bay Company.[2]

These men were primarily domestic retailers, excluded from membership in the powerful overseas companies that dominated London trade.[3] Only twelve of one hundred twenty-nine members of the Massachusetts Bay Company could be considered merchants.

Three (Matthew Craddock, Samuel Vassall, and Nathan Wright) were later named associates in the Massachusetts Bay Company Charter.

"THE WEST COUNTRY" refers to Dorset in southwest England and remnants of the *Dorchester Company,* which went bankrupt in 1626. Its founder, Rev. John White, and John Humfrey, its treasurer, sought to attract investors in London to restart their venture and appealed to Mathew Craddock and his cohort of London tradesmen. Later, Humfrey orchestrated a meeting between Craddock's London tradesmen and the *Boston Men.*

In April 1627, John Humfrey was in Boston for the birth of his son and was asked to witness the signing of Isaac Johnson's Will. Humfrey's ties to Boston stem from his wife, Elizabeth, whose half-brother, Herbert Pelham II, was buried in Boston in 1624.[4]

His son, Herbert Pelham III, inherited his father's Boston estate, was described as *"of Boston"* in his 1626 marriage record, and was one of ten *Boston Men* who joined the Massachusetts Bay Company.[5]

Not only was Herbert Pelham III a first cousin to Humfrey's wife, Elizabeth, but the two also shared an aunt, Elizabeth West, who married Richard Saltonstall in 1631. Saltonstall likely joined the Massachusetts Bay Company due to his ties to the Pelham and Humfrey families.[6]

As a member of the Inns of Court, John Humfrey associated with members Herbert Pelham III and Isaac Johnson and as a member of Lincoln's Inn, Humfrey befriended Preston and Bellingham.[7]

Bellingham had been elected to represent Boston in Parliament in February 1628 and helped found both the New England and Massachusetts Bay Companies.[8] Later, in New England, Bellingham married Herbert Pelham III's sister, Penelope, and served as governor of the Massachusetts Bay Company for ten years.[9]

"IT WAS LIKEWISE DELIBERATELY THOUGHT UPPON, AND AT LENGTH WITH OFTEN NEGOTIATION SOE RIPENED" refers to the *Boston Men* coming to terms with Matthew Craddock and his cohort of London tradesmen. In the Massachusetts Bay Company records, Craddock's group was referred to as the *adventurers*. The *Boston Men* and those who desired to emigrate were called the *planters*. Both groups sought a land grant from the *Council for New England*, then under Warwick's control since Ferdinando Gorges had been assigned command of Plymouth in the Thirty Years War.

As a result, Gorges paid little attention to the Council for New England, so the Earl of Warwick did much as he pleased.[10]

Warwick demanded that *men of blood* apply. As a result, Henry Rosewell, John Younge, and Thomas Southcote were solicited in conformance with the earlier Dorchester Company grant.

In March 1628, the *Rosewell Grant* was secured and enabled the formation of the *New England Company* a month later. Richard Bellingham reportedly drafted the *Rosewell Grant* and served as legal counsel for the group.[11]

New England Company patentees listed in the *Rosewell Grant* were Henry Rosewell, John Younge, Thomas Southcote, John Humfrey, John Endecott, and Simon Whitcombe. These six men are also listed as patentees in the *Massachusetts Bay Company Royal Charter*.

Regardless of being named, Rosewell, Younge, and Southcote played no active role in the company.[12]

Although no copy of the *Rosewell Grant* is known to exist, C.M. Andrews argues *that* the *Rosewell Grant* is assumed to be embedded in the *Massachusetts Bay Company's Royal Charter*.

> *In the absence of the originals of any of the possible documents, the original patent to Warwick and his associates, its transfer to the New England Company, or the supposed grant by the New England Council—any conclusions are bound to be more or less conjectural.*
>
> *It has always been assumed that the copy of the New England Company's patent, embedded in the Massachusetts Bay Company's charter of 1629, is to be taken at its face value as accurately reproducing the original text.*[13]

The New England Company had a total of forty-four members, twenty-four of whom were members from London, and comprised a majority. As a result, Matthew Craddock was elected governor.

Isaac Johnson and Richard Saltonstall were listed first among the associates in the grant, as each had pledged £100 to the venture.

Other associates, like Richard Bellingham, John Venn, and Matthew Craddock, pledged £50 each.[14]

In June 1628, the New England Company selected John Endicott to head its first voyage to Massachusetts. Endicott departed aboard the *Abigail* for Salem with fifty or so settlers.

Before his association with the New England Company, Endicott was relatively unknown. Some historians assume he was from Dorchester, and his willingness to migrate resulted in his being selected to lead the New England Company's first expedition.

Soon after Endicott departed for Massachusetts, death visited the company. In July 1628, John Preston died of tuberculosis, and in November, John Humfreys' wife, Elizabeth, died in childbirth.[15] In August, Thomas Dudley's sixteen-year-old daughter, Anne, was stricken with smallpox and revealed in her fevered state that she was in love with Simon Bradstreet. By the end of the year, the two were wed.

"IN THE YEAR 1629, WEE PROCURED A PATENT FROM HIS MAJESTY FOR OUR PLANTING" refers to the New England Company morphing into the Massachusetts Bay Company and obtaining a Royal Charter on March 4th, 1629.[16] Massachusetts Bay Company records first mentioned the *Boston Men* as a discrete group on March 2nd, 1629, when Thomas Coney presented the *Boston Men*'s desire to each pledge £25 for stock in the company.

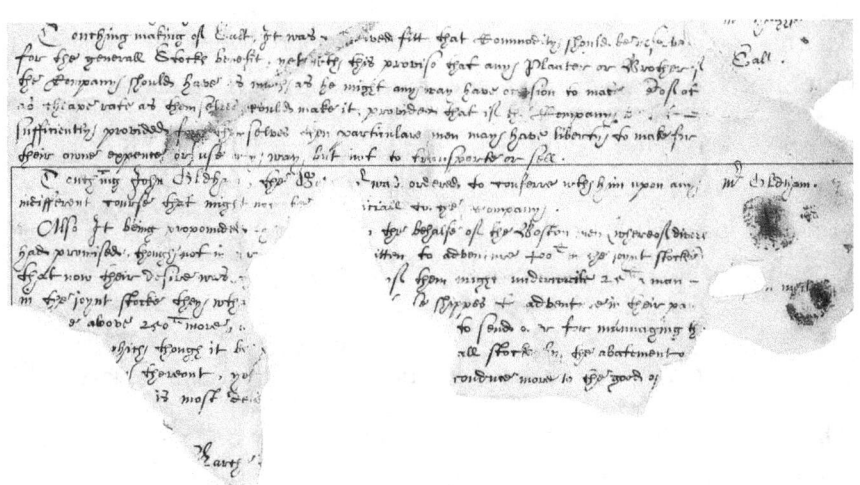

Boston Men's first appearance in Massachusetts Bay Company records.

Mr. Coney proposed that ten Boston Men now desire to invest £25 each in joint stock. Some promised to invest £400 in joint stock, although it is not shown in our records. An additional £250 was promised to purchase ships and provide men to sail to New England.[17]

At the time, Thomas Coney served as Boston's town clerk and was in London to renew Boston's charter and solicit Parliament for repairs to the town's sluice.[18]

Atherton Hough then served as Boston's mayor and likely facilitated Coney's attendance at the meeting. Hough was one of ten *Boston Men* who desired to invest in the company.

Although Isaac Johnson had earlier pledged £400, it did not appear in company records and may have prejudiced the company's general stock.

Regardless, the *Boston Men's* investment was accepted as being *conducive to the good of the plantation*.[19]

It is important to note that the timing of the *Boston Men's* investment was well thought out and strategic.

To ensure success, Lord Saye solicited Robert Wolseley, a clerk of Patents in the Chancery, to secure a Royal Charter.

Twenty years later, Wolseley's son, Charles, married Lord Saye's daughter, Anne Fiennes, in a match that appears to have been arranged in reward for Wolseley having secured and signed a Royal Charter for the Massachusetts Bay Company.[20]

As a result, the Massachusetts Bay Company is the only venture in the twenty years of the Great Migration to obtain a Royal Charter.[21]

The *Boston Men* finalized their investment two days before the company received its Royal Charter—at which time, John Humfreys remarked,

> We are all much bound to Lord Saye for his cordial advice and true affections.[22]
>
> As also my Lord of Warwick. Sir Nathaniel Rich deserves very much acknowledgment for his wise handling of Sir Ferdinando Gorges.[23]

Samuel Skelton, chaplain to the Earl of Lincoln, set sail for Salem aboard the *George Bonaventure* two months after the Royal Charter was granted. It was the company's second expedition.

Upon arrival in New England, Skelton became Salem's first pastor.

In June 1629, a rift developed between the company's founding members, who intended to settle New England—called *the Planters*, and those London tradesmen who intended to remain in England as investors—called *the Adventurers*.

To resolve the rift, the *Adventurers* met in London, and the *Planters* met at Sempringham, on the same day in July, to discuss ways to ensure that *the Planters* could govern their affairs in America without interference from *the Adventurers* in England.

Governor Craddock realized a *Planter* was needed to replace John Endicott as the governor in Massachusetts to divide governance of the company between England and New England.

Despite Isaac Johnson's commitment to migrate, he was not a suitable candidate because the London investors were wary of Johnson's wealth and connections with nobility.

Similarly unsuitable were Dudley and Bradstreet for being too close to the Earl of Lincoln, and Bellingham represented the Boston faction in Parliament.

Had he not been courting the Earl of Lincoln's sister, Lady Susan, John Humfrey would have been an ideal candidate.

A compromise had to be found.

As it happened, Isaac Johnson and Emmanuel Downing were both members of Gray's Inn at the Inns of Court along with Downing's brother-in-law, John Winthrop. As a result, Johnson invited Downing and Winthrop to attend the *Planters'* meeting at Sempringham in July and later wrote to confirm their attendance.[24]

> *It had beene an excellent Tyme for mr. Winthorpe to haue beene this Commencement att Cambridge, where I heare are many reverend Divines, to Consider of mr. Whites call. Lett mee entreat to bee remembered to him, when yow haue occasion to write to him.*
>
> *So expecting yow both heere ere it bee long, with the acknowledgment of much beholdingnes to yow, for many undeserved fauours, I am forced to break off, restinge Your assured frend*
>
> *Isa: Johnson: Sempringham July. 8. 1629*[25]

Three weeks later, Winthrop's diary shows that he and Downing traveled to the meeting at Sempringham.

> *July 28: 1629 My Bro: Downing and myself ridinge into Lincolnshire by Ely, my horse fell under me in a bog in the fennes, so as I was allmost to the waiste in water; but the Lorde preserved me from futher danger. Blessed be his name.*[26]

Despite Winthrop later having been elected the governor of the Massachusetts Bay Company, he traveled to Sempringham with misgivings about leaving England.

When his son, John Jr., considered joining Endicott's expedition to Salem in 1628, Winthrop wrote him saying,

> *"I am loth you should thinke of settlinge there."*[27]

Those men from Boston, who intended to settle New England, and three clerics: John Cotton, Thomas Hooker, and Roger Williams, joined Winthrop, Downing, Dudley, and Johnson at Sempringham.

Although some historians believe that the Earl of Lincoln hosted the Sempringham Meeting, the Earl no longer frequented Sempringham after having severed ties with his mother in 1622.

The Earl and his wife lived at his Tatteshall estate while his mother, younger siblings and the Dudley family remained at Sempringham.

As a result, Thomas Dudley and Isaac Johnson likely hosted the meeting at Sempringham. Dudley lived there with his wife and children, and Johnson and his wife, Lady Arbella, often frequented Sempringham to visit Lady Elizabeth, Arbella's mother.

The Sempringham Meeting focused on issues concerning *the Planters,* and both Dudley and Johnson were committed to settling in New England.

While *the Planters* met at Sempringham, *the Adventurers* met at the London home of Thomas Goffe, the company's deputy governor. Matthew Craddock opened the London meeting, stating,

> *For the advancement of the plantacon, the inducing and encouraging persons of worth an quality to transplant themselves and famylyes thether, and for other weighty reasons therein contained, to transfer the government of the plantacon to those that shall inhabite there, and not to continue the same in subordination to the Company heer, as now is.*[28]

A month later, on August 26th, twelve (12) *Planters* who attended the Sempringham Meeting gathered at Queens' College in Cambridge, to commit to settling in New England in what is known as *The Cambridge Agreement.*

> *It is fully and faithfully agreed amongst us, and every one of us doth hereby freely and sincerely promise and bind himself, in the word of a Christian, and in the presence of God, who is the searcher of all hearts, that we will so really endeavor the prosecution of this work, as by God's assistance, we will be ready in our persons, and with such of our several families as are to go with us, and such provision as we are able conveniently to furnish ourselves withal, to embark for the said*

> *Plantation by the first of March next, at such port or ports of this land as shall be agreed upon by the Company, to the end to pass the Seas (under God's protection) to inhabit and continue in New England.*
>
> *Provided always, that before the last of September next, the whole Government, together with the Patent for the said plantation, be first, by an order of Court, legally transferred and established to remain with us and others which shall inhabit upon the said plantation."* [29]

The most significant signers of the *Cambridge Agreement* were Isaac Johnson, Thomas Dudley, John Humfrey, John Winthrop, and Richard Saltonstall.

All but two of the twelve signers eventually settled in New England.

More importantly, *the Planters'* commitment *"to embark for the said Plantation"* was contingent upon:

> *The whole Government, together with the Patent for the said plantation, be first, by an order of Court, legally transferred and established to remain with us and others which shall inhabit upon the said plantation.*

As a result, the issue of transferring the company's government and its charter to New England was hotly debated at the next meeting of the Massachusetts Bay Company on August 28th, and two committees were formed.[30]

The *Adventurers* were represented by Nathaniel Wright, Theophilus Eaton, Thomas Adams, and William Spurstow, who argued against the transfer.

The *Planters* were represented by Richard Saltonstall, Isaac Johnson, and John Venn, who argued for the transfer.[31]

For over two months, the legality of transferring the company's government and charter to New England preoccupied the company as *the Adventurers* repeatedly insisted that the transfer was illegal.

Finally, on October 15th, 1629, a combined committee of *Adventurers* and *Planters* was established to resolve the matter.

Surprisingly, both Dudley and Winthrop attended their first meeting of the Massachusetts Bay Company that day.

Both men had signed the *Cambridge Agreement,* and both were committed *Planters,* and both supported transferring the company's government and charter to New England; yet neither had ever attended a company meeting before October 15th, 1629.[32]

At the meeting,

- Thomas Dudley, John Winthrop, Richard Saltonstall, Isaac Johnson, John Humfrey, William Vassell, William Pynchon, and Emmanuel Downing represented *the planters*.

- John Davenport, Nathaniel Wright, Richard Perry, Henry Waller, John Venn, Thomas Adams, Simon Whitcombe, Sir John Young, William Spurstow, and John Revell represented *The Adventurers*.

The following day, October 16th, 1629, an agreement was reached, and it was announced that:

> It was thought fitt & natural that the gouvmn^t of psons (persons) bee held there & the gouvmn^t of trade & merchandise to be heere.[33]

This result was made possible because the Royal Charter failed to stipulate where company meetings were to be held.

> *The said Governor, Deputy Governor, and Assistants of the said Company, for the time being, shall or may once every month, or oftener at their pleasures, assemble and hold and keep a Court or Assembly of themselves for the better ordering and directing of their affairs*
>
> *....and that any seven or more persons of the Assistants, together with the Governor, or Deputy Governor so assembled, shall be said, taken, held, and reputed to be, and shall be a full and sufficient Court or Assembly of the said Company, for the handling, ordering all businesses and occurrences as shall from time to time happen, touching or concerning the said Company or plantation*
>
> *....and that there shall or may be held and kept by the Governor, or Deputy Governor of the said Company*
>
> *...upon every last Wednesday in Hillary, Easter, Trinity, and Michaelmas terms respectively forever, one great general and solemn Assembly, which four general Assemblies shall be styled and called the four great and general Courts of the said Company.*

Annual elections were to be held on the last Wednesday of the Easter Term at a place and time chosen by the company. As a result, the Royal Charter did not stipulate where the company would meet, nor that the charter must remain in England.

In short, the company's *planter faction* manipulated a Royal Charter before fully committing to the enterprise, ensuring that those intending to settle in Massachusetts could govern themselves without interference from the company's investors in London.

As a result, the Royal Charter was deliberately worded to prevent oversight by the Crown.

Despite commonly held views that Massachusetts was founded by those fleeing religious persecution, it was established as a *for-profit* venture.

Although the Mayflower story better fits a scenario of religious persecution, it too was established as a *for-profit enterprise*. The Pierce Patent, by which the *Mayflower* sailed, was a commercial venture established by the *Virginia Company of London*.

In 1620, the Earl of Warwick and Ferdinando Gorges established the Council for New England to assimilate the *Virginia Company of London* and the *Virginia Company of Plymouth* into a single venture. Their agent, Thomas Weston, recruited sixty-five (65) individuals as paying passengers or indentured servants to help finance the voyage.[34]

Of the *Mayflower's* one hundred and two (102) passengers, only thirty-seven (37) were religious separatists known as the *pilgrims*. The other sixty-five (65) passengers paid for their passage or were indentured to the Council for New England.

On October 29, 1629, the company held an election to determine who would be governor of *the Planters* in New England.

Johnson, Humfrey, Saltonstall, and Winthrop were nominated, and Winthrop was elected due to:

> his integritie & sufficiencie, as being one every well fitted & accomplished for the place Govno^r.[35]

John Humfrey was elected Deputy Governor. Thomas Dudley and Isaac Johnson were elected Assistants.

In March 1630, the company relocated to South Hampton, where what is known as the *Winthrop Fleet* lay at anchor.

An old warship named the *Eagle* had been purchased and refurbished, primarily due to Isaac Johnson's contribution of £ 5,000.

The *Eagle* was christened the *Arbella* after Johnson's wife and made the fleet's flagship.[36]

On March 18th, 1630, Simon Bradstreet and William Coddington were elected Assistants.

Five days later, John Humfrey announced his intention to remain in England, and Thomas Dudley was elected Deputy Governor to replace him.

Humfrey's reason for remaining in England became apparent later in December, when, after having married Lady Susan Clinton, he began addressing Isaac Johnson as *'brother'*. [37]

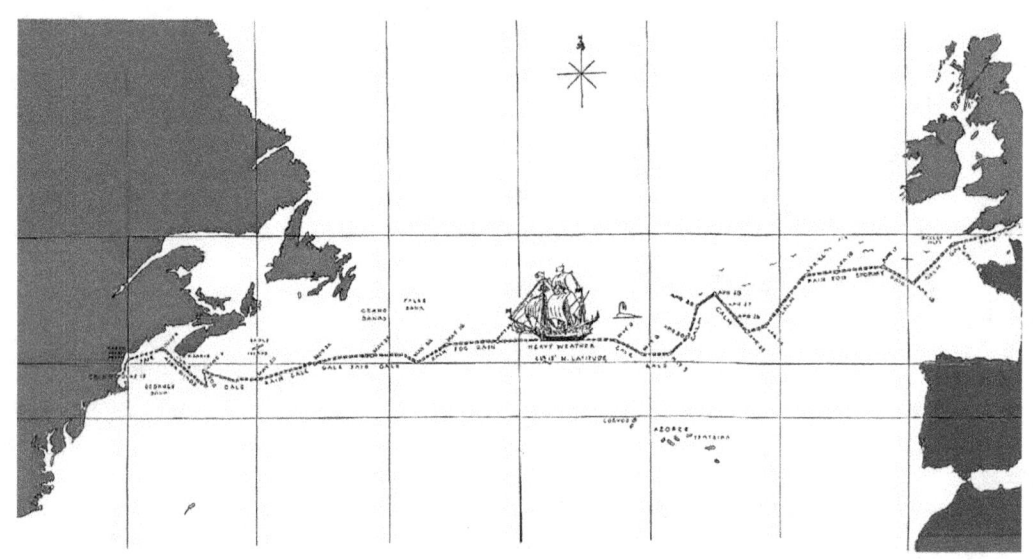

Route of the Arbella, flagship of the Winthrop Fleet, April 11 to June 30, 1630

CITY ON A HILL

When Rev. John Cotton was asked to preach a farewell sermon to the departing Massachusetts Bay Company in April 1630, his sermon likened those departing England to the Israelites chosen to inhabit the promised land.[1]

> *Moreover, I will appoint a place for my people Israel, and I will plant them, that they may dwell in a place of their owne, and move no more.*[2] Samuel 2: 7.10

What is called the Winthrop Fleet sailed from Southampton to the Isle of Wight on April 8th, with approximately 210 passengers aboard, and then departed for New England on April 11th.[3] The *Boston Men* who sailed with the fleet were:

- Isaac Johnson and his wife, Lady Arbella
- Simon Bradstreet and his wife, Anne Dudley
- Thomas Dudley and his family of six.
- Charles Fiennes, the younger brother of Lady Arbella.
- William Coddington and his wife, Mary.

A TALE OF TWO BOSTONS

The Cotton Window in St. Botolph's Church - Boston, England

Governor John Winthrop delivered *A Model of Christian Charity* to passengers aboard the *Arbella* in April 1630.

> *We must delight in each other; make others' conditions our own; rejoice together, mourn together, labor and suffer together, always having before our eyes our commission and community in the work, as members of the same body.*

> *So shall we keep the unity of the spirit in the bond of peace. The Lord will be our God, and delight to dwell among us, as his own people... for we must consider that we shall be as a City upon a Hill. The eyes of all people are upon us.*

Two additional men from Boston who were not members of the Massachusetts Bay Company also sailed with the Winthrop Fleet.

- William Pelham, younger brother of Herbert Pelham III, migrated to New England later in 1638.
- William Cheeseborough, his wife, Anne Stevenson, and four children, Peter, Samuel, Nathaniel, and Sarah.[4]

Upon arriving in New England, William Coddington returned to England to remarry after the death of his wife, Mary. He returned aboard the *Mary & John* in 1633 with his new wife, Mary Mosely, and five servants.

After preaching the Winthrop Fleet farewell sermon, John Cotton returned to Boston, Lincolnshire, to remain vicar of the local parish.

Within a month of returning, Cotton and his wife, Elizabeth, were stricken with malaria, known locally as *fen fever*; and in January 1631, were invited to convalesce at the Earl of Lincoln's Sempringham estate. Cotton Mather wrote of the event,

> Being invited unto the Earl of Lincoln's, in pursuance of the Advice of his Physicians, that he (Cotton) should change the Air, he removed thither; and thereupon he happily recovered.[5]

Boston town records show that on February 7, 1631,

> Three pounds & seven shillings were laid down to Mr. Doctor Coozen & his Apothecary for theire charddges to advise about Mr Cottons sickness.[6]

Slow to recover, Cotton complained as late as the summer of 1633:

> The dregs of the ague still hang about me.

Elizabeth, Cotton's beloved wife of eighteen years, however, did not recover and died. Though it is unknown when her funeral occurred or where she was buried, Boston town records reflect that John Brown, Boston's mayor, was paid seven pounds ten shillings in November 1631 to cover Elizabeth Cotton's funeral expenses.[7]

> *Paid to Mr Maior for soe much expended by him about Mrs Cottons funeral.*[8]

Returning to those who migrated, Thomas Dudley provided a detailed account of the *Winthrop Fleet's* Atlantic crossing in a 1631 letter to Lady Bridget, Countess of Lincoln.[9]

> *Wee came to such resolution that in April, 1630, wee set sail from old England with 4 good shipps.*[10] *And in May following, 8 more followed;*[11] *2 having gone before in February and March;*[12] *and 2 more following in June and August, besides another set out by a private merchant.*[13] *These 17 shipps arrived all safe in New England for the increase of the plantation here this yeare 1630—but made a long, troublesome and costly voyage, beeing all windbound long in England, and hindered with contrary winds, after they set sail and soe scattered wth. mists and tempests that few of them arrived together.*
>
> *Our 4 shipps which sett out in April arrived here in June and July, where wee found the Colony in a sadd and unexpected condition, above 80 of them beeing dead the winter before, and many of those alive were weak and sick; all the corne and bread amongst them all, hardly sufficient to feed upon a fortnight, insomuch that the remainder of 180 servants wee had the two yeares before sent over, cominge to us for victualls to sustain them, wee found ourselves wholly unable to feed them by reason that the provisions shipped for them were taken out of the shipp they were put in, and they who were trusted to shipp them in another, failed us, and left them behind; whereupon necessity enforced us to our extreme loss to give them all*

> libertie, who had cost us about 16 or 20 £ a person furnishing and sending over.[14] But bearing theis things as wee might, wee beganne to consult of the place of our sitting downe; for Salem, where wee landed, pleased us not.[15]

Dudley further reported at least two hundred people died between April and December 1630.

> Many of our people brought with us beeing sick of feavers and the scurvy ... wherein many were interrupted with sickness and many dyed weekly, yea almost dayley. Amongst whom were Mrs. Pinchon, Mrs. Coddington, Mrs. Philips, and Mrs. Alcock, a sister of Mr. Hookers. Wee were forced to change counsaile for... Charlestowne, which stands on the North side of the mouth of Charles River.[16]

Soon after landing at Salem, Lady Arbella, Isaac Johnson's wife, died of what is thought to have been scurvy and was buried in an unmarked grave off Bridge Street near Arbella Street in present-day Salem.

In England, John Cotton remarried to Sarah (Hawkred) Story, who was seventeen years his junior.

Cotton had known Sarah from her childhood, as he had conducted baptisms, burials, and marriages for the Hawkred family for over twenty years.

Sarah's first husband, William Story, apprenticed with her father. They married in May 1619, and William died ten years later, in 1628, leaving Sarah widowed with a six-year-old daughter named Elizabeth.

In Massachusetts, the Winthrop moved the company from Salem to Charlestown, in the hope of finding a plentiful source of fresh water, but none was found.

A TALE OF TWO BOSTONS

William Blaxton contacted Isaac Johnson to inform him that there was a good source of fresh water on the Shawmut Peninsula—called *Trimountaine* by the French.

Johnson—still grieving the loss of Lady Arbella—led the company to freshwater on the Shawmut Peninsula.[17]

Records of the Governor and Company of the Massachusetts Bay document that on September 7, 1630:

> It is ordered, that Trimountaine shallbe called Boston.[18]

Dudley's letter to Lady Bridget also referenced Boston's naming.

> Which place we named Boston, as we intended to have done the place wee first resolved on.[19]

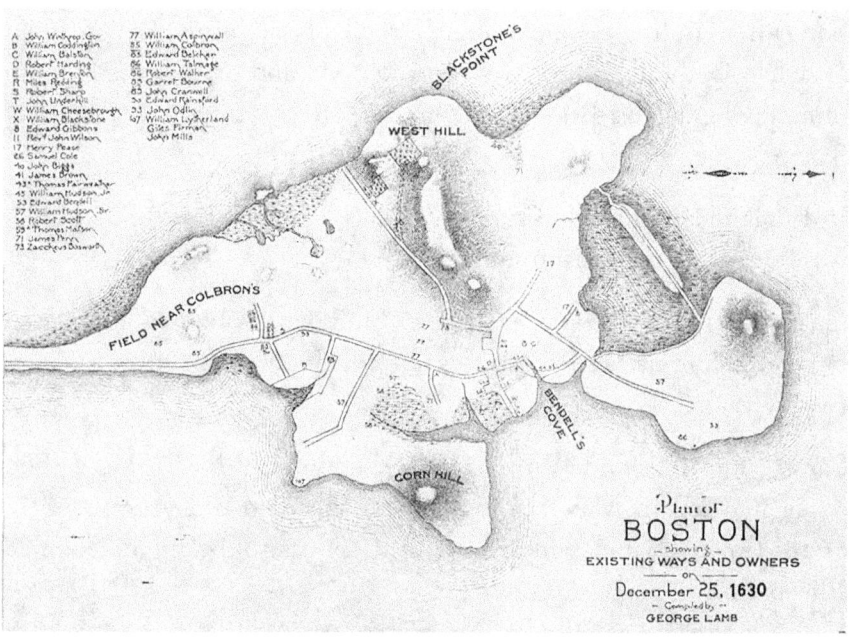

Winthrop noted in his journal that death continued to plague the company despite finding an excellent source of fresh water.

> *About the beginning of September, died Mr. Gager, a right godly man, a skilful chirurgeon, and one of the deacons of our congregation; and Mr. Higginson, one of the ministers of Salem, a zealous and a profitable preacher—this of a consumption, that of a fever, and on the 30th of September, dyed Mr. Johnson another of the five undertakers (the Lady Arrabella, his wife, being dead a month before.) This gentleman was a prime man amongst us, having the best estate of any, zealous for religion and greatest furtherer of this plantation. He made a most godly end, dying willingly, professing his life better spent in promoting this plantatacon than it would have beene any other way. He left to us a loss greater than the most conceived.[20]*

The town of Boston inherited Isaac Johnson's land and buried him in what they called *Isaac Johnson's Burying Ground*, which is now known as *King's Chapel Burying Ground*.

Back in England, after Bishop of London, William Laud, issued a warrant for his arrest, John Cotton, his pregnant wife, Sarah, her daughter, Elizabeth, eight servants, and forty-six (46) members of his congregation boarded the *Griffin* on July 22, 1633, bound for Massachusetts. Accompanying him were founding members of the Massachusetts Bay Company: Atherton Hough, Thomas Leverett, and Abraham Mellows. Cotton's 1633 migration amounted to a 240% increase over the nineteen individuals from Boston that sailed with the *Winthrop Fleet* in 1630.

The final eight years of the Great Migration, from 1633 to 1640, account for approximately 80% of the Great Migration due to William Laud becoming Archbishop and his subsequent persecution of Puritans and is now termed—the *Laudian Migration*.[21]

On the voyage to New England, at age 49, John Cotton became a father for the first time as, in retrospect, it seems that his first wife, Elizabeth, was unable to bear children.

Sarah Cotton boarded the *Griffin* nine months pregnant and gave birth to a son at sea, whom they fittingly named *Seaborn*. Since Cotton held the congregational view that election by a congregation bestows sanctity on a vicar, Seaborn could not be baptized at sea. Winthrop's Journal entry for September 4, 1633, noted Cotton's arrival.

> *Sept. 4. The Griffin, a ship of three hundred tons, arrived (having been eight weeks from the Downs). In this ship came Mr. Cotton, Mr. Hooker and Mr. Stone, ministers, and Mr. Pierce, Mr. Haynes (a gentleman of great estate), Mr. Hoffe, and many other men of good estates. They got out of England with much difficulty, all places being belaid to have taken Mr. Cotton and Mr. Hooker, who had been long sought for to have been brought into the high commission, but the master being bound to touch at the Wight, the pursuivants attended there, and, in the meantime, the said ministers were take in at the Downs. Mr. Hooker and Mr. Stone went presently to Newtown, where they were to be entertained, and Mr. Cotton stayed at Boston.*[22]

Less than a week after arriving, John and Sarah Cotton were admitted to the Church of Boston, and their son, Seaborn, was baptized by John Wilson, pastor of Boston's Church.

Wilson had received his Master's from King's College, Cambridge. Before migrating with the Winthrop Fleet, Wilson had been considered more of a scholar than a preacher.

On October 10th, the Church of Boston kept fast and elected Cotton, their teacher, and Thomas Leverett, their ruling elder.[23]

John Winthrop reflected on Cotton's impact on the Church of Boston in December 1633 as follows:

> *It pleased the Lord to give special testimony of his presence in the Church of Boston after Mr. Cotton was called to office there.*

> *More were converted and added to that church than to all the other churches in the bay... divers profane and notorious evil persons came and confessed their sins and were comfortably received into the bosom of the church. Yea, the Lord gave witness to the exercise of Prophecy.*[24]

As a new father and a Fellow of Emmanuel College, Cambridge, John Cotton had a vested interest in education and in April 1635, established America's first public school to educate Boston's youth.

The Boston Latin School was modeled after the Boston Grammar School in Boston, Lincolnshire, which Cotton had helped manage as the town's vicar.

Philemon Pormort, from Alford, Lincolnshire, was selected as the school's first master. In October 1627, Portmort married Susanna Bellingham, a distant relative of Richard Bellingham, and migrated to Massachusetts with Anne Hutchinson and her family in 1634.[25]

On October 6th, 1635, Sir Henry Vane arrived in Boston aboard the *Abigail,* accompanied by Hugh Peters and John Winthrop Jr., who had been appointed the Governor of the Saybrook Colony in what is now Connecticut by its founders, Lord Saye and Lord Brooke.

Originally, Vane intended to accompany John Winthrop Jr. to settle the Saybrook Colony. However, the citizens of Boston found him so dashing and charismatic that they refused to let him leave.

Though raised in luxury, young Vane became a Puritan, which resulted in his dismissal from Oxford University. His father was Comptroller and Treasurer of the Royal Household of Charles I. Frustrated by his son's Puritanism, young Vane was sent to Vienna as an assistant to Robert Anstruther, the English ambassador.[26]

Upon his return, his father encouraged his son to seek a position in the king's Privy Chamber and asked Charles I how to best rid his son of his nonconformist views.

Charles arranged an audience with Archbishop Laud, during which Laud quickly lost his patience with Vane, who contemptuously tossed his long hair aside and departed, ending the interview.

Upon his arrival in New England, John Cotton became a father figure and mentor to Vane, who was then but twenty-two years old. Cotton invited Vane to join his family, so Vane built an addition to the Cotton house at his own expense, which he later endowed to Cotton's firstborn son, Seaborn.

Both Cotton and Vane were university-educated and spoke several languages. Cotton had been the head lecturer at Emmanuel College, Cambridge, was fluent in Latin, Greek, and Hebrew, and wrote poetry in Greek. Vane was fluent in Greek and Latin and spoke several European languages.

At the time, John Cotton was fifty years old and the most distinguished cleric and scholar in New England.

As a new father, Cotton had already established the Boston Latin School and likely discussed the need for a place of higher education with Vane during long evenings by the fire.

This idea incubated for several years before becoming a reality when Vane was elected Governor.

On October 28, 1636, the General Court, headed by Vane, allocated £400 to establish a place of higher education.

Josiah Quincy, past President of Harvard University, later said,

> *The General Court appointed twelve of the most eminent men of the colony to take order for a college at Newtown, all of them names dear to New England, on account of their sacrifices, their sufferings, and virtues. Of the twelve, six were magistrates, and six were clergy. The most influential were John Winthrop, Thomas Dudley, and Rev. John Cotton.*

CITY ON A HILL

To these, the name of Sir Henry Vane must be added, as he was governor and head of the court that first proposed a college in 1636.[27]

A timeline of Harvard College's founding follows:

- On October 28, 1636, the General Court voted that *the good people of Massachusetts would provide £400 for the establishment of a place of education, with £200 to be paid the following year and £200 upon completion of the work.* The next Court then appointed the location and type of building.
- In May 1637, John Harvard emigrated to New England with his wife and settled in Charlestown, Massachusetts.
- On November 15, 1637, the College is ordered to be at New Towne.

Harvard College founding plaque

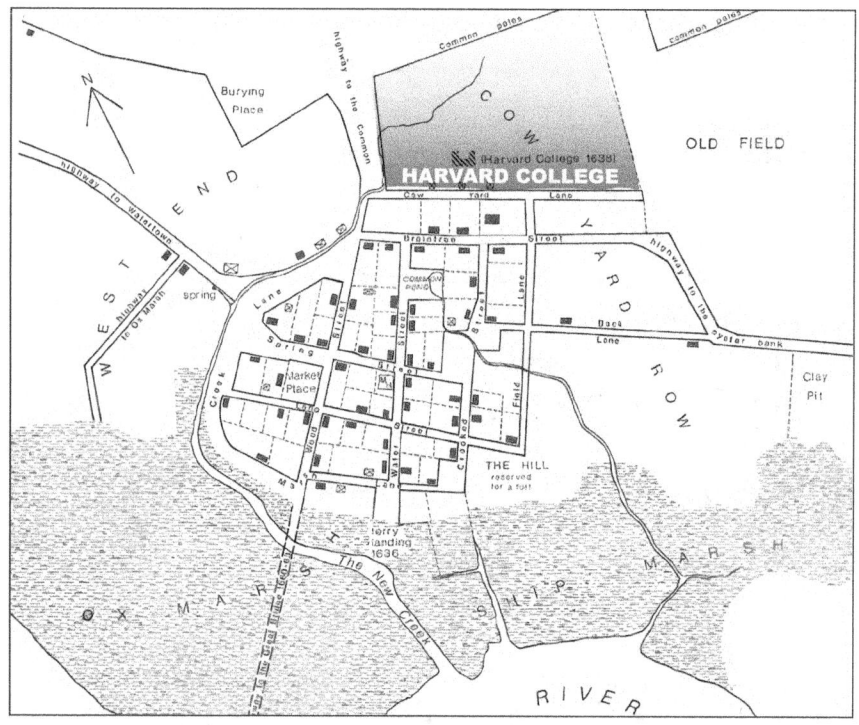

1638 Map showing Harvard College's proposed location in New Towne

- November 27, 1637, Court Records show: *For the College, the Governor, Mr. Winthrope; the Deputy, Mr. Dudley; the Treasurer, Mr. Bellingham; along with Mr. Cotton that these or the greater part of them, whereof Mr. Winthrope, Mr. Dudley, or Mr. Bellingham, to be always be one, to take order for a College at Newetowne.*[28]
- Mr. Nathaniel Eaton, a graduate of Trinity College, Cambridge, was appointed the first professor and master of Harvard College.
- May 2, 1638, Court records state: *It is ordered that Newetowne shall henceforth be called Cambridge.*[29]

CITY ON A HILL

- May 11, 1638, nearly three acres were granted *to the professor and to the Town's use forever, for a public school or college; and the use of Mr. Nathaniel Eaton as long as he shall be employed in that work; so that at his death, or ceasing from that work, he or his shall be allowed according to the charges he hath been at, in building or fencing.*
- 1638 - Nathaniel Eaton commenced teaching.[30]
- On September 14, 1638, John Harvard died at age thirty-one and verbally disposed of his property in place of a written will, with half of his estate and all his library going to the new college proposed for the New Towne. The remainder of his estate was left to his wife.
- March 18, 1639 - In recognition of John Harvard's endowment, Court records state, *It is ordered that the College agreed upon formerly to be built at Cambridge shall be called Harvard College.*[31]
- On September 4, 1639, Nathaniel Eaton was censured for beating Nathaniel Briscoe with a cudgel by striking him over two hundred blows.
- Mrs. Eaton confessed to the ill and scant diet she served students, including skimpy portions of bad food. However, she denied any knowledge of *goat dung being added to their hasty pudding.*[32]
- The Court fined Mr. Eaton £40 and *debarred him from teaching children within our jurisdiction.* Eaton fled to Virginia before it was discovered that he had taken over £200 and received £500 in cash for worthless bills of exchange.
- As a result, the court seized his estate, and the college was closed for a year.[33]

Old Harvard College 1638-1670

- On September 23, 1642, the first commencement at Harvard College was held as *nine bachelors gave good proof of their proficiency in the tongues and arts.* All nine graduates lined up in front of President Henry Dunster. He conferred degrees on the group in order of their parents' prominence, which made Benjamin Woodbridge Harvard's first graduate. After delivering an address in Latin, Dunster handed each new scholar *"a Booke of Arts,"* wrote one witness.
- The General Court decided that magistrates and teaching elders of the six nearest churches would be governors of the college, and most of these dined with the students at commencement.[34]
- December 27, 1643, *By order of the General Court all the magistrates and the teaching elders of the six nearest churches were appointed to be forever governors of the*

college, and this day they met at Cambridge and considered of the officers of the college, and chose a treasurer, H. Pelham, Esq., being the first of that office.[35] John Cotton was elected to represent the First Church of Boston as one of Harvard College's six governors.

John Harvard graduated from John Cotton's *alma mater*, Emmanuel College, Cambridge University—as did Isaac Johnson, William Blaxton, Simon Bradstreet, and the Earl of Warwick.

When Harvard was admitted to Emmanuel College in 1627, John Preston was its Master. Though Preston was in the habit of sending promising Emmanuel graduates to John Cotton for finishing, by the time Harvard completed his Master of Arts in 1636, Cotton had already migrated to America.

In 1636, John Harvard married Anne Sadler of Ringmer, Sussex. That same year, he inherited nearly £1,600 from his mother, Katherine Rogers, who was born at Stratford-upon-Avon to Thomas Rogers, a well-to-do butcher, master, and grazier who undoubtedly knew William Shakespeare and his younger brother, Edmund. Katherine Rogers married twice: first to Robert Harvard and then to John Elleston of London.

Both husbands left her sizeable estates. With his inheritance, John Harvard purchased over £200 in books and set sail for New England in the spring of 1637 after being offered a teaching post as best Charlestown could provide. Within a year of his arrival at Charlestown, Harvard died of consumption on September 14, 1638, at the age of thirty.

Having no written will, Harvard verbally dictated that half his estate and library be given to the *'new college'* while the other half should go to his wife.

On March 18, 1639, the *'new college'* was named Harvard College by the Massachusetts Court in recognition of Harvard's contribution.

A stained-glass window in the Emmanuel College Chapel at Cambridge University commemorates John Harvard's role in helping fund the founding of Harvard College.

An idealized image of John Harvard in stained glass in the chapel at Emmanuel College Cambridge

In 1634, Anne Hutchinson arrived in Boston, Massachusetts, and moved across the street from John Winthrop, who soon became furious with her community involvement and outspoken nature. Four years later, Winthrop wrote,

> *When Mrs. Hutchinson was cast out of the church. Mrs. Dyer going forth with her, a stranger asked what young woman it was.*
>
> *The others answered, it was the woman which had the monster which gave the first occasion to some that heard it to speak of it.*[36]

The *monster* referred to was a miscarriage Mary Dyer suffered six months earlier while Anne Hutchinson assisted as midwife.

This ultimately led to Anne's banishment and Henry Vane's decision to return to England.

Anne consulted John Cotton regarding the legality of concealing the birth and disposing of the fetus.

Anne had long been a member of John Cotton's St. Botolph's congregation in England, and Cotton told her that if the fetus were buried, it would be best to conceal the matter, because he *"would want it so if it had happened to him."*

When news of the incident leaked, Governor Winthrop confronted Cotton, who famously replied,

> *Mistress Hutchinson, Cotton, and God buried the fetus that day!*[37]

Noted historian Robert Winthrop, a descendant of John Winthrop, shied away from the affair, saying,

> *The story of Mrs. Hutchinson and the Antinomian Controversy belongs to another writer and is gladly left to him.*

A TALE OF TWO BOSTONS

Winthrop's March 27, 1638 diary entry continued,

> *The governor, with advice of some other of the magistrates and elders of Boston, caused the said monster to be taken up, and though it were much corrupted, yet most of those things were to be seen, as the horns and claws, the scales, etc.*
>
> *When it died in the mother's body, (which was about two hours before the birth,) whereon the mother lay, and withal there was such a noisome savor, as most of the women were taken with extreme vomiting and purging, so as they were forced to depart; and others of them their children were taken with convulsions, (which they never had before nor after,) and so were sent for home, so as by these occasions it came to be concealed.*[38]

Winthrop's diary continues regarding the miscarriage Anne Hutchinson recently suffered.

> *Mistress Hutchison being big with child, and growing towards the time of her labor, as other women doe, she brought forth not one, (as Mistress Dyer did) but (what was more strange to amazement) thirty monstrous births or thereabouts, at once; some of them bigger, some lesser, some of one shape, some of another; few of any perfect shape, none at all of them (as far as I could ever learn) of human shape.*[39]

Winthrop's smear campaign did not end there. Wild rumors were circulated regarding Anne Hutchinson's promiscuity. One of these rumors claimed Henry Vane had fathered the deformed births.

By tragic coincidence, Mary Dyer and Anne Hutchinson each suffered a miscarriage within six months of each other, only to be disparaged by Winthrop's politicization of the miscarriages as the work of the devil in a smear campaign perpetrated to justify the persecution of two of New England's best and brightest minds.

Anne Hutchinson **Mary Dyer**

After having been governor for four of the six preceding terms, Winthrop was defeated by Vane in 1636. Sir Henry Vane was a follower of Anne Hutchinson and had been Winthrop's chief political rival since his arrival in Boston in 1635.

During what was known as the Antinomian Controversy, the town of Boston split into rival camps, with Winthrop, Endicott, and Wilson on one side and Vane, Hutchinson, and Cotton on the other. Cotton survived the controversy, but Anne Hutchinson and her family were banished from the colony. They first moved to Rhode Island and then to what is now the Borough of Bronx in New York City near Pelham Bay Park, where, in the summer of 1643, they were inadvertently killed in a raid on a Dutch village by members of the Lenape tribe.

Sir Henry Vane packed his things, willed his portion of Cotton's house to Seaborn Cotton, and returned to England in August 1637, after Winthrop was again elected governor. Relieved, Winthrop ordered *his honorable dismission* with *divers vollies of shot.*

In 1640, John Cotton turned fifty-five, and his wife, Sarah, gave birth to their second son, John Cotton Jr. That same year, Charles I asked Parliament to fund his campaign against the Scots, which had bogged down.[40]

In a *Quid pro quo*, Parliament demanded that Charles reform the English church. Charles refused and dissolved Parliament.

Soon after, England was plunged into civil war, and the Massachusetts Bay Company was out of danger of having its royal charter revoked.[41]

Despite having been knighted by Charles I, Sir Henry Vane was elected to head the Long Parliament, which convened from November 1640 until 1660. During this period, the English Civil Wars took place, and Charles I was executed.

Cotton's teleological interpretation of these events, based on *Revelation 16,* assumed that God willed the Great Migration to reform the church because,

> *The time of the Fifth Vial was upon them, and the second coming of Jesus Christ would be nigh.*[42]

Maria, the daughter of John and Sarah Cotton, was born in 1642 and later married Increase Mather. Cotton Mather was their son.

That same year, Charles I was forced to flee London for Hampton Court and the Westminster Assembly convened to discuss potential church reforms as three New Englanders: Cotton, Hooker, and Davenport, were urged:

> *to come ovar with all possible speed, all or any of them towards the seatlinge and composeing the affaires of the church.*[43]

Perhaps sensing the coming chaos, the three declined, and in response, Cotton authored *The Keys of the Kingdom of Heaven*, which gave rise to *the Congregational Way,* and occasioned a leading opponent at Westminster to refer to Cotton as,

> *The prime man of them all in New England.*

Between 1643 and 1650, the Massachusetts Bay Colony maintained close ties with its English brethren as the crown was undone and Cromwell came to power.

John Cotton's third son, Roland, was born in December 1644, and a month later, on January 10, 1645, Archbishop William Laud was tried and beheaded on Tower Hill.

In 1646, congregational ministers petitioned the General Court of Massachusetts to convene a Synod of Churches to determine whether Presbyterianism or Congregationalism offered the most effective church governance.

The synod opened in Cambridge in September 1646, and Ralph Partridge, Richard Mather, and John Cotton were appointed to propose models of church government.

Richard Mather concluded what is known as the Cambridge Platform by citing *The Keys of the Kingdom of Heaven,* Cotton's work, which established the *Congregational Way.*

In 1648, as John Cotton turned sixty-three, Charles I surrendered his crown, ending England's Civil Wars.

Between 1649 and 1659, the pace of English history accelerated so rapidly that the Massachusetts Bay Colony could hardly keep up with events.

A TALE OF TWO BOSTONS

The trial of Charles I began on January 19, 1649, and he was beheaded on January 30, 1649. The following year, in 1650, tea was introduced to England for the first time.

At a Thanksgiving sermon, Rev. John Cotton discussed the causes of the English Civil Wars to justify the trial and execution of Charles I to his congregation.

Frances J. Bremer says of the upheaval in England,

> *New Englanders continued to look eagerly for news from England, relying on reports from proven friends to help them sift fact from rumor and thus to understand the nature of the debates and changes in the motherland.*

> *Both before and after the execution of the king, New Englanders cast their lot with their English Puritan friends. When Oliver Cromwell became Lord Protector, the Massachusetts General Court instructed its agent in England, John Leverett, to take the first convenient opportunity to let his Highness understand how thankfullie we accept and at all tymes readilie acknowledge his Highness favour and clemencie towards us.*[44]

John Cotton corresponded with Cromwell, who communicated his belief that

> *The Lord hath set you forth a vessel honour to his name, in working many and great deliverances for his people, and for his truth.*

In 1650, a smallpox epidemic ravaged Boston and took the Cotton's eldest daughter, Sarah, and their youngest son, Roland.

In his grief, John Cotton found an outlet in poetry and composed a poem for each child in Greek[45]. His touching verse for Sarah, translated from Greek, reads:

> *Εὔξαι, πάτερ φίλτατε· νῦν ἐπίτρεψόν μοι ἀπελθεῖν*
> Pray, dearest father, now allow me to go home.
>
> *εἰς οἶκον· ταῦτ᾽ ἦν ἔσχατα ῥήματ᾽ ἐμοί.*
> To my home; these were the last words I spoke.
>
> *Σάρρα γλυκυτάτη, πορεύου· κατάπαυσιν ἔχουσα*
> Go then, sweetest Sarah; possessing your rest.
>
> *σαββατισμὸν λάβε μετὰ Κυρίου καὶ μακάρων.*
> Take the Sabbath-rest with your Lord be blessed. 46

In 1651, Seaborn Cotton graduated from Harvard College. Across the Atlantic, while Cromwell was ill, recovering from the Battle of Dunbar, Charles II was crowned King of Scotland in Edinburgh. Later that September, after the Battle of Worcester, Cromwell wrote Cotton saying,

> *Surely, Sir, the Lord is greatly to be feared, as to be praised! We need your prayers in this as much as ever. How shall we behave ourselves after such mercies? What is the Lord a-doing? What prophecies are now fulfilling? Who is a God like ours?*[47]

In November 1652, John Cotton crossed the Charles River by boat to preach a sermon to the students at Harvard College entitled, *Thy Children shall be taught of the Lord.*

The return trip was bitterly cold, and Cotton became ill after exposure to the river's dampness. An evening or two later, Cotton left his study and said to his wife, Sarah, "*I shall go into that room no more,*" and took to his bed ill for over three weeks.

During his illness, Harvard College's President, Henry Dunster, visited Cotton to ask for his blessing by saying, "*I know in my heart, they whom you bless shall be blessed.*" The pastor of the First Church in Boston, Rev. John Wilson, asked *God to lift the light of his countenance* on Cotton. To which he replied, "*God hath done it already, brother!*"

John Cotton died at home in bed on December 23, 1652, and was interred in Isaac Johnson's Burying Ground. Later, in 1720, a memorial stone was erected in King's Chapel Burying Ground that reads:

> Here Lyes Intombed the Bodyes of the Famous Reverend & Learned Pastors of the First Church of Christ in BOSTON.
>
> Mr JOHN COTTON Aged 67 Years. Dec^d Decm^{br} the 23rd 1652.

Memorial to John Cotton & pastors of Boston's First Church

By the time Cotton died, his wife, Sarah, had borne him six children.

Cotton's sons, Seaborn and John Jr., attended Harvard College and followed in their father's footsteps into the clergy.

CITY ON A HILL

Sarah and Rowland died of smallpox in 1650.

Their daughter, Elizabeth, married Jeremiah Eggington and died the following year in 1656. Daughter Maria married Increase Mather, the son of Richard Mather. Their son, Cotton Mather, achieved fame for his role in the Salem Witch Trials, was a prolific author, and eventually became president of Harvard College.

Between the death of John Cotton in 1652 and the 1677 death of his wife, Sarah, the following events occurred,

- In 1654, Seaborn Cotton married Dorothy Bradstreet, daughter of Governor Simon Bradstreet, whose wife, Anne Bradstreet, became New England's most famous poet and author of *The Tenth Muse*.
- In 1656, Sarah Cotton remarried to Richard Mather, father of her son-in-law, Increase Mather. Thus, mother and daughter (Sarah and Maria Cotton) married father and son (Richard and Increase Mather). Richard Mather preceded Sarah in death and was buried in Dorchester.
- In 1657, Oliver Cromwell declined an offer of the crown, and John Cotton Jr. graduated from Harvard College.
- In 1658, Oliver Cromwell died in England, and Seaborn's wife, Dorothy, gave birth to Sarah's first grandson, John.
- In 1659, under pressure from Sir Henry Vane, Oliver Cromwell's son Richard resigned as the Lord Protector of England.
- In 1660, John Cotton Jr. married Joanna Rossiter, daughter of Dr. Bryan Rossiter, in Guilford, Connecticut.
- In England, despite Sir Henry Vane's protests, Parliament reinstated the Stuart monarchy and made Charles II king.

Despite having been banished from Boston in 1638, Mary Dyer returned in May 1660 and was brought before Governor Endicott, who condemned her to death.

Mary's executioner publicly proclaimed her

> *guilty of her own blood,*

Pastor John Wilson then urged Mary to repent of her sin and not be

> *"so deluded and carried away by the deceit of the devil."*

Mary replied,

> *"Nay man, I am not now to repent."*[48]

On June 1, 1660, Mary Dyer was hanged from a tree in the Boston Common.

Sarah (*Hawkred, Story, Cotton*) Mather died on May 27, 1676, at age seventy-five, twenty-five years after John Cotton, her husband of twenty years, and is the only woman born in Boston, England, to have been buried in Boston's oldest burying ground.

The only other person from Boston, England, buried in King's Chapel Burying Ground is John Leverett, who served as Governor of Massachusetts from 1673 to 1679.

Sarah's headstone, located near John Cotton, is easily missed as there is no mention of her being Cotton's wife. Her headstone reads:

> *Sarah Mather*
> *The Wife of Richard*
> *Mather aged 75*
> *yeares departed*
> *this life y^e 27 day*
> *of may 1677*

CITY ON A HILL

Sarah (Hawkred /Story/Cotton) Mather is the only woman born in Boston, England, to be buried in Boston's King's Chapel Burying Ground. The only other person from Boston, England, buried in King's Chapel Burying Ground is John Leverett, who served as Governor of Massachusetts from 1673 to 1679.

FOUNDING FACTORS

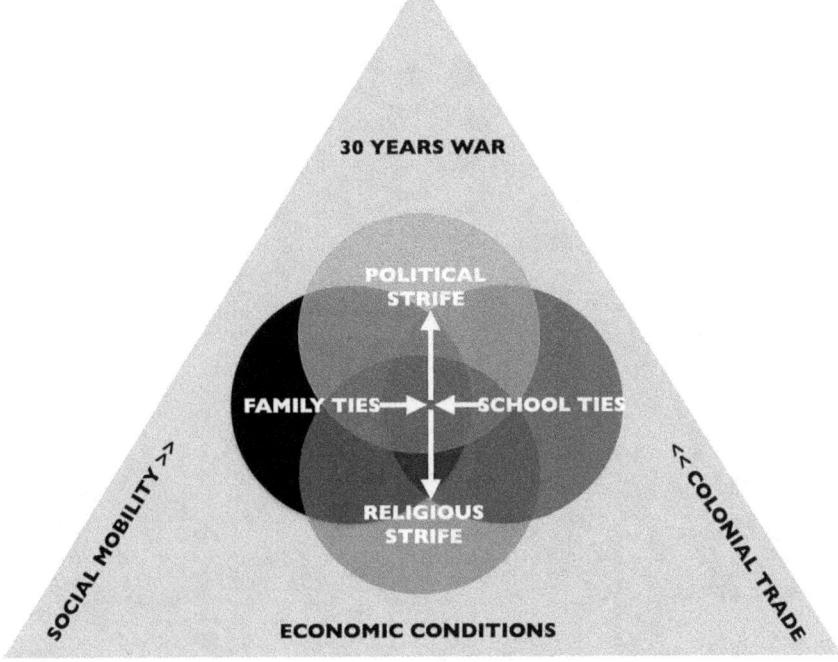

The Massachusetts Bay Company was created during a period of unprecedented turmoil in early 17th-century England due to:

- Political strife as a result of the accession of the Stuart Dynasty to the English throne.
- Religious strife as a result of Archbishop Laud's obsession with restoring the church to its former Catholic splendor.

Cohesive elements in English society helped to mitigate this strife by fostering resistance to Stuart oppression that facilitated the formation of the Massachusetts Bay Company as follows:

- Family ties fostered solidarity through blood and marriage.
- School ties transcended social standing, fostering unity.

POLITICAL STRIFE

JAMES STUART
King of England, Scotland & Ireland

GEORGE VILLIERS
Duke of Buckingham

CHARLES STUART
King of England, Scotland & Ireland

Rex fuit Elizabeth - nunc est regina Jacobus
Elizabeth was King - now James is Queen[1]

The Stuart reign was born in violence when Elizabeth I executed Mary, Queen of Scots, in 1587. Elizabeth died without an heir in 1603, and Mary's son, James, was crowned King of England. Ascension of a Scot to the English throne initiated unrest and political strife that culminated in the assassination of James' homosexual lover, civil war, and the only regicide in English history— the beheading of James' successor, Charles I.

A TALE OF TWO BOSTONS

Not long after Elizabeth ordered the execution of Mary, Queen of Scots, her the court turned its attention away from the aging sovereign to an uncertain future that would follow her death.

In 1601, parliament attempted to prohibit the writing or publications regarding succession to suppress an issue too dangerous for public exposure.[2]

Censorship, however, was not enough to contain England's anxiety. By the end of the 1590s—after years of failed harvests, rising prices, plague, and population pressure—the issue of succession became common talk in taverns and market stalls.

Elizabeth watched with growing melancholy. Her body was failing her, and her court, sensing the shift of power, drifted toward the rising star of James VI of Scotland.

Robert Cecil, Elizabeth's most loyal minister, began secret correspondence with James many years before her death, carefully cultivating a king he believed England would one day need.

Although Elizabeth's correspondence with James grew warmer and more frequent, she never revealed what James wanted most—naming him her successor.

For over thirty years Elizabeth managed James carefully, increased his pension and suppressed potential rivals like Arbella Stuart who was brilliant, unpredictable, and dangerously close in blood.

Elizabeth's final weeks were shrouded in secrecy as she withdrew to her chamber, refusing food, sleep, or medicine.

> *I am a wretch forsaken. My estate is turned topside turvey.*[3]

Finally, Elizabeth, who had outlasted every crisis of her age, died on March 24, 1603.

POLITICAL STRIFE

The council kept her death quiet while Cecil and his colleagues prepared the machinery of succession.

It is said that Elizabeth raised her hand to her head when James's name was spoken as the likely heir—a gesture interpreted as approval.

But this tale, like so many surrounding her final hours, was likely the narrative Cecil needed to justify James' succession.

Within hours, Robert Cecil proclaimed James VI of Scotland as James I of England—*by law, by lineal succession, and undoubted right.*

The men of Lincolnshire—future founders of the Massachusetts Bay Company—watched with growing unease as the new king arrived, confident in divine right, hungry for union, and determined to rule a kingdom he did not yet understand.

Surprisingly, James I is considered one of England's most intellectual monarchs, Henry IV of France called him, T*he wisest fool in Christendom.*[4]

James' works, *The True Law of Free Monarchies and Basilikon Doron,* demonstrated both intellectual prowess and folly by advocating *the divine right of the king.*

His assertion that monarchs are not accountable to any earthly authority alienated England's Parliament, which considered James an uncouth, homosexual Scottish upstart.

One foreign ambassador recorded in his diary that James's court was:

> *altogether undignified.*

ΒΑΣΙΛΙΚΟΝ ΔΩΡΟΝ.

OR

HIS MAIESTIES INSTRVCTIONS TO HIS DEAREST SONNE, HENRY THE PRINCE.

AT LONDON
Imprinted by *Felix Kyngston*, for *Iohn Norton*, according to the copie printed at *Edenburgh*. 1603.

POLITICAL STRIFE

James came to England believing he understood kingship. In Scotland, his rule had been shaped by conflict, the need to tame fractious nobles, and by a Parliament that never presumed to challenge the crown's prerogatives.

For him, monarchy was not a political arrangement—it was a divine vocation. God had placed the king above his subjects, answerable only to Heaven. It was a comforting doctrine for a man raised amid the insecurities of Scottish politics, but it left him ill-prepared for the more intricate, more balanced structures of English governance.

He arrived in England with a scholar's confidence and a foreigner's blind spots. His belief in the divine right of kings—articulated in *The True Law of Free Monarchies*—met an English political nation accustomed to negotiation and precedence of the Magna Carta.

Elizabeth had understood this instinctively and cloaked power by speaking of herself as *married to her people*. By contrast, James, asserted his divine prerogative and insisted that kings *make the laws and break them*.[5]

To the English, steeped in the common law, this sounded dangerously like absolutism.

To support his extravagant lifestyle, James circumvented Parliament's authority and imposed taxes without their approval.

When Parliament blocked his ability to levy taxes, James countered by peddling titles and honors.

During the first year of his reign, he sold over a thousand knighthoods and peerages and increased the aristocratic titles in England by 40%.

Then, in 1611, James exploited England's newly emerging merchant class by creating and selling newly created title called *Baronet* to supplement his lavish lifestyle.

Hungry for the respectability they hoped a title would bestow, over three hundred wealthy merchants paid £1,095 each for a *Baronet*.[6]

James's first attempt at diplomacy was the 1613 marriage of his daughter, Elizabeth Stuart, to Frederick V, the Elector Palatine.

In 1618, Frederick ignited the Thirty Years' War by deposing the Holy Roman Emperor, Ferdinand II, King of Bohemia.

Frederick V, Elector Palatine

Ferdinand II, King of Bohemia & the Holy Roman Emperor

In response, the Catholic Habsburg Empire invaded Bohemia to recover Ferdinand's throne.

When James asked Parliament to fund recovery of the Palatine, they refused, and Frederick fled to the Dutch Republic in 1622, where he established a court in exile at The Hague.

Ironically, the marriage of Elizabeth Stuart to Frederick V produced an only child, Sophia, whose son, George.

Ironically in 1714, George inherited the English throne and supplanted the Stuarts by establishing the Hanover Dynasty.

At the center of James I's court, stood George Villiers.

Young, handsome, and ambitious, the future Duke of Buckingham became James's inseparable companion and homosexual lover. Their closeness—emotional, political, and physical—became the defining feature of James' reign.

The English, proud and sensitive to foreign influence, saw in Buckingham the corruption of the monarchy. The more Buckingham rose, the more James's credibility fell. Buckingham's presence inflamed Parliament, alienated courtiers, and provoked whispers that the king was ruled by favoritism rather than by law or reason.[7]

Religion, the linchpin of Tudor unity, proved equally contentious. Catholics had hoped James would grant tolerance; Puritans hoped he would reform the church. Both were disappointed.

The Gunpowder Plot of 1605 hardened laws against Catholics and fueled an atmosphere of suspicion. Puritans found James impatient with their demands, seeing in their zeal a challenge to episcopal authority and thus to the crown.

James's obsession with witchcraft, inflamed by the publication of his book, *Daemonologie,* led to witchcraft trials in Scotland and influenced anti-witchcraft laws in England. These policies gave the impression of a king preoccupied with theological phantoms while neglecting the more pressing concerns of governance.

However, the greatest blow to his popularity came not from religion but from foreign policy. James's *Treaty of London* in 1604, which made peace with Spain, was wise in theory but unpopular in practice.

When Sir Walter Raleigh, the nation's favorite adventurer, returned from a failed expedition against Spain—his men having attacked a Spanish outpost in Venezuela—the Spanish ambassador demanded Raleigh' execution. Raleigh's death in 1618 outraged the public, who saw it as a betrayal of English honor and a capitulation to Spain.[8]

England had fought Spain for decades under Elizabeth and the memory of the defeat of the Spanish Armada remained a point of national pride.

By the end of his reign, James no longer commanded the loyalty Elizabeth had enjoyed. Rumors of Catholic sympathies circulated. Comparisons between the late Queen's majesty and James's slovenly manners were rampant. Parliament grew increasingly assertive, and challenged his prerogatives and rejected his vision of monarchy.[9] As he aged, James grew increasingly dependent on George Villiers, his lover, and declared this love before Parliament.

> *I, James, am neither a god nor an angel but a man, like any other. Therefore I act like a man and confess to loving those dear to me more than other men. You may be sure that I love the Earl of Buckingham more than anyone else and more than you who are here assembled. I wish to speak in my own behalf and not to have it thought to be a defect, for Jesus Christ did the same, and therefore I cannot be blamed. Christ had John, and I have George.*[10]

When James elevated Villiers to the Duke of Buckingham, Parliament sought his impeachment for a monopoly patent granted to his half-brother, Sir Edward Villiers, which made him the kingdom's sole distributor of gold and silver thread. In December 1621, Parliament presented a *Great Protestation* to James stating,

> *That the liberties, franchises, privileges, and jurisdictions of parliament are the ancient and undoubted birthright and inheritance of the subjects of England; and that the arduous and urgent affairs concerning the king, state, and the defense of the realm, and the church of England, and the making and maintenance of laws, and redress of mischiefs, and grievances which daily happen within this realm, are proper subjects and matter of counsel and debate in parliament.*

POLITICAL STRIFE

> *The commons in parliament have like liberty and freedom to treat of those matters, in such order as in their judgments shall seem fittest: and every such member of the said house hath like freedom from all impeachment, imprisonment, and molestation.*[11]

In response, James dissolved Parliament, which did not resume until shortly before his death.

James died on March 27, 1625, leaving behind a kingdom weary of his rule and anxious about the character of his heir. The hope that England had pinned on him in 1603 had long since faded. In his place, James left something more dangerous than disillusionment: he left Charles, a young king trained to believe in divine right without ever seeing its limits. Unlike his father, Charles did not know how to bend.

Those who would one day sail to New England—men shaped by Elizabeth's balance and embittered by James's failures—watched the succession with a wary patience. They knew that the peace Elizabeth had bought with ambiguity had finally run its course. Under Charles, the excesses of the Stuart monarchy would ultimately lead to his downfall and execution.

Charles ascended the throne in the spring of 1625 with the bearing of a man who believed that monarchy was not a political office but a sacrament.

By any measure, James' successor, Charles, was not suited for the throne and would never have been king were it not for the death of his older brother, Henry, in 1612.

If James had spoken of divine right as theory, Charles lived it as instinct. Every inch of him—his reserve, his ceremonial exactness, his cold dignity—revealed a temperament shaped by isolation, insecurity, and instruction without contradiction.

From the first months of his reign, Charles's actions revealed the dangers of a king who confuses consistency with virtue. His marriage to Henrietta Maria, the French Catholic princess, alarmed a country still haunted by the memory of Mary I and still scarred by the Gunpowder Plot. Henrietta Maria arrived with priests, a chapel, and a French retinue that seemed to mock the Protestant identity so laboriously built under Elizabeth. Charles assured Parliament that he would protect the Church of England, yet he had already, in secret, promised to relax anti-Catholic laws in negotiations with France. The newly crowned king began his reign with a divided heart and a divided kingdom.

Charles dissolved Parliament again in 1626 and decided he would have money regardless of consent. What followed was one of the most fateful decisions in English history: *The Forced Loan.*

It was not called a tax. It was a matter of language that was presented as a *loan*, with the pretense that subjects might someday be repaid. Englishmen were commanded to appear before commissioners, declare their means, and *"lend"* the king a sum equivalent to what Parliament might have granted.

Refusal meant interrogation, imprisonment, or worse. Social pressure weighed as heavily as the law.

In Lincolnshire, Norfolk, Suffolk, and other counties with strong traditions of local autonomy, the loan was met with quiet but stubborn resistance. Gentlemen, merchants, ministers—some wealthy, some not—refused not out of miserliness but principle.[12]

If the king could demand money without Parliament, what remained of the ancient compact between king and people?

What remained of Magna Carta?

Those who refused were imprisoned.

POLITICAL STRIFE

Five—the *Five Knights*—petitioned for a *writ of habeas corpus*, insisting that their detention without charge violated the very liberties the crown was sworn to protect.

Judges, anxious and intimidated, ruled ambiguously, granting the king authority to hold them without formally addressing the legality of the loan.

The effect was unmistakable: Charles had asserted the right to tax without Parliament and imprison without cause. To men raised in the tradition of the common law, this struck to the very core of English identity.

The Petition of Right was Parliament's attempt to save the kingdom from fracture. It asked only for what Englishmen believed they already possessed: no taxation without parliamentary consent; no imprisonment without cause shown; no billeting of soldiers in private homes; no use of martial law on civilians in peacetime.

Charles accepted the Petition publicly to secure subsidies, then disregarded its provisions almost immediately. The ink was hardly dry before he resumed collecting customs duties without grant and defending the Forced Loan as lawful prerogative.[13]

This duplicity—this mingling of royal promise and royal violation—broke something deeper than political trust. It broke the sense that king and subject shared a common moral universe.

In February 1626, despite needing Parliament to fund his uncle, King Christian IV of Denmark, in the Thirty Years' War, Charles suspended Parliament to preempt the impeachment of Buckingham, who had mentored Charles while he was the Crown Prince and became his his closest confidant and advisor after he ascended the throne.

When Charles dissolved Parliament for the final time in 1629, the Boston Men saw that the old world could no longer be repaired.

A TALE OF TWO BOSTONS

In the years that followed, their plans solidified in an enterprise that became the Massachusetts Bay Company. Thomas Dudley embraced the project with the conviction of a man who believed history was turning a page.

Atherton Hough, a Boston alderman and loyal supporter of the Massachusetts venture, prepared to leave behind the fenlands that had shaped him.

And John Cotton—who would eventually flee England under the threat of Archbishop Laud's crackdown—gave the movement its moral center.

In April 1630, a fleet of eleven ships sailed from Southampton. On board were more than 700 souls, including twenty-one from Cotton's own parish of Boston. They carried with them not only their families and possessions but a vision: to build a *"city upon a hill,"* a community governed by covenant, consent, and the disciplined practice of faith.

They carried, too, the memory of a monarchy that had forgotten its limits and a determination never to repeat its mistakes. The Founders of Massachusetts Bay did not leave England because they despised it.

They left because they loved what it had been, and what they believed it could be again—if only they could plant its best ideals on new ground.

The Forced Loan had taught them a bitter truth: that a kingdom ruled by prerogative could no longer sustain the liberties of a free people. Across the Atlantic, they sought to make those liberties flesh.

Thus the story of New England begins not with the wilderness but with the fenlands of Lincolnshire, with men who said no when saying no mattered, and with a king who mistook obedience for affection.

Their departure was not an act of exile but of creation—a new beginning shaped by old principles.

POLITICAL STRIFE

In that act, the Boston Men carried forward something the Stuarts had forgotten: that authority, unbounded by law and conscience, ceases to be authority at all.

Buckingham, being the omnipresent favorite, worsened matters. Charles clung to him even more fiercely than James had. Together they plunged into reckless foreign adventures: the failed Cádiz expedition, the disastrous attempt to relieve the Huguenots at La Rochelle. Men died, money vanished, and England gained nothing but humiliation.

Parliament moved to impeach Buckingham twice, and twice Charles dissolved it to shield him. It was a revealing moment—the king choosing loyalty to one man over the judgment of an entire political nation.

When an aggrieved soldier finally stabbed Buckingham to death in 1628, Parliament lost its scapegoat and turned its fury directly upon the king.

Ultimately, in January 1649, Cromwell's Rump Parliament tried Charles I for treason, found him guilty, and executed him.[14]

Oliver Cromwell rose from relative obscurity to be elected to Parliament in 1629.

Later, when Cromwell attempted to migrate to the Saybrook Colony in New England, which the Earl of Warwick granted to Lords Saye and Lord Booke in 1631, the crown prevented Cromwell from leaving.

——*Oliver Cromwell*——

In 1640, Cromwell was again elected to the Parliament and networked with *godly aristocrats*, including Lord Saye, Warwick, and Oliver St. John.[15]

A TALE OF TWO BOSTONS

At the start of the English Civil Wars in 1644, Cromwell rose to the rank of lieutenant general and participated in defeating a large Royalist Army at the Battle of Naseby in 1645.[16]

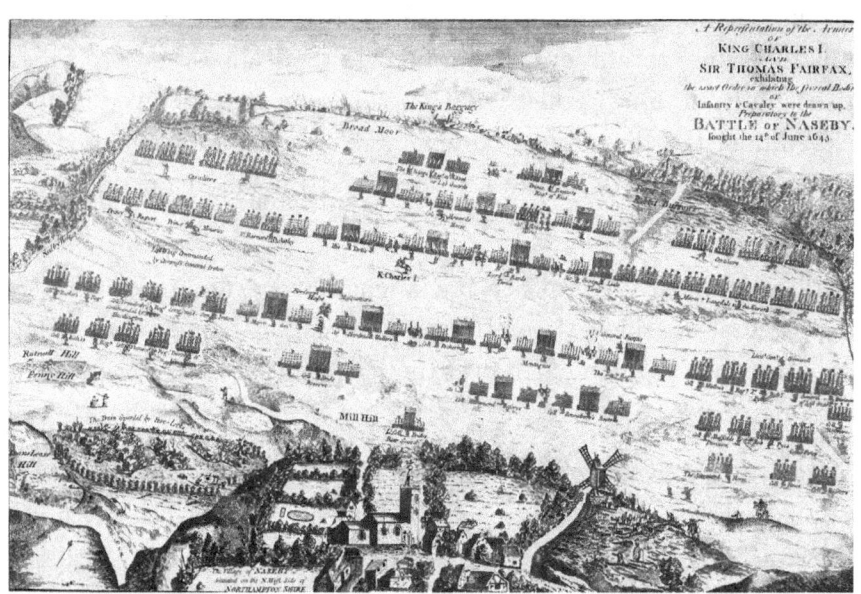

Diagram showing the Battle of Naseby

Portrait of Cromwell at the Battle of Naseby in 1645

POLITICAL STRIFE

Early in 1648, Charles I was arrested and confined at Carisbrooke Castle on the Isle of Wight.

Later, on December 6, 1648, Colonel Thomas Pride purged Parliament of all who objected to trying Charles I for treason, and England's Long Parliament transitioned into the *Rump Parliament*.

On December 15, 1648, Cromwell's New Model Army Officers voted to imprison Charles I at Windsor Castle,

> *In order to the bringing of him speedily to justice.*[17]

Although the House of Lords objected, the House of Commons voted to set up a High Court of Justice and try Charles I for treason.

Charles requested that his trial begin on January 20, 1649, at Westminster, saying,

> *I would know by what power I am called hither. I would know by what authority - I mean lawful authority.*

Although the House of Commons found him guilty, Charles' execution was postponed to pass an emergency act that prohibited:

> *proclaiming any person to be King of England or Ireland or the Dominions thereof.*

On Tuesday, January 30, 1649, around two in the afternoon, Charles was forced to exit a window of Whitehall's banqueting hall to a scaffold erected special for the occasion and with a single blow of an axe was beheaded.[18]

A TALE OF TWO BOSTONS

German print of the Execution of Charles I on January 30, 1649

Painting of Charles I's execution by an unknown artist.

POLITICAL STRIFE

A regicide is shown holding the head of Charles I up for display.

Thomas Hobbes published *The Leviathan* in 1651 in response to the execution of Charles I.

Hobbes's illustration of an ideal sovereign represented the collective will of the people as a multitude of individuals comprising the Leviathan's body.[19]

In *The Leviathan,* society's need for a benevolent, omnipotent monarch was advocated, as shown in the frontispiece (*below*).

Thomas Hobbes' depiction of Charles I as the Leviathan

RELIGIOUS STRIFE

Archbishop William Laud loved the remnants of Catholic splendor that remained after Henry VIII separated from the Church of Rome.

Henry's motive for breaking from the Pope was to divorce Catherine of Argon and marry Anne Boleyn. To do so, he established the Church of England, dissolved the monasteries, confiscated their wealth, and added half a billion dollars—*in today's dollars*—to his treasury.[1]

Having achieved his goal of marrying Anne Boleyn and becoming the wealthiest monarch in Europe, Henry cared little about Catholic practices that remained in his newly established Church of England.

Catholic religious images, vestments, surplices, anointed priests, stained glass, and music continued as precursors to what is now known as the *high church*.

Following Henry's death in 1547, John Calvin's teachings became popular in England, and a movement emerged to purify the church of its Catholic remnants.

William Laud and other traditionalists in the Church of England abhorred this movement and disparagingly referred to its followers as *Puritans*.

Puritans aspired to destroy the very elements of the church that Laud struggled to preserve. Matters of doctrine concerned Laud less than his obsession to restore Catholic splendor to the English church..

The most alarming aspect of Puritanism for the Crown was its demand for freedom from intervention by the Church of England's hierarchy of bishops, including the monarch as head of the church.[2]

To defeat Puritanism, Laud embraced Arminianism and ingratiated himself with the Duke of Buckingham, who made him his chaplain.[3]

When Charles I ascended the throne in 1625, Laud became his sycophant and publicly advocated Charles's *divine right* as king.

In 1628, Charles elevated Laud to Bishop of London. Then, in 1630, appointed him Chancellor of Oxford University.

After George Abbot died in August 1633, Laud was elevated to Archbishop of Canterbury and began restoring churches to their pre-Reformation grandeur by reinstating the *beauty of holiness*.

Laud forced compliance by inspecting churches and using the *Star Chamber* as a tool of tyranny to enforce change and punish non-conformists.[4]

As a result, traditional vestments, religious images, and stained glass re-emerged in churches and cathedrals throughout England.

Puritans who refused to comply were convicted of being *Seditious and Libel* by the *Star Chamber* had their cheeks branded with the letters 'SL' and their nose or ears cut off.

During Laud's term as Archbishop, being branded with 'SL' came to be known as the *Sign of Laud*.

RELIGIOUS STRIFE

In 1640, a Calvinist-leaning Parliament accused Laud of treason and imprisoned him in the Tower of London. By 1641, the House of Commons elevated indictments against Laud to the House of Lords, and articles of impeachment were finalized in October 1643.

The manner and forme of the Arch-Bishops Triall in the House of Peeres.

PROVERBS 11. 8.
The Righteous is delivered out of Trouble, and the wicked commeth in his stead.

A. The Arch-Bishop of *Canterbury*.
B. The Gentleman Vsher with his Black-Rod.
C. The Leiutenant of the Tower. D. The Bishops Councell.
E. The Clarke that reades the Evidence.
F. The Table where the Books and Papers given in evidence lay.
G. The Members of the House of Commons, and Mr. *Prynne* standing in the midst of them.
I. I. I. The witnesses, H. Mr. *Henry Burton*, Mittris *Bastwicke*. Mr. *Baker* the Messenger.
K. K. K. The People and Auditors, within and without the Barre.
L. L. The LORDS. M. M. The Judges and Assistants.
N. The Speaker of the Lords House. T. The Hangings of 88. S. Mich. *Sparke*.

William Prynne was Laud's most vocal critic, was branded S.L. (*seditious libeller*) on his cheeks, had his ears cut off, was fined £5,000, sentenced to life in prison, and was pilloried with John Bastwick, another of Laud's enemies.

While being led back to his cell, Prynne mocked the SL (*seditious libeller*) scars on his cheeks as *stigmata laudis*—signs of praise or signs of Laud.[5]

———William Prynne———

In recognition of his suffering, Parliament granted Prynne the satisfaction of assisting in Laud's trial and execution by helping the prosecution collect evidence to prove the charges against Laud. Consequently, some have accused Prynne of witness tampering as he chose who testified against Laud. Laud's trial started on March 12, 1644, and continued through July. During this period, civil war broke out, so Parliament resorted to an *ordinance of attainder* to convict Laud.[6]

Laud was beheaded at Tower Hill on January 10, 1645.[7] Prynne was then asked to search Laud's room in the Tower to confiscate his papers. Prynne redacted Laud's diary and published it as *A Breviate of the Life of William Laud*. Later, in 1645, Prynne published a summary of Laud's trial titled *Hidden Works of Darkness Brought to Public Light*, and in 1646, Parliament asked him to publish a complete account of Laud's trial and execution, which Prynne titled,

> *Canterburies Doom or the first part of a complete History of the Commitment, Trial, & Execution of William Laud, Late Arch-Bishop of Canterbury.*[8]

Canterburies Doome.

OR

THE FIRST PART OF A COMPLEAT

HISTORY

OF

The *Commitment, Charge, Tryall, Condemnation, Execution* of WILLIAM LAVD Late Arch-Bishop of CANTERBURY.

Containing the severall *Orders, Articles,* Proceedings in PARLIAMENT against him, from his first Accusation therein, till his *Tryall*: Together with the *Various Evidences* and *Proofs* produced against him at the LORDS *Bar*, in justification of the first branch of the COMMONS Charge against him; to wit, *His Trayterous Endeavours to Alter and Subvert Gods True Religion, by Law established among us; to introduce and set up Popish Superstition and Idolatry in lieu thereof, by insensible Degrees; and to Reconcile the Church of England to the Church of Rome, by sundry Jesuiticall Policies, Practises*: with his severall *Answers* to these *Evidences*, *Proofs*, and the COMMONS Reply thereunto.

Wherein this Arch-Prelates manifold Trayterous Artifices to Usher in Popery by Degrees, are cleerly detected, and the *Ecclesiasticall History* of our Church-affaires, during his *Pontificall Domination*, faithfully presented to the publike View of the World.

By WILLIAM PRYNNE, of Lincolns Inne, Esquire; Specially deputed to this publike Service, by the House of Commons Order; Dated 4 *Martii.* 1644.

PSAL. 7. 14. 15, 16.
Behold he travelleth with Iniquity, and hath conceived Mischiefe, and brought forth Falshood: He made a pit and diggedit, and is fallen into the Pit that he digged: His Mischiefe shall return upon his own Head, and his Violent dealing shall come down upon his own Pate.

PSAL. 9. 16.
The Lord is known by the Judgement which he executeth; the Wicked is snared in the Works of his own hands.

LONDON,
Printed by *John Macock*, for *Michael Spark* senior, at the signe of the *Blue Bible* in *Green Arbour*. 1646.

William Laud's execution was lampooned in the satirical leaflet (*shown right*). The top of the leaflet reads:

> *Great was surnam'd Gregorie of Rome, Our Little by Gregorie comes short home.*

London's executioner Gregory Brandon was succeeded by his son Richard, and the two were referred to as *Gregory & Young Gregorie*. Laud is shown satirized as *Pope Gregory the Great of Rome*, and is about to be beheaded by *Our Little Gregorie*. Gregory also alludes to Laud having demolished St. Gregory's church merely to improve the view of St. Paul's Cathedral. Laud is shown vomiting his works: *Canons and Constitution, Sunday no Sabbath,* and *Order of the Star Chamber*. The tobacco pamphlet refers to Laud's participation in the lucrative tobacco monopoly.[9] Standing next to Laud, with a bleeding ear, is Henry Burton. In 1637, Laud had ordered the disfigurement of William Prynne, Henry Burton, and John Bastwick for attacking him in print. The couplets shown streaming from their mouths read:

> Laud (bottom): *O Mr. Burton, I am sick at heart.*
> Burton (top): *And so you will till head from body part.*

The verse below reads:

> Raw-meats, o Bishop bredd Sharp Crudities
> Eares from the Pillory? Other Cruelties[10]
> As Prisonments, by your high Inquisition
> That makes your vomits have no intermission
>
> My disease bredd by too much Plentitude
> Of Power, Riches: The rude multitude
> Did yae invy, and curbing of zeale
> Of lamps, now shyning in the Common weale.[11]

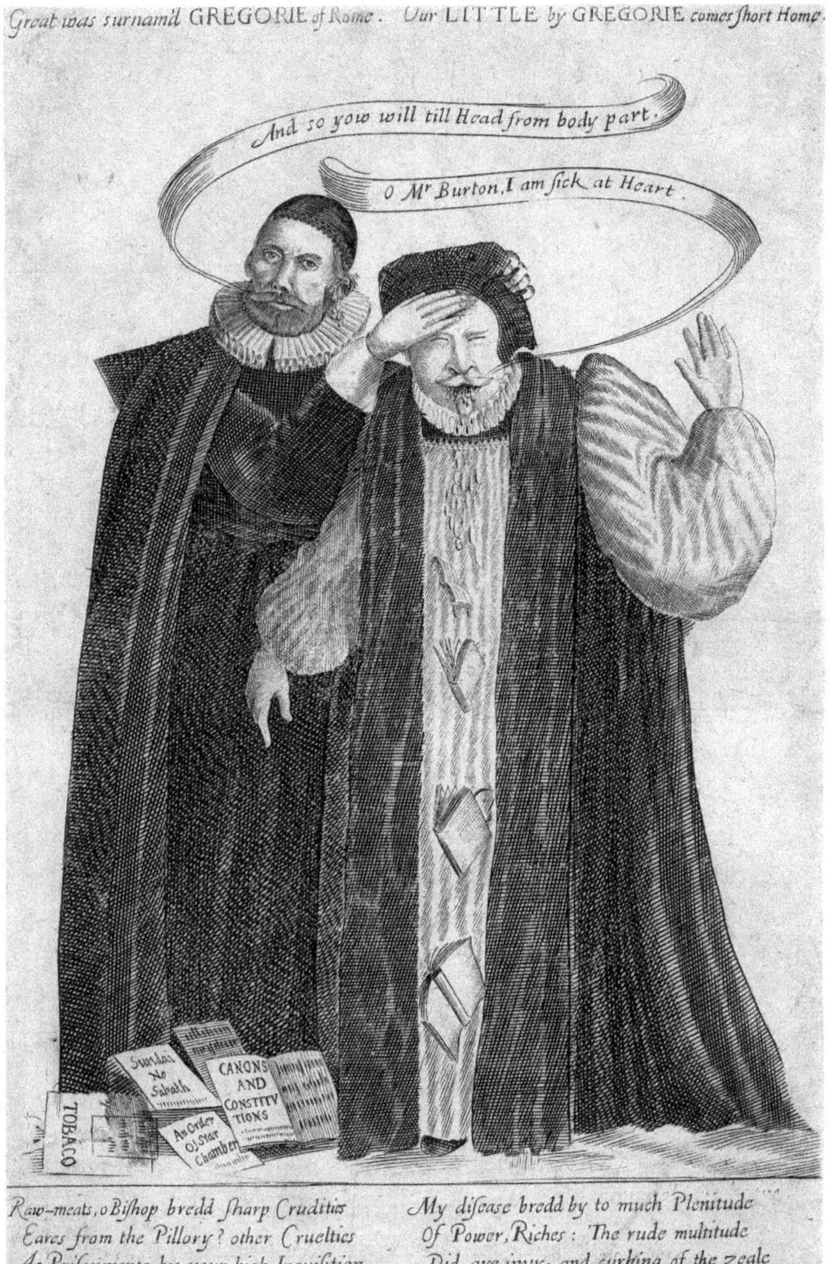
Great was surnam'd GREGORIE of Rome. Our LITTLE by GREGORIE comes short Home.
And so yow will till Head from body part.
O Mr Burton, I am sick at Heart.
Sunday No Sabath
CANONS AND CONSTITUTIONS
An Order Of Star Chamber
TOBACO
Raw-meats, o Bishop bredd sharp Cruditis
Eares from the Pillory? other Cruelties
As Prisoniments, by your high Inquisition
That makes your vomits have no intermision.
My disease bredd by to much Plenitude
Of Power, Riches: The rude multitude
Did aye invy, and curbing of the zeale
Of lamps, now shyning in the Common Weale.

A TALE OF TWO BOSTONS

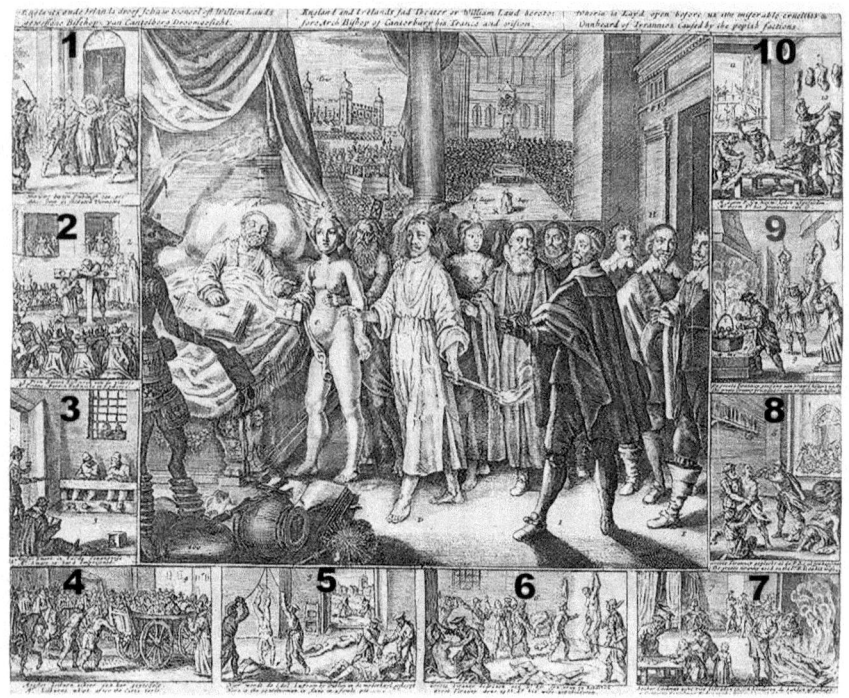

Broadside showing atrocities Archbishop William Laud commited in Ireland by an anonymous Dutch artist 1645

The central panel of this Dutch Broadside shows William Laud dreaming that *TIME*, as the Earl of Strafford's ghost, pushes *NAKED TRUTH* forward to confront him while he sleeps with Calvin's book (*ironically*) on his lap. Behind, winged *RELIGION* leads those Laud persecuted (*Peter Smart, Henry Burton, Alexander Leighton, John Lilburne, John Bastwick, and William Prynne*) to join in. The right panel in the background shows Laud kneeling before Parliament. The left panel shows Laud's beheading on Tower Hill. Side panels display 1) a Dublin preacher being murdered, 2) Prynne, Burton, and Bastwick being pilloried, 3) Peter Smart in prison, and 4) Lilburne being whipped on a cart. Side panels 5 through 10 show the many atrocities committed by Laud against the people of Ireland, including women and children.

> *Laud's narrowness of outlook and sharpness of temper, and especially his use of the Prerogative Court of High Commission (Star Chamber) to punish dissidents and subversives, contributed to the gathering unpopularity of the royal government. Many thought him likely to convert to Catholicism, which he was far from doing, but confusing his love of ceremony with popery, his critics feared and detested him, thinking him a quasi-papist. His unpopularity was extreme, but Charles trusted him implicitly, disastrously.*[12]

Some in the modern church, like Rev. Lucius Waterman, consider Laud a hero and a martyr.

> *That we have our Prayer Book, our Altar, even our Episcopacy itself, we may, humanly speaking, thank Laud. That our Articles have not a Genevan sense tied to them and are not an intolerable burden to the Church is due to Laud. Laud saved the English Church. The English Church, in her Catholic aspect, is a memorial to Laud.*[13]

Cambridge University's Professor Emeritus, Patrick Collinson, disagrees, saying Laud was:

> *The greatest calamity ever visited upon the English Church.*[14]

In private life, Laud was a bachelor who kept a personal diary in which he recorded his lifelong homoerotic desires and insecurities.

In 1625, he recorded a dream in which the Duke of Buckingham visited him in bed.

> *That night it seemed to me that the duke of Buckingham came into bed with me, where he behaved himself with great kindness towards me, after that rest, wherewith wearied persons are won't to solace themselves.*[15]

FAMILY TIES

The Fiennes Family

William Fiennes, Viscount Saye & Sele, secured a Royal Charter for the Massachusetts Bay Company by soliciting help from Robert Wolseley, who signed and issued the charter in 1629. Twenty years later, in 1649, his daughter, Anne Fiennes, married Charles Wolseley, son of Robert Wolseley.

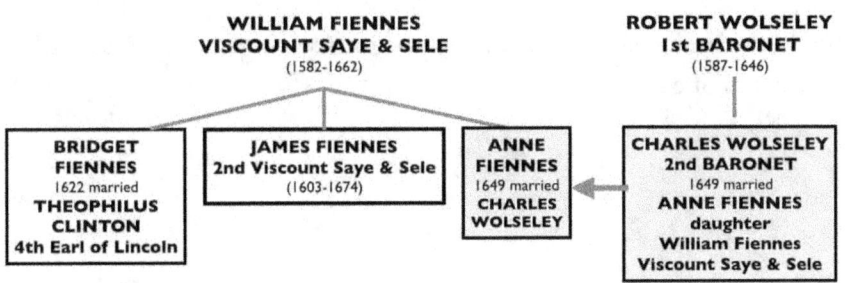

Lord Saye's oldest daughter, Bridget, married Theophilus Clinton, 4th Earl of Lincoln. Lord Saye mentored the Clinton in the House of Lords and supported his protest against the Forced Loan in 1626.

He also supported the *Petition of Right* and addressed the House of Lords on May 24, 1628, by saying:

> *It is the due right of the subject not to be committed without cause expressed.*
>
> *The refusing to join in petition* (with the Commons) *to enjoy this right will seem strange to posterity and make us hateful to posterity if we thus degenerate from our ancestors.*
>
> *I desire my name may be recorded amongst those Lords who shall agree to join with the Commons herein for preservation of our just rights.*[1]

One year later, on March 4, 1629, Robert Wolseley signed the Royal Patent for the Massachusetts Bay Company.[2]

> *"By writ of Privy Seal, Wolseley"*

The match of Robert Wolseley's son, Charles, to Anne Fiennes, the daughter of Lord Saye and younger sister of Bridget Fiennes, wife of the 4th Earl of Lincoln, twenty years later, appears to have been payback by Lord Saye to Robert Wolseley, for having secured the Massachusetts Bay Company's Royal Patent.[3]

Such payback was typical in 17th-century England to manipulate matters in one's favor.

FAMILY TIES

The Gorges Family

Gorges' family ties to the Clintons date back to Nicholas Gorges, a retainer of the 1st Earl of Lincoln, Edward Clinton, Lord High Admiral of the Royal Navy from 1558 to 1585.[4]

Under Clinton's command, Gorges captained the *Swiftsure* and was appointed by Clinton to represent the town of Boston, Lincolnshire in Parliament in 1584.

The Gorges family married into the Clinton family on three different occasions:

- In 1597, Arthur Gorges, the nephew of Nicholas Gorges, married Elizabeth Clinton, Theophilus Clinton's aunt.
- In 1620, John Gorges, the son of Ferdinando Gorges, married Frances Clinton, Theophilus Clinton's sister.
- In 1643, Elizabeth Gorges, Arthur Gorges's daughter, married her cousin, Theophilus Clinton.

After the death of his first wife in 1620, Ferdinando Gorges twice married his widowed cousins.

1. In 1627, Ferdinando married his second cousin, Elizabeth, the daughter of Tristram Gorges and the widow of William Bligh.
2. In 1629, Ferdinando's third marriage was to his first cousin, Elizabeth, the daughter of Thomas Gorges and Hugh Smyth's widow.

Elizabeth Gorges - 3rd wife of Ferdinando Gorges

A TALE OF TWO BOSTONS

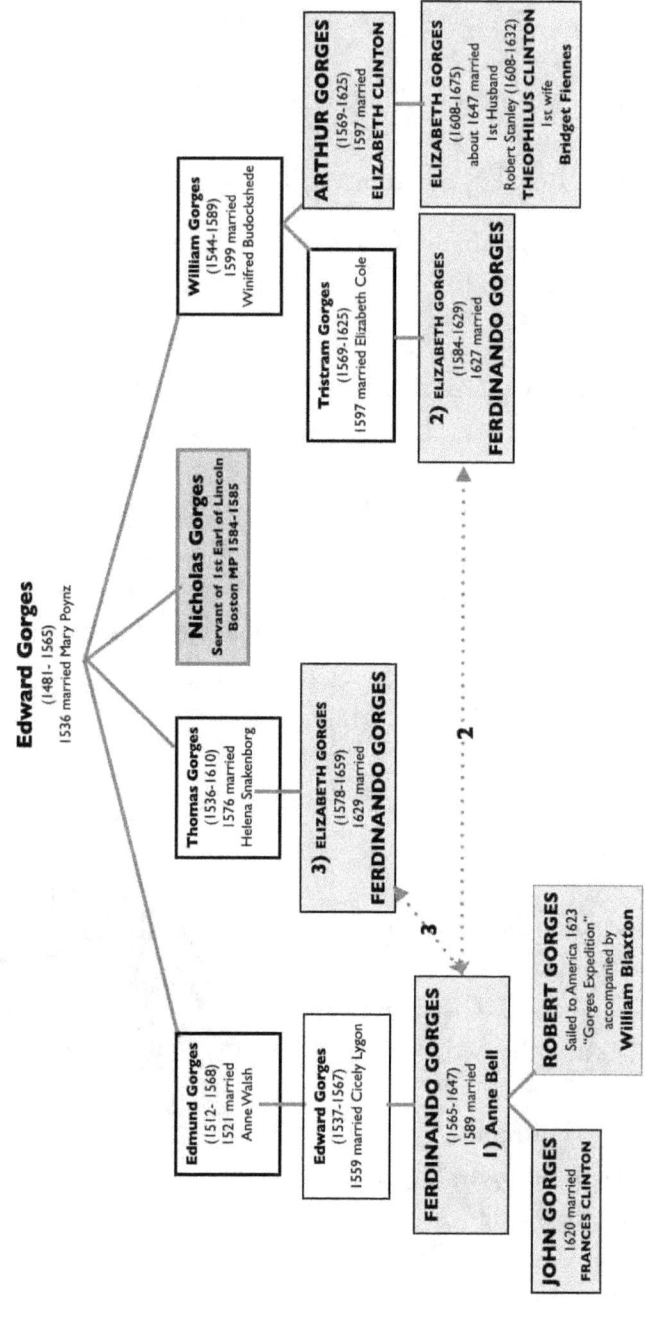

FAMILY TIES

Clinton and Gorges' family ties enabled William Blaxton to join the Gorges' expedition in August 1623 and become the first European to settle on Massachusetts's Shawmut Peninsula, later renamed Boston.

In April 1623, Blaxton attended the wedding of Lady Arbella Clinton and his dear friend, Isaac Johnson. Blaxton and Johnson lived together for seven years at Cambridge's Emmanuel College.

Through Isaac Johnson and Arbella Clinton's marriage, Blaxton met Arbella's sister, Frances, the wife of John Gorges, son of Ferdinando Gorges, then head of the Council for New England. John's brother, Robert Gorges, had recently been named governor of all New England by his father. Within months of Isaac Johnson's wedding, Blaxton accompanied Robert Gorges to New England, where he settled the Shawmut Peninsula in 1625.

A TALE OF TWO BOSTONS

The Knyvett Sisters

The Knyvett Sisters: Katherine - Elizabeth - Frances

Knyvett sisters' marriages tied the 4th Earl of Lincoln and his siblings to two of 17th-century England's most notorious nobles: the Duke of Buckingham and the Earl of Warwick.

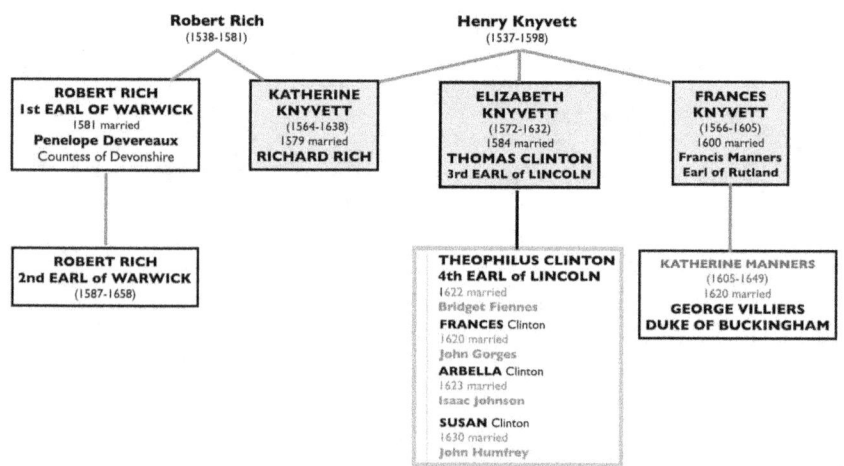

FAMILY TIES

Clinton family ties to the Earls of Warwick stem from the 1584 marriage of Katherine Knyvett to Richard Rich, brother of Robert Rich, the 1st Earl of Warwick. Katherine's nephew, the 2nd Earl of Warwick, Robert Rich, was associated with the Earl of Lincoln's father-in-law, Lord Saye, and helped mentor Theophilus in the House of Lords.

Warwick exploited colonial ventures in the early 17th century as head of the Council for New England and was a notorious pirate.

Between 1626 and 1632, over half of all privateering ships sailed under the patronage of the Earl of Warwick.[5]

Through their aunt, Frances Knyvett, the Earl of Lincoln and his siblings were cousins to Katherine Manners, the only child and sole heir to the Earl of Rutland.

As a result, Katherine was England's second richest woman outside the Royal family and eventually married the Duke of Buckingham, George Villiers.

Francis Manners
6th Earl of Rutland

Frances Knyvett Manners
Countess of Rutland

Katherine Manners
Duchess of Buckingham

The Duke of Buckingham's mother, Mary Villers, was known for her relentless ambition and greed.

In 1620, Katherine Manners fell prey to Mary Villers' plot to contrive a marriage for her son when she was invited to the Villers' home, mysteriously fell ill, and was forced to spend the night.[6]

Suspecting that his daughter's virtue had been compromised, Katherine's father, the Earl of Rutland, was outraged and demanded that Buckingham immediately marry his daughter.[7]

Mary Villiers
Mother of George

George Villiers
Duke of Buckingham

Though ill-suited for life at court, Katherine devoted herself to Buckingham despite his failure to reciprocate.

> *There is none more miserable than I am, and till you leave this life of courtier which you have been ever since I knew you, I shall think myself unhappy.*[8]

Their doomed marriage ended shortly after Charles I asked Buckingham to defeat the Huguenots occupying La Rochelle.

In a *quid pro quo* arrangement, Charles I agreed to help the French defeat the Huguenots, and in turn, the French would help Charles I defeat the Spanish occupying the Palatinate.

Parliament objected to the war with the Huguenots. Buckingham switched allegiance to the Huguenots to placate Parliament, but not before seven ships were delivered to the French, who had to man the vessels themselves after English crews refused.

After his expedition to free La Rochelle failed, Buckingham joined Charles I at Portsmouth to organize another expedition in 1628.

FAMILY TIES

Katherine followed in hopes of dissuading him from attacking the French again.

Von Honthorst's painting in the National Portrait Gallary was commissioned by Charles I in 1628.

Unknown to Buckingham, an embittered army lieutenant named John Felton had been passed over for promotion and was headed to Portsmouth to seek revenge.

Felton had borrowed money from his mother to purchase a dagger at Tower Hill and was intent on murdering Buckingham.

On August 23, 1628, while Katherine slept in her room at the Greyhound Inn, John Felton waited for Buckingham, who, despite warnings, refused to wear a protective coat of mail.

Felton found Buckingham, thrust a knife into his chest, ran to the Inn's kitchen, and confessed his crime.[9]

A TALE OF TWO BOSTONS

An eyewitness account reported,

> (Buckingham) *turned about, uttering only this word, villaine, and never spoke more: but presently, plucking out the knife from himself, before he fell to the ground, he made towards the traitor two or three paces, and then fell against a table.*[10]

Von Honthorst's 1628 painting of Buckingham as Mercury and his wife paying homage to Charles I and his Queen (upper left as Apollo and Diana). The Painting now hangs in the entry hall at Hampton Court.

FAMILY TIES

The Pelham-West Families

The Pelham-West families shaped 17th-century Anglo-American history by participating in the Dorchester Company, the Virginia Colony, the Plymouth Colony, and the Massachusetts Bay Company.

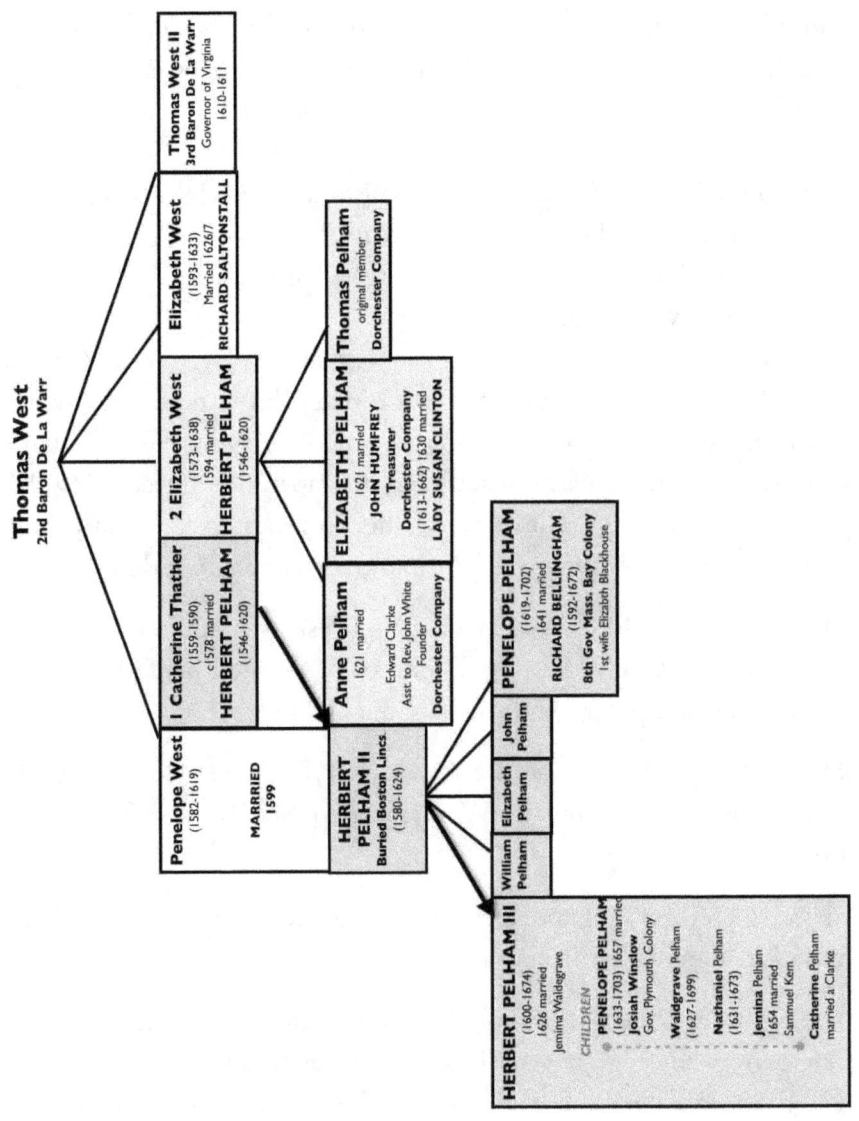

A TALE OF TWO BOSTONS

Herbert Pelham, the elder, first married Catherine Thatcher in 1578. His son and grandson, Herbert Pelham II & Herbert Pelham III, followed in this line.

After Catherine's death, Herbert Pelham married Elizabeth West and produced a second family tied to the Dorchester Company.

Son Thomas was a founding member of the Dorchester Company. Daughters Anne and Elizabeth married two Dorchester Company founders on the same day in a dual ceremony in 1621.

- Anne married Edward Clarke, assistant to Rev. John White, founder of the Dorchester Company.
- Elizabeth married John Humfrey, the Dorchester Company's treasurer.

John Humfrey connected to Boston, Lincolnshire, through his wife, Elizabeth, and played a pivotal role in establishing the New England Company and the Massachusetts Bay Company by introducing the *Boston Men* to the remnants of the Dorchester Company and Matthew Craddock's cohort of Puritan tradesmen in London.

The 2nd Baron De La Warr, Thomas West, was Herbert Pelham's second wife's father. His son, Thomas II, inherited his father's title and was the first governor of the Virginia Colony.

The Delaware River and the Colony of Delaware both bear his name. His sister, Elizabeth West, married Sir Richard Saltonstall around 1630.

In 1599, Herbert Pelham II married Penelope West, the sister of his father's second wife, Elizabeth West.

Their son, Herbert Pelham III, joined the Massachusetts Bay Company and migrated to Boston, Massachusetts, in 1638. His daughter, Penelope, married Josiah Winslow, Governor of the Plymouth Colony.

FAMILY TIES

Gov. Josiah Winslow   Penelope (Pelham) Winslow

Herbert Pelham III's younger brother, William, sailed with the Winthrop Fleet in 1630.

William's three siblings, Elizabeth, John, and Penelope, joined him in New England in 1635.

Penelope later married Governor Richard Bellingham in 1641.

Governor Bellingham was twenty years older than Penelope and conducted their controversial marriage ceremony himself.[11]

A TALE OF TWO BOSTONS

The Bulkeley Family

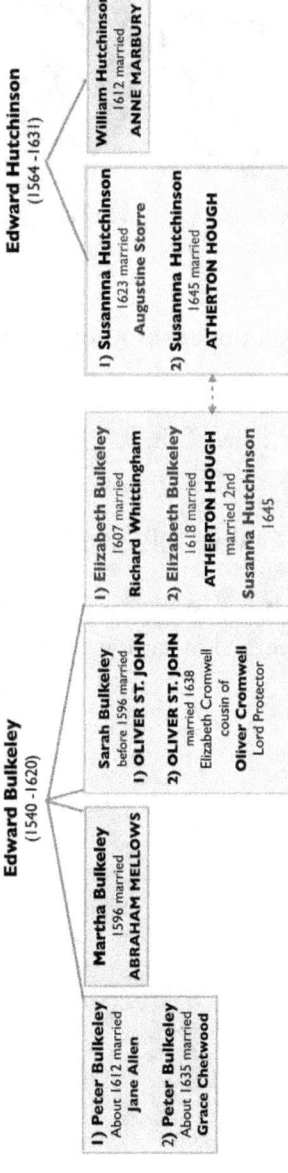

FAMILY TIES

The marriages of three Bulkeley sisters, Martha, Sarah, and Elizabeth, reverberate throughout 17th-century Anglo-American history. Martha Bulkeley married Abraham Mellows, a Massachusetts Bay Company founding member, in 1596.

It was a second marriage for both. Together they migrated to Boston, Massachusetts, on January 1st, 1633, and were admitted to the First Church in Boston on July 20th, 1634.

Their son, Oliver Mellows, married Elizabeth Hawkred, the sister of John Cotton's second wife, Sarah Hawkred.

Martha Bulkeley's sister, Sarah, married Oliver St. John around 1596. Their son, Oliver Jr., was born in 1598.

Later, upon entering Cambridge University, he befriended Oliver Cromwell and joined Lincoln's Inn in 1619 and the Providence Island Company in 1630.

In 1638, Oliver St. John married Oliver Cromwell's cousin, Elizabeth, and the bond between the two grew stronger.

———Oliver St. John, Jr———

After Cromwell's army killed 2,000 Royalists and captured 9,000 others at the *Battle of Preston* in 1648, St. John distanced himself from Cromwell when those captured were sent to New England in servitude.[12]

Like St. John, peers in the House of Lords, like Lord Saye, were torn between the crown's tyranny and Cromwell's military dictatorship.[13]

St. John's sister, Elizabeth, married Samuel Whiting of Boston, Lincolnshire, in August 1629.

> Mr. Whiting having lost his first wife and his two sons.[14]

Earlier in 1612, Samuel Whiting's father approached John Cotton and asked him to facilitate Samuel's matriculation to his alma mater, Emmanuel College, Cambridge.

Samuel Whiting and his wife, Elizabeth St. John, migrated to Boston, Massachusetts, in 1636.

After Cotton died in 1652, Samuel Whiting authored the first published account of Cotton's life titled,

> Concerning the Life of the Famous Mr. Cotton, Teacher to the Church of Christ at Boston, in New England.

Martha and Sarah's sister, Elizabeth Bulkeley, married Atherton Hough in 1618 after her first husband, Richard Whittingham, died.

Hough was a founding member of the Massachusetts Bay Company.

On July 22, 1633, Atherton Hough, his wife, Elizabeth Bulkeley, and her sister, Martha Bulkeley, wife of Abraham Mellows, boarded the *Griffin* together with John Cotton and with his wife, Sarah Hawkred, her daughter, Elizabeth Story, and eight servants, as follows:

- Elizabeth Bulkeley, wife of Atherton Hough, and six servants;
- Martha Bulkeley, wife of Abraham Mellows, son Oliver Mellows, his wife, Elizabeth (Hawkred/Coney), their son John, and one servant.
- Thomas Leverett, his wife, Anne Fitche, daughters Jane and Ann, son John, and four servants;

Atherton Hough married for a third time after his second wife, Elizabeth Bulkeley, died in 1643. His third wife was Susanna Hutchinson, the widow of Augustine Storre. Susanna's brother, William Hutchinson, married Anne Marbury, who was later exiled from Massachusetts and helped found Rhode Island.

FAMILY TIES

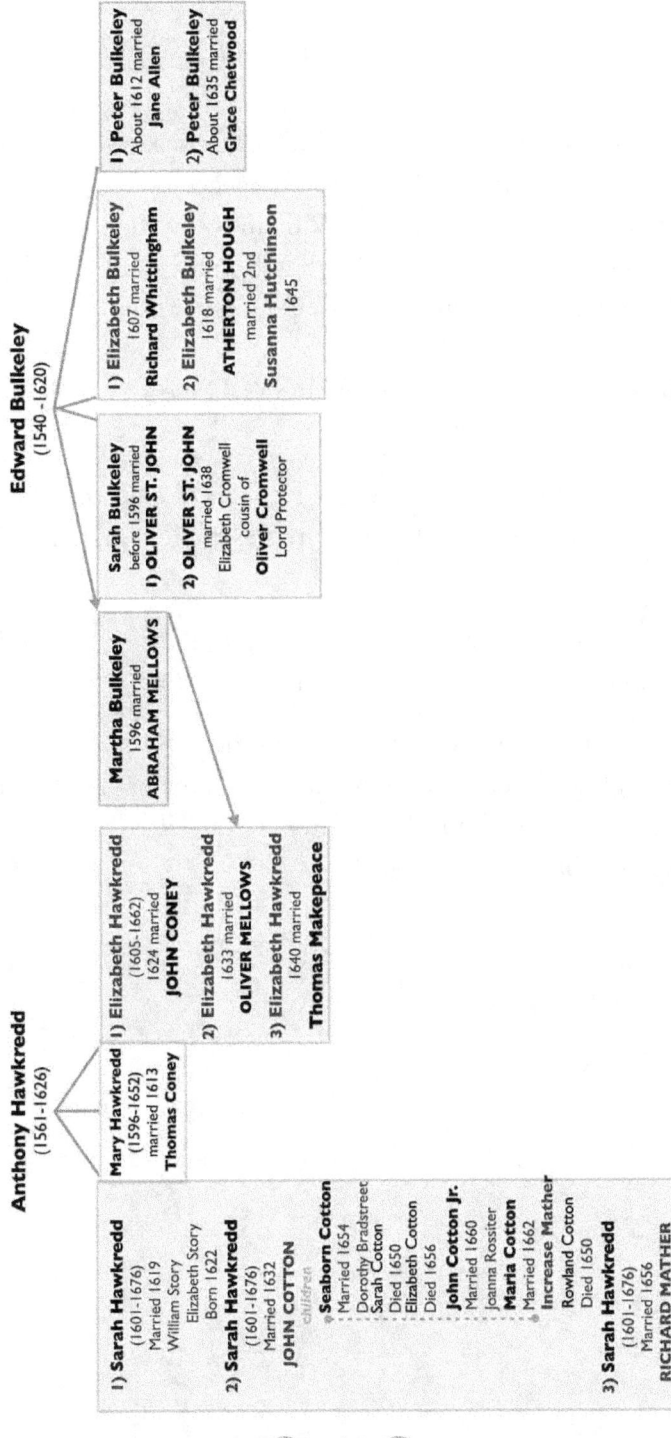

Elizabeth Hawkred and her sister, Sarah, each married three times.

- Elizabeth Hawkred married John Coney, secondly Oliver Mellows, and, finally, Thomas Makepeace.
- Sarah Hawkred first married William Story, then John Cotton, and lastly Richard Mather. Sarah and Elizabeth migrated to Massachusetts with Cotton in 1633.

Peter Bulkeley graduated from St. John's College, Cambridge, and was ordained in 1608.

He married Jane Allen on April 12, 1613, and they had nine children—the last of whom died with his mother in childbirth on December 2, 1626.

Peter then married Grace Chetwood, and they sailed to Boston, Massachusetts, aboard the *Susan and Ellen* in 1635.

In America, he was ordained at Cambridge in April 1637 and became the first minister of Musketaquid—later named Concord in what became New Hampshire—*having carried a good number of planters with him into the woods.*[15]

FAMILY TIES

Three Frances Wrays

Three successive generations of Frances Wrays are deeply rooted in 17th-century Lincolnshire history.

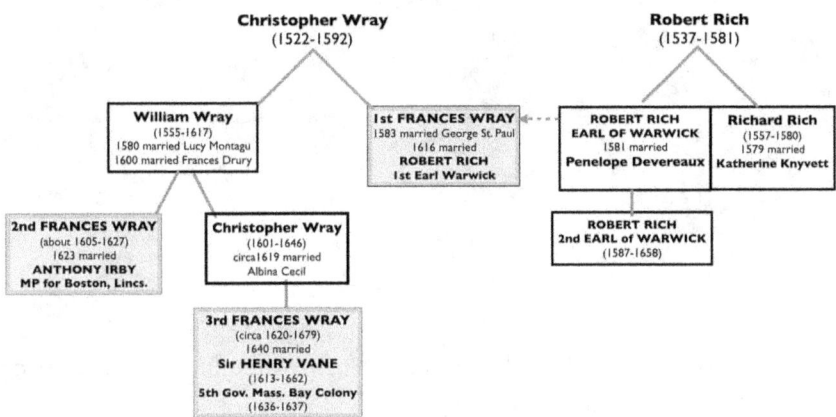

The first Frances Wray was the daughter of Sir Christopher Wray, *"a man of shining conversation and eminent bounty"* who served as Chief Justice of the King's Bench until he died in 1592.

Frances first married George St. Paul and, upon his death, became one of the wealthiest women in Lincolnshire.

This made her an attractive match for Robert Rich, the 1st Earl of Warwick, after his first wife, Penelope Devereaux, died.

Penelope Devereux was Anne Boleyn's great-grandniece and inherited her fiery temperament and beauty. At a young age, Penelope fell in love with Charles Blount and secretly promised herself to him in marriage.

Against her will, Penelope was forced to marry Robert Rich, the 1st Earl of Warwick, in 1585.

Despite her forced marriage, Penelope cohabited with Charles Blount and bore him five children.

Throughout her twenty-year marriage to Robert Rich, Penelope bore him seven children. The two eventually separated in 1601, and in 1605, Penelope was granted a divorce—*mensa et thoro*.[16]

1st Earl of Warwick, Robert Rich
2nd wife Lady Frances Wray

Lady Penelope Devereaux
1st wife of Robert Rich
Mother of 2nd Earl of Warwick

2nd Earl of Warwick
Robert Rich

Though divorced, Robert Rich waited until Penelope died in 1607 before marrying Lady Frances Wray. His son, Robert Rich Jr., opposed his father's marriage to Lady Frances as he feared for his inheritance. As a result, Lady Frances agreed that if she died first, her husband would inherit her entire estate, and if he died first, she would inherit a considerable portion of his.

Lady Frances failed to disclose that despite receiving an annual income of £1,700 from her first husband's estate, she only owned a home in Snarford, Lincolnshire. Before he died in 1619, Robert Rich purchased the title Earl of Warwick from James I for £10,000. After Warwick's death, Lady Frances retired to her estate at Snarford in Lincolnshire. Her stepson, the 2nd Earl of Warwick, then asked John Preston to recommend someone to steward her estate. Preston recommended Simon Bradstreet.

The second Frances Wray, daughter of William Wray of Glentworth, Lincolnshire, married Sir Anthony Irby in 1623.

Irby graduated from Emmanuel College, Cambridge, and was knighted in 1624. In 1628, Irby challenged Richard Oakeley to represent the Borough of Boston in the House of Commons.

Irby was narrowly defeated because the Bishop of Lincoln endorsed his opponent, Oakley, and only Boston Borough Council members were allowed to vote.

Irby demanded a new election in which all freemen of Boston could vote.

Despite protests by the Borough Council to Parliament, the first election was overturned when Parliament ruled in Irby's favor by allowing a larger franchise of all freemen of Boston to vote.[17]

Sir Anthony Irby
MP for Boston

Sir Henry Vane Jr.
Governor Massachusetts

The third Frances Wray, at age sixteen, married Sir Henry Vane. She was the niece of the second Frances, wife of Sir Anthony Irby, and daughter of Christopher Wray of Glentworth, Lincolnshire.

Sir Henry Vane served as governor of the Massachusetts Bay Colony from May 1636 to May 1637 and remains the youngest person ever elected governor, having been twenty-three years old when elected.

Three years after returning to England, Vane was elected to head the Long Parliament from 1640 to April 20th, 1653, when Oliver Cromwell, the Lord Protector of England, burst into the chambers of Parliament shouting,

> *I will put an end to your prating. You are no Parliament. I say you are not Parliament. I will put an end to your sitting.*

As head of Parliament, Sir Henry Vane, responded,

> *This is not honest, yea it is against morality and common honesty.*

To which Cromwell famously replied,

> *O, Sir Henry Vane, Sir Henry Vane, the Lord deliver me from Sir Henry Vane.*[18]

Cromwell's Protectorate ended when his son, Richard Cromwell, ceded power at Sir Henry Vane's urging, and Charles II was restored to the crown in 1661.

Charles II proceeded to arrest all those who had executed his father, and despite Vane having opposed the regicide, he was arrested and imprisoned in the Tower of London.

After passing the Indemnity Act, Parliament petitioned Charles II to grant Vane clemency and spare his life.

Though Charles granted the petition, Vane remained confined in the Tower of London, and the Crown seized all income from his estates.

In consultation with his minions, Charles II deemed Vane too dangerous to let live.

Sir Henry Vane was tried for treason, found guilty by a jury of royalists, taken to Tower Hill, and executed on June 14, 1662.

Vane's execution stands as one of the most attended executions in English history. Samuel Pepys, the famous diarist, recorded the event as follows:

> *He made a long speech, many times interrupted by the Sheriff and others there, and they would have taken his paper out of his hand, but he would not let it go.*

FAMILY TIES

But they caused all the books of those that writ after him to be given the Sheriff; and the trumpets were brought under the scaffold that he might not be heard.

Then he prayed, and so fitted himself, and received the blow; but the scaffold was so crowded that we could not see it done.

He had a blister, or issue, upon his neck, which he desired them not hurt.

He changed not his colour or speech to the last, but died justifying himself and the cause he had stood for; and spoke very confidently of his being presently at the right hand of Christ; and in all things appeared the most resolved man that ever died in that manner, and showed more of heat than cowardize, but yet with all humility and gravity.

One asked him why he did not pray for the King.

He answered, "Nay," says, "You shall see I can pray for the King: I pray God to bless him!" [19]

Robert Winthrop, president of the Massachusetts Historical Society from 1855 to 1885, said of the matter.

There was so much that was noble in Vane's character, and so much that was sad in his fate, that it is pleasant to remember that Winthrop afterwards makes record that he (Vane) showed himself in later years a true friend to New England, and a man of noble and generous mind.

A friendly correspondence was kept up between him (Vane) and Winthrop as late as 1645, and their relations were cordial and affectionate.

A TALE OF TWO BOSTONS

Statue of Sir Henry Vane in the Boston USA Public Library

SCHOOL TIES

INDIVIDUALS	BOSTON AREA	CAMBRIDGE COLLEGE	INNS OF COURT	COMPANY/COMPANIES
Blaxton, William	YES	EMMANUEL		Gorges Expedition
BELLINGHAM, RICHARD	YES		LINCOLN'S INN	NEW-ENGLAND CO. & MBC
BRADSTREET, SIMON	YES	EMMANUEL		MBC
Clinton, Theophilus Earl of Lincoln	YES	Queens'	GRAY'S INN	
Cotton, John	YES	EMMANUEL		
DUDLEY, THOMAS Dudley (Samuel & Thomas)	YES YES	EMMANUEL		MBC
Humfrey, John (Treasurer Dorchester Co.)	through marriage	Trinity	LINCOLN'S INN	DORCHESTER CO. NEW ENGLAND CO. & MBC
JOHNSON, ISAAC	YES	EMMANUEL	GRAY'S INN	NEW-ENGLAND CO. & MBC
Pelham, Herbert II PELHAM, HERBERT III Pelham, William	YES YES	EMMANUEL	GRAY'S INN	MBC
Preston, John		EMMANUEL	LINCOLN'S INN	
Earl of Warwick Robert Rich		EMMANUEL	GRAY'S INN	MBC-Bermuda-Saybrook
Winthrop, John		Trinity	GRAY'S INN	MBC

SCHOOL TIES

Although 17th-century English society was extremely class-conscious, university and Inns of Court ties often transcended class distinctions.

The *Boston Men* and members of the Massachusetts Bay Company forged lasting friendships through their mutual ties to Cambridge University and the Inns of Court.

Most *Boston Men* attended Emmanuel College, Cambridge, and were either Gray's or Lincoln's Inn members at the Inns of Court.[1]

The Inns of Court functioned as *England's third university* and provided legal education to nobles, gentry, and aspiring barristers.

The Inns of Court maintained a monopoly on legal training in England until the 19th century, as the only law taught in universities was ecclesiastical canon law.[2]

The four institutions that comprise the Inns of Court are Gray's Inn, Lincoln's Inn, the Inner Temple, and the Middle Temple.

FOUNDING FACTIONS

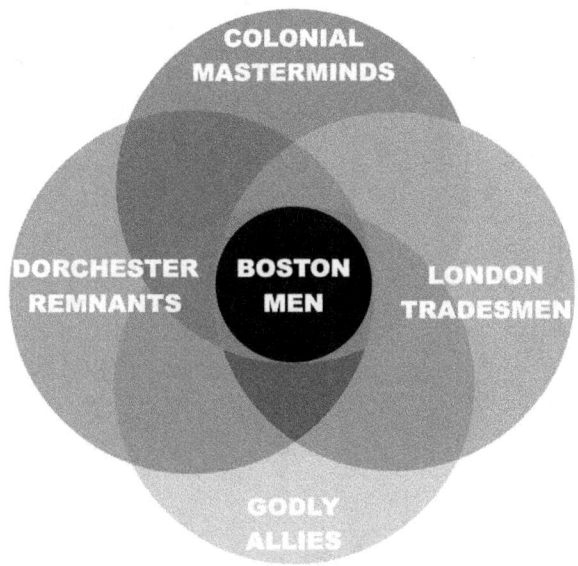

The *Boston Men* networked with four factions in 17th-century English society to establish the *Massachusetts Bay Company*.

- COLONIAL MASTERMINDS, *who sought to exploit the Crown's patronage of colonial ventures.*
- GODLY ALLIES, *who sought to counter the suppression of Calvinism by restoring the Feoffees for Impropriations.*
- DORCHESTER REMNANTS, *who hoped to restart their failed New England fishing venture.*
- LONDON TRADESMEN, *who hoped to become fully-fledged merchants by investing in the Massachusetts Bay Company.*

COLONIAL MASTERMINDS

Peers in the House of Lords collaborated with *godly allies* to attract investment in their colonial ventures.

> *In particular, the Earl of Warwick and Lord Saye & Sele worked very closely with the ministers John Preston at court, Hugh Peter in London, and Thomas Hooker in Essex, and this collaboration was almost certainly crucial in facilitating broader cooperation between oppositionists from the greater landed class on the one hand and those from the lesser gentry and from the middle- and lower-class citizenry on the other.[1]*

The Earl of Warwick, Robert Rich, his brother, the Earl of Holland, Henry Rich, and Lord Saye & Sele, William Fiennes, leveraged their positions in the House of Lords to take advantage of the Crown's endorsement of Colonial ventures.

In particular, the Earl of Warwick and the Earl of Holland held unique positions in the colonizing movement by manipulating the crown's patronage of their privateering ventures to plunder Spanish gold routes.

These two peers held leadership roles in almost every early Stuart period colonial venture, including the Virginia Company. Robert Rich, who became the 2nd Earl of Warwick in 1619, followed in his father's footsteps and maintained England's largest privateering fleet.

Between 1628 and 1630, Warwick, Holland, and Lord Saye supported the founding of the Massachusetts Bay Company and its subsequent royal charter.[2]

Later, as head of the Council for New England, the Earl of Warwick rewarded Lord Saye for obtaining a Royal Charter for the Massachusetts Bay Company by granting him the *Sayebooke Colony*, together with Lord Brooke, which, later under the *Warwick Patent*, became the Colony of Connecticut, as follows:

> *All that part of New England in America which lies and extends itself from a river there called Narraganset River the space of forty leagues upon a straight line near the sea shore towards the southwest, west and by south, or west, as the coast lieth towards Virginia, accounting three English miles to the league; and also all and singular the lands and hereditaments whatsoever, lying and being within the lands aforesaid, north and south in latitude and breadth, and in length and longitude of and within all the breadth aforesaid, throughout the main lands there, from the western ocean to the south sea.[3]*

WARWICK PATENT listing patentees: Viscount Saye & Sele, Lord Brooke, Lord Holland, Charles Fiennes, Nathaniel Rich, Richard Saltonstall, Richard Knightly, John Pim, John Hamdon, John Humfrey and Herbert Pelham.

GODLY ALLIES

John Cotton   Thomas Hooker   Hugh Peter   John Preston   Richard Sibbes

The Earl of Warwick and Lord Saye & Sele networked with *godly allies* from Cambridge University, like John Cotton, John Preston, Thomas Hooker, Hugh Peter, and Richard Sibbes, to leverage solidarity in opposition to the crown's suppression of Puritanism.

These *Colonial Masterminds* and their *Godly Allies* united to reestablish the *Feoffees of For Impropriations* in February 1626 in response to the crown's rejection of Calvinism at the York House Conference.

In particular, the Earl of Warwick orchestrated opposition to the Crown's religious and political policies—especially *The Force Loan*—through his network of godly allies.

The rise in the educational level of the clergy in general by the seventeenth century and the importance of Cambridge as a center of Puritan education are well known. Warwick chose clergy who were not only predictably university-educated but also Cambridge men.

Although identification is sometimes uncertain, it seems that of sixty-five incumbents of Rich livings between 1619 and 1658, some forty-eight had been Cambridge undergraduates, of whom eighteen were appointed by Warwick before 1642; thus, only five of his chosen ministers were not Cambridge-educated.

Emmanuel provided a disproportionate number; the college's evangelizing Puritanism and Warwick's links as a former student, when he and his brother Holland had lived in the house of its famous Puritan master Laurence Chaderton, resulted in ten Emmanuel men holding family livings between 1619 and 1658, five of them appointed by Warwick himself.[1]

In the fall of 1626, Warwick called Hugh Peter to London to preach at Christ Church and commune with the king's heart—*in secret and reveal unto him those things which were necessary for the government and his kingdom.*[2]

Other Puritan ministers allied with the Earl of Warwick preached sermons warning against the crown's misguided rule.

On Guy Fawkes Day 1626, Thomas Hooker warned of "*wickedness in high places,*" saying that the godly would lead God to bring about the fall of Protestant England at the hands of the Spanish military if the crown did not correct its ways.

Similarly, John Preston warned the king that God would destroy him if he did not further exert himself in support of the Protestant Cause at home and abroad.

Preston was exceptionally well-connected with the Earl of Warwick and had facilitated his son's entry to Cambridge University.

GODLY ALLIES

When John Preston was appointed preacher at Lincoln's Inn, his influence extended to other Inns of Court, like Gray's Inn, where the Earl of Warwick, the Earl of Lincoln, Isaac Johnson, John Winthrop, and Herbert Pelham Jr. were members.

Richard Sibbes, John Cotton's mentor, served as preacher at Gray's Inn from 1617 to 1635 and was the chief cleric and *feoffee* among the *Feoffees of For Impropriations*.

In addition, these men shared ties to Cambridge University, as most shared a mutual alma mater, Emmanuel College, where John Cotton served as a Fellow from 1606 to 1613, and John Preston was made Master in 1622.

Preston was especially dear to William Fiennes, Lord Saye & Sele.

> *So dear was Preston to Lord Saye that Saye was at his side when Preston died of tuberculosis in 1628 and was named executor of Preston's Will.*[3]

DORCHESTER REMNANTS

In 1622, Richard Bushrod and his Dorchester associates secured a fishing license from the Council for New England to access the lucrative North Atlantic cod trade. Before their venture was formalized into a joint-stock company, a small ship, the *Fellowship*, was purchased and set sail for New England in the summer of 1623. However, the *Fellowship* sailed too late for a productive fishing season and was forced to return to England, leaving fourteen men to winter on Cape Ann.

Rev. John White, head of the fledgling Dorchester Company, contacted Roger Conant at Nantasket and asked him to lead those remaining at Cape Ann to protect cattle, supplies, and the trappings of a salt-making operation to preserve cod. Conant established a trading post at Nantasket with John Oldham and Rev. John Lyford, who had been banished from Plymouth Colony by Governor Bradford for expressing *"dangerous ideas."*

Meanwhile in England, Sir Walter Earle of Dorchester requested a patent from the Council for New England to expand the fishing operation to a permanent settlement on Cape Ann.

The Dorchester Company was established with one hundred nineteen members, each investing twenty-five pounds in the fledgling company.

However, in 1626 the company failed to meet its debt obligations and declared bankruptcy. Soon after, the company's assets at Stage Head were disputed by three parties:

- THE DEFUNCT DORCHESTER COMPANY represented by Roger Conant and his group Dorchester fishermen, who planned to abandon the site.
- THE PLYMOUTH COLONY represented by Myles Standish, whom Governor Bradford sent to claim the site for the Plymouth Colony.
- LONDON INVESTORS represented by John Hewes who was sent to recover investors losses from the bankruptcy.

In 1907, Gloucester, Massachusetts, citizens commemorated their view that Rev. John White founded the Massachusetts Bay Colony.

William Peirce, Master of the *Anne*, discovered that Hewes was planning to attack Stage Head while fishing off Cape Ann and sent word to Governor Bradford, who sent Myles Standish to protect Plymouth's interests. Standish threatened to open fire on anyone occupying the Dorchester Company site.

According to Bradford's account, Conant and his men *"rushed from their huts"* and declaring that their equipment and salt was the rightful property of the Dorchester Company.[1] Conant then led his group to Naumkeag (Salem).

In 1930, during Boston's Tercentenary Anniversary, a second historical marker commemorated the 1623 settlement of Cape Ann, claiming that *"Dorchester adventurers found the nucleus of the Massachusetts Bay Colony."*

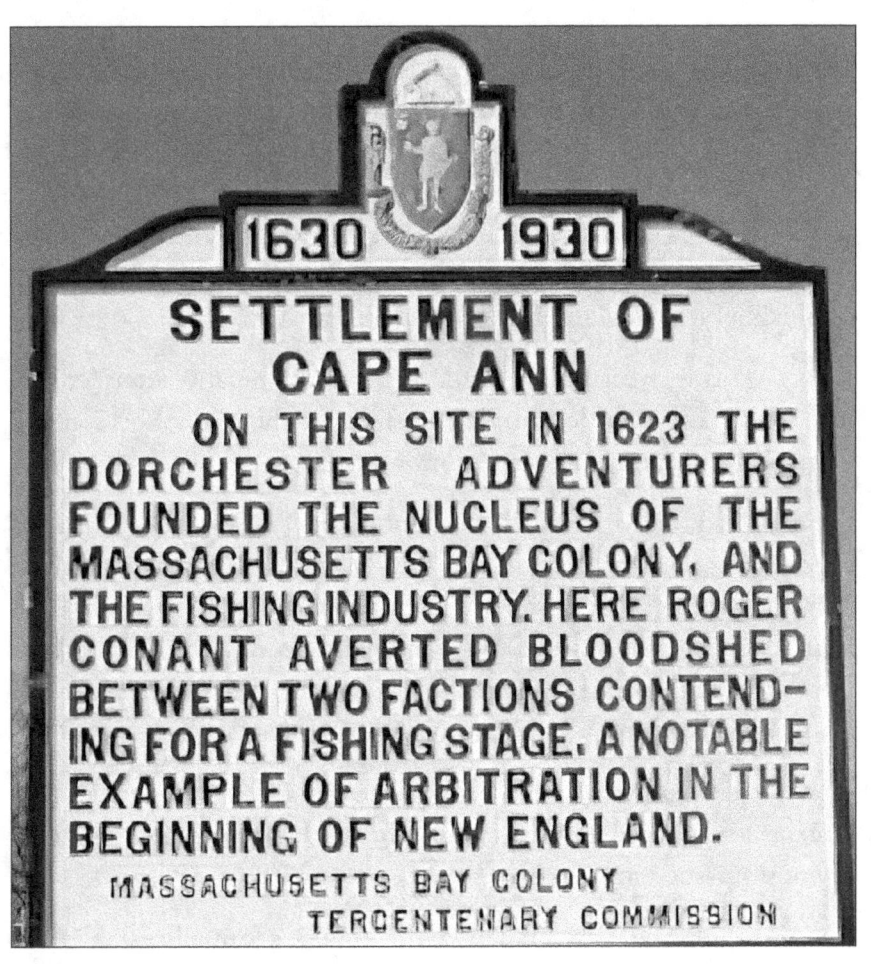

Regardless, the Dorchester Company failed to gain a foothold in New England, ran out of working capital, and, despite receiving an infusion of borrowed money, the company went bankrupt in 1626.

The same year, the Dorchester Company declared bankruptcy, Charles I declared a Forced Loan in 1626 to finance his uncle's participation in the Thirty Years' War.

In an attempt to restart the bankrupt Dorchester Company, Rev. John White, together with John Humfrey, solicited help from:

- Mathew Craddock and his cohort of London tradesmen
- Isaac Johnson and the *Boston Men* Who Resisted the *Forced Loan* of 1626

In the summer of 1627, Isaac Johnson and the *Boston Men* met in Lincolnshire with others opposed to the *Forced Loan* and discussed colonizing New England.[2]

John Humfrey, treasurer of the Dorchester Company, attended the meeting as he was in Boston, Lincolnshire, for the birth of his son and witnessed the signing of Isaac Johnson's will.

Ultimately, Humfrey forged a coalition between Craddock and his cohort of London tradesmen and the *Boston Men* to seek a grant in New England.[3] To accomplish this, Isaac Johnson solicited help from Lord Saye and the Earl of Warwick, who headed the Council for New England, to issue a grant for New England. As head of the council, Warwick required that *gentlemen of blood* apply.

In response, Humfrey and Rev. White secured three gentlemen from Dorchester for this purpose, and what is known as the *Rosewell Grant* was issued in March 1628.

A month later, the New England Company was formally established, and a year later, it morphed into the Massachusetts Bay Company.

LONDON TRADESMEN

Although wealthy nobles controlled the large companies that dominated trade and wholesale prices in 17th-century England, socially mobile tradesmen in London challenged this control and aspired to become merchants.

Puritan peers in the House of Lords, like the Earl of Warwick and Lord Saye, encouraged such aspirations in hopes of gaining investors for their colonial ventures.

One such tradesman, Matthew Craddock, rose from an apprentice in the Skinner's Company in 1606 to eventually gain merchant status. Later, he served as director of the East India Company from 1634 until he died in 1641.[1]

Craddock organized a cohort of London tradesmen to join a venture that later morphed into the Massachusetts Bay Company, and was later elected the company's first governor. Soon after, he was named an associate in its Royal Charter.

Similarly, brothers William and Samuel Vassall aspired to become full-fledged merchants and were named associates in the Massachusetts Bay Company's Royal Charter. The brothers had escaped the Huguenot persecution in France and supported the Puritan cause in England.

William Vassall was a signatory of the Cambridge Agreement and served as an assistant to the Governor of the Massachusetts Bay Company. Samuel secured a future as a merchant by marrying Frances Cartwright, the daughter of a wealthy London merchant member of the Levant Company that traded throughout the Mediterranean.[2]

When Thomas Dudley wrote to the Countess of Lincolnshire, Lady Bridget, in 1631, he mentioned a meeting in Lincolnshire to discuss a venture in New England that imparted *'letters and messages to some in London and the West Country.'*[3]

"*Some in London*" in Dudley's letter referred to Matthew Craddock and his cohort of London tradesmen eager to invest in Colonial ventures.

Those in *'the West Country'* were remnants of the Dorchester Company led by Rev. John White and the company's former treasurer, John Humfrey.

Jointly, John Humfrey, the *Boston Men,* and Craddock's London tradesmen obtained the *Rosewell Grant* in March 1628.

A month later, in April, the New England Company was established with forty-four (44) members, twenty-six (26) of whom were from London.

LONDON TRADESMEN

Twenty (20) of the twenty-six (26) Londoners were craftsmen and tradesmen working as brewers, clothiers, armorers, goldsmiths, drapers, fishmongers, glovers, haberdashers, leather sellers, skinners, tailors, and vintners.

Only two of the twenty-six New England Company members from London migrated to New England.

By the time the New England Company morphed into the Massachusetts Bay Company and received a Royal Charter on March 4th, 1629, total membership had grown to one hundred twenty-nine (129), sixty-five (65) of whom were from London.

Only twelve (12) of the sixty-five from London eventually migrated to New England.

FOUNDING STORY

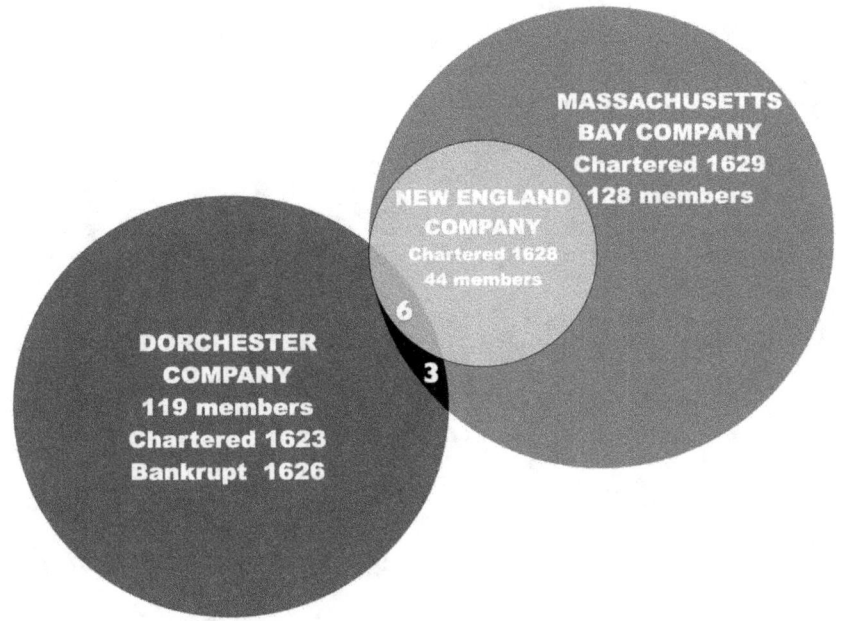

The Council for New England issued the Dorchester Company a license to establish a base for fishing with access to the lucrative North Atlantic cod trade in 1623. Three years later, in 1626, the Dorchester Company went bankrupt. A year later, the company's treasurer, John Humfrey, was in Boston, Lincolnshire, for the birth of his son and witnessed the signing of Isaac Johnson's Will. While in Boston, Humfrey conferred with Isaac Johnson, Thomas Dudley, and Richard Bellingham about a colonial venture.

In March 1628, they obtained the Rosewell Grant and, in April, formed the New England Company consisting of 44 members. Six of the 44 had been members of the Dorchester Company. A year later, in 1629, the New England Company morphed into the Massachusetts Bay Company with 129 members, including three additional members from the original Dorchester Company.

TIMELINE

The *Boston Men's* involvement in founding the Massachusetts Bay Company can be divided into four periods:

- 1618 - 1622 - *The Earl of Lincoln comes of age*
- 1623 - 1626 - *Lead-up to the Forced Loan*
- 1627 - 1628 - *Formation of the New England Company*
- 1629 - 1630 - *Formation of the Massachusetts Bay Company*

Theophilus Clinton, the 4th Earl of Lincoln, was central to the founding of the Massachusetts Bay Company, as acknowledged by Michael Winship in: <u>Godly Republicanism: Puritans, Pilgrims, and a City on a Hill</u>.

> The Massachusetts Bay Company emerged out of agitation against the Forced Loan in Lincolnshire. This agitation has been called 'one of the most effective protests against Crown policy in the entire pre-Civil War period.' The Earl of Lincoln, Theophilus Clinton, active in the organization of the Massachusetts Bay Company, spearheaded the protest. [1]

A TALE OF TWO BOSTONS

YR	DATE	EVENTS 1618 and 1622
1618	Feb/March	Theophilus Clinton enters Cambridge due to Cotton & Preston
1618	15-Apr	Theophilus Clinton enters Queen's College, Cambridge
1618	3-Jul	Theophilus Clinton granted MA Degree from Queen's College
1619	15-Jan	Theophilus Clinton becomes the 4th Earl of Lincoln
1619	May 26	Dowager Countess of Lincoln sponsors a Patent for the *Mayflower*
1619	yearend	Thomas Dudley hired as steward to the Earl of Lincoln
1620	Feb	Earl of Lincoln admitted to Inns of Court (Gray's Inn)
1620	31-Jul	Frances Clinton marries John Gorges
1620	3-Nov	Great Council for New England established by James I
1620	yearend	Earl of Lincoln's peerage acknowledged by the House of Lords
1621	30-Jan	Earl of Lincoln attends his first session of Parliament
1621	31-Jan	Isaac Johnson admitted to Inns of Court (Gray's Inn)
1621	1-Jul	John Preston appointed chaplain to Prince Charles
1621	4-Sep	John Humfrey marries Elizabeth Pelham
1621	yearend	Simon Bradstreet hired to assist Thomas Dudley
1622	April	Earl of Lincoln marries Lady Bridget Fiennes
1622	21-May	John Preston appointed Preacher at Lincoln Inn
1622	July	Dowager Countess dedicates a book to Lady Bridget
1622	July/Aug	Earl of Lincoln & Lady Bridget move to Tattershall Castle
1622	Aug/Sep	Lord Saye & Sele imprisoned for six months
1622	23-Oct	John Preston elected Master of Emmanuel College, Cambridge

In 1618, Theophilus Clinton entered Queen's College, Cambridge, in preparation for elevation to the 4th Earl of Lincoln through the efforts of John Cotton's dear friend, John Preston.

In 1619, Theophilus' father died, and he became the 4th Earl of Lincoln. To pay the debt inherited by Theophilus, his mother, Lady Elizabeth, the Dowager Countess of Lincoln, hired Thomas Dudley to steward his estate and facilitate the repayment of the Earl's debt.

The following year, the House of Lords acknowledged Theophilus' peerage, and he was admitted to the Inns of Court at Gray's Inn.

In 1621, Theophilus attended his first session of Parliament, and Simon Bradstreet was hired to assist Thomas Dudley in stewarding the Earl's estate.

In 1622, Theophilus married Lady Bridget Fiennes, daughter of William Fiennes, Lord Saye & Sele.

TIMELINE

Soon after, the couple estranged themselves from the Earl's mother, Lady Elizabeth, after she dedicated her book extolling the merits of breastfeeding to her son's new wife, Lady Bridget.

That same year, the Duke of Buckingham elevated John Preston to unparalleled status by appointing him chaplain to Prince Charles, making him a preacher at Gray's Inn and Master of Emmanuel College, Cambridge.

Four years later, Preston's relationship with Buckingham soured when Buckingham made it clear he favored Arminianism over Calvinism.

Theophilus' father-in-law, Lord Saye & Sele, was imprisoned for six months by James I for speaking against "The Divine Right of the King" in the House of Lords.

A TALE OF TWO BOSTONS

PRELUDE TO THE FORCED LOAN

YR	DATE	EVENTS 1623 and 1626
1623	5-Apr	Isaac Johnson marries Lady Arbella, sister of Earl of Lincoln
1623		Anthony Irby maries Frances Wray
1623	3-May	Herbert Pelham's son, Anthony, baptized in Boston
1623	7-Aug	William Blaxton sails to New-England with Robert Gorges
1623	yearend	Council of New-England gives Dorchester Company a grant
1624	March/April	Robert Gorges returns from New-England
1624	20-Jul	Herbert Pelham buried at St. Botolph's Church in Boston
1624	July/Aug	Simon Bradstreet fills in as steward to the Earl of Lincoln
1624	July/Aug	Thomas Dudley & family relocate from Sempringham to Boston
1624	Nov/Dec	Earl of Lincoln provides horse troops to the Thirty-Years War
1625	27-Mar	Charles I assumes the crown after death of his father, James I
1625	23-Jul	Isaac Johnson inherits $5 million from his grandfather
1625	Aug/Sep	Earl of Lincoln sues his mother for custody of siblings
1625	1-Nov	Richard Bellingham elected Recorder for the town of Boston
1625	yearend	William Blaxton settles the Shawmut Peninsula in New England
1626	30-Jan	Isaac Johnson becomes a freeman of Boston
1626	Feb	York House Conference endorses Arminianism over Calvinism
1626	15-Jun	Charles I suspends Parliament
1626	Sep	Charles I imposes the Forced Loan
1626	Sep/Oct	Earl of Lincoln & others refuse to pay the Forced Loan
1626	Nov	Earl of Lincoln imprisoned in the Tower of London
1626	Dec	Lady Bridget petitiones to visit her husband in the Tower
1626	yearend	Dorchester Company goes bankrupt and disbands

On April 5th, 1623, Isaac Johnson married Lady Arbella Clinton, sister of the 4th Earl of Lincoln, and entered the Earl's circle of family and friends.

More importantly, Johnson's best friend, William Blaxton, was introduced to Lady Frances Clinton's husband, John Gorges, and in August 1623, joined the New England expedition of Robert Gorges.

Late in 1623, the Council of New England granted the Dorchester Company a fishing license to establish a base in New England.

In 1624, Thomas Dudley moved into Boston to associate more closely with John Cotton, and Simon Bradstreet took over stewardship of the Earl of Lincoln's estate.

TIMELINE

That same year, in 1624, James I requested the Earl to command a horse troop to support his son-in-law in the Thirty Years War.

The Earl asked Thomas Dudley for advice before proceeding, and Dudley consulted with John Preston.

The following year, in 1625:

- Charles I became king
- Isaac Johnson inherited the equivalent of $5 million from his grandfather
- Richard Bellingham was elected the recorder of the Borough of Boston
- William Blaxton settled the Shawmut Peninsula to become the first English inhabitant of what would later become Boston, Massachusetts.

Charles I suspended Parliament on June 15, 1626, and imposed a Forced Loan on England in September.

Earlier that year, Isaac Johnson became a freeman of Boston.

The Earl of Lincoln resisted the Forced Loan and encouraged others to do the same.

As a result, he was imprisoned in the Tower of London in November, and in December, his wife, Lady Arbella, petitioned to visit him in the tower.

By the end of 1626, the Dorchester Company went bankrupt and disbanded.

A TALE OF TWO BOSTONS

NEW ENGLAND COMPANY FORMATION

YR	DATE	EVENTS 1627 and 1628
1627	all year	Earl of Lincoln remaines imprisoned in the Tower of London
1627	Jan-Feb	Arraignments sought for Boston Men refusing the Forced Loan
1627	21-Mar	Arrest warrant issued for Earl of Lincoln's household staff
1627	April	John Humfrey witnesses Isaac Johnson's Will in Boston
1627	3-May	John Humfrey's son, Johnathan, baptized in Boston
1627	summer	Meeting at Semprinham to discuss settling New England
1627	autumn	Simon Bradstreet becomes steward for Warwick's stepmother
1627	autumn	Thomas Dudley returns to Sempringham as steward to the Earl
1628	25-Feb	Richard Bellingham elected to represent Boston in Parliament
1628	March	Earl of Lincoln released from the Tower of London
1628	2-Mar	Troops burn down Banbury- the estate of Lord Saye & Sele
1628	17-Mar	Atherton Hough elected the Mayor of Boston
1628	19-Mar	Remnants of Dorchester Company receive grant from Warwick
1628	April	New-England Company is formally established with 41 members
1628	April	Matthew Craddock elected governor of the New-England Company
1628	7-Jun	The House of Commons passes the Petition of Right
1628	20-Jun	John Endecott sets sail for Salem for the New-England Company
1628	20-Jul	John Preston dies of tuberculosis
1628	Aug/Sep	Thomas Dudley's daughter, Anne, stricken with small pox
1628	1-Nov	Wife of John Humfrey, Elizabeth Pelham, dies at Dorset
1628	Dec	Simon Bradstreet marries Anne Dudley

The impact of the 1626 Forced extended into 1627.

While the Earl of Lincoln remained a prisoner in the Tower of London, arrest warrants were issued for his steward, Thomas Dudley, other household staff, and members of the Boston Borough Council.

In 1627, a nascent Massachusetts Bay Company was conceived while John Humfrey was in Boston, Lincolnshire, for the birth of his son, Johnathan. During this time, he witnessed the signing of Isaac Johnson's will.

In the summer of 1627, Thomas Dudley met with , Johnson, and other Boston Men to discuss settling in New England.

That autumn, Dudley and his family returned to Sempringham from Boston after the Earl of Warwick appropriated Simon Bradstreet to steward the estate of his aging stepmother, Lady Francis Wray.

TIMELINE

Resistance to the Force Loan peaked in 1628. Richard Bellingham was elected to represent Boston in the House of Commons, and the New England Company was formed.

That same year, the Earl of Lincoln was released from the Tower of London, and in March 1628, the town of Branbury was nearly burnt to the ground when an army cooking fire raged out of control at the estate of the Earl's father-in-law, Lord Saye.

Atherton Hough was elected Mayor of Boston, Lincolnshire, and Isaac Johnson, Richard Bellingham, and John Humfrey networked with the remnants of the defunct Dorchester Company and tradesmen in London to obtain a grant from the Council of New England under the control of the Earl of Warwick.

In April 1628, Mathew Craddock was elected governor of the newly formed New England Company, and on June 7th, the House of Commons passed the Petition of Right in protest of the Forced Loan.

On June 20th, the New England Company selected John Endicott as its governor in America, and he sailed to Salem. John Preston died of tuberculosis on July 20th, and in August or September, Thomas Dudley's daughter Anne was stricken with smallpox.

Elizabeth, the wife of John Humfrey, died in Dorset on November 1st, and in December, Simon Bradstreet married Thomas Dudley's daughter, Anne.

A TALE OF TWO BOSTONS

MASSACHUSETTS BAY COMPANY FORMATION

YR	DATE	EVENTS 1629 and 1630
1629	2-Mar	Boston Men's invest in Massachusetts Bay Company
1629	4-Mar	Massachusetts Bay Company granted a Royal Charter
1629	10-Mar	Charles I dissolves Parliament
1629	4-May	Samuel Skelton sails to Salem for the Massachusetts Bay Company
1629	3-Jul	John Winthrop goes to Cambridge to hear John White
1629	28-Jul	Sempringham Meeting held to discuss settling New-England
1629	26-Aug	Cambridge Agreement signed
1629	15-Oct	Thomas Dudley & John Winthrop attend their first MBC meeting
1629	20-Oct	John Winthrop elected Governor of MBC
1629	20-Oct	Thomas Dudley & Isaac Johnson elected Assistants of MBC
1630	18-Mar	William Coddington & Simon Bradstreet elected Assistants of MBC
1630	23-Mar	Thomas Dudley replaces John Humfrey as Deputy Gov. of MBC
1630	8-Apr	Rev. John Cotton preaches farewell sermon to departing MBC
1630	8-Apr	MBC ships depart South Hampton for New-England
1630	12-Jun	*Arbella* arrives at Salem in New England
1630	July/Aug	Lady Arbella, wife of Isaac Johnson, died of scurvy.
1630	July/Aug	Blaxton invites MBC to share fresh water on Shawmut Peninsula
1630	7-Sep	MBC orders "*Trimountaine shallbe called Boston*"
1630	30-Sep	Isaac Johnson died
1630	yearend	John Humfrey and Lady Susan Clinton wed late in 1630

In March 1629, the Massachusetts Bay Company emerged from the nascent venture conceived in the summer of 1627.

In May 1629, Samuel Skelton, chaplain to the Earl of Lincoln, was recruited to sail to New England and head the church in Salem.

In July 1629, John Winthrop attended Rev. John White's talk on settling in New England at Cambridge University.

He later attended the Sempringham Meeting, where the *Boston Men* and others, known as the planters, who desired to migrate, discussed their need for autonomy in New England.

August 25th, 1629, at Queen's College, Cambridge University, *the planters'* need for autonomy was articulated in what became known as the *Cambridge Agreement*.

On October 15th, Thomas Dudley and John Winthrop attended their first meeting of the Massachusetts Bay Company in London.

TIMELINE

On October 20th, Winthrop was elected governor of the Massachusetts Bay Company for New England.

Thomas Dudley and Isaac Johnson were elected assistants.

Early in 1630, the Massachusetts Bay Company moved to South Hampton.

William Coddington and Simon Bradstreet were elected assistants, and Dudley replaced John Humfrey as Deputy Governor.

On April 8th, Reverand John Cotton preached a farewell sermon to the departing Winthrop Fleet at South Hampton.

On June 12th, the Winthrop Fleet's flagship, the *Arbella,* and three other ships arrived at Salem, Massachusetts.

Soon after landing at Salem, Lady Arbella died of scurvy.

In midsummer of 1630, the Massachusetts Bay Company relocated from Salem to Charlestown, seeking a source of fresh water.

William Blaxton contacted his dear friend, Isaac Johnson, and led them to the Shawmut Peninsula, where fresh water was plentiful.

On September 7th, the Massachusetts Bay Company ordered.

Trimountaine shallbe called Boston.

Later that month, Isaac Johnson died and was buried in what the company called *"Isaac Johnson's Burial Ground."*

In late 1630, John Humfrey married Lady Susan Clinton, younger sister of the Earl of Lincoln, in London.

MEMBERSHIP

London men comprised half of the Massachusetts Bay Company's 129 members. Disregarding fourteen (14) members whose origins are unknown and seventeen (17) from miscellaneous English counties, eleven (11) men from Boston, Lincolnshire, comprised the second-largest autonomous group in the company. Ten of the eleven were *Boston Men* central to the company's evolution.[1]

POINTS OF ORIGIN

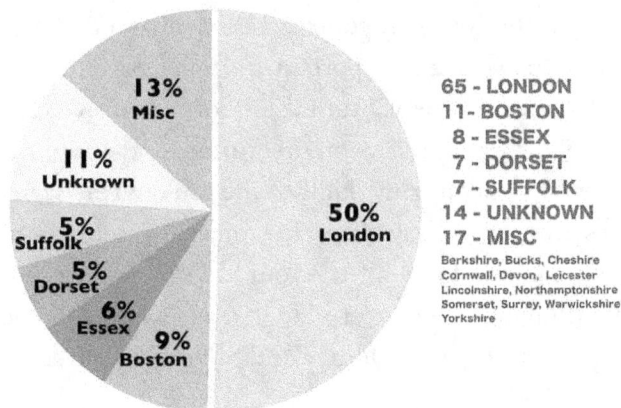

Thirty-six percent (36%) of the company's membership consisted of tradesmen like apothecaries, brewers, clothiers, drapers, fishmongers, goldsmiths, grocers, haberdashers, skinners, tailors, and vintners, who were excluded from membership in the powerful overseas companies that dominated London trade.[2]

OCCUPATIONS

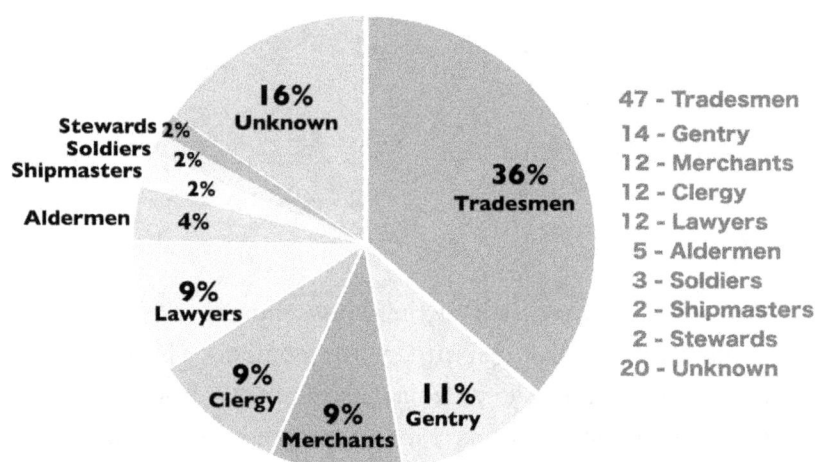

More than half of the tradesmen had been members of the company's predecessor, the *New England Company*. *Boston Men*—Isaac Johnson, Charles Fiennes, Abraham Mellows, and Herbert Pelham—are included in the fourteen gentry. The twelve members identified as merchants played an important role in organizing Calvinist tradesmen to invest in the venture. Eight of the twelve clergy settled in New England, and five were recruited and employed by the Massachusetts Bay Company. Half of the ten lawyers were members of Lincoln's Inn—including three Boston Men, John Humfrey and Richard Bellingham. Three of the four aldermen were *Boston Men*: William Coddington, Atherton Hough, and Thomas Leverett. The two stewards were Thomas Dudley and Simon Bradstreet.

MEMBERSHIP

Twenty percent (41) of the company's total membership (129) emigrated to New England. The graph below shows the percentage by point of origin for these 41 individuals. Over half originated from London (13) and Boston (11). Although 32% of total migrants were from London (13), only ten (10) remained in New England, as three of the thirteen returned to England within two years.

NEW ENGLAND MIGRATION

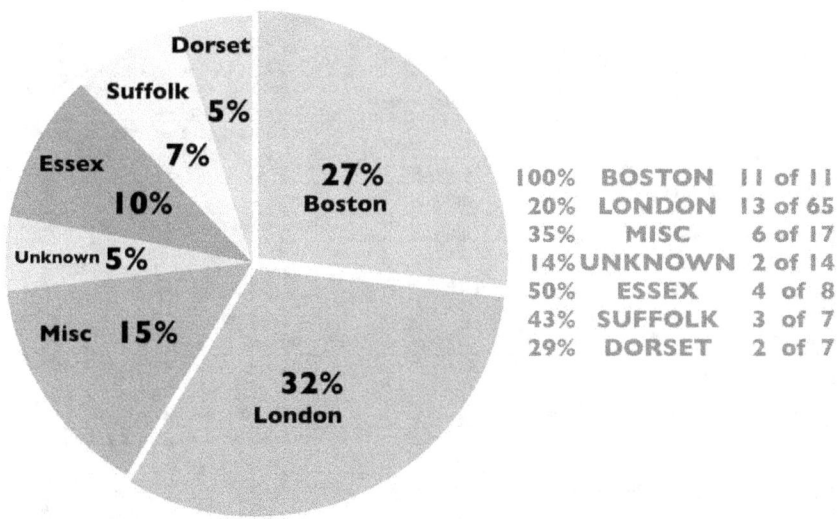

Boston Men migrated *en masse*—eleven out of eleven men—and were the only group to do so. Ten of the eleven were *Boston Men* who led the *planter* faction of the Massachusetts Bay Company, intending to settle New England. To ensure the success of their venture, the *Boston Men* manipulated a Royal Charter through their connections with the Earl of Lincoln's father-in-law, Lord Saye & Sele, to secure their autonomy in New England. One of the eleven, Samuel Skelton, was the Earl of Lincoln's chaplain and curate of Sempringham's St. Andrew's Church. In 1629, Skelton was employed by the New England Company to sail to America and head the First Church in Salem, Massachusetts.

A TALE OF TWO BOSTONS

SURNAME	GIVEN NAME	LOCATION	OCCUPATION	COMMENTS
Rosewell	Henry	Devon	Gentry Knight	Heads list of Patentees & New England Company member
Younge	John	Devon	Gentry Knight	New England Company member
Southcote	Thomas	Devon	Gentry	Original patentee & Dorchester & New England Company member
Humfrey	John	Dorchester	Lawyer Lincoln's Inn	Migrated 1634 - Treasurer of Dorchester Co. signer Cambridge
Whetcombe	Simon	London	Tradesman Draper	Initial MBC Assistant & New England Company member
Endecott	John	Dorchester	Soldier	Migrated 1628 - first Governor in MA and was New England Company
Saltonstall	Ricahrd	London	Knight	Initial MBC Assistant- Migrated in 1630 and New England Company member & signer Cambridge Agreement
Johnson	Isaac	Boston	Gentry	Migrated 1630 founder of New England Company & signer
Aldersey	Samuel	London	Haberdasher	Initial MBC Assistant & New England Company member
Venn	John	London	Tradesman Tailor	Initial Assistant of MBC & New England Company member
Cradock	Matthew	London	Tradesman Skinner	First Governor of MBC & New England Company member
Harwood	George	London	Haberdasher	One of twelve Feoffees & Treasurer of New England Co.
Nowell	Increase	Warwickshire	Tradesman Grocer	Migrated in 1630 - Initial MBC Assistant & signer Cambridge Agreement
Perry	Richard	London	Tradesman Tailor	Initial MBC Assistant
Bellingham	Richard	Boston	Lawyer Lincoln's Inn	Migrated 1634 & MP for Boston & New England Company member
Wright	Nathan	London	Merchant	Initial MBC Assistant
Vassall	Samuel	London	Tradesman Draper	Initial MBC Assistant & signer Cambridge Agreement
Eaton	Theophilus	Bucks	Merchant	Migrated 1637 - Initial MBC Assistant
Goffe	Thomas	London	Merchant	Migrated 1631 - Deputy Governor of MBC
Adams	Thomas	London	Tradesman Draper	Initial MBC Assistant & New England Company member
Browne	John	Essex		Migrated 1629 but returned to England 1629 Dorchester Company
Browne	Samuel	Essex	Lawyer Lincoln's Inn	Migrated 1629 but returned to England 1629 One of twelve Feoffees
Hutchins	Thomas			Initial MBC Assistant & New England Company member
Vassall	William	London	Merchant	Migrated in 1630 - signer Cambridge Agreement Initial MBC Assistant
Pyncheon	William	Essex	Tradesman Fur	Migrated in 1630 - signer Cambridge Agreement
Foxcroft	George	London	Fishmonger	Initial MBC Assistant & New England Company member

Massachusetts Bay Company Royal Patent had 6 Patentees & 20 Associates

MEMBERSHIP

The Massachusetts Bay Company's Royal Charter included six patentees and twenty associates. The patentees included Sir Henry Rosewell, Sir John Young, Thomas Southcott, John Humfrey, John Endecott, and Simon Whetcombe. Historians assume these six are identical to those in the *Rosewell Grant* issued by the Earl of Warwick on March 9, 1628.

The said Council established at Plymouth for the planting, ruling, ordering, and governing of New England in America, have by their deed, indented under their common seal, bearing date the nineteenth day of March last past, in the third year of Our reign, given, granted, bargained, sold, enfeoffed, aliened, and confirmed to Sir Henry Rosewell, Sir John Young, knights, Thomas Southcott, John Humfrey, John Endecott, and Simon Whetcombe, their heirs and assignees, and their associates forever, all that part of New England in America aforesaid.[3]

Sir Henry Rosewell, Sir John Young, and Thomas Southcott were listed in name only an never participated in any of the company's meetings.

Only two of the six patentees migrated to New England: Humfrey and Endecott.

John Humfrey is listed fourth among Patentees as he was key in organizing support for the *Rosewell Grant* and introduced the Boston Men to Matthew Craddock's cohort of London Tradesmen. He also facilitated the participation of Isaac Johnson, Sir Richard Saltonstall, and Richard Bellingham in securing the Rosewell Grant.[4]

Most historians agree that the Massachusetts Bay Company's Charter was based on the Rosewell Grant. Therefore, the twenty Associates named in the Royal Charter are assumed to be identical to those listed in the Rosewell Grant. Ten of the twenty migrated to America, one died en route, and four returned to England.

> *By these presents of Our especial grace, certain knowledge, and mere motion, do grant and confirm unto the said Sir Henry Rosewell, Sir John Young, Thomas Southcott, John Humfrey, John Endecott, and Simon Whetcombe, and to their associates hereafter named;* (videlicet) Sir Richard Saltonstall, knight, Isaac Johnson, Samuel Aldersey, John Ven, Mathew Cradock, George Harwood, Increase Nowell, Richard Perry, Richard Bellingham, Nathaniel Wright, Samuel Vassall, Theophilus Eaton, Thomas Goffe, Thomas Adams, John Browne, Samuel Browne, Thomas Hutchins, William Vassall, William Pinchion, and George Foxcrofte, *their heirs and assignees, all the said part of New England in America.*[5]

The order in which the Royal Charter lists the twenty Associates demonstrates their importance in the *Rosewell Grant*.

Due to his status as a knight, Sir Richard Saltonstall was listed first among the Associates. Second was Isaac Johnson, who helped obtain the Royal Charter through his father-in-law, Lord Saye & Sele.

Mathew Craddock, head of the London cohort of tradesmen, is listed fifth. Richard Bellingham is listed ninth among Associates due to his role as a legal advisor who likely drafted the *Rosewell Grant*.[6]

PATENTEES

1. Sir Henry Rosewell from Ford Abbey in Devon County was listed first among the *Patentees*. Although the *Rosewell Grant* bore his name and title to satisfy the Earl of Warwick's requirement that *men of blood* apply for the grant, he played no active role in the Massachusetts Bay Company.[7]

2. Sir John Younge is listed second as a *Patentee* and, like Rosewell, was used to obtain the Rosewell Grant as *a man of blood* but had no further association with the Massachusetts Bay Company. Younge was from Devonshire, represented Devonshire in the Long

MEMBERSHIP

Parliament in 1640, and was a member of Cromwell's Second Parliament in 1654.[8]

3. Thomas Southcoat, third among Patentees, was *a man of blood* used to obtain the Rosewell Grant. Little else is known of him.[9]

4. John Humfrey is listed fourth among Patentees and was a prime mover in helping obtain the Rosewell Grant and establishing both the New England Company and the Massachusetts Bay Company. Humfey was the Treasurer of the Dorchester Company, which received a grant for fishing rights at Cape Ann in 1623.[10]

5. Simon Whetcombe was an active member of the New England and Massachusetts Bay Companies but did not migrate to America. He helped purchase the *Eagle*, the flagship of the Winthrop Fleet, which was renamed the *Arbella*.[11]

6. John Endicott is relatively unknown other than his birth in Dorchester in 1558 and marriage to a cousin of Matthew Craddock, the first governor of the Massachusetts Bay Company. Endicott is said to have been associated with Samuel Skelton, the Earl of Lincoln's chaplain.[12]

ASSOCIATES

1. Sir Richard Saltonstall is first among the associates listed in the Royal Charter of the Massachusetts Bay Company due to his status as a knight. Although he sailed to New England with the *Winthrop Fleet* in 1630, he returned to England the following year, leaving his two eldest sons to manage his affairs.[13]

2. Isaac Johnson was preeminent among the *Boston Men* and is listed second as the primary financer of the Massachusetts Bay Company.[14]

3. Samuel Aldersey subscribed to the company but never left England, though he helped purchase the *Arbella*.[15]

A TALE OF TWO BOSTONS

4. John Venn intended to migrate to New England but changed his mind. He was an MP for London during the Long Parliament.[16]

5. Matthew Craddock was elected the first governor of the New England Company and the Massachusetts Bay Company, but never left England. As a wealthy London merchant, he had agents who managed his affairs in New England. Later, he represented London in the Long Parliament.[17]

6. George Harwood was elected Treasurer of the company and served as a *feoffee*.[18]

7. Increase Nowell migrated with the Winthrop Fleet in 1630 and settled in Charlestown, where he died in 1655.[19]

8. Richard Perry never left England and served on a committee that audited company accounts.[20]

9. Richard Bellingham is the second *Boston Man* listed in the Royal Patent and is said to have drafted the *Rosewell Grant*.[21] Though he did not attend company meetings in London, he migrated to Massachusetts in 1634. He served the Massachusetts Bay Company for 42 years: 10 years as Governor, 13 years as Deputy Governor, and 19 years as an Assistant.

10. Nathan Wright appears in company records as a merchant and owned one-eighth of the *Winthrop Fleet's* flagship, the *Arbella*.[22]

11. Samuel Vassall was an eminent merchant and alderman for the City of London. Later, he represented London in the Long Parliament.[23]

12. Theophilus Eaton was a wealthy London merchant who migrated to New England with Rev. John Davenport and settled in New Haven, where he was elected governor.[24]

13. Thomas Goffe was a London merchant and was elected Deputy

MEMBERSHIP

Governor of the company at its founding. He never migrated but owned several ships that serviced the company in New England.[25]

14. Thomas Adams attended the company's London meetings and owned one-eighth of the *Arbella* but never sailed to America.[26]

15 & 16. Brothers John and Samuel Browne are always mentioned together in company records. John was the senior of the two and had been a member of the Dorchester Company. The two brothers sailed to New England with Francis Higginson in 1629 but clashed with Governor Endicott and were forcibly returned to England.[27]

17. Thomas Hutchins is unknown, except for being listed as an associate in the Royal Patent.

18. William Vassall was the brother of Samuel Vassall and sailed with the *Winthrop Fleet* in 1630 but returned to England that same year. Later, in 1635, he returned to America and settled in Scituate, part of the Plymouth Colony.[28]

19. William Pyncheon sailed with the *Winthrop Fleet* in 1630 and established the town of Springfield, Massachusetts, on the Connecticut River.[29]

20. George Foxcroft actively attended company meetings in London but never left England.[30]

MEMBERS

In addition to the six patentees and twenty associates listed in the Massachusetts Bay Company Royal Charter, a total of one hundred and three (103) individuals were listed as company members.

Ninety-five (95) of these individuals were stockholders and eight were clergy employed by the company.[31]

Members of the company follow arranged in five (5) groups of approximately twenty individuals per group.

- A - B with twenty (20) individuals
- C - G with twenty-three (23) individuals
- H - O with twenty-one (21) individuals
- P - S with twenty-one (21) individuals
- T - Y with eighteen (18) individuals

MEMBERS: A - B

Arbie	?	London	Merchant	perhaps John Aubrey of Cheapside
Andrews	Richard	London	Haberdasher	wealthiest & most liberal Adventurer
Andrews	Thomas	London	Tradesman	
Archer	Henry	London	Clergy	
Arnold	Andrew	Somerset		New England Company member
Backhouse	William	Berkshire	Apothecary	
Ballard	Daniell			associated with John White & New England Co member
Barnardiston	Nathaniel	Suffolk	Gentry Knight	
Bateman	(Mr.)	London	Gentry	likely Robert Bateman
Bilson	(Mr.)			may be William Balston
Bowles	John	London		
Bradshawe	Job	London	Tradesman	New England Company member
Bradshawe	Joseph	London	Tradesman	New England Company member
Bradstreet	Simon	Boston	Steward	Migrated 1630
Brereton	William	Cheshire	Gentry/Knight/MP	
Bridges	Francis	Surrey	Salter & Gentry	One of twelve Feoffees
Bright	Francis	London	Clergy	Migrated 1629 and returned 1630
Browne	Keliam	Essex		signer Cambridge Agreement
Burnell	Thomas	London	Tradesman Cloth	
Bushrod	Richard	Dorchester	MP and Haberdasher	Member of Dorchester Company & New England Company member

1. Arbie was likely John Arburey from Cheapside near St. Paul's Cathedral in London.

2. Richard Andrews was perhaps the wealthiest and most liberal of the London-based adventurer. In 1619, a group of adventurers, including Andrews, gathered in London to consider financing a voyage of the *Mayflower*.[32]

MEMBERSHIP

Later, in July 1639, Andrews wrote to Gov. John Winthrop requesting help to recover the debt owed him by the Plymouth Plantation.[33] In 1641, the leaders of Plymouth repaid Andrews £500, which he used to buy cattle and provisions to relieve the poor in the Massachusetts Bay Colony.[34]

3. Thomas Andrews was a senior member of the Massachusetts Bay Company who derived his wealth through association with the Craddock family. Andrews began as a linen draper and, in 1638, became Master of the Leather-Sellers Company of London.[35]

4. John Archer was the Rector of All Hallows Church on Lombard Street in London. He was admitted to the company through a motion proposed by the Rev. John White.

5. Andrew Arnold- Very little is known of Arnold other than he was from Somerset and was a member of the New England Company.

6. William Blackhouse was from Swallowfield, Berkshire. He *"became a most renowned chymist, Rosicrucian, and a supporter of those that studied chymistry and astrology, especially Elias Ashmole, whom he adopted as his son."* At a meeting on April 5, 1629, he presented the company with several books, including an English Bible, The Booke of Common Prayer, Calvin's Institutes, and The French Country Farm.[36]

7. Daniell Ballard was a member of the New England Company and attended a company meeting on April 17, 1629. Later, in 1645, he was associated with the lawyer John 'Century' White.[37]

8. Sir Nathaniel Barnardiston was a knight from Suffolk. In 1630, Winthrop mentioned the possibility of Barnardiston sailing to New England. His will was proved in September 1653, and he left a legacy for children in New England to attend college.[38]

9. Bateman was known by "Mr. Bateman" in company records dated

September 29, 1629, and may have been the Robert Bateman known to have been interested in the First Virginia Company.[39]

10. Bilson was shown as "Mr. Bilson" on May 21, 1629, company records, and is likely William Baulston, who sailed with the Winthrop Fleet in 1630.[40]

11. John Bowles - is an unknown—no further information exists.

12. Job Bradshawe was the son of Joseph Bradshawe, a brewer from Westminster, London. He is mentioned as having attended a company meeting on October 20, 1629.[41]

13. John Bradshawe, the brother of Job Bradshawe, was mentioned in company records on July 28, 1629.[42]

14. Simon Bradstreet was a *Boston Man* who assisted Dudley as a steward of the estate of the 4th Earl of Lincoln, Theophilus Clinton. Later, he married Dudley's daughter, Anne, and served the Massachusetts Bay Company—48 years as an assistant and eight years as governor, the youngest of the *Boston Men* to do so.[43]

15. Sir William Brereton obtained a land grant in Massachusetts from John Gorges. He also attempted to obtain a land grant from Massachusetts Bay Company, but the company refused and suggested he invest as a shareholder—which he did. During the English Civil Wars, Brereton served as a general on the side of Parliament and was a member of the House of Commons.[44]

16. Francis Bridges never left England and was one of the twelve feoffees of the *Feoffees for Impropriations*.[45]

17. Rev. Francis Bright of London sailed to Salem with Samuel Skelton aboard the *George Bonaventure* in May 1629. It was the company's second expedition. Bright returned to England the following year, in 1630.[46]

MEMBERSHIP

18. Kellam Browne signed the *Cambridge Agreement* and was the brother of John & Samuel Browne (*discussed in Associates*).[47]

19. Thomas Burnell was a cloth worker in London and was a brother-in-law to Samuel Aldersey.[48]

20. Richard Bushrod obtained a fishing license for the Dorchester Company from the Council for New England and represented the town of Dorchester in Parliament from 1614 to 1626.[49]

MEMBERS: C - G

SURNAME	GIVEN NAME	LOCATION	OCCUPATION	COMMENTS
C	A	Essex		widow of John Clement & New England Company member
Caron	Joseph	London	Tradesman	New England Company member
Clarke	Edward	Dorchester		married sister of John Humfrey's 1st wife & Dorchester Company member
Coddington	Willaim	Boston	Alderman	Migrated in 1630
Colbron	William	Essex		Migrated 1630 - signer Cambridge Agreement
Cole	Samuel		Innkeeper	Migrated 1630
Cook	Edward	London	Apothecary	
Coulson	Christopher			
Crane	Robert	London	Tradesman	
Crowther	William	London	Haberdasher	New England Company member
Darley	Henry	Yorkshire	Lawyer Inner Temple	
Davenport	John	London	Clergy	Migrated 1637 - One of twelve
Davis	Richard	London	Tradesman Vintner	One of twelve Feoffees & New England Company member
Derby	William	Dorchester	Tradesman silk	Dorchester & New England Company member
Downing	Emanuel	London	Lawyer Inner Temple	Migrated in 1638
Dudley	Thomas	Boston	Steward	Migrated 1630 - signer Cambridge Agreement
Durley	Henry	Yorkshire	Gentry	New England Company member
Fiennes	Charles	Boston	Noble	Migrated in 1630 and returned same year
Flyer	Francis	London	Merchant	
Foord	Edward		Tradesman	New England Company member
Glover	Josse	London	Clergy	Migrated in 1638
Glover	John	London	Soldier	New England Company member
Goodwin	John	Suffolk	Tradesman	

1. C.A. was likely Anne Clement, the widow of John Clement from Shenfield in Essex.[50]

2. Joseph Caron was a resident of London who, in 1641, was listed as a member of the Skinners Company.[51]

3. Edward Clarke was an original member of the Dorchester Company who joined the Massachusetts Bay Company without becoming a member of the New England Company. Clarke and John Humfrey married two daughters of Herbert Pelham in Dorchester on the same day in 1621. As a result, Clark was likely influenced by John Humfrey to join the Massachusetts Bay Company.[52]

MEMBERSHIP

4. William Coddington was a *Boston Man* who sailed with the *Winthrop Fleet* in 1630 and later moved to Rhode Island, where he became governor.[53]

5. William Colbron supported the transfer of the company governance and its charter to New England. He sailed with the Winthrop Fleet in 1630 and became a deacon and ruling elder of the First Church in Boston, Massachusetts.[54]

6. Samuel Cole sailed with the Winthrop Fleet in 1630. In 1653, he was granted 400 acres of land after paying £50 in common stock twenty-three years earlier.[55]

7. Edward Cook was a London apothecary who invested £100 in joint stock in the company. In October 1650, his share of the company stock was converted to shares in Harvard College.[56]

8. Christopher Coulson was elected an Assistant in the company's first recorded election on May 13, 1629. He attended meetings in London but did not migrate.[57]

9. Robert Crane was a London tradesman who purchased stock in the company on June 17, 1629, and served on the committee that audited company accounts.[58]

10. William Crowther was mentioned as a subscriber in May 1628 and was present at the first company election on May 13, 1629, but is not mentioned in company records after this date. In 1640, he became a member of the House of Commons representing the London Borough of Weebly.[59]

11. Henry Darley joined the Massachusetts Bay Company in 1630. Later, in 1632, he became a member of the Providence Island and Sayebrook Companies. He represented various Yorkshire constituencies as MP from 1628 to 1656 and supported Parliament during the English Civil Wars.[60]

12. John Davenport is listed as a company member by Haven, though he was not shown in company records. Davenport was a feoffee of the *Feoffees for Impropriations* and fled England for Holland to avoid prosecution by Archbishop Laud. In 1637, John Cotton encouraged Davenport to migrate to New England, where he later founded New Haven, Connecticut. In 1667, John Wilson, pastor of Boston's First Church, died, and Davenport moved to Boston to take his place.[61]

13. Richard Davis was a London vintner and *feoffee* of the *Feoffees for Impropriations*. He was recorded as attending a company meeting on June 17, 1629.[62]

14. William Derby was a member of the Dorchester and New England Company but is not shown in company records.[63] The Port Books of Weymouth for 1625 show two cargos for William Derby & Co.

- The first was in September 1625 from Virginia with a cargo of dry fish, codfish, train oil, quarters of oak, and 300 fox, raccoon, martins, otter, and beaver skins.
- The second was in September 1626 from Newfoundland of fish and oil.

15. Emanuel Downing migrated to New England in March 1638 and settled near Salem. He was John Winthrop's brother-in-law.[64]

16. Thomas Dudley sailed with the *Winthrop Fleet* in 1630 and served the company as governor, deputy governor, and assistant for over twenty years.[65]

17. Henry Durley does not appear in company records but is thought to have been the son of Sir Richard Durley of Yorkshire and brother of John Durley, the London tailor.[66]

18. Charles Fiennes accompanied his sister, Lady Arbella, in the 1630 *Winthrop Fleet* and was one of ten *Boston Men*.[67]

MEMBERSHIP

19. Francis Flyer is shown in company records on October 20, 1629, and was a London merchant.[68]

20. Edward Foord purchased stock in the company in May 1628 but was not mentioned in company records until October 15, 1629. Although listed as a London tradesman, he was an ingenious inventor who invented a machine that raised water from the Thames to the streets of London[69]

21. Josse Glover- was the eldest son of Roger Glover.[70] He sailed between England and America several times and was suspended as rector of St. Nicholas parish church in 1634. Shortly after his scheduled arrival in Boston, Massachusetts. John Winthrop wrote,

> *A printing house was begun at Cambridge by one Daye, at the charge of Mr. Glover, who died on sea hitherward.*

22. John Glover is listed in numerous company records from 1637 through 1641. Haven reported that he was commander of a military company in Dorchester for many years.[71]

23. John Goodwin was a Suffolk clothier who left £50 to Matthew Cradock in his will.[72]

MEMBERS: H - O

Harvey	Anne			
Hewson	Thomas	London	Merchant	New England Company member
Higginson	Francis	Leicester	Clergy	Migrated with Skelton in 1629
Hills	Joseph	Essex	Tradesman	
Hodson	Daniel	London	Tradesman	New England Company member
Hough	Atherton	Boston	Alderman	Migrated in 1633 - 1629 Boston
Hubbard	William	Suffolk	Alderman	Migrated in 1635
Ironside	Edward		Lawyer Lincoln's Inn	
Janson	Brian	London	Gentry Knight	
Keane	Robert		Tradesman Tailor	Migrated in 1635
Kirby	Francis	London	Tradesman	brother-in-law of Emmanuel
Leverett	Thomas	Boston	Alderman	Migrated in 1633 with Cotton
Ludlowe	Roger	Wiltshire	Lawyer Inner Temple	Migrated in 1630
Malbon	John		Craftsman Iron	
Manesty	Nathaniel	London	Craftsman	New England Company member
Marsh	Thomas	London		
Mellowes	Abraham	Boston	Gentry	Migrated in 1633 with Cotton
Milburne	Peter	London	Ship's Master	Migrated in 1630 - Captained the *Arbella*
Nichols	Mathias	Bucks	Clergy	Dorchester Co. member
Nye	Philip	London	Chaplain	
Oldfield	Joseph		Fishmonger	New England Company member

1. Anne Harvey invested £25 in the company and was the aunt of Thomas Browne of Sudbury, Massachusetts, who in 1640 was granted 200 acres by his aunt.[73]

2. Thomas Hewson was an active company member who purchased a one-sixteenth share in the *Arbella*. However, he is only mentioned once in company records as a member.[74]

3. Francis Higginson sailed to Salem with Samuel Skelton in May 1629, soon after the company received its Royal Charter. The company employed Francis Higginson as a cleric. He was educated at Emmanuel College, Cambridge University, and arrived in Salem on June 29, 1629. He died in August the following year. Higginson never owned stock in the company.[75]

MEMBERSHIP

4. Joseph Hills was a woolen draper from Maldon, Essex, of whom it was said in 1639,

> "he came to New England as an undertaker (adventurer) *in the ship called the Susan and Ellen, of London, in* 1635."[76]

5. Daniel Hodson was a London clothier but is not mentioned in company records.[77]

6. Atherton Hough was a *Boston Man* who sailed to Massachusetts with John Cotton aboard the *Griffin* in 1633.[78]

7. William Hubbard was from Cambridge, England, and sailed aboard the *Defense* to New England in 1635 but never appeared in company records. He became a freeman of Massachusetts in 1638 and was granted 300 acres by the General Court.[79]

8. Edward Ironside became a member of Lincoln's Inn in 1627 and attended a company meeting on August 29, 1629.[80]

9. Sir Brian Janson attended a company meeting in Southampton on March 18, 1630. John Winthrop wrote,

> *There is newly come into our company and sworn an assistant, one Sir Brian Janson, of London, as he hath given 50li to our common stock and 50li to the joint stock.*[81]

10. Robert Keane was a tailor who had invested in the Plymouth Colony. He migrated to Boston, Massachusetts, in 1635 and was granted 400 acres in 1639.[82] He had a tailor shop on State Street in Boston and co-founded the Ancient and Honorable Artillery Company of Massachusetts. He was buried in the King's Chaple Burying Ground, and every year on the 1st Monday in June, the Ancient and Honorable Artillery Company leads a procession to his gravesite and lays a wreath in his memory.

11. Francis Kirby was a *"skinner"* (including leather dealers, hides, skins, furs, and pelts) who exported supplies and received payment mainly in beaver skins. His marriage to Susan Downing, the sister of Emanuel Downing, occurred about 1616. In company records, he is shown as:

> Brother of Mr. Downing, who corresponded with John Winthrop, Jr. advising him on the selection of beaver skins and acted as agent, forwarding goods in payment.[83]

12. Thomas Leverett was one of the *Boston Men* who sailed to Massachusetts with John Cotton aboard the *Griffin* in 1633.[84]

13. Roger Ludlowe was elected an Assistant at the company's last meeting in London at the house of Deputy Governor Goffe. He was reportedly a brother-in-law of Endicott, who migrated with Edward Rossiter and was one of the first settlers of Dorchester. In 1634, he succeeded Thomas Dudley as deputy governor and, a year later, moved to Connecticut, where he founded the town of Windsor.[85]

14. John Malbon- Company records dated March 2, 1629, state:

> Also for Mr. Malbon, it was propounded, he having skyll in iron works and willing to put up £25 in stock, it should be accepted as £50 and his charges to be borne out and home for New England; and up his return and report what may be done about iron works, consideration to be had of proceeding therein accordingly, and further recompense if there is cause to entertain him.[86]

15. Nathaniel Manesty was a goldsmith of Foster Lane, London.[87]

16. Thomas Marsh paid *"33li 6s 8d...to have land according to the proportion agreed on for such an adventure."*[88]

17. Abraham Mellowes was a *Boston Man* who sailed to Massachusetts with John Cotton aboard the *Griffin* in 1633.[89]

MEMBERSHIP

18. Peter Milburne was the master of the Wintrhop Fleet's flagship. He owned a one-eighth share in the *Arbella* and was made a company member due to his service as her captain.[90]

19. Mathias Nicols was an original member of the Dorchester Company who joined the Massachusetts Bay Company without becoming a member of the New England Company. He attended New College, Oxford University with Rev. John White. Together, they bid farewell to passengers of the *Mary & John* in March 1630 before it set sail for New England. Matthias died in Plymouth on 15 July 1631 and left a will that was proved on the 10th of October, which left money

> *unto the common stock for New England, towards the advancement of that plantation.*[91]

20. Philip Nye was Curate of St. Michael's Church in London and was admitted to the company by Rev. White's motion that

> *Their meetings might be sanctioned by the prayers of some faithful ministers here in London, whose advice would likewise be requisite on many occasions.*[92]

21. Joseph Oldfield was a London fishmonger and an original member of the New England Company that subscribed to the *Feoffees for Impropriations*. His sister Sarah married Josse Glover.[93]

MEMBERS: P - S

SURNAME	GIVEN NAME	LOCATION	OCCUPATION	COMMENTS
Palmer	Abraham	London	Merchant	Migrated in 1629 with Skelton & New England Company member
Paynter	(Mr.)			
Pelham	Herbert	Boston	Gentry	Migrated in 1639
Pemberton	James	London		
Perkins	William	London	Tradesman Tailor	
Peter	Hugh	Cornwall	Clergy	Migrated in 1635 & New England Company member
Phillips	George	Suffolk	Clergy	Migrated in 1630
Pocock	John	London	Tradesman	supporter of the Pilgrims
Puliston	Thomas	London	Tradesman	
Revell	John	London	Fishmonger	Migrated in 1630 then returned
Rich	Robert	London	Noble	Earl of Warwick
Rossiter	Edward	Somerset	Gentry	Migrated in 1630
Rowe	Owen	London	Merchant Silk	
Sharpe	Thomas	London	Merchant	Migrated in 1629 with Skelton - Cambridge Agreement signer
Sharpe	Samuel	London	Tradesman Leather	Migrated in 1629 with Skelton - Cradock's agent
Skelton	Samuel	Boston	Clergy	Migrated in 1629
Smyth	John	Lincolnshire		possibly Capt. John Smith
Spenser	John	London		
Spurstowe	William	London	Merchant	
Steevens	Thomas	London	Craftsman Armourer	Initial MBC Assistant & New England Company member
Stileman	Elias	London	Tradesman Tailor	Migrated in 1629 with Skelton

1. Abraham Palmer was a London merchant who invested £50 in the company and accompanied Skelton and Higginson to New England in 1629. He was granted 200 acres in 1638 and later relocated to Barbados, where he died in 1652.[94]

2. Paynter is mentioned in company records on September 28. 1630 as Thomas Paynt^r and on September 3, 1634, as Mr. Paynter.[95]

3. Herbert Pelham was one of the *Boston Men* and the last to migrate to New England in 1639.[96]

4. James Pemberton was mentioned once in company records on March 12, 1638.[97]

5. William Perkins was mentioned once in company records on

MEMBERSHIP

October 10, 1638.[98] He was a London tailor whose son, Rev. William Perkins, was granted 400 acres "for his father's £50."

6. Hugh Peter was mentioned in company records on three occasions from March 3, 1635, to June 6, 1639, when the court granted him 500 acres of land.[99]

Through the patronage of the Earl of Warwick, Hugh Peter was ordained in June 1623. Due to his participation in the *Feoffees for Impropriations,* he was imprisoned and released after Warwick posted bail.

In 1627, Peter was suspended by the Bishop of London, William Laud.

Rev. Hugh Peter, the Regicide

In 1628, he subscribed £50 to the New England Company and attended company meetings as early as May 1629. He then went to Europe and became pastor of a church in Rotterdam.

He returned to England in June 1635 and sailed to New England with Sir Henry Vane and three agents of the *Sayebrook Company.*

In December 1636, after Roger Williams's banishment, Peter became Salem's minister. He returned to England in 1641, promoted the republican cause, and became chaplain to Oliver Cromwell.

Hugh Peter supported the regicide, was tried as a regicide, and executed with his head displayed on London Bridge.[100]

7. George Phillips was mentioned in company records on October 19, 1630, and May 18, 1631.[101] He sailed with the *Winthrop Fleet* in 1630 and was the first minister of Watertown, Massachusetts.[102]

8. John Pocock was a woolen draper from London who had invested in the Plymouth Plantation and was an early subscriber to the Massachusetts Bay Company.[103]

9. Thomas Pulliston was a London draper listed in company records on May 11, 1629.[104]

10. John Revell sailed with the *Winthrop Fleet* in 1630 but returned immediately. He was shown in company records on July 28, 1629, and again on December 10, 1629, when he was elected an Assistant. He resided in London and worked as a fishmonger.[105]

11. Robert Rich, 2nd Earl of Warwick, though not listed in the Massachusetts Bay Company's Royal Patent, participated in every colonial grant he issued. Warwick assumed the presidency of the Council for New England before 1628 and was responsible for issuing the Rosewell Grant that enabled the establishment of the New England Company, the precursor to the Massachusetts Bay Company.

In 1631, as president of the Council for New England, Warwick issued a controversial grant known as the *Warwick Patent* that granted membership to eleven of his closest friends and relatives, including Viscount Saye & Sele and Lord Brooke.[106]

12. Edward Rossiter was mentioned in company records as elected an Assistant on October 20, 1629. He sailed with the Winthrop Fleet in 1630 and died within a year of his arrival.[107]

13. Owen Rowe- On February 18, 1636, Rowe wrote to Winthrop, expressing his desire to settle in Massachusetts and have a farm.[108] Rowe was a London silk merchant who became Lieutenant Colonel in the London Militia during the Commonwealth. When Charles II was restored to the throne, Rowe was tried and sentenced to life imprisonment.

MEMBERSHIP

14. Thomas Sharpe was from London. He was mentioned in company records on March 3, 1629, and elected Assistant on October 20, 1629. He sailed with the *Winthrop Fleet* in 1630 but returned to England in March 1631. In 1641, Sharpe became Warden of the Company of Leathersellers.[109]

15. Samuel Sharpe was Matthew Craddock's private agent in New England and sailed to Salem with Samuel Skelton in May 1629.[110]

16. Samuel Skelton was chaplain to the Earl of Lincoln and migrated to Salem aboard the *George Bonaventure* in 1629. The New England Company employed him as the first pastor of the Salem Church, but he was not a member of the company.[111]

17. John Smyth may have been Captain John Smith of Plymouth Plantation fame. A 'Mr. Smyth' is shown once in company records on November 20, 1629.[112]

18. John Spenser- Little is known of John Spenser, though he was thought to have been the brother of Thomas Spenser of Westminster, who, in his will dated 22 June 1648, referred to land in New England, which was bequeathed to his wife and children.[113]

19. William Spurstowe was a London mercer who, through marriage, is thought to be connected with Aldersey, Craddock, and other company members.[114]

20. Thomas Steevens was a member of the New England Company and is shown in company records as an armorer on Botolph Lane near Billingsgate, next to Pudding Lane in London.[115]

21. Elias Stileman settled in Salem in 1629 and was granted 100 acres in 1636. Earlier in 1635, he was granted a license to keep a tavern to sell beer and provisions. This license was upgraded to sell '*strong waters*' in March 1656.[116]

MEMBERS: T - Y

SURNAME	GIVEN NAME	LOCATION	OCCUPATION	COMMENTS
Tuffneale	Richard	London	Brewer	New England Company member
Wade	Thomas	Northampton		
Waldgrave	Thomas	Suffolk		
Waller	Henry	London	Tradesman	London MP 1628
Ward	Nathaniel	Suffolk	Clergy	Migrated in 1634
Warren	(Mr.)	London		
Way	George	Dorchester	Tradesman	New England Company member
Webbe	Francis			Initial MBC Assistant & New England Company member
West	Nicholas			signer Cambridge Agreement
Whitchcote	Charles	London	Soldier Colonel	New England Company member
White	John	London	Lawyer Lincoln's Inn	One of twelve Feoffees known as Century White New England Company member
White	Edmond	London	Haberdasher	
White	Richard		Ship's Master	possible master of the *'Peter'*
Wince	Daniel	London	Tradesman	
Winthrop	John	Suffolk	Lawyer Gray's Inn	Migrated in 1630 - signer Cambridge Agreement
Woodgate	(Mr.)			
Young	Richard	London	Haberdasher	New England Company member
Young	James	London	Merchant	

Of the eighteen members listed below (T - Y), six were members of the New England Company, and two were original members of the Dorchester Company. None of the eighteen were *Boston Men*.

John Winthrop, the first elected governor of the company in New England, is listed here.

The only other member listed who migrated to New England is Nathaniel Ward, who graduated from Emmanuel College, Cambridge, in 1603 to become one of England's leading Puritan ministers. Ward migrated to Massachusetts in 1634 after being dismissed from the Church of England by Archbishop Laud.

1. Richard Tuffneale was a London brewer who served as a member of Parliament from Southwark, London. He was not mentioned in company records.[117]

MEMBERSHIP

2. Thomas Wade- Little is known of Thomas Wade other than he was from Northampton. Wade's son, Johnathan, migrated in 1632 and petitioned the company for land worth:

> 60li formerly disbursed by Thomas Wade for his use in the Country Stocke, for the furtherance of this plantation.[118]

3. Thomas Waldgrave was only mentioned in company records by his surname. He served on a committee appointed on April 30, 1629, to compose oaths of office to be taken by the Governor and his council. In a letter from Winthrop to his son, John Jr., mention of Walgrave appears as follows:

> I have had some speech lately with my cousin Walgrave about matching you with his younger daughter, which I have referred to your own liking. It is a religious and worshipful family; but how the woman will like you, I know not, for she is somewhat crooked.[119]

4. Henry Waller was called 'Captain Waller' in company records, though he was reportedly both a tradesman and a member of Parliament for London in 1628. Rev. George Hughes, a noted Puritan divine, then preacher at Allhallows' Bread Street, preached his funeral sermon on October 31, 1631, and said of him,

> The worshipful Captain Henry Waller, the worthy commander of the renowned martial band of the honorable city of London, exercising arms in the Artillery.[120]

5. Nathaniel Ward was not a company subscriber and was employed as a cleric. He graduated from Emmanuel College, Cambridge University, in 1603 and later practiced as a European barrister. In 1628, he became rector of Stondon Massey in Essex and was reprimanded by William Laud, then Bishop of London.

In 1633, he was dismissed as a Puritan and migrated to New England in 1634, where he became pastor of the Ipswich church. At the end of the English Civil Wars, he returned to England and died shortly after.[121]

6. Warren- A "Mr. Warren" is mentioned by his surname in company records on April 27, 1629.[122]

7. George Way was a Dorchester tradesman who partnered with his brother-in-law, Thomas Purchase, to send ships to New England. He was a Dorchester Company member who joined the New England and Massachusetts Bay Companies.[123]

8. Francis Webbe was listed in company records on April 2, 1629, and was a member of the New England Company. He married Samuel Aldersey's sister and was granted 200 acres by the company on September 28, 1640.[124]

9. Nicholas West signed the Cambridge Agreement but did not migrate.[125]

10. Charles Whitchote was listed as Colonel Charles Whicheote, Governor of Windsor Castle, who refused to allow the Prayer Book to be used at Charles I's burial.

> *The Common Prayer Book was put down and he would not suffer it to be used where he commanded.*[126]

11. John White is often confused with Rev. John White, the patriarch of Dorchester, when, in fact, he is called John "Century" White in company records. He was a member of Lincoln's Inn at the Inns of Court, a counselor for the Massachusetts Bay Company, and a member of the House of Commons from Southwark, London. Lord Clarendon referred to him as,

> *A grave lawyer notoriously disaffected to the Church.*[127]

MEMBERSHIP

12. Edmond White was a member of the Haberdashers Company and was only mentioned once in company records on June 17, 1629, as having underwritten to lend the company £25.[128]

13. Richard White may have been the shipmaster of the *Peter* out of Weymouth.[129]

14. Daniel Wince was a London grocer but does not show company records.[130]

15. John Winthrop is covered in Chapter 8, Adventurers & Planters, in Section I, *The Emergence of the Boston Men.*

16. Woodgate was present at a company meeting as 'Mr. Woodgate' on July 28, 1629.[131]

17. Richard Young was a London haberdasher. On May 10, 1648, company records show that

> *John Tod was granted 100 acres in consideration of the sum Mr. Richard Young ventured.*[132]

18. James Young was a London merchant admitted to the company on December 10, 1629.[133]

HANDWRITTEN SAMPLE OF ORIGINAL MASSACHUSETS BAY COMPANY RECORDS

Oct. 20, 1629, handwritten copy of John Winthrop's election as Governor

A Gen̄rall Court holden at Mr Goff the Deputyes House, on Tewsday, the 20th of Octo., 1629.

Prsent, Mr Matthew Cradock, Gor,
Sr Richard Saltonstall,
Mr Isack Johnson,
Capt Jo: Venn,
Mr Aldersey,
Mr Nath: Wright,
Mr Geo: Harwood, Trēr,
Mr Jo: Humfry,
Mr Wm Vassall,
Mr Wm Pinchon,
Mr Geo: Foxcroft,
Mr Increase Noell,
Mr Chr: Colson,
Mr Rich: Perry,
Mr Tho: Adams,
Mr Jo: Pocock,
Mr Tho: Hutchins,
Assistants;

Mr Davenport, } Clerks;
Mr Whyte,
Mr Wenthrop,
Mr Dudley,
Mr Puliston,
Mr Ballard,
Mr Job Bradshaw,
Mr Cooke,
Mr Revell,
Capt Waller,
Mr Ballard,
Mr Woodgate,
Mr Stephens,
Mr Fr: Flyer,
Mr Spurstowe,
Mr Huson,
Mr Roe,
Mr Webb; wth some others of the geñalitie./

*And now the Court, pceeding to the elecc̄on of a new Goūnor, Deputie, & Assistants, wch, vpon serious deliƀacōn, hath bin and is conceived to bee for the espetiall good & advancemt of their affaires, and having received extraordinary great comēndacōns of Mr John Wynthrop, both for his integritie & sufficiencie, as being one every well fitted & accomplished for the place of Goūnor, did putt in nominacōn for that place the said Mr John Winthrop, Sr R: Saltonstall, Mr Is: Johnson, and Mr John Humfry; and the said Mr Winthrop was, wth a geñall vote & full consent of this Court, by erecc̄on of hands, chosen to bee Goūnor for the ensuing yeare, to begin on this p̄sent day;

Eleccōn of Gor̄nor, Mr John Winthrop

who was pleased to accept therof, and thervpon tooke the oath to that place apptainẽ. In like manñ, & wth like free & full consent, Mr John Humfry was chosen Deputie Goūnor,

and Sr R: Saltonstall,
Mr Is: Johnson,
Mr Tho: Dudley,
Mr Jo: Endecott,
Mr Noell,
Mr Wm Vassall,
Mr Wm Pinchon,
Mr Sam: Sharpe,
Mr Edw: Rossiter,

Mr Thomas Sharpe,
Mr John Revell,
Mr Matt: Cradock,
Mr Thomas Goff,
Mr Aldersey,
Mr John Venn,
Mr Nath: Wright,
Mr Theoph: Eaton, &
Mr Tho: Addams,

were chosen to bee Assistants; wch said Deputie, and the greatest p̄t of the sd Assistants, being p̄sent, tooke the oaths to their said places apptaining respectively./

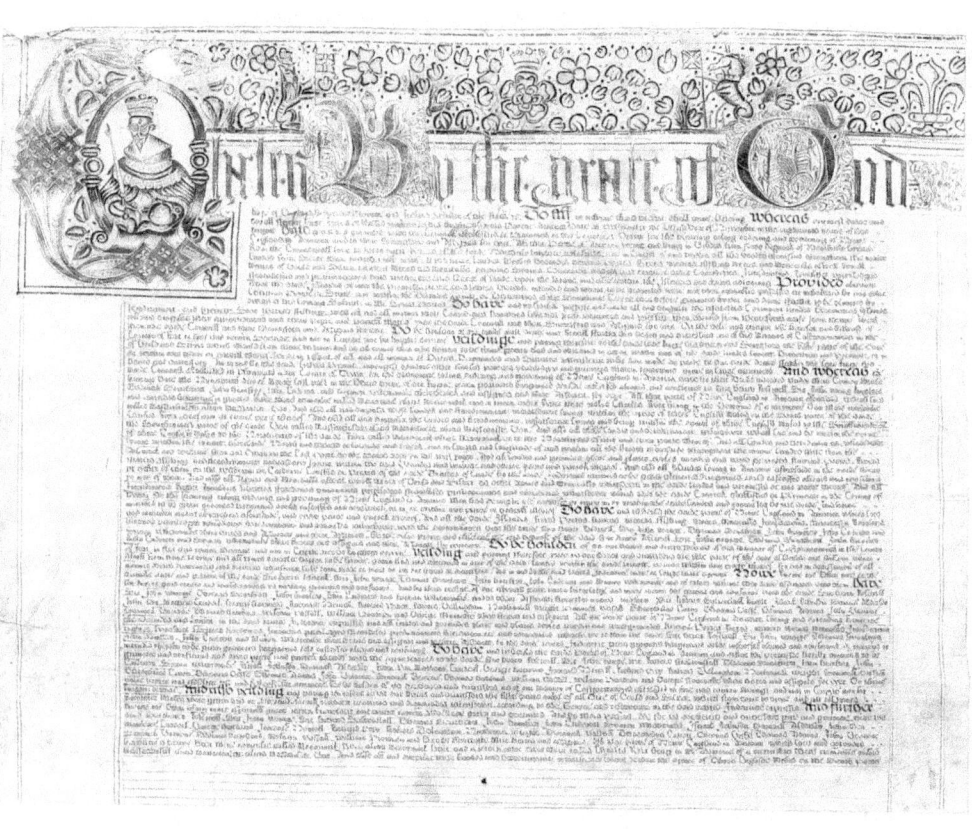

The Royal Charter of the Massachusetts Bay Company ~ March 4th 1629

ROYAL CHARTER

The role the Council for New England played in granting the Massachusetts Bay Company a Royal Charter has long puzzled historians. The Council was created by James I in 1620 as a grand aristocratic enterprise with dukes, earls, and courtiers among its patentees but soon degenerated into a struggle for control between Robert Rich, 2nd Earl of Warwick and Sir Ferdinando Gorges. Ultimately, the Council transformed from the *great noble project* James envisioned to a Puritan-controlled springboard that established the Massachusetts Bay Company due to:

- The façade of its 1620 aristocratic charter;
- Aristocratic appointees failure to participate;
- Gorges's assignment to defend the Plymouth Fort; and
- Warwick's control of the council from 1627 on.[1]

The Council for New England was presented as a *'great noble project,'* to transplant the hierarchical order of England into North America and emerged from the failure of the Northern Virginia Company.

A TALE OF TWO BOSTONS

After the Popham Colony collapsed in 1607, Sir Ferdinando Gorges worked tirelessly to secure a new patent. In November 1620, James I granted a sweeping charter to forty noblemen and gentlemen, styled as *the Council established at Plymouth in the County of Devon*. This charter granted them lands from 40° to 48° north latitude — effectively all of New England — together with monopolistic rights over fishing and trade.

The membership list included some of the most powerful figures of the realm: the Duke of Lennox, Marquis of Hamilton, Earls of Pembroke and Arundel, and Viscount Haddington. But these grandees essentially lent their names and prestige, while the practical leadership quickly gravitated toward Gorges.[2]

Gorges, a soldier and loyal royalist, was elected governor of the Council and presided over its meetings in London.[3] He envisioned a feudalized New England, with manors and baronies modeled on English society, overseen by bishops and noble proprietors. From the start, he issued patents to allies, including John Mason and his own family. His influence dominated Council records through the early 1620s.

Robert Rich, 2nd Earl of Warwick, entered the Council with a very different agenda. A militant Puritan and naval magnate, Warwick championed ventures hostile to Spain and friendly to Puritan investors. By the late 1620s, Warwick had become the leading broker of colonial patents. Most importantly, in 1627–28, while Gorges was occupied at Plymouth fort, Warwick consolidated control in London. During this interval, he facilitated the Massachusetts Bay patent (1628) and guided the Company in securing a Royal Charter directly from Charles I on March 4th, 1629.[4]

In *History of Grants Under the Great Council for New England*, Samuel F. Haven lumped the grants for the New England Company and the Massachusetts Bay Company together in a single entry, *Grant No. 11,* and stated that the New England Company grant issued on March 19, 1628, was converted to a Royal Charter for the Massachusetts Bay Company on March 4th, 1629.[5] C.M. Andrews concluded in *The Colonial Period of American History* that the Rosewell Grant and subsequent New England Company Charter were embedded in the Massachusetts Bay Company's Royal Charter.

> *In the absence of the originals of any of the possible documents, the original patent to Warwick and his associates, its transfer to the New England Company, or the supposed grant by the New England Council—any conclusions are bound to be more or less conjectural. It has always been assumed that the copy of the New England Company's patent, embedded in the Massachusetts Bay Company's charter of 1629, is to be taken at its face value as accurately reproducing the original text.*[6]

As originals are lost, conclusions remain conjectural. However, both Haven and Andrews overlooked the Dorchester Company, which was organized in 1623 by 119 investors and failed in 1626. Treasurer John Humfrey, with Isaac Johnson and Lord Saye & Sele, obtained the Rosewell Grant from the Earl of Warwick in March 1628 based on Dorchester Company precedence.

With the Rosewell Grant, the New England Company was formed in April 1628 with forty-four members. Six were original Dorchester investors; twenty-four London tradesmen elected Matthew Craddock governor. Patentees included Sir Henry Rosewell, Sir John Younge, Thomas Southcote, John Humfrey, John Endecott, and Simon Whitcombe. Isaac Johnson and Richard Saltonstall pledged £100, while Craddock, John Venn, and Richard Bellingham each pledged £50.[7]

By February 1629, membership expanded to 129, and the Company reorganized as the Massachusetts Bay Company and approached Lord Saye & Sele to obtain a Royal Charter.

A TALE OF TWO BOSTONS

~Sir Thomas Coventry~

Royal Charters were obtained through Chancery procedures to lobby the Privy Council or secured under the Great Seal by the Lord Keeper, Sir Thomas Coventry (1625–1640).[8]

The *Lord Keeper of the Great Sea*l was formalized during the reign of Elizabeth I when Parliament passed an act that provided *a place of pre-eminence, jurisdiction, execution of laws, and all customs, commodities, and advantages as lord chancellor.*

Serving under the *Lord Keeper of the Great Seal* were: a personal staff of four secretaries, a clerk for engrossing patents and four under-clerks, an examiner of letters patent, the clerk of the Crown and three under-clerks, the Keeper of the Wax Seal, three clerks of the Petty Bag, and six Patents-in-the-Chancery clerks.[9]

Among the six Patents-in-the-Chancery clerks was Robert Wolseley, who had risen from under-clerk to baronet in 1628, purchasing his office and baronetcy through controversial means.[10]

A Royal Charter for the Massachusetts Bay Company was approved as follows:

> *Per breve de Privato Sigillo, Wholesales*
>
> (By writ of the Privy Seal, Wolseley.)
>
> *Praedictus Matthaeus Cradock juratus est 18 Martii 1628. Coram me Carolo Caesare, Milite, in Cancellaria Mro.*
>
> (Aforesaid Matthew Craddock was sworn 18 March 1628 O.S. —
>
> [3/4/1629 N.S.] before Sir Charles Caesar, Master in Chancery.)

Thus, the charter was processed by Robert Wolseley's office, and Craddock's oath was taken in the Chancery and not before the King.

ROYAL CHARTER

Robert Wolseley arrived in London around 1620 and secured a position as an under-clerk in the Chancery despite having no formal legal training, never having attended university, nor ever having been a member of the Inns of Court. In 1625, Wolseley purchased a half-share of a Patent of Chancery clerkship worth £500 per annum. To accomplish this, he engaged in several shady financial transactions, including mortgaging property he and his brother inherited.

Wolsleley Manor near the village of Colwich, Staffordshire.

Wolseley rose from a gentleman to Esquire to become a *Baronet* in 1628 after paying less than one-tenth the standard fee of £1,095 for a *Baronetcy* established by James I in 1611.

In 1630, Royal commissioners investigated Wolseley after he was accused of charging £ 4 12 shillings for a gunner's patent when the actual fee was just 13 shillings.

During his career, Wolseley negotiated several pardons and granted himself a full pardon for any offenses he may have committed while in office.

Twenty years later, Robert Wolseley's son, Sir Charles Wolseley, married Anne Fiennes, the youngest daughter of William Fiennes, Lord Saye & Sele. Lord Saye, a patron of Puritan ventures, who had supported the founding of the Massachusetts Bay Company from its inception. The marriage reflects the reciprocal favor system of the time: just as Warwick granted Saye the Sayebrook Patent in 1635, so too did Saye reward Wolseley's role in the 1629 charter by marrying his daughter to Wolseley's heir.

Within months of the charter, conflict arose between planters bound for New England and London adventurers. The planters pressed to govern themselves overseas. Because the charter did not stipulate where meetings must be held, they lawfully carried it to Massachusetts. This omission enabled the Winthrop fleet to transplant the company's government to New England in 1630, ensuring self-governance independent of investors in London.

The Royal Charter was deliberately worded to prevent Crown oversight. By tracing the charter through Chancery and Robert Wolseley's office, and by noting the Wolseley–Fiennes marriage alliance, we can see how aristocratic favor, Puritan finance, and Chancery paperwork intersected in the foundation of Massachusetts Bay.

Within months of receiving a Royal Patent, a rift developed in the Massachusetts Bay Company between the *planters* committed to migrating to New England and Craddock's cohort of London tradesmen— the *adventurers*.[11]

The conflict centered on the *planters'* need to ensure they could govern themselves in New England without interference from the *adventurers* in London.

ROYAL CHARTER

For the advancement of the plantacon, the inducing and encouraging persons of worth an quality to transplant themselves and famylyes thether, and for other weighty reasons therein contained, to transfer the government of the plantacon to those that shall inhabite there, and not to continue the same in subordination to the Company heer, as now is.[12]

The *adventurers* argued that the Crown prohibited transferring the company's governance to New England. Although the company received its Royal Charter in March 1629, from July through October 1629, the issue of transferring governance dominated company meetings until it was finally resolved.

On October 16th, a joint committee of *adventurers* and *planters* agreed,

It was thought fitt & natural that the gouvmnt of psons (persons) bee held there & the gouvmnt of trade & merchandise to be heere.[13]

This result was made possible because the Royal Charter failed to stipulate where company meetings were to be held.

The said Governor, Deputy Governor, and Assistants of the said Company, for the time being, shall or may once every month, or oftener at their pleasures, assemble and hold and keep a Court or Assembly of themselves for the better ordering and directing of their affairs....and that any seven or more persons of the Assistants, together with the Governor, or Deputy Governor so assembled, shall be said, taken, held, and reputed to be, and shall be a full and sufficient Court or Assembly of the said Company, for the handling, ordering all businesses and occurrences as shall from time to time happen, touching or concerning the said Company or plantation....and that there shall or may be held and kept by the Governor, or Deputy Governor of the said Company...upon every last Wednesday in

> Hillary, Easter, Trinity, and Michaelmas terms respectively forever, one great general and solemn Assembly, which four general Assemblies shall be styled and called the four great and general Courts of the said Company.

Annual elections were to be held on the last Wednesday of the Easter Term at a place and time chosen by the company.

As a result, the Royal Charter did not stipulate where the company would meet, nor that the charter must remain in England. In short, the company's *planter faction* manipulated a Royal Charter before fully committing to the enterprise, ensuring that those intending to settle in Massachusetts could govern themselves without interference from the company's investors in London. Thus, the Royal Charter was deliberately worded to prevent oversight by the Crown.

While popular memory often emphasizes religious persecution as the reason for establishing the Massachusetts Bay Colony, in fact, it began as a for-profit venture.

Only later did narratives of persecution dominate memory; and despite the Mayflower story better fitting one of religious persecution, it was too established as a *for-profit enterprise*.

The Pierce Patent, by which the *Mayflower* sailed, was a commercial venture established by the *Virginia Company of London*.

In 1620, the Earl of Warwick and Ferdinando Gorges established the Council for New England to assimilate the *Virginia Company of London* and the *Virginia Company of Plymouth* into a single venture. Their agent, Thomas Weston, recruited sixty-five (65) individuals as paying passengers or indentured servants to finance the voyage.[14]

Of the *Mayflower*'s one hundred and two (102) passengers, only thirty-seven (37) were religious separatists known as the *pilgrims*. The other sixty-five (65) passengers paid for their passage or were indentured to the Council for New England.

ROYAL CHARTER

*Timeline of The Great Council for New England (1606–1638)**

- 1606 – The First Virginia Charter creates the northern (Plymouth) and southern (London) companies.
- 1607 – The Popham Colony was founded in Maine, but it collapsed within the year.
- 1620 – James I issues a charter creating the *Great Council for New England*, which covered the area between 40° and 48° latitude.
- 1622 – John Mason and Ferdinando Gorges receive a patent for the Province of Maine.
- 1623 – Council asserts monopolistic rights over fishing, provoking resistance from Bristol merchants.
- 1627–28 – Gorges stationed at Plymouth fort; Warwick consolidates control of the Council and secures the Massachusetts Bay patent.
- 1629 – The Royal charter of Massachusetts Bay was granted by Charles I by *writ of the Privy Seal, through the office of Wolseley, Clerk of the King's Letters Patent* and bypassed his Privy Council to be enacted.
- 1630 – Winthrop fleet sails; charter carried to New England.
- 1635 – Council formally surrenders charter to the Crown; ceases to function as a corporate body.
- 1638 – Last recorded references to the Council; Gorges left with only a proprietary claim to Maine

---

* See APENDIX: History of Grants under the Great Council for New England

APPENDICIES

- Boston Men's Motives
- Lincolnshire & the Massachusetts Bay Company
- Dudley's Letter to the Countess of Lincoln
- Charter of the Great Council for New England
- Grants Under the Great Council for New England
- Petition of Right
- Massachusetts Bay Company Royal Charter
- Cambridge Agreement
- The Humble Request
- James I & Witchcraft
- James I - Published Works
- Thomas Knyvett & the Gunpowder Plot

BOSTON MEN'S MOTIVES

The departure of the Boston Men in 1630 was the culmination of disappointments, betrayals, and broken covenants. Men rarely uproot their lives for one cause alone.

The founders of the Massachusetts Bay Company—Isaac Johnson, Thomas Dudley, Richard Bellingham, John Humphrey, Atherton Hough, and John Cotton—did not abandon England lightly.

To understand why the Boston Men left, one must follow their world from the late days of Elizabeth through the troubled reigns of James and Charles—through the laws broken, the liberties strained, and the promises abandoned.

The world of Elizabeth I had taught these men that monarchy and liberty could coexist. Under her long, disciplined reign, England experienced something precious: a careful equilibrium between crown and Parliament, prerogative and consent, majesty and restraint. Even when Elizabeth demanded obedience, she did so with the instinctive understanding that her subjects' trust mattered as much as her commands.[1]

When James I ascended the throne, he brought with him a foreign doctrine—the divine right of kings—which Elizabeth had never embraced. His writings, especially *The True Law of Free Monarchies and Basilikon Doron,* insisted that kings answer only to God.[2] This clashed with the English understanding that kings were bound by the common law as much as by conscience.

The Boston Men witnessed:

- favoritism toward Scottish courtiers,
- failed foreign policies,
- heightened religious anxieties,
- An openly homosexual monarch.

James's attempt to revise the national chronicle through Camden's *Annals* revealed his deeper insecurity: a king who wished to curate history rather than honor it.[3]

Yet many still hoped the kingdom could recover its balance. This hope ended under Charles.

Charles inherited his father's theology but not his tact. Silent, ceremonious, and rigid, he believed the king's will was the kingdom's law. His marriage to Henrietta Maria alarmed the Protestant conscience.

His loyalty to Buckingham angered Parliament. His disregard for the Petition of Right—Parliament's plea to restore ancient liberties—betrayed the last trust between monarch and nation.[4]

But nothing struck the Boston Men as deeply as the Forced Loan. In 1626–27, Charles demanded money without Parliament's approval.

Boston men refused and were imprisoned without charge. The Five Knights case revealed that the courts would not protect them. The Petition of Right affirmed their liberties, but Charles broke its promises as soon as he spoke them.

BOSTON MEN'S MOTIVES

By 1629, when Charles dissolved Parliament for the final time, the Boston Men understood a stark truth:

- The monarchy they had inherited was gone.
- The England they loved had become unrecognizable.

For them, the Magna Carta, the Confirmation of the Charters, and ancient parliamentary rolls, proved that:

- Kings are bound by law.
- Taxation requires consent.
- Imprisonment requires cause.
- Authority requires accountability.[5]

When Charles violated these principles, the Boston Men concluded that England's constitutional order was broken as three realities emerged:

- The king would not honor the Petition of Right.
- Parliament could no longer protect the nation.
- Personal Rule meant the end of lawful restraint.

The Boston Men left not to escape England but to preserve it—in this sense—the Forced Loan did more than finance failed wars. It financed the birth of New England.

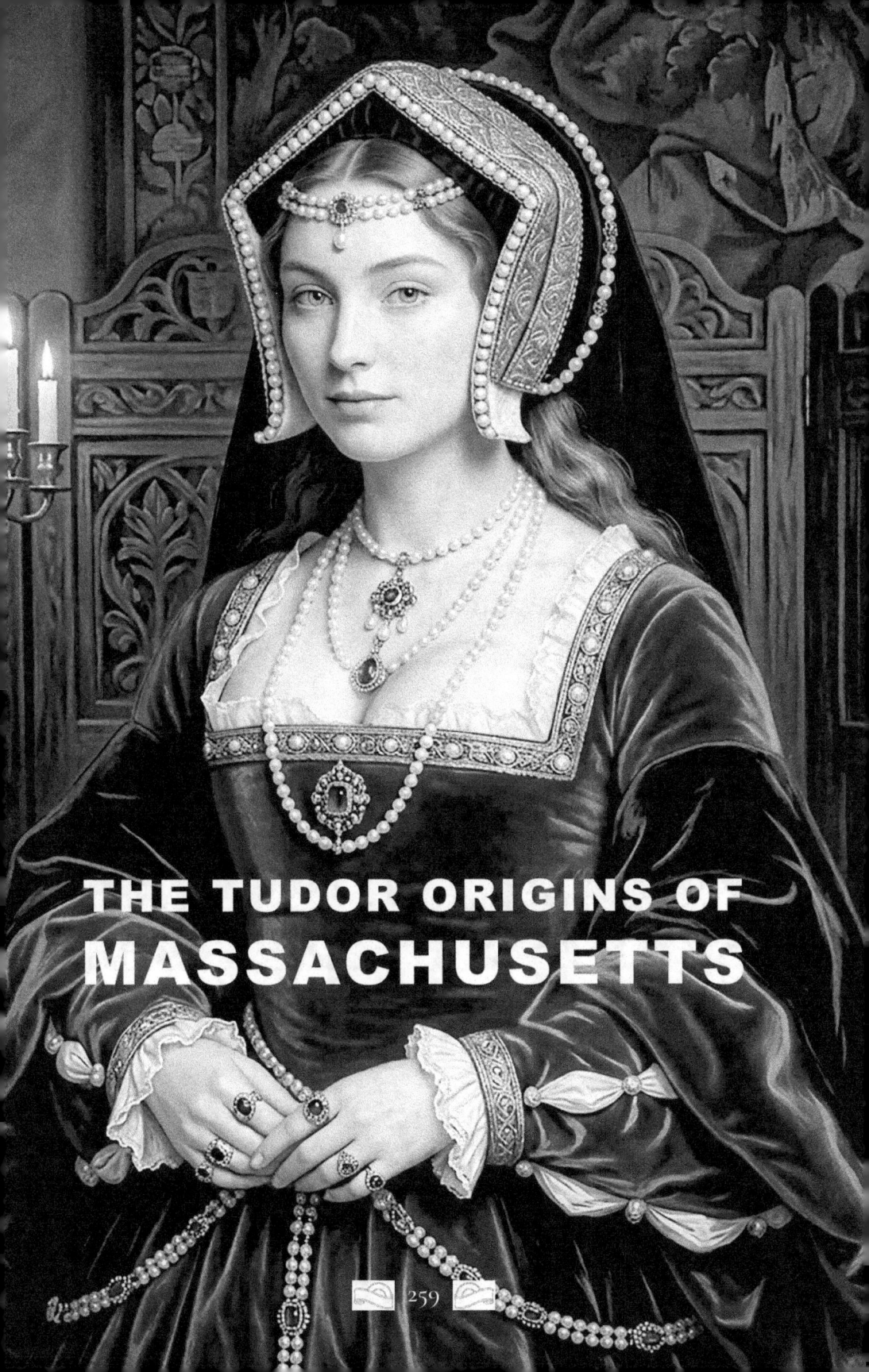

A TALE OF TWO BOSTONS

—Bessie Blount and Henry VIII—

The historical significance that Sempringham Manor played in the founding the Massachusetts began in Tudor England when Henry VIII seduced Elizabeth "Bessie" Blount.[1]

Around 1517, Bessie Blount, a maid of honor to Queen Catherine of Aragon, entered the intimate circle of Henry VIII.

The king, still in the vigor of youth and keenly conscious of dynastic uncertainty, pursued Bessie during court revels and masques.[2] Unlike Henry's later conquests like Anne Boleyn, Bessie Blount failed to resist the king's advances and in June 1519 she gave birth to his son, Henry FitzRoy.[3]

In a kingdom lacking a legitimate male heir, Cardinal Wolsey ensured that the king's personal affair did not become a destabilizing dynastic crisis and orchestrated the delicate matter of Bessie Blount's pregnancy and removal to Syon Abbey, where the birth occurred under careful supervision.

Syon Abbey 10 miles north of London on the Thames River

The birth of FitzRoy forced the Crown to confront an awkward constitutional problem: how to acknowledge royal paternity without disturbing the structure of lawful succession.

Wolsey understood that FitzRoy's recognition required orchestration such that FitzRoy was honored excluded from the line succession.[4] The surname *"FitzRoy"*—literally *"son of the king"*—proclaimed royal blood while preserving illegitimacy.[5]

—*Cardinal Thomas Wolsey*—

Bessie's removal from court and subsequent marriage were likewise handled by Wolsey's administrative machinery and ensured that both Bessie and their child were well cared for.[6]

In 1522, Henry asked Wolsey to arrange the marriage of Bessie to Gilbert Tailboys of South Kyme, a substantial Lincolnshire landholder, who was knighted shortly after the marriage.[7]

The match ensured Bessie's future and granted her a life interest in property sufficient to secure her independence and when Gilbert Tailboys died in 1530, Bessie, then Lady Tailboys, retained all his estates.

The marriage of Edward Clinton & Elizabeth "Bessie" Blount

In 1534 Bessie married Edward Clinton, a rising Lincolnshire gentleman. This second marriage appears to have been a personal union rather than a courtly arrangement.[8] And yet it could not be disentangled from Tudor politics.

Edward Clinton's ascent had begun earlier. Born in 1512, he became a royal ward in 1517 upon the death of his father, Thomas Clinton, 8th Baron Clinton.[9] As a minor heir holding lands of the Crown, his estates fell under the king's control. Wardship in Tudor England was not merely financial supervision; it was political formation.[10] Young Clinton was raised within a culture of service to the Crown, and his advancement depended upon royal favor.

By the 1530s he had entered active military service. His loyalty proved decisive during the Lincolnshire Rising of October 1536, when popular resistance to the Dissolution of the Monasteries threatened royal authority in the north. Clinton raised forces from his estates and stood firmly with Henry VIII.[11] In a county convulsed by unrest, he aligned himself publicly with the king. His action during crisis marked him as reliable.

The Dissolution of the Monasteries transformed loyalty into land and in January 1539 Henry VIII granted Elizabeth Blount and Edward Clinton the site of the dissolved Sempringham Priory.[12]

The vast redistribution of monastic property was overseen by the Court of Augmentations and Sempringham, once a Gilbertine foundation, became a secular estate embedded within Edward Clinton's expanding influence.[13]

Sempringham Manor reimagined

By serving in campaigns against France and Scotland, Edward Clinton steadily rose in royal service. In May 1550 he was appointed Lord High Admiral under Edward VI.[14] Under Elizabeth I, he commanded England's fleet in defensive operations against French intervention in Scotland.[15] In recognition of decades of service, Elizabeth elevated him to Earl of Lincoln.[16]

By the late sixteenth century, Sempringham was no longer defined by its Gilbertine origins but by its place within the Clinton ascendancy. Marriage alliances, ecclesiastical patronage, and land consolidation transformed the estate into a regional seat where local administration intersected with national governance.[17]

Edward Clinton died on 16 January 1585 and was buried at St George's Chapel, Windsor.[18] Thomas Fuller later described him as a "Wise, Valiant and Fortunate Gentleman."[19]

Edward's successor, Henry Clinton, the 2nd Earl of Lincoln, inherited his father's title at age forty-six.

Henry however, was reputed to be mad and was distinguished as the most despised peer in the House of Lords.[20]

Tattershall Castle (reimagined)

Although Henry chose to reside at Tattershall Castle, the importance of Sempringham Manor endured well beyond mad Henry's individual temperament. At his death, Thomas Clinton, third Earl of Lincoln, inherited mad Henry's title and his debt—estimated at £20,000, which in turn passed to his son. Theophilus Clinton, in 1619.[21]

To manage this crisis, the family turned to Thomas Dudley, whose administrative skill rapidly restored the estate's financial stability.[22]

Dudley's role extended beyond financial management. He entered the Sempringham household of the Dowager Countess of Lincoln.

During the Earl's imprisonment in the Tower of London for defying the Forced Loan, Dudley served in his place and networked John Preston, John Cotton, and a wider Puritan network of dissidents that extended beyond Lincolnshire.[23]

These relationships were not incidental. They formed the connective tissue between local estate management and broader religious and political movements.

By the 1626, Sempringham evolved as a center of dissent and alliances that eventually culminated in transatlantic migration.

Marriage alliances within the Clinton-Fiennes family were central to this transformation. Lady Arbella Clinton married Isaac Johnson, a principal financier of the Massachusetts Bay Company.[24] Lady Susannah Clinton married John Humphrey, treasurer of the failed Dorchester Company.[25]

These alliances created a network in which religious conviction, financial investment, and familial obligation converged at the Sempringham Meeting after the Massachusetts Bay Company and obtained a Royal Charter on March 4th, 1629.[26]

Later, Dudley later wrote to Bridget (Fiennes) Clinton, Countess of Lincoln, from Boston, Massachusetts in 1630,

> *In the year 1629, wee procured a patent from his Majesty for our planting.*[27]

Sempringham Manor was not just a residence.
It was a birthing center for the Massachusetts Bay Company.

DUDLEY'S LETTER TO THE COUNTESS OF LINCOLN

To the Right Honorable, my very good Lady, the Lady BRIDGET, Countess of Lincoln.[1]

MADAM,

Your letters (which are not common nor cheap) following me hither into *New England*, and bringing with them renewed testimonies of the accustomed favours you honored me with in the *old*, have drawn from me this narrative retribution, which (in respect of your proper interest in some persons of great note amongst us) was the thankfullest present I had to send over the seas. Therefore I humbly intreat your Honour this be accepted as payment from him, who neither hath, nor is any more, than

Your Honor's

Old Thankful Servant

THOMAS DUDLEY

Boston in New England,

March 12th 1631[2]

For the satisfaction of your Honour, and some friends, and for the use of such as shall hereafter intend to increase our plantation in *New England*, I have in the throng of domestick, and not altogether free from publick business, thought fit to commit to memory our present condition, and what hath befallen us since our arrival here; which I will do shortly, after my usual manner, and must do rudely, having yet no table, nor other room to write in, than by the fireside upon my knee, in this sharp winter; to which my family must have leave to resort, though they break good manners, and make me sometimes forget what I would , and what I would not.

Here commences the ancient MS copy, which probably contained an account of the Bays and Rivers, and then a brief notice of the Indian tribes living on them.

Sachim in New England who I saw the last somer. Upon the river of Naponset neere to the Mattachusetts fields dwells *Chicka Talbott*, who hath between 50 and 60 subjects. This man least favors the English of any Sagamore (for soe are the kings with us called, as they are called Sachims southwards) wee are acquainted with, by reason of the old quarrel betweene him and those of Plymouth, wherein hee lost 7 of his best men, yet hee lodged one night the last winter at my house in friendly manner. About 70 or 80 miles westward from theis, are seated the Nipnett men, whose Sagamore wee know not, but we heare their numbers exceed any but the Pecoates and the Narragansets, and they are the only people wee yet heare of in the inland Country. Upon the river of Mistick is seated *Sagamore John*[3], and upon the river Sawgus, *Sagamore James*[4] his brother, both so named by the English. The elder brother *John* is a handsome young... (*one line missing*)...conversant with us, affecting English apparell and houses and speaking well of our God. His brother *James* is of a farr worse disposition, yet repaireth often to us. Both these brothers command not above 30 or 40 men for aught I can learn. Near to

Salem dwellth two or three families, subject to the Sagamore of Agawam, whose name he told me, but I have forgotten it. This Sagamore hath but few subjects and them and himself tributary to Sagamore James, having beene before the last year (in James his minority) tributary to *Chicka Talbott*. Upon the river Merimack is seated Sagamore *Passaconaway*, having under his command 4 or 500 men, being esteemed by his countrymen a false fellow, and by us a wich. For any more northerly I know not, but leave it to after relacons. Having thus briefly and disorderly, especially in my description of the Bays and Rivers, set down what is come to hand touching the...(*one line is missing*)

Now concerning the English that are planted here, I find that about the year 1620, certaine English set out from Leyden, in Holland, intending their course for Hudson's river; the mouth whereof lies south of the river of the Pecoates, but ariseth as I am informed, northwards in about 43 degrees, and soe a good part of it within the compass of our Patent. Theis being much weather beaten and wearied with seeking the river after a most tedious voyage, arrived at length in a small Bay, lyeing northeast from Cape Cod, where, landing about the moenth of December, by the favor of a calm winter, such as was never seen here since, beganne to build their dwellings in that place, which now is called New Plymouth, where, after much sicknes, famine, povertie and great mortality, (through all which God by an unwonted Providence caryed them) they are now groune upp to a people, healthfull, wealthy, politique and religious: such things doth the Lord for those that wait for his mercies. Theis of Plymouth came with Patents from King James, and have since obtained others from our Sovereigne King Charles, havinge a Governour and Councaile of their owne. There was about the same time one Mr. Wesen[5], an English merchant, who sent diverse men to plant and trade who sate downe by the river Wesaguscus, but this not comeing for soe good ends as those of Plymouth, spedd not soe well, for the most of them dyinge and languishing away, they who survived were rescued by those of Plymouth out of the hands of *Chicka Talbott* and his Indians, who oppressed these weake English, and intended to have destroyed them, and the Plymotheans also, as is set down in a tract written by Mr. Winslow[6] of Plymouth. Also since, one Capt. Wollaston[7] wth. some 30 with him, came neer to the same place, and built on a hill, which he named Mount Wollaston; but being not supplied with renewed provisions, they vanished away as the former did. Also, diverse merchants of Bristow and some other places have yearly for theis 8 years or thereabouts sent ships hether at the fishing times to trade for Beaver where there factors dishonestly for their gaines, have furnished the Indians with guns, swords, powder and shott.

Touching the plantation which wee here have begun, it fell out thus: About the yeare 1627. some friends beeing togeather in Lincolnshire, fell into some discourse about New England, and the plantinge of the gospell there; and after some deliberation wee imparted our reasons by lers. and messages to some in London and the west country[8] where it was likewise deliberately thought uppon, and at length with often negotiation soe ripened that in the year 1628[9], wee procured a patent from his Matie[10] for our planting between the Matachusets Bay and Charles River on the south and the river of Merimack on the North; and 3 miles on eyther side of those Rivers and Bay; as allso for the government of those who did or should inhabit wth in that compass: and the same yeare, we sent Mr. John Endicott[11] and some with him to beginne a plantacon; and to strengthen such as hee should find there, which wee sent hether from Dorchester and some places adjioyning; from whom the same year receivinge hopeful newes, the next yeare, '1629, wee sent diverse shipps over wth. about 300 people, and some cowes, goates and horses, many of which arrived safely. These, by their too large commendacons of the Country and the commodities thereof, invited us soe strongly to go on that Mr. Wenthropp of Suffolke (who was well knowne in his own country and well approved heere for his pyety, liberality, wisedom and gravity) cominge in to us, wee came to such resolution that in April, 1630, wee set sail from old England with 4 good shipps.[12] And in May following, 8 more followed[13]; 2 having gone before in February and March[14], and 2 more following[15] in June and August, besides another set out by a private merchant. These 17 shipps arrived all safe in New England for the increase of the plantation here this yeare 1630—but made a long, troublesome and costly voyage, beeing all windbound long in England, and hindered with contrary winds, after they set sail and soe scattered wth. mists and tempests that few of them arrived together. Our 4 shipps which sett out in April arrived here in June and July, where wee found the Colony in a sadd and unexpected condition, above 80 of them beeing dead the winter before, and many of those alive were weak and sick; all the corne and bread amongst them all, hardly sufficient to feed upon a fortnight, insomuch that the remainder of 180 servants wee had the two yeares before sent over, cominge to us for victualls to sustain them, wee found ourselves wholly unable to feed them by reason that the provisions shipped for them were taken out of the shipp they were put in, and they who were trusted to shipp them in another, failed us, and left them behind; whereupon necessity enforced us to our extreme loss to give them all libertie[16], who had cost us about 16 or 20 £. a person furnishing and sending over. But bearing theis things as wee might, wee beganne to consult of the place of our sitting downe; for Salem[17], where wee landed, pleased us not. And to that purpose, some were sent to the Bay to search upp the rivers for a convenient place; who uppon their returne, reported to have found a good place uppon Mistick; but some other of us seconding theis to approove or dislike of their judgment, wee found a place [that] liked us better, 3 leagues up Charles river; and thereupon unshipped our goods into other vessells and with much cost and labor, brought them in July to Charlestowne: but there receiving advertisements by some of the late arrived shipps from London and Amsterdam, of some French preparations against us (many of our people brought with us beeing sick of feavers and the scurvy, and wee thereby unable to carry up our ordinance and baggage soe farr) wee were forced to change counsaile and for our present shelter to plant dispersedly, some at Charlestowne which stands on the North side of the mouth of Charles river; some on the south side thereof, which place we named Boston; (as we intended to have done the place wee first resolved on) some of us upon Mistick, which we named Meadford; some of us westwards on Charles River, four miles from Charlestown, which place wee named Watertown; others of us two miles from Boston, in a place we named Rocksbury; others upon the river of Sawgus between Salem and Charlestowne; and the western men[18] four miles South from Boston, at a place wee named Dorchester. This dispersion troubled some of us, but help it wee could not; wanting ability to remoove to any place fitt to build a Towne upon, and the time too short to deliberate any longer, least the winter should surprise us before we had builded our houses. The best counsel wee could find out was, to build a fort to retire to, in some convenient place, if an enemy pressed thereunto, after wee should have fortified ourselves against the injuries of wet and cold. So ceasing to consult further for that time, they who had health to labor fell to building, wherein many were interrupted with sickness and many dyed weekly, yea almost dayley. Amongst whom were Mrs. Pinchon, Mrs. Coddington, Mrs. Philips, and Mrs. Alcock, a sister of Mr. Hookers. Insomuch that the shipps beeing now uppon their returne, some for England, some for Ireland, there was, as I take it not much less than a hundred (some think many more) partly out of dislike of our government which restrained and punished their excesses, and partly through fear of famine, not seeing other means than by their labour to feed themselves, which returned back againe. And glad were wee so to be ridd of them. Others also afterwards heareing of men of their owne disposition, which were planted at Pascataway, went from us to them, whereby though our numbers were lessened, yet we accounted ourselves nothing weakened by their removall. Before the departure of the shipps, we contracted with Mr. Pierce[19] Mr. of the *Lyon* of Bristow, to returne to us with all speed with fresh supplies of victuals, and gave him directions accordingly. With this shipp returned Mr. (*John*) Revell, one of the five undertakers here for the joint stock of the company; and Mr. Vassall, one of the assistants, and his family; and also Mr. Bright, a minister, sent hither the yeare before. The shipps beeing gone, victuals wastinge, and mortality increasinge, wee held diverse fasts in our severall congregations, but the Lord would not yet bee depricated; for about the beginning of September, died *Mr. Gager*, a right godly man, a skilful chirurgeon, and one of the deacons of our congregation; and *Mr. Higginson*, one of the ministers of Salem, a zealous and a profitable preacher; — this of a consumption, that of a fever, and on the 30th of September, dyed *Mr. Johnson* another of the five undertakers (the Lady *Arrabella*, his wife, being dead a month before.) This gentleman was a prime man amongst us, having the best estate of any, zealous for religion and greatest furtherer of this plantation. He made a most godly end, dying willingly, professing his life better spent in promoting this plantatacon than it would have beene any other way. He left to us a loss greater than the most conceived. — Within a month after, died *Mr. Rossiter*, another of our assistants, a godly man, and of a good estate, which still weakened us more; so that there now were left of the 5 undertakers but the Governour, Sir Richard Saltonstall and myself, and 7 other of the Assistants. And of the people who came over with us, from the time of their setting saile from England in Aprill, 1630, until December followinge, there died by estimacon about 200 at the least — Soe lowe hath the Lord brought us! Well, yet they who survived were not discouraged, but bearing God's corrections with humilitye and trusting in his mercies, and considering how after a greater ebb hee had raised upp our neighbors at Plymouth, wee begaune again in December to consult about a fit place to build a towne upon, leavinge all thoughts of a Fort, because uppon any invasion wee were necessarily to loose our howses when wee should retire thereunto; soe after diverse meetings at Boston, Roxbury and Waterton on the 28th day of December, wee grew to this resolution to bind all the

Assistants (Mr. Endicott and Mr. Sharpe excepted, which latter purposeth to return by the next shipps to England) to build howses at a place[20], a mile East from Waterton, neere Charles river, the next spring, and to winter there the next year, that soe by our examples and by removeing the ordinance and munition thether, all who were able, might be drawne thether, and such as shall come to us hereafter to their advantage bee compelled soe to doe, and soe if God would, a fortified Towne might there grow upp, the place fitting reasonably well thereto. I should before have mentioned how both the English and Indian corne beeinge at tenne shillings[21] a strike, and beaver beeinge valued a. 6 shillings a pound, wee made laws to restrain the selling of corn to the Indians, and to leave the price of beaver at liberty, which was presently sold for ten and 20 shillings a pound. I should alsoe have remembered how the halfe of our cowes, and almost all our mares and goats, sent us out of England dyed at sea in their passage hither, and that those intended to be sent us out of Ireland were not sent at all; all which together with the loss of our six months building, occasioned by our intended removall to a town to be fortified, weakened our estates, especially the estates of the undertakers, who were 3 or 4000£. engaged in the joynt stock, which was now not above many hundreds[22]; yet many of us laboured to beare it as comfortably as wee could, remembering the end of our comeinge hether and knowinge the power of God who canne support and raise us againe, and useth to bring his servants lowe that the meek may bee made glorious by deliverance. *Psalms 112.*

In the end of this December, departed from us the ship *Handmaid* of London, by which wee sent away one Thomas Morton, a proud insolent man who has lived here diverse years, and had beene an Attorney in the West Countryes while he lived in England. Multitude of complaintes were received against him for iniuries doone by him both to the English and Indians, and amongst others for shootinge hail shott at a troop of Indians, for not bringing a Cannowe unto him to cross a river withall, whereby her hurt one, and shott through the garments of another; for the satisfaction of the Indians wherein, and that it might appear to them and to the English that wee meant to doe justice impartially, wee caused his hands to be bound behind him and set his feet in the bill bowes, and burned his howse to the ground, all in the sight of the Indians, and soe kept him prisoner till wee sent him for England, whither we sent him, for that my Lord Chiefe Justice there soe required that he might punish him cappitally for fouler misdemeaners there perpetrated as wee were informed.

I have no leisure to review and insert things forgotten, but out of due time and order must sett them downe as they come to memory. — About the end of October this year, 1630, I ioined with the Governor and Mr. Maverecke[23] in sending out our pinnace[24] to the Narragansetts to trade for corne to supply our wants, but after the pinnace had doubled Cape Cod, shee putt into the next harbour shee found, and there meetinge with Indians, who shewed their willingness to truck[25], shee made her voyage their, and brought us 100 bushells of corne, at about 4 shillings a bushel, which helped us somewhat. From the coast where they traded, they saw a very large island, four leagues to the east,[26] which the Indians commended as a fruitful place, full of good vines, and free from sharp frosts, having one only entrance into it, by a navigable river, inhabited by a few Indians, which for a trifle would leave the island, if the English would sett them upon the maine; but the pynace haveinge no direction for discovery, returned without sailing to it, which in 2 houres they might have done. Upon this coast, they found store of vines full of grapes dead ripe, the season being past — whether wee purpose to send the next yeare sooner, to make some small quantitie of wine, if God enable us, the vines growinge thinne with us and we not having yet any leasure to plant vineyards. But now having some leasure to discourse of the motives for other men's comeinge to this place, or their abstaining from it, after my brief manner I this: That if any come hether to plant for worldly ends that canne live well at home, he commits an errour, of which he will soone repent him. But if for spirituall, and that noe particular obstacle hinder his removall, hee may finde here what may well content him, vizt: materialls to build, fewell to burn, ground to plant, seas and rivers to fish in, a pure ayer to breathe in, good water to drinke, till wine or beare canne be made; which, together with the cowss, hoggs and goates brought hether allready, may suffice for food; for as for foule and venison, they are dainties here as well as in England. For cloaths and bedding, they must bring them with them, till time and industry produce them here. In a word, wee yett enjoy little to be envied, but endure much to be pittyed in the sickness and mortallitye of our people. And I do the more willingly use this open and plaine dealinge, lest other men should fall short of their expectacons when they come hether, as wee to our great preiudice did, by meanes of letters sent us from hence into England, wherein honest men out of a desire to draw over others to them, wrote somewhat hyperbolically of many things here. If any godly men, out of religious ends, will come over to help us in the good worke wee are about, I think they cannot dispose of themselves nor of their estates more to God's glory, and the furtherance of their own reckoning; but they must not bee of the poorer sort yett, for diverse years; for wee have found by experience that they have hindered, not furthered the worke. And for profaine and deboshed persons, their oversight in comeinge hether is wondered at, where they shall find nothing to content them. If there bee any endowed with grace and furnished with meanes to feed themselves and theirs for 18 months, and to build and plant, lett them come over into our Macedonia and helpe us, and not spend themselves and their estates in a less pr.fitable employment; for others I conceive they are not yet fitted for this business.

Touching the discouragements which the sickness and mortality which every first year hath seized upon us, and those of Plymouth as appeared before, may give to such who have cast any thoughts this way (of which mortality it may be said of us allmost as of the Egyptians, that there is not an howse where there is not one dead, and in some howses many) the naturall causes seem to bee in the want of warm lodginge, and good dyet, to which Englishmen are habittuated at home; and in the suddain increase of heate which they endure that are landed here in somer, the salted meates at sea having prepared their bodyes thereto, for those only 2 last year dyed of fevers who landed in June and July; as those of Plymouth who landed in the winter dyed of the scirvy, as did our poorer sort, whose houses and bedding kept them not sufficiently warm, nor their dyet sufficiently in heart. Other causes God may have, as our faithful minister Mr. Wilsoune (lately handling that pointe) showed unto us, which I forbear to mention, leaving this matter to the further dispute of phisitions and divines—Wherefore to returne, upon the third of January died the daughter of Mr. Sharpe, a godly virginne, making a comfortable end, after a long sicknes. The plantacon here received not the like loss of any woman since wee came hether, and therefore she well deserves to be remembered in this place; and to add to our sorrows, upon the 5th day, came letters to us from Plymouth, advertiseinge us of this sadd accident followinge—About a fortnight before, there went from us in a shallop to Plymouth six men and a girle, who in an hour or two before night, on the same day they went forth, came near to the mouth of Plymouth Bay, but the wind then cominge strongly from the shore, kept them from entering and drove them to sea wards, and they having no better means to helpe themselves, let down their killick[27], that soe they might drive the more slowly, and bee nearer land when the storm should cease. But the stone slipping out of the killick, and thereby they driving faster than they thought all the night, in the morninge, when they looked out, they found themselves out of sight of land, which soe astonished them, the frost being extreme and their hands so benumbed with cold, that they could not handle their oares, neyther had any compass to steare by, that they gave themselves for lost, and lay downe to dye quietly, only one man who had more naturall heate and courage remaining then the rest, continued soe long looking for land, that the morning waxing clearer, hee discovered land, and with difficulty hoysted the saile, and so the winde a little turninge, 2 days after they were driven from Plymouth Bay, they arrived at a shore unknowne unto them. The stronger helped the weaker out of the boate and taking their saile on shore, made a shelter thereof, and made a fire; but the frost had soe pierced their bodyes that one of them died about 3 days after their landinge, and most of the others grew worse, both in bodye and courage; —noe hope of reliefe beeinge within their view. Well, yett the Lord pittyinge them and two of them who onely could use their leggs goeing abroad, rather to seeke then to hope to find helpe, they mett first with 2 Indian women, who sent unto them an Indian man, who informed them that Plymouth was within 50 miles, and offered together to procure reliefe for them, which they gladly accepting, hee perfourmed, and brought them 3 men from Plymouth (the governour and counsell of Plymouth liberally rewarding the Indian who tooke care for the safety of our people) who brought them all alive in their boate thether, save one man, who with a guide chose rather to goe over land, but quickly fell lame by the way, and getting harbour at a trucking house the Plymoutheans had in those parts, there he yet abides. At the others landing at Plymouth, one of them dyed as hee was taken out of the boate; another (and he the worst in the company) rotted from the feete upwards where the frost had gotten most hold, and soe died within in a few days. The other 3, after God had blessed the Chirurgeon's skill used towards them, returned safe to us. I sett downe this the more largely, partly because the first man that died was a godly man of our congregation; one *Richard Garrad*, who, at the time of his death, more feared he should dishonor God than cared for his own life; — As allso because diverse boats have been in manifest perill this year, yett the Lord preserved them all, this one excepted.

Amongst those who dyed about the end of this January, there was a girle of 11 years old, the daughter of one *John Ruggles* of whose family and kindred dyed so many, that for some reason it was matter of observacon amongst us; who in the time of her sicknes expressed to the minister and to those about her, soe much faith and assurance of salvation, as is rarely found in any of that age, which I thought not unworthy here to committ to memory; and if any taxe mee for wasting paper with recordinge theis small matters, such may consider that little mothers bring forth little children, small common wealths; — matters of small moment, the reading whereof yett is not to be despised by the judicious, because small things in the beginning of naturall or politique bodyes are as remarkable as greater things in bodyes full growne.

Upon the 5th of February, arrived here Mr. *Pierce* with the ship *Lyon* of Bristow[28] with supplyes of victuals from England, who had sett fourth from Bristow the first of December before. He had a stormy passage hether, and lost one of his lors not far from our shore, who in a tempest having helped to take in the spritt saile, lost his hold as he was comeinge downe and fell into the sea; where after long swimminge he was drouned, to the great dolour of those in the shipp, who beheld so lamentable a spectacle, without beeing able to minister help to him; the sea was soe high and the ship drove soe fast before the wind, though her sails were taken downe. By this shipp wee understood of the fight of 3 of our shipps and 2 English men of war comeing out of the straites[29] with 14 Dunkirkes[30] upon the coast of England as they returned from us in the end of the last summer, who through God's goodness with the loss of some 13 or 14 men out of our 3 shipps; and I know not how many out of the 2 men of war gott at length clear of them. The *Charles,* one of our 3, a stout shipp of 300 tunne, beeing soe torne, that shee had not much of her left whole above water.

By this shipp wee also understood the death of many of those who went from us the last year to Old England, as likewise of the mortality there, whereby wee see are graves in other places as well as with us.

Also to increase the heape of our sorrows, wee received advertisement by lers. from our friends in England, and by the reports of those who came hether in this shipp to abide with us, (who were about 26) that they who went discontentedly from us the last year, out of their evill affections towards us, have raised many false and scandalous reports against us, affirminge us to be Brownists in religion, and ill affected to our state at home, and that theis vile reports have wonne credit with some who formerly wished us well. But wee do desire, and cannot but hope, that wise and imp.tial men will at length consider that such malcontents have ever p.sed this manner of casting dirt to make others seeme as foule as themselves, and that our godly friends, to whome wee have beene known, will not easily believe that wee are not soe soon turned from the profession wee soe long have made in our native country: And for our further clearinge, I truely affirm, that I know noe one person who came over with us the last year to bee altered in judgment and affection, eyther in ecclesiasticall or civill respects since our comeing hither; but wee doe continue to pray dayly for our Soveraigne lord the King, the Queene, the Prince, the royal blood, the counsaile and whole state, as duty bindes us to doe, and reason perswades others to believe, for how ungodly and unthankful should wee bee if we should not thus doe, who came hether by vertue of his Majstie's letters patent, and under his gracious protection, under which shelter wee hope to live safely, and from whome [whose?] kingdom and subjects, wee now have received and hereafter expect reliefe. Lett our friends therefore give noe credit to such malicious aspersions, but be more ready to answer for us, then wee hear they have been: we are not like those which have dispensations to lye; but as wee were free enough in Old England, to turne our in sides outwards, sometimes to our disadvantage, very unlike is it that now (beeinge *procul a fulmine*[31]) wee should be so unlike ourselves: lett therefore this bee sufficient for us to , and others to heare in this matter.

Amongst others who died about this time was Mr. *Robert Welden*, whom in the time of his sickness, wee had chosen to bee Captaine of 100 foote,[32] but before hee tooke possession of his place, he dyed the

16 of this February, and was buried as a soldier with 3 volleys of shott. Upon the 22nd day of February, wee held a general day of Thanksgiveinge throughout the whole Colony for the safe arrivall of the shipp which came last with our provisions.

About this time, wee apprehended one *Robert Wright*, who had been sometimes a lynnen draper in Newgate market, and after that a brewer on the Banke side and on Thames Streete. This man wee lately understood had made an escape in London from those who came to his howse to apprehend him for clipping the Kinges coyne [*one or two words wanting*] had stolen after us. — Uppon his examinacon, he confessed the fact and his escape, but affirmed hee had the kinges pardon for it, under the broade seal, which hee yett not being able to provcue, and one to whome he was known chargeing him with untruth in some of his answers, we therefore committed him to prison, to be sent by the next shipp into England.

Likewise, we were lately informed that one Mr. *Gardiner*, who arrived here a month before us (and who had passed here for a knight by the name of Sr. *Christopher Gardiner* all this while) was noe knight, but instead thereof, had two wives now liveinge in a house at London, one of which came about September last from Paris in France (where her husband had left her years before) to London, where she had heard her husband had marryed a second wife, and whom by enquiryg she found out, and they both condoling each others estate, wrote both their lres. to the governour (by Mr. *Pierce* who had conference with both the women in the presence of Mr. *Allerton* of Plymouth;) his first wife desiring his returne and conversion; his second, his destruceon for his foule abuse, and for robbing her of her estate, of a part whereof she sent an Inventory hether, compriseinge therein many rich jewels, much plate and costly lynnen. This man had in his family (and yet hath) a gentlewoman whom he called his kinswoman, and whom one of his wives in her letter, names *Mary Grove*, affirming her to be a known harlot, whose sending back into Old England shee allso desired, togeather with her husband. Shortly after this intelligence, wee sent to the house of the said *Gardiner* (which was 7 miles from us) to apprehend him and his woman, with a purpose to send them both to London to his wives there; but the man, who having heard some rumour from some who came in the shipp, that lres were come to the Governor, requiring justice against him, was readily prepared for flight, soe soon as he should see any crossinge the river, or likely to apprehend him, which hee accordingly perfourmed; for hee dwelling aloone, easily discerned such who were sent to take him, halfe a mile before they approached his house, and with his peece[33] on his neck, went his way, as most men think northwards, hopeing to find some English there like to himselfe; but likely enough it is, which way so ever hee went, hee will loose himselfe in the woods and be stopped with some rivers in his passing, notwithstanding his compass in his pockett, and so with hunger and cold, will perish before hee find the place he seekes. His woman was brought unto us and confessed her name, and that her mother dwells 8 miles from Beirdly in Salopshire, and that *Gardiner's* father dwells in or neare Gloucester, and was (as she said) brother to Stephen Gardiner, Bishop of Winchester, and did disinherit his sonne for his 26 years absence in his travailes in France, Italy, Germany and Turkey; that he had (as he told her) married a wife in his travailes, from whom hee was divorced, and the woman long since dead; that both herselfe and *Gardiner* were both Catholiques till of late, but were now Protestants; that shee takes him to be a knight, but never heard when he was knighted. The woman was impenitent and close,[34] confessing noe more then was wrested from her by her owne contradictions, soe we have taken order to send her to the two wives in Old England to search her further.

Upon the 8 of March, from after it was faire day light untill about 8 of the clock in the forenoon, there flew over all the towns in our plantacons so many flocks of doves,[35] each flock containyng many thousands, and some soe many that they obscured the light, that passeth credit, if but the truth should bee written; and the thing was the more strange, because I scarce remember to have seen tenne doves since I came into this country. They were all turtles,[36] as appeared by diverse of them we killed flying, somewhat bigger than those of Europe, and they flew from the north east to the south west; but what it portends I know not.

The shipp now waits but for wind, which when it blows, there are ready to go aboard therein for England Sr. Richard Saltonstall, Mr. Sharpe, Mr. Coddington, and many others, the most whereof purpose to returne to us again, if God will. In the meane time, wee are left a people poor and contemptible, yet such as trust in God and are contented with our condition, beeing well assured that he will not faile us nor forsake us.

I had almost forgotten to add this, that the wheate we received by this last shipp stands us in 13 or 14 shillinges a strike, and the pease about 11s. a strike, besides the adventure[37], which is worth 3 or 4 shillinges a strike, which is an higher price than I ever tasted bread of before.

Thus, MADAM, I have as I canne, told your Hon. all our matters, knowinge your wisedome can make good use thereof. If I live not to perform the like office of my duty hereafter, likely it is some other will doe it better.

Before the departure of the Shipp (wch. yet was wind bound) there came unto us *Sagamore John* and one of his subjects requireinge sattisfaction for the burning of two wigwams by some of the English, which wiggwams were not inhabitted, but stod in a place convenient for their shelter, when uppon occasion they should travaile that wayes. By examination, wee found that some English fowlers having retired into that which belonged to the subject and leaveinge a fire there in carelessly which they had kindled to warm them, were the cause of burninge thereof; for that which was the Sagamores, wee could find no certaine proofe how it was fired, yet least hee should thinke us not scedulous enough to find it out, and soe should depart discontentedly from us, we gave both him and his subject satisfaction for them both.

The like accident of fire also befell Mr. *Sharpe* and Mr. *Colborne* upon the 17 of this March, both whose howses, which were as good, and as well furnished as the most in the plantacon, were in 2 hours space burned to the ground, togeather with much of their household stuff, apparell and other thinges, as allsoe some goods of others who soiourned wth. them in their howses; God soe pleasing to exercise us with corrections of this kind, as hee hath done with others: for the prevention whereof in our new towne, intended this somer to bee built, wee have ordered that noe man there shall build his chimney with wood, nor cover his howse with thatch, which was readily assented unto, for that diverse other howses have been burned since our arrival (the fire alwaies begininnge in the woodden chimneys) and some English wigwams, which have taken fire in the roofes covered with thatch or boughs.

And that this shipp might returne into Old England with heavy newes, upon the 18 day of March, came one from Salem and told us, that upon the 15 thereof, there died Mrs. *Skelton*, the wife of the other minister there, who, about 18 or 20 dayes before, handling cold thinges in a sharpe morning, put herselfe into a most violent fitt of the wind colleck and vomitting, which continuinge, she at length fell into a feaver and soe dyed as before. She was a godly and a helpfull woman, and indeed the maine pillar of her family, havinge left behind her a husband and 4 children, weake and helpeles, who canne scarce tell how to live without her. She lived desired and dyed lamented, and well deserves to bee honorably remembered.

Upon the 25th of this March, one of Watertown having lost a calfe, at about 10 of the clock at night, hearinge the howlinge of some wolves not farr off, raysed many of his neighbours out of their bedds, that by dischardginge their musketts neere about the place where hee heard the wolves, hee might so putt the wolves to flight, and save his calf—

The wind serveing fitt to cary the report of the musketts to Rocksbury, 3 miles off at such a time; the inhabitants there tooke an alarme beate upp their drume, armed themselves, and sent in post to us in Boston to raise us allsoe. Soe in the morninge the calfe beeinge found safe, the wolves affrighted, and our danger past, we went merrily to breakfast.

I thought to have ended before; butt the stay of the shipp and my desire to informe your honr. of all I canne, hath caused this addition, and every one having warninge to prepare for the shipps departure tomorrow, I am now this 28th of March, 1631, sealing my lrs.

CHARTER OF THE GREAT COUNCIL FOR NEW ENGLAND

JAMES, by the Grace of God, King of England, Scotland, France and Ireland, Defender of the Faith, &c. to all whom these Presents shall come, Greeting, Whereas, upon the humble Petition of divers of our well disposed Subjects, that intended to make several Plantations in the Parts of America, between the Degrees of thirty-ffoure and ffourty-five; We according to our princely Inclination, favouring much their worthy Disposition, in Hope thereby to advance the in Largement of Christian Religion, to the Glory of God Almighty, as also by that Meanes to streatch out the Bounds of our Dominions, and to replenish those Deserts with People governed by Lawes and Magistrates, for the peaceable Commerce of all, that in time to come shall have occasion to traffique into those Territoryes, granted unto Sir Thomas Gates, Sir George Somers, Knights, Thomas Hanson, and Raleigh Gilbert, Esquires, and of their Associates, for the more speedy Accomplishment thereof, by our Letters-Pattent, bearing Date the Tenth Day of Aprill, in the Fourth Year of our Reign of England, France and Ireland, and of Scotland the ffourtieth, free Liberty to divide themselves into two several Collonyes; the one called the first Collonye, to be undertaken and advanced by certain

Knights, Gentlemen, and Merchants, in and about our Cyty of London; the other called the Second Collonye, to be undertaken and advanced by certaine Knights, Gentlemen, and Merchants, and their associates, in and about our Citties of Bristol, Exon, and our Towne of Plymouth, and other Places, as in and by our said Letters-Pattents, amongst other Things more att large it doth and may appears. And whereas, since that Time, upon the humble Petition of the said Adventurers and Planters of the said first Collonye, We have been graciously pleased to make them one distinct and entire Body by themselves, giving unto them their distinct Lymitts and Bounds, and have upon their like humble Request, granted unto them divers Liberties, Priveliges, Enlargements, and Immunityes, as in and by our severall Letters-Patents it doth and may more at large appears. Now forasmuch as We have been in like Manner humbly petitioned unto by our trusty and well beloved Servant, Sir fferdinando Gorges, Knight, Captain of our ffort and Island by Plymouth, and by certain the principal Knights and Gentlemen Adventurers of the said Second Collonye, and by divers other Persons of Quality, who now intend to be their Associates, divers of which have been at great and extraordinary Charge, and sustained many Losses in seeking and discovering a Place fitt and convenient to lay the Foundation of a hopeful Plantation, and have divers Years past by God's Assistance, and their own endeavours, taken actual Possession of the Continent hereafter mentioned, in our Name and to our Use, as Sovereign Lord thereof, and have settled already some of our People in Places agreeable to their Desires in those Parts, and in Confidence of prosperous Success therein, by the Continuance of God's Devine Blessing, and our Royall Permission, have resolved in a more plentifull and effectual Manner to prosecute the same, and to that Purpose and Intent have desired of Us, for their better Encouragement and Satisfaction herein, and that they may avoide all Confusion, Questions, or Differences between themselves, and those of the said first Collonye, We would likewise be graciously pleased to make certaine Adventurers, intending to erect and. establish fishery,

CHARTER OF THE GREAT COUNCIL FOR NEW ENGLAND

Trade, and Plantacion, within the Territoryes, Precincts, and Lymitts of the said second Colony, and their Successors, one several distinct and entire Body, and to grant unto them, such Estate, Liberties, Priveliges, Enlargements, and Immunityes there, as in these our Letters-Pattents hereafter particularly expressed and declared. And for asmuch as We have been certainly given to understand by divers of our good Subjects, that have for these many Years past frequented those Coasts and Territoryes, between the Degrees of Fourty and Fourty-Eight, that there is noe other the Subjects of any Christian King or State, by any Authority from their Soveraignes, Lords, or Princes, actually in Possession of any of the said Lands or Precincts, whereby any Right, Claim, Interest, or Title, may, might, or ought by that Meanes accrue, belong, or appertaine unto them, or any of them. And also for that We have been further given certainly to knowe, that within these late Yeares there hath by God's Visitation reigned a wonderfull Plague, together with many horrible Slaugthers, and Murthers, committed amoungst the Sauages and brutish People there, heertofore inhabiting, in a Manner to the utter Destruction, Deuastacion, and Depopulacion of that whole Territorye, so that there is not left for many Leagues together in a Manner, any that doe claime or challenge any Kind of Interests therein, nor any other Superiour Lord or Souveraigne to make Claime "hereunto, whereby We in our Judgment are persuaded and satisfied that the appointed Time is come in which Almighty God in his great Goodness and Bountie towards Us and our People, hath thought fitt and determined, that those large and goodly Territoryes, deserted as it were by their naturall Inhabitants, should be possessed and enjoyed by such of our Subjects and People as heertofore have and hereafter shall by his Mercie and Favour, and by his Powerfull Arme, be directed and conducted thither. In Contemplacion and serious Consideracion whereof, Wee have thougt it fitt according to our Kingly Duty, soe much as in Us lyeth, to second and followe God's sacred Will, rendering reverend Thanks to his Divine Majestie for his gracious favour in laying open and revealing the same unto us, before any other Christian Prince or State, by which Meanes without Offence, and as We trust to his Glory, Wee may with Boldness goe on to the settling of soe hopefull a Work, which tendeth to the reducing and Conversion of such Sauages as remaine wandering in Desolacion and Distress, to Civil Societie and Christian Religion, to the Inlargement of our own Dominions, and the Aduancement of the Fortunes of such of our good Subjects as shall willingly intresse themselves in the said Imployment, to whom We cannot but give singular Commendations for their soe worthy Intention and Enterprize; Wee therefore, of our especiall Grace, mere Motion, and certaine Knowledge, by the Aduice of the Lords and others of our Priuy Councell have for Us, our Heyrs and Successors, graunted, ordained, and established, and in and by these Presents, Do for Us, our Heirs and Successors, grant, ordaine and establish, that all that Circuit, Continent, Precincts, and Limitts in America, lying and being in Breadth from Fourty Degrees of Northerly Latitude, from the Equnoctiall Line, to Fourty-eight Degrees of the said Northerly Latitude, and in length by all the Breadth aforesaid throughout the Maine Land, from Sea to Sea, with all the Seas, Rivers, Islands, Creekes, Inletts, Ports, and Havens, within the Degrees, Precincts and Limitts of the said Latitude and Longitude, shall be the Limitts; and Bounds, and Precints of the second Collony: And to the End that the said Territoryes may forever hereafter be more particularly and certainly known and distinguished, our Will and Pleasure is, that the sa.ne shall from henceforth be nominated, termed, and called by the Name of New-England, in America; and by that Name of New-England in America, the said Circuit, Precinct, Limitt, Continent, Islands, and Places in America, aforesaid, We do by these Presents, for Us, our Heyrs and Successors, name, call, erect, found and establish, and by that Name to have Continuance for ever.

And for the better Plantacion, ruling, and governing of the aforesaid New-England, in America, We will, ordaine, constitute, assigne,

CHARTER OF THE GREAT COUNCIL FOR NEW ENGLAND

limits and appoint, and for Us, our Heyrs and Successors, Wee, by the Advice of the Lords and others of the said priuie Councill, do by these Presents ordaine, constitute, limett, and appoint, that from henceforth, there shall be for ever hereafter, in our Towne of Plymouth, in the County of Devon, one Body politicque and corporate, which shall have perpetuall Succession, which shall consist of the Number of fourtie Persons, and no more, which shall be, and shall be called and knowne by the Name the Councill established at Plymouth, in the County of Devon for the planting, ruling, ordering, and governing of New-England, in America; and for that Purpose Wee have, at and by the Nomination and Request of the said Petitioners, granted, ordained, established, and confirmed; and by these Presents, for Us, our Heyres and Successors, doe grant, ordaine, establish, and confirme, our right trusty and right well beloved Cosins and Councillors Lodovick, Duke of Lenox, Lord Steward of our Houshold, George Lord Marquess Buckingham, our High Admiral of England, James Marquess Hamilton, William Earle of Pembrocke, Lord Chamberlaine of our Houshold, Thomas Earl of Arundel, and our right trusty and right well beloved Cosin, William Earl of hathe, and right trusty and right well beloved Cosin and Councellor, Henry Earle of Southampton, and our right trusty and right well beloved Cousins, William Earle of Salisbury, and Robert Earle of Warwick, and our right trusty and right well beloved John Viscount Haddington, and our right trusty and well beloved Councellor Edward Lord Zouch, Lord Warden of our Cincque Ports, and our trusty and well beloved Edmond Lord Sheffield, Edward Lord Gorges, and our well beloved Sir Edward Seymour, Knight and Baronett, Sir Robert Manselle, Sir Edward Zouch, our Knight Marshall, Sir Dudley Diggs, Sir Thomas Roe, Sir fferdinando Gorges, Sir Francis Popham, Sir John Brook, Sir Thomas Gates, Sir Richard Hawkins, Sir Richard Edgcombe, Sir Allen Apsley, Sir Warwick Hale, Sir Richard Catchmay, Sir John Bourchier, Sir Nathaniel Rich, Sir Edward Giles, Sir Giles Mompesson, and Sir Thomas Wroth, Knights; and our well beloved Matthew Sutcliffe, Dean of Exeter,

Robert Heath, Esq; Recorder of our Cittie of London, Henry Bourchier, John Drake, Rawleigh Gilbert, George Chudley, Thomas Hamon, and John Argall, Esquires, to be and in and by these Presents; We do appoint them to be the first modern and present Councill established at Plymouth, in the County of Devon, for the planting, ruling, ordering, and governing of New-England, in America; and that they, and the Suruiuours of them, and such as the Suruluours and Suruinor of them shall, from tyme to tyme elect, and chuse, to make up the aforesaid Number of fourtie Persons, when, and as often as any of them, or any of their Successors shall happen to decease, or to be removed from being of the said Councill, shall be in, and by these Presents, incorporated to have a perpetual Succession for ever, in Deed, Fact, and Name, and shall be one Bodye corporate and politicque; and that those, and such said Persons, and their Successors, and such as shall be elected and chosen to succeed them as aforesaid, shall be, and by these Presents are, and be incorporated, named, and called by the Name of the Councill established at Plymouth, in the County of Devon, for the planting, ruling, and governing of New-England, in America; and them the said Duke of Lenox, Marquess Buckingham, Marquess Hamilton, Earle of Pembroke, Earle of Arundell, Earle of hathe, Earle of Southampton, Earle of Salisbury, Earle of Warwick, Viscount Haddington, Lord Zouch, Lord Sheffleld, Lord Gorges, Sir Edward Seymour, Sir Robert Mansell, Sir Edward Zouch, Sir Dudley Diggs, Sir Thomas Roe, Sir fferdinando Gorges, Sir ffrancis Popham, Sir John Brooks, Sir Thomas Gates, Sir Richard Hawkins, Sir Richard Edgcombe, Sir Allen Apsley, Sir Warwick Heale, Sir Richard Catchmay, Sir John Bourchier, Sir Nathaniell Rich, Sir Edward Giles, Sir Giles Mompesson, Sir Thomas Wroth, Knights; Matthew Suttcliffe, Robert Heath, Henry Bourchier, John Drake, Rawleigh Gilbert, George Chudley, Thomas Haymon, and John Argall, Esqrs. and their successors, one Body corporate and politick, in Deed and Name, by the Name of the Councell established att Plymouth, in the County of

CHARTER OF THE GREAT COUNCIL FOR NEW ENGLAND

Devon for the planting, ruling, and governing of New-England, in America. Wee do by these Presents, for Us, our Heyres and Successors, really and fully incorporate, erect, ordaine. name, constitute, and establish, and that by the same Name of the said Councill, they and their Successors for ever hereafter be incorporated, named, and called, and shall by the same Name have perpetual Succession. And further, Wee do hereby for Us, our Heires and Successors, grant unto the said Councill established aft Plymouth, that they and their Successors, by the same Name, be and shall be, and shall continue Persons able and capable in the Law, from time to time, and shall by that Name, of Councill aforesaid, have full Power and Authority, and lawful Capacity and Habilily, as well to purchase, take, hold, receive, enjoy, and to have, and their Successors for ever, any Manors, Lands, Tenements, Rents, Royalties, Privileges, Immunities, Reversions, Annuities, Hereditaments, Goods, and Chattles whatsoever, of or from Us, our Heirs, and Successors, and of or from any other Person or Persons whatsoever, as well in and within this our Realme, of England, as in and within any other Place or Places whatsoever or wheresoever; and the same Manors, Lands, Tenements, and Hereditaments, Goods or Chattles, or any of them, by the same Name to alien and sell, or to do, execute, ordaine and performe all other Matters and Things whatsoever to the said Incorporation and Plantation concerning and-belonging.

And further, our Will and Pleasure is, that the said Councill, for the time being, and their Successors, shall have full Power and lawful authority, by the Name aforesaid, to sue, and be sued; implead, and to be impleaded; answer, and to be answered, unto all Manner of Courts and Places that now are, or hereafter shall be, within this our Realme and elsewhere, as well temporal as spiritual, in all Manner of Suits and Matters whatsoever, and of what Nature or Kinde soever such Suite or Action be or shall be. And our Will and Pleasure is, that the said flourty Persons, or the greater Number of them, shall and may, from time to time, and at any time hereafter, at their owne Will and Pleasure, according to the Laws, Ordinances, and Orders of or by them, or by the greater Part of them, hereafter in Manner and forme in these Presents mentioned, to be agreed upon, to elect and choose amongst themselves one of the said dourty Persons for the Time being, to be President of the said Councill, which President soe elected and chosen, Wee will, shall continue and be President of the said Councill for so long a Time as by the Orders of the said Councill, from time to time to be made, as hereafter is mentioned, shall be thought fitt, and no longer; unto which President, or in his Absence, to any such Person as by the Order of the said Councill shall be thereunto appointed, Wee do give Authority to give Order for the warning of the said Council, and summoning the Company to their Meetings. And our Will and Pleasure is, that from time to time, when and so often as any of the Councill shall happen to decease, or to be removed from being of the said Councell, that then, and so often, the Survivors of them the said Councill, and no other, or the greater Number of them, who then shall be from time to time left and remaininge, and who shall, or the greater Number of which that shall be assembled at a public Court or Meeting to be held for the said Company, shall elect and choose one or more other Person or Persons to be of the said Councill, and which from time to time shall be of the said Councill, so that the Number of Bounty Persons of the said Councill may from time to time be supplied: Provided always that as well the Persons herein named to be of the said Councill, as every other Councellor hereafter to be elected, shall be prevented Lord Chancellor of England, or to the Lord High Treasurer of England, or to the Lord Chamberlaine of the Household of Us, our Heires and Successors for the Time being, to take his and their Oath and Oathes of a Councellor and Councellors to Us, our Heirs and Successors, for the said Company and Collonye in New-England.

And further, Wee will and grant by these Presents, for Us, our Heires and Successors, unto the said Councill and their Successors, that they and their Successors shall have and enjoy for ever a Common Seale, to be engraver according to their Discretions; and that it shall be lawfull for them to appoint whatever Seale or Seales, they shall think most meete and necessary, either for their Use, as they are one united Body incorporate here, or for the publick of their Gouvernour and Ministers of New-England aforesaid, whereby the Incorporation may or shall scale any Manner of Instrument touching the same Corporation, and the Manors, Lands, Tenements, Rents, Reversions, Annuities, Hereditaments, Goods, Chattles, Affaires, and any other Things belonging unto, or in any wise appertaininge, touching, or concerning the said Councill and their Successors, or concerning the said Corporation and plantation in and by these our Letters-Patents as aforesaid founded, erected, and established.

And Wee do further by these Presents, for Us, our Heires and Successors, grant unto the said Councill and their Successors, that it shall and may be lawfull to and for the said Councill, and their Successors for the Time being, in their discretions, from time to time to admits such and so many Person and Persons to be made free and enabled to trade traffick unto, within, and in New-England aforesaid, and unto every Part and Parcell thereof, or to have, possess, or enjoy, any Lands or Hereditaments in New-England aforesaid, as they shall think fitt, according to the Laws, Orders, Constitutions, and Ordinances, by the said Councill and their Successors from time to time to be made and established by Virtue of, and according to the true Intent of these Presents, and under such Conditions, Reservations, and agreements as the said Councill shall set downe, order and direct, and not otherwise. And further, of our especiall Grace, certaine Knowlege, and mere Motion, for Us, our Heires and Successors, Wee do by these Presents give and grant full Power and Authority to the said Councill and their Successors, that the said Councill for the Time being, or the greater Part of them, shall and may, from time to time, nominate, make, constitute, ordaine, and confirms by such Name or Names, Style or Styles, as to them shall seeme Good; and likewise to revoke, discharge, change, and alter, as well all and singular, Governors, Officers, and Ministers, which hereafter-shall be by them thought fill and needful to be made or used, as well to attend the Business of the said Company here, as for the Government of the said Collony and Plantation, and also to make, ordaine, and establish all Manner of Orders, Laws, Directions, Instructions, Forms, and Ceremonies of Government and Magistracy fitt and necessary for and concerning the Government of the said Collony and Plantation, so always as the same be not contrary to the Laws and Statutes of this our Realme of England, and the same att all Times hereafter to abrogate, revoke, or change, not only within the Precincts of the said Collony, but also upon the Seas in going and coming to and from the said Collony, as they in their good Discretions shall thinke to be fittest for the good of the Adenturers and Inhabitants there.

And Wee do further of our especiall Grace, certaine Knowledge, and mere Motion, grant, declare, and ordain, that such principall Governor, as from time to time shall be authorized and appointed in Manner and Forme in these Presents heretofore expressed, shall haue full Power and Authority to use and exercise marshall Laws in Cases of Rebellion, Insurrection and Mutiny in as large and ample Manner as our Lieutenants in our Counties within our Realme of England have or ought to have by Force of their Commission of Lieutenancy. And for as much as it shall be necessary for all our lovinge Subjects as shall inhabit within the said Precincts of New-England aforesaid, to determine to live together in the Feare and true Worship of Allmighty God, Christian Peace, and civil Quietness, each with other, whereby every one may with more Safety, Pleasure, and Profist, enjoye that whereunto they shall attaine with great Pain and Perill, Wee, for Us, our Heires and Successors, are likewise pleased and contented, and by these Presents do give and grant unto the said Council and their Successors, and to such Governors, Officers, and

Ministers, as shall be by the said Councill constituted and appointed according to the Natures and Limitts of their Offices and Places respectively, that they shall and may, from time to time for ever heerafter, within the said Precincts of New-England, or in the Way by the Seas thither, and from thence have full and absolute Power and Authority to correct, punish, pardon, governe, and rule all such the Subjects of Us, our Heires and Successors, as shall from time to time adventure themselves in any Voyage thither, or that shall aft any Time heerafter inhabit in the Precincts or Territories of the said Collony as aforesaid, according to such Laws, Orders, Ordinances, Directions, and Instructions as by the said Councill aforesaid shall be established; and in Defect thereof, in Cases of Necessity, according to the good Discretions of the said Governors and Officers respectively, as well in Cases capital and criminal, as civill, both marine and others, so allways as the said Statutes, Ordinances, and Proceedings, as near as conveniently may be, agreeable to the Laws, Statutes, Government and Policie of this our Realme of England. And furthermore, if any Person or Persons,-Adventurers or Planters of the said Collony, or any other, aft any Time or Times heereafter, shall transport any Moneys, Goods, or Merchandizes, out of any of our Kingdoms, with a Pretence or Purpose to land, sell, or otherwise dispose of the same within the Limitts and Bounds of the said Collony, and yet nevertheless being att Sea, or after he hath landed within any Part of the said Collony shall carry the same into any other fforaigne Country with a Purpose there to sell and dispose thereof, that then all the Goods and Chattles of the said Person or Persons so offending and transported, together with the Ship or Vessell wherein such Transportation was made, shall be forfeited to Us, our Heires and Successors.

And Wee do further of our especial Grace, certaine Knowledge, and meere Motion for Us, our Heirs and Successors for and in Respect of the Considerations aforesaid, and for divers other good Causes and Considerations, us thereunto especially moving, and by the Advice of the Lords and Others of our said Privy Councill have absolutely giuen, granted, and confirmed, and do by these Presents absolutely give, grant, and confirm unto the said Councill, called the Counceil established att Plymouth in the County of Devon for the planting, ruling, and governing of New-England in America, and unto their Successors for ever, all the aforesaid Lands and Grounds, Continent, Precinct, Place, Places and Territoryes, viz, the aforesaid Part of America, lying, and being in Breadth from ffourty Degrees of Northerly Latitude from the Equinoctiall Line, to ffourty-eight Degrees of the said Northerly Latitude inclusively, and in Length of, and within all the Breadth aforesaid, throughout the Maine Land from Sea to Sea, together also, with the Firme Lands, Soyles, Grounds Havens, Ports, Rivers, Waters, Fishings, Mines, and Mineralls, as well Royall Mines of Gold and Silver, as other Mine and Mineralls, precious Stones, Quarries, and all, and singular other Comodities, Jurisdictions, Royalties, Priveliges, Franchises, and Preheminences, both within the same Tract of Land upon the Maine, and also within the said Islands and Seas adjoining: Provided always, that the said Islands, or any of the Premises herein before mentioned, and by these Presents intended and meant to be granted, be not actually possessed or inhabited by any other Christian Prince or Estate, nor he within the Bounds, Limitts, or Territoryes, of that Southern Collony Heretofore by us granted to be planted by diverse of our loving Subjects in the South Parts, to have and to hold, possess and enjoy, all, and singular, the aforesaid Continent, Lands, Territoryes, Islands, Hereditaments and Precincts, Sea Waters, Fishings, with all, and all Manner their Commodities, Royalties, Liberties, Preheminences and Profitts, that shall arise from thence, with all and singular. their Appertenances, and every Part and Parcell thereof, and of them, to and unto the said Councell and their Successors and Assignes for ever, to the sole only and proper Use, Benefit and Behooffe of them the said Council and their Successors and Assignes for ever, to be holden of Us, our Heires, and Successors, as of our Manor of East-Greenwich, in our County of Kent, in free and common Soccage and not in in Capite, nor by Knight's Service; yielding and paying therefore to Us, our Heires, our Successors, the fifth Part, of the Ores of Gold and Silver, which from time to time, and aft all times hereafter, shall happen to be found, gotten, had, and obtained, in or within any the said Lands, Limitts, Territoryes, and Precincts, or in or within any Part or Parcell thereof, for, or in Respect of all, and all Manner of Dutys, Demands, and Services whatsoever, to be done, made, or paid to Us, our Heires, and Successors.

And Wee do further of our especiall Grace, certaine Knowledge and meere Motion, for Us, and our Heires, and Successors, give and grant to the said Councell, and their Successors for ever by these Presents, that it shall be lawfull and free for them and their Assignes, att all and every time and times hereafter, out of our Realmes or Dominions whatsoever, to take, load, carry, and transport in, and into their Voyages, and for, and towards the said Plantation in New-England, all such and so many of our loveing Subjects, or any other Strangers that will become our loving Subjects, and live under our Allegiance, as shall willingly accompany them in the said Voyages and Plantation, with Shipping, Armour, Weapons, Ordinances, Munition, Shott, Victuals, and all Manner of Cloathing, Implements, Furniture, Beasts, Cattle, Horses, Mares, and all other Things necessary for the said Plantation, and for their Use and Defence, and for Trade with the People there, and in passing and returning to and fro, without paving or yielding, any Custom or Subsidie either inwards or outwards, to Us, our Heires, or Successors, for the same, for the Space of seven Years, from the Day of the Date of these Presents, provided, that none of the said Persons be such as shall be hereafter by special Name restrained by Us, our Heire, or Successors.

And for their further Encouragement, of our especial Grace and Favor, Wee do by these Presents for Us, our Heires, and Successors, yield and grant, to and with the said Councill and their Successors, and every of them, their Factors and Assignes, that they and every of them, shall be free and quits from all Subsidies and Customes in NewEngland for the Space of seven Years, and from all Taxes and Impositions for the Space of twenty and one Yeares, upon all Goods and Merchandizes aft any time or times hereafter, either upon Importation thither, or Exportation from thence into our Realme of England, or into any our Dominions by the said Councill and their Successors their Deputies, Factors, and Assignes, or any of them, except only the five Pounds per Cent. due for Custome upon all such Goods and Merchandizes, as shall be brot and imported into our Realme of England, or any other of our Dominions, according to the ancient Trade of Marchants; which five Pounds per Cent. only being paid, it shall be thenceforth lawful and free for the said Adventurers, the same Goods and Merchandize to export and carry out of our said Dominions into fforraigne Parts, without any Custom, Tax, or other Duty to be paid to Us, our Heires, or Successors, or to any other Officers or Ministers of Us, our Heires, or Successors; provided, that the said Goods and Merchandizes be shipped out within thirteene Months after theire first Landing within any Part of those Dominions.

And further our Will and Pleasure is, and Wee do by these Presents charge, comand, warrant, and authorize the said Councill, and their Successors, or the major Part of them, which shall be present and assembled for that Purpose, shall from time to time under their comon Seale, distribute, convey, assigne, and sett over, such particular Portions of Lands, Tenements, and Hereditaments, as are by these Presents, formerly granted unto each our loveing Subjects, naturally borne or Denisons, or others, as well Adventurers as Planters, as by the said Company upon a Comission of Survey and. Distribution, executed and returned for that Purpose, shall be named, appointed, and allowed, wherein our Will and Pleasure is, that Respect be had as well to the Proportion of the Adventurers, as to the special Service,

CHARTER OF THE GREAT COUNCIL FOR NEW ENGLAND

Hazard, Exploit, or Meritt of any Person so to be recompensed, advanced, or rewarded, and wee do also, for Us, our Heires, and Successors, grant to the said Councell and their Successors and to all and every such Governours, other Officers, or Ministers, as by the said Councill shall be appointed to have Power and Authority of Government and Command in and over the said Collony and Plantation, that they and every of them, shall, and lawfully may, from time to time, and aft all Times hereafter for ever, for their severall Defence and Safety, encounter, expulse, repel, and resist by Force of Arms, as well by Sea as by Land, and all Ways and Meanes whatsoever, all such Person and Persons, as without the speciall Licence of the said Councell and their Successors, or the greater Part of them, shall attempt to inhabitt within the said severall Precincts and Limitts of the said Collony and Plantation. And also all, and every such Person or Persons whatsoever, as shall enterprise or attempt att any time hereafter Destruction, Invasion, Detriment, or Annovance to the said Collony and Plantation; and that it shall be lawfull for the said Councill, and their Successors, and every of them, from Time to Time, and att all Times heereafter, and they shall have full Power and Authority, to take and surprize by all Ways and Means whatsoever, all and every such Person and Persons whatsoever, with their Ships, Goods, and other Furniture, trafficking in any Harbour, Creeke, or Place, within the Limitts and Precintes of the said Collony and Plantations, and not being allowed by the said Councill to be adventurers or Planters of the said Collony. And of our further Royall Favor, Wee have granted, and for Us, our Heires, and Successors, Wee do grant unto the said Councill and their Successors, that the said Territoryes, Lands, Rivers, and Places aforesaid, or any of them, shall not be visited, frequented, or traded unto, by any other of our Subjects, or the Subjects of Us, our Heires, or Successors, either from any the Ports and Havens belonging or appertayning, or which shall belong or appertayne unto Us, our Heires, or Successors, or to any forraigne State, Prince, or Pottentate whatsoever: And therefore, Wee do hereby for Us, our Heires, and

Successors, charge, command, prohibit and forbid all the Subjects of Us, our Heires, and Successors, of what Degree and Quality soever, they be, that none of them, directly, or indirectly, presume to vissitt, frequent, trade, or adventure to traffick into, or from the said Territoryes, Lands, Rivers, and Places aforesaid, or any of them other than the said Councill and their Successors, Factors, Deputys, and Assignes, unless it be with the License and Consent of the said Councill and Company first had and obtained in Writing, under the comon Seal, upon Pain of our Indignation and Imprisonment of their Bodys during the Pleasure of Us, our Heires or Successors, and the Forfeiture and Loss both of theire Ships and Goods, wheresoever they shall be found either within any of our Kingdomes or Dominions, or any other Place or Places out of our Dominions.

And for the better effecting of our said Pleasure heerein Wee do heereby for Us, our Heires and Successors, give and grant full Power and Authority unto the said Councill, and their Successors for the time being, that they by themselves, their Factors, Deputyes, or Assignes, shall and may from time to time, and at all times heereafter, attach, arrest, take, and seize all and all Manner of Ship and Ships, Goods, Wares, and Merchandizes whatsoever, which shall be bro't from or carried to the Places before mentioned, or any of them, contrary to our Will and Pleasure, before in these Presents expressed. The Moyety or one halfe of all which Forfeitures Wee do hereby for Us, our Heires and Successors, give and grant unto the said Councill, and their Successors to their own proper Use without Accompt, and the other Moyety, or halfe Part thereof, Wee will shall be and remaine to the Use of Us, our Heires and Successors. And we likewise have condiscended and granted, and by these Presents, for Us, our Heires and Successors, do condiscend, and grant to and with the said Councill and their Successors, that Wee, our Heires or Successors, shall not or will not give and grant any Lybertye, License, or Authority to any Person or Persons whatsoever, to saile, trade, or trafficke unto the aforesaid parts of New-England, without the good

CHARTER OF THE GREAT COUNCIL FOR NEW ENGLAND

Will and Likinge of the said Councill, or the greater Part of them for the Time Hinge, let any their Courts to be assembled. And Wee do for us, our Heires and Successors, give and grant unto the said Councill, and their Successors, that whensoever, or so often as any Custome or Subsidie shall growe due or payable unto Us, our Heires or Successors, according to the Limitation and Appointment aforesaid by Reason of any Goods, Wares, Merchandizes, to be shipped out, or any Returne to be made of any Goods, Wares, or Merchandizes, unto or from New-England, or any the Lands Territoryes aforesaid, that then so often, and in such Case the ffarmers, Customers, and Officers of our Customes of England and Ireland, and every of them, for the Time being, upon Request made unto them by the said Councill, their Successors, Factors, or Assignes, and upon convenient Security to be given in that Behalfe, shall give and allowe unto the said Councill and their Successors, and to all Person and Persons free of the said Company as aforesaid, six Months Time for the Payment of the one halfe of all such Custome and Subsidie, as shall be due, and payable unto Us, our Heires and Successors for the same, for which these our Letterspattent, or the Duplicate, or the Enrolrnent thereof, shall be Onto our said Officers a sufficient Warrant and Discharge. Nevertheless, our Will and Pleasure is, that if any of the said Goods, Wares, and Merchandizes, which be, or shall be, aft any Time heereafter, ended and exported out of any of our Realmes aforesaid, and shall be shipped with a Purpose not to be carried to New-England aforesaid, that then such Payment, Duty, Custome, Imposition, or Forfieture, shall be paid and belong to Us, our Heires and Successors, for the said Goods, Wares, and Merchandices, so fraudulently sought to be transported, as if this our Grant had not been made nor granted: And Wee do for Us, our Heires and Successors, give and grant unto the said Councill and theire Successors for ever, by these Presents, that the said President of the said Company, or his Deputy for the Time being, or any two others of the said Councill, for the said Collony in New-England, for the Time beinge, shall and may, and aft all Times heereafter, and from time to time, have full Power and Authority, to minister and give the Oath and Oaths of Allegiance and Supremacy, or either of them, to all and every Person and Persons, which shall aft any Time and Times heereafter, goe or pass to the said Collony in New-England. And further, that it shall be likewise-be lawful for the said President, or his Deputy for the Time being, or any two others of the said Councill for the said Collony of New-England for the Time being, from time to time, and aft all Times heerafter, to minister such a formal Oath, as by their Discretion shall be reasonably devised, as well unto any Person and Persons imployed or to be imployed in, for, or touching the said Plantation, for their honest, faithfull, and just Discharge of their Service, in all such Matters as shall be committed unto them for the Good and Benefit of the said Company, Collony, and Plantation, as also unto such other Person or Persons, as the said President or his Deputy, with two others of the said Councill, shall thinke meete for the Examination or clearing of the Truth in any Cause whatsoever, concerning the said Plantation, or any Business from thence proceeding, or "hereunto belonging.

And to the End that now lewd or ill-disposed Persons, Saylors, Soldiers, Artificers, Labourers, Husbandmen, or others, which shall receive Wages, Apparel, or other Entertainment from the said Councill, or contract and agree with the said Councill to goe, and to serve, and to be imployed, in the said Plantation, in the Collony in NewEngland, do afterwards withdraw, hide, and conceale themselves, or refuse to go thither, after they have been so entertained and agreed withall; and that no Persons which shall be sent and imployed in the said Plantation, of the said Collony in New-England, upon the Charge of the said Councill, doe misbehave themselves by mutinous Seditions, or other notorious Misdemeanors, or which shall be imployed, or sent abroad by the Governour of New England or his Deputy, with any Shipp or Pinnace, for Provision for the said Collony, or for some Discovery, or other Business or Affaires concerninge the same, doe from thence either treacherously come back againe, or returne into the Realme of Englande by Stealth, or without Licence of the Governour of the said Collony in New-England for the Time being, or be sent hither as Misdoers or Offendors; and that none of those Persons after theire Returne from thence, being questioned by the said Councill heere, for such their Misdemeanors and Offences, do, by insolent and contemptuous Carriage in the Presence of the said Councill shew little Respect and Reverence, either to the Place or Authority in which we have placed and appointed them and others, for the clearing of their Lewdness and Misdemeanors committed in New-England, divulge vile and scandalous Reports of the Country of New-England, or of the Government or Estate of the said Plantation and Collony, to bring the said Voyages and Plantation into Disgrace and Contempt, by Meanes whereof, not only the Adventurers and Planters already engaged in the said Plantation may be exceedingly abused and hindered, and a great number of our loveing and well-disposed Subjects, otherways well affected and inclined to joine and adventure in so noble a Christian and worthy Action may be discouraged from the same, but also the Enterprize itself may be overthrowne, which cannot miscarry without some Dishonour to Us and our Kingdome: Wee, therefore, for preventing so great and enormous Abuses and Misdemeanors, Do, by these Presents for Us, our Heires, and Successors, give and grant unto the said President or his Deputy, or such other Person or Persons, as by the Orders of the said Councill shall be appointed by Warrant under his or their Hand or Hands, to send for, or cause to-be apprehended, all and every such Person and Persons, who shall be noted, or accused, or found at any time or times hereafter to offend or misbehave themselves in any the Affaires before mentioned and expressed; and upon the Examination of any such Offender or Offenders, and just Proofe made by Oathe taken before the said Councill, of any such notorious Misdemeanours by them comitted as aforesaid, and also upon any insolent, contemptuous, or irreverent Carriage or Misbehaviour, to or against the said Councill, to be shewed or used by any such Person or Persons so called, convened, and appearing before them as aforesaid, that in all such Cases, our said Councill, or any two or more of them for the Time being, shall and may have full Power and Authority, either heere to bind them over with good Sureties for their good Behaviour, and further therein to proceed, to all Intents and Purposes as it is used in other like Cases within our Realme of England, or else at their Discretions to remand and send back the said offenders, or any of them, to the said Collony of New-England, there to be proceeded against and punished as the Governour's Deputy or Councill there for the Time being, shall think meete, or otherwise according to such Laws and Ordinances as are, and shall be, in Use there, for the well ordering and good Government of the said Collony.

And our Will and Pleasure is, and Wee do hereby declare to all Christian Kings, Princes, and States, that if any Person or Persons which shall hereafter be of the said Collony or Plantation, or any other by License or Appointment of the said Councill, or their Successors, or otherwise, shall at any time or times heereafter, rob or spoil, by Sea or by Land, or do any Hurt, Violence, or unlawfull Hostillity to any of the Subjects of Us, our Heires, or Successors, or any of the Subjects of any King, Prince, Ruler, or Governour, or State, being then in League and Amity with Us, our Heires and Successors, and that upon such Injury, or upon just Complaint of such Prince, Ruler, Governour, or State, or their Subjects, Wee, our Heires, or Successors shall make open Proclamation within any of the Ports of our Realme of England commodious for that Purpose, that the Person or Persons having committed any such Robbery or Spoile, shall within the Term limited by such a Proclamation, make full Restitution or Satisfaction of all such Injuries done, so as the said Princes or other, so complaining, may hold themselves fully satisfied and contented. And if that the said Person or Persons having committed such Robery or Spoile, shall not make or cause to be made Satisfaction accordingly within such Terme so to be limited, that then it shall be lawful for Us, our Heires, and Successors, to put the said

Person or Persons our of our Allegiance and Protection; and that it shall be lawful and free for all Princes to prosecute with Hostillity the said Offenders and every of them, their, and every of their Procurers, Aidors, Abettors, and Comforters in that Behalfe. Also, Wee do for Us, our Heires, and Successors, declare by these Presents, that all and every the Persons, beinge our Subjects, which shall goe and inhabitt within the said Collony and Plantation, and every of their Children and Posterity, which shall happen to be born within the Limitts thereof, shall have and enjoy all Liberties, and ffranchizes, and Immunities of free Denizens and naturall Subjects within any of our other Dominions, to all Intents and Purposes, as if they had been abidinge and born within this our Kingdome of England, or any other our Dominions.

And lastly, because the principall Effect which we can desire or expect of this Action, is the Conversion and Reduction of the People in those Parts unto the true Worship of God and Christian Religion, in which Respect, Wee would be loath that any Person should be permitted to pass that Wee suspected to affect the Superstition of the Chh of Rome, Wee do hereby declare that it is our Will and Pleasure that none be permitted to pass, in any Voyage from time to time to be made into the said Country, but such as shall first have taken the Oathe of Supremacy; for which Purpose, Wee do by these Presents give full Power and Authority to the President of the said Councill, to tender and exhibit the said Oath to all such Persons as shall at any time be sent and imployed in the said Voyage. And Wee also for us, our Heires and Successors, do covenant and grant to and with the Councill, and their Successors, by these Presents, that if the Councill for the time being, and their Successors, or any of them, shall at any time or times heereafter, upon any Doubt which they shall conceive concerning the Strength or Validity in Law of this our present Grant, or be desirous to have the same renewed and confirmed by Us, our Heires and Successors, with Amendment of such Imperfections and Defects as shall appear fitt and necessary to the said Councill, or their

Successors, to be reformed and amended on the Behalfe of Us, our Heires and Successors, and for the furthering of the Plantation and Government, or the Increase, continuing, and flourishing thereof, that then, upon the humble Petition of the said Councill for the time being, and their Successors, to us, our Heires and Successors, Wee, our Heires and Successors, shall and will forthwith make and pass under the Great Seall of England, to the said Councill and theire Successors, such further and better Assurance, of all and singular the Lands, Grounds, Royalties, Privileges, and Premisses aforesaid granted, or intended to be granted, according to our true Intent and Meaneing in these our Letters-patents, signified, declared, or mentioned, as by the learned Councill of Us, our Heires, and Successors, and of the said Company and theire Successors shall, in that Behalfe, be reasonably devised or advised. And further our Will and Pleasure is, that in all Questions and Doubts, that shall arise upon any Difficulty of Instruction or Interpretation of any Thing contained in these our Letters-pattents, the same shall be taken and Interpreted in most ample and beneficial Manner, for the said Council and theire Successors, and every Member thereof. And Wee do further for Us, our Heires and Successors, charge and comand all and singular Admirals, Vice-Admirals, Generals, Commanders, Captaines, Justices of Peace, Majors, Sheriffs, Bailiffs Constables, Customers, Comptrollers, Waiters, Searchers, and all the Officers of Us, our Heires and Successors, whatsoever to be from time to time, and att all times heereafter, in all Things aiding, helping, and assisting unto the said Councill, and their Successors, and unto every of them, upon Request and Requests by them to be made, in all Matters and Things, for the furtherance and Accomplishment of all or any the Matters and Things by Us, in and by these our Letters-pattents, given, granted, and provided, or by Us meant or intended to be given, granted, and provided, as they our said Officers, and the Officers of Us, our Heires and Successors, do tender our Pleasure, and will avoid the contrary att their Perills. And Wee also do by these Presents, ratifye and confirm unto the said Councill and their

CHARTER OF THE GREAT COUNCIL FOR NEW ENGLAND

Successors, all Priveliges, Franchises, Liberties, Immunities granted in our said former Letters-patents, and not in these our Letters-patents revoked, altered, changed or abridged, altho' Expressed, Mentioned, &c. In Witness, &c.

Witnes our selfe at Westminster, the Third Day of November, in the Eighteenth Yeare of our Reign over England, &c.[1]

GRANTS UNDER THE GREAT COUNCIL FOR NEW ENGLAND

History Of Grants © Under The Great Council For New England: A Lecture Of A Course By Members Of The Massachusetts Historical Society, Delivered before the Lowell Institute, Jan. 15, 1869. By Samuel F. Haven, A.M. Boston: Press Of John Wilson And Son,1869.

The subject assigned to me for a lecture tonight is " History of Grants under the Great Council for New England."

However important this may be from a historical point of view, so far as pleasurable interest is concerned, it certainly has a rather dry and unpromising aspect.

Moreover, it was said of this Great Council for New England, by the learned Dr. Belknap, after he had tried in vain to harmonize their proceedings, that—

Hither from the jarring interests of the members, or their indistinct knowledge of the country, or their inattention to business, or some other cause which does not fully appear, their affairs were transacted in a con- fused manner from the beginning; and the grants which they made were so inaccurately described, and interfered so much with each other, as to occasion difficulties and controversies, some of which are not yet ended.

So, too, Governor Sullivan, in his work on *Land Titles in Massachusetts,* declares that the legislative acts of the Council for New England and their judicial determinations *were but a chain of blunders;* and *their grants, from the want of an accurate knowledge of the geography of the territory, were but a course of confusion.*

Possibly, it was with the hope of obtaining additional light upon these obscurities and perplexities, to the extent of reconciling apparent discrepancies, that the subject was selected for treatment in this series of historical lectures. But intricacies which learned historians and acute lawyers have failed to elucidate, it may be presumed are not susceptible of a distinct and definite solution, such as Courts require for the establishment of a title to property; and we may be compelled to find in a narrative of the circumstances under which they had their origin ∼ their only reasonable explanation.

You will therefore be spared a technical dissertation upon charters, patents, grants, and other methods of conveying territorial rights, and be asked to listen to a relation of the rise, the character, the operations, and the end of the great corporation in England created by James I. on the 3d of November, 1620, consisting of forty noblemen, knights, and gentlemen, and called *The Council established at Plymouth, in the County of Devon, for the Planting, Ruling, and Governing of New England in America.*

It will be necessary to go back a little; not indeed to the days of Adam and Eve, as did our distinguished New England chronologer, Dr. Prince, who devoted so much time and space to the preliminary annals of the world, that he died before completing those of this limited portion of the globe, which were the real object of his work, — but to the beginning of England's conventional title to American possessions. It was a conventional title, inasmuch as it rested upon an understanding among the so-called Christian powers, that the rights of nations and peoples, who were not at least nominally Christian, should be entirely disregarded. The sovereigns of Europe carried out in practice the principle which the Puritans of Cromwell's parliament were said to have asserted in theory, and apparently regarded the scripture promise _ that the saints shall inherit the earth as a mere statement of their own just prerogative. Among Catholics, the Pope, as an inspired administrator, distributed newly discovered regions according to his inclination and infallible discretion. His assignments of continents and seas by the boundaries of latitude and longitude were valid in Spain and Portugal and France; but in England the King, when he had become also the head of a church, claimed authority to empower his subjects to discover *remote, heathen, and barbarous lands, not actually possessed of any Christian prince or people, and the same to hold, occupy, and enjoy, with all commodities, jurisdictions, and royalties, both by sea and land;* of course, in subordination to his own paramount authority, but with no reference to the supremacy of the Roman pontiff.

John and Sebastian Cabot were commissioned, in like phraseology, by Henry VII, *to seek out countries or provinces of the heathen and infidels, wherever situated, hitherto unknown to all Christians, and to subdue and possess them as his subjects.* If their discoveries had been followed at once by possession, the papal sanction might have been deemed essential to a sound title; but England had long been a Protestant country before steps were taken to maintain her claims to a portion of the New World. Remote events, like distant objects, are apt to seem crowded together, for want of a perspective to make the intervals which separate them evident to our perceptions. Thus, we often fail to realize the duration of uneventful periods of history which come between the strifes and commotions, or other great occurrences which chiefly occupy the attention of both the historian and his reader. From a.p. 1495, the date of the commission to the Cabots, to A.D. 1578, the date of the letters patent to Sir Humphrey Gilbert, under which possession was first taken for the English crown, the lapse of time exceeds that of two generations of men, as these are usually estimated.

Meanwhile, circumstances were silently and indirectly, as well as slowly, preparing for the settlement of this portion of the American continent. Unrecorded voyages were annually made to our coasts for fish by the Spaniards, Portuguese, and French; the fasts of the church causing a large demand for that article of food in Catholic countries. The people bordering on the Bay of Biscay were hereditary fishermen. Their ancestors had captured whales in their own tempestuous sea; and Biscayans, or Basques, as they were more frequently termed, were in great re- quest as experts for the fisheries at Newfoundland, and along the shores of New England. They professed to believe that their countrymen visited the same fishing-grounds before Columbus crossed the ocean. 'The business was so lucrative that the re- ports first brought home by the Cabots of the great abundance of codfish in those regions produced an excitement among the people engaged in that trade, not unlike that which rumors of gold in California and Australia have created in more recent times.

No account has been preserved of the *commencement* of fishing voyages to the American seas; but they can be traced back to within half a dozen years of the return of the Cabots; and twelve or fifteen years later, as many as fifty vessels of different nations were employed on the Grand Banks.

Of such voyages no journal was kept and no history was writ- ten; because it was the policy of the adventurers to keep these prolific sources of wealth, as much as possible, from attracting - the attention of competitors.

The presence of European vessels on our shores, in consider- able numbers, a century before the arrival of the Pilgrims, may ~ account for traditions among the natives, and the occasional discovery of articles of European manufacture in their graves, that have been supposed to point to the visits of the Northmen at far more distant periods.[1]

A process of preparation not less marked and effective was at the same time going on in England itself. Until the reign of Henry VII, that kingdom had been behind all other European States in mercantile enterprise.- Italy, Spain, Portugal, Holland, and even Germany, were before her in commerce or manufactures. The fluctuations of trade, in the removal of its seats from one place or country to another, are among the marvels and curiosities of history. The chief wonders of the world —the costly and gigantic remains of decayed cities, where now all is silence and desolation—are the fruits of accumulated capital in what were once the forwarding and distributing stations of trade. Thebes, Babylon, Nineveh, Palmyra, Tyre, and Carthage were great and magnificent, because, as the prophet Nahum saith of Nineveh, *they multiplied their merchants above the stars of heaven.*

Wherever traffic has found a seat and centre, art, architecture, enterprise, and political power have been its inevitable fruits. 'The growth and decay of these local influences, and their distribution — in turn among the kingdoms of the earth, though springing from ~ natural causes, belong no less to the mysterious operations of Providence. It was the commercial decline of Italy (the "industrial Italy of the Middle Ages), whose prodigal remains of aesthetic splendor are the memorials of her merchant princes, that carried Venetian navigators to England, among them the family of Cabots, seeking employment for the exercise of their native arts.[2] At the same time, the incessant wars upon the continent were driving tradesmen and manufacturers from the free cities of central Europe, which they had built up and enriched; many of whom took refuge in the British Isles, which thus easily acquired the advantages of skill and experience in the production and sale of imported fabrics. England's opportunity had come. Though not lying in the course of the world's great thoroughfares, yet, by insular position, favorably formed for maritime pursuits, her chances of wealth and power from the magic agencies of commerce had at length arrived. Through the reigns of Henry VII, Henry VIII, Edward VI, and Bloody Mary, to their full fruition in the Augustan era of Queen Elizabeth, these causes were not only increasing the riches, but. developing wonderfully the mental and physical character and capacities of the British people. More independent, politically and socially, than their neighbors in Holland, they shared with them the accumulation of the precious metals which flowed from American mines, through Spain and Portugal, to the chief marts of trade, and experienced the stimulating effects of capital in all departments of life and action. Enterprise, extravagance, ambition, emulation, and greed were the healthy and unhealthy consequences of a prosperous and excited community.

The tendency to a sort of theatrical exaggeration in sentiment and manners that followed upon this development of physical resources and mental energies was perhaps a natural result. Man has often been declared to be the product of the peculiarities of the period in which he was born. Well might Shakespeare say of his own time, *All the world is a stage, and all the men and women are mere players;*" for the whole reign 'of Elizabeth was a theatrical pageant, where Leicester and Essex, Sidney, Southampton, and Raleigh, and not excepting Bacon, the representative of philosophy, personated the various characters of an heroic drama; while the many-sided Shakespeare was himself a dramatic embodiment of the entire intellectual expansion of his age.

There lived then a certain remarkable woman, remarkable for having two sons of different fathers, whose heroic temperament and versatile talents must have been derived from their common mother. The half-brothers, Humphrey Gilbert and Walter Raleigh, were more alike in tastes and genius than is often seen in a nearer relationship. It was the blood of the Champernons,—a name that has a place of its own in our colonial history,— and not that of the Gilberts or Raleighs, which made them what they were. To these two men, of honorable birth and social standing, each of whom combined the habits and qualities of a soldier with those of a studious scholar, and could handle with equal skill the pen and the sword, we owe it that this New England where we live, and this entire Union of vigorous States, are not dependencies of France or Spain, or such as are those feeble provinces which sprang from French or Spanish colonization.

Whatever constructive right or title England had acquired by the discoveries of the Cabots, a little more delay, and their assertion would have been no longer practicable, except at the point of the sword. It was Gilbert and Raleigh who, in the nick of time, gave this direction to British energies; and apparently nothing but the grand ideas and exhaustless resolution of these great minds, and their inspiring influence amid disappointment and disaster, saved an indefinite and uncertain claim by means of a positive and substantial possession.

The rival claims of the leading European powers, at this juncture, to the soil of our continent north of the Gulf of Mexico, were not better defined, or more easy of satisfactory adjustment upon legal and equitable principles, than are those of the grantees of the Great Council for New England, which are, now the particular subject of consideration. The rules and precedents of national and international law furnish a convenient phraseology for the discussion of questions relating to territorial ownership and boundaries, as phrenology provides a convenient nomenclature for describing the faculties of the mind, although it may not be admitted to determine their actual position and limits. In larger divisions of land, even where private citizens, alone are concerned, the most tenacious grasp is apt ultimately to acquire the legal title. 'Time heals defects, and the pertinacious possessor finds his right to hold and convey secured by circumstances, and protected by judicial tribunals.

The English jurists of the reign of Elizabeth maintained, that discovery and possession united could alone give a valid title to a new country. But how far asunder in point of time might these acts be, and yet retain their virtue when brought together? And what if another discovery and a possession came between them? Will a possession fairly taken, but not continued by uninterrupted occupancy, avail for a completion of title?

The answers to these questions are not so distinctly given as to enable us to found upon them, clearly, the right of the British crown to issue patents and charters, empowering its subjects to hold and distribute the regions which, under the names of Virginia and New England, embraced a large portion of the North American continent.

John and Sebastian Cabot discovered, and to some extent explored, the American coast (4. D. 1497-8) from Labrador to the Carolinas, more than a year before the continent had been seen by Columbus or by Americus Vespucius; but the subjects of other powers had visited these shores familiarly, and some of them had taken formal possession in the name of their sovereign, long before Sir Humphrey Gilbert came to Newfoundland in 1583.

On behalf of the King of Portugal, Cortereal ranged the northern coast only two years later than the Cabots, and gave the name Labrador to the country still so called. A map of the Gulf of St. Lawrence and the neighboring country was made by the French, from their own observations, as early as 1507.

It is said, that in 1522 there were fifty houses at Newfound- land occupied by people of different nations. There were probably some English among them, although the English fisheries were then chiefly in the direction of Iceland.

In 1524, an expedition for discovery was sent by Francis I of France, under John De Verazzano, a Florentine, who explored our coast from the Carolinas to Newfoundland, as the Cabots had done, but with more particularity, and called the country The New France; and in the same year Stephen Gomez, in the service of Spain, sailed from

GRANTS UNDER THE GREAT COUNCIL FOR NEW ENGLAND

Florida to Cape Race; his object being, as was then the case with almost all the navigators that preceded him here, to find a passage through to the Pacific Ocean, then called the South Sea.

After this, while the Spaniards were seeking a foothold in Florida, the French, in a series of expeditions from 1534 to 1542, with Cartier as chief leader, were, on behalf of France, erecting monuments in token of possession, and planting colonies, in the region of the Gulf of St. Lawrence. Having endured several seasons of trial and suffering, these colonies came to an end, as settlements ; leaving, it is claimed, some of their members still in the country. With the exception of a disastrous expedition in 1549, when Roberval and a numerous train of adventurers were supposed to have perished at sea, no farther measures were taken by the French to re-establish themselves in the North till near the close of that century.

Thus, while England had neglected to maintain her rights as a discoverer, Spain, Portugal, and France had explored the same parts of North America; and France had planted her subjects on the soil, without formal remonstrance, so far as is known, from any other power. The English fishery at Newfound- land had become important in 1548; but no record has been preserved of any attempt at colonization.

This negligence, or indifference, was first broken by Sir Humphrey Gilbert. He had written a discourse to show the probability of a passage by the north-west to India, which may have promoted the voyage of Frobisher to the Arctic Sea in 1576; and, in 1578, he received from Queen Elizabeth authority to discover and take possession of remote and barbarous lands unoccupied by any Christian prince or people, as the Cabots had been empowered to do by Henry VII. It is noticeable, that the patent to Gilbert contains no allusion to the Cabots, or to any rights of the crown derived from former discoveries. For aught that appears in the instrument itself, this was an independent and original enterprise for discovery and conquest, with a right on the part of Gilbert to possess and govern the discovered and conquered lands in subordination to the Queen. But such was not the view of the grantee himself. He did not survive to be his own historian; but we learn from the narrative of Edward Haies, *a principall actour in the same voyage,*

1st, That the enterprise of Gilbert was based upon the consideration, that "John Cabot, the father, and Sebastian, his son, an Englishman born, were the first finders out of all that great tract of land stretching from the Cape of Florida unto those Islands which we now call the Newfoundland; all of which they brought and annexed unto the crown of England."

2d, That if a man's motives " be derived from a virtuous and heroical mind, preferring chiefly the honor of God, compassion of poor infidels captives by the devil, tyrannizing in most wonderful and dreadful manner over their bodies and souls," and other honorable purposes specified, *God will assist such an actor beyond the expectation of man.* Especially as, *in this last age of the world, the time is complete for receiving also these Gentiles into his mercy; . . . it seeming probable by the event of precedent attempts made by the Spaniards and French sundry times, that the country lying North of Florida God hath reserved to be reduced unto Christian civilization by the English nation.*

> *Then seeing the English nation only hath right unto these countries of America, from the Cape of Florida northward, by the privilege of first discovery, . . . which right also seemeth strongly defended on our behalf by the powerful hand of almighty God, withstanding the enterprises of other nations; it may greatly encourage us upon so just ground, as is our right, and upon so sacred an intent as to plant religion, to prosecute effectually the full possession of these so ample and pleasant countries appertaining unto the crown of England; the same (as is to be conjectured by infallible arguments of the world's end approaching) being now arrived unto the time by God prescribed*

of their vocation, if ever their calling unto the knowledge of God may be expected.

This conviction, that the end of the world was near, was the source of much of the heroic adventure and the excuse for much of the merciless barbarity towards the natives, which attended the occupation of this continent by Europeans. The Word was first to be preached among all nations, and soldiers and priests alike believed themselves agents of heaven in the fulfillment of prophecy, when, acting under papal or royal authority, they compelled the submission of heathen nations to the Christian faith by violence and bloodshed. Columbus thought he had ascertained by calculation that there remained but one hundred and fifty years from his time before the final catastrophe. *My enterprise,* said he, *has accomplished simply that which the prophet Isaiah had predicted— that, before the end of the world, the gospel should be preached upon all the earth, and the Holy City be restored to the church.* Nearly ninety years of that remnant of time had expired when, influenced by similar sentiments, Sir Humphrey Gilbert set forth on a similar errand.

It was his intention to take possession at Newfoundland for the northern portion of the country, and at some point nearer Florida for the southern portion of the English claim; going first to Newfoundland to gain the advantage of a favorable season of the year, and the period when fishing vessels were most numerous at that station. The ships of different nations then engaged in that employment, were one hundred from Spain, fifty from Portugal, and one hundred and fifty from France, to fifty from England. But England had become full-blooded and dangerous, and already aspired to rule the seas. She had the best ships, which, as Haies expresses it, were *admirals* over the rest, and controlled the harbors.

Gilbert landed, and calling together the merchants and ship-masters of the several nations, took possession with all the prescribed formalities. He promulgated laws, to which the people, by general voice, promised obedience ; and made grants of land, the recipients covenanting to pay an annual rent, and yearly to maintain possession of the same by themselves or their assigns as his representatives.

We know that Gilbert was lost at sea, without having been able to make a like demonstration elsewhere. But his proceedings at Newfoundland have been regarded by all English writers as substantiating the English title to the whole country. No distinct colony was left behind him; but the British domination continued to be recognized by the mixed population on the shore, and was, when necessary, enforced by summary process among the ships.

On learning the death of his heroic half-brother, Sir Walter Raleigh, his partner in the enterprise, immediately obtained a similar commission and patent in his own name, and sought to complete their purpose by planting a colony at the South. It was his fortune, too, to fail in that part of his design which contemplated the establishment of settlements under his own rule and tributary to himself; but he was the first to possess and occupy the soil of Virginia; and, although interrupted for a time, the occupancy of British subjects in that region became permanent, without the interference of rival attempts at colonization.

It was under such circumstances, and in such manner, that the title of England, be it good or bad, to a portion of our continent, was originally acquired and maintained.

It seemed to be desirable to refer to the nature of that title, to the civil condition of England, to the operations of trade and fishery, and to the colonial projects which preceded the incorporation of that semi-commercial, semi-political body known as the Great Council for New England. For it was the wealth of the mercantile classes, resulting in some degree from the discovery of new sources and new courses of trade in distant regions, that made the nobility and gentry eager to partake of their gains. The " Fellowship of English Merchants for the Discovery of New Trades," sometimes called also the Muscovy or Russian Company, which had a charter as early as 1554-5, had been remarkably successful. Immense fortunes, like those of Sir Thomas Smith and Sir John Wolstenholm, and others who took part in the Virginia enterprises, had been realized by merchants who became knights and baronets. The wealth of the House of Commons far exceeded that of the House of Lords. The great increase of extravagance in private expenditure had become a serious drain upon the resources of the nobility; and it was the hope of profit from the fur trade and fisheries, combined with the advantage and dignity of territorial proprietor- ship, that caused the formation and governed the conduct of the New-England Company, while ignorance of business and embarrassments arising from conflicting claims, domestic and foreign, brought it to an end.

There is another preliminary fact, which is of great interest to New England, and especially to Massachusetts. At the beginning of a new century, A.D. 1602, Raleigh's colonies had disappeared, and all traces of them were lost. Dr. Holmes, in his Annals, remarks, that then "in North America north of Mexico not a single European family could be found." If we understand by family a household of men, women, and children, this statement may be nearly correct; and yet it is estimated that there were at that time, at Newfoundland, as many as ten thousand men and boys employed on board and on shore in the business of taking and curing fish. Colonization, however, had been virtually abandoned in despair. At that critical period, it was revived by two men whose service to this country in that respect has never been properly or sufficiently acknowledged. These were the Earl of Southampton and Bartholomew Gosnold: the first, the friend and patron of Shakespeare, and the subject of many of his sonnets, who had impaired his fortune by his liberality to men of letters; the other, an intrepid mariner from the west of England, who became the leading spirit, and one of the first victims, of the attempt to renew the settlements of Virginia.

A TALE OF TWO BOSTONS

You are all familiar with the story of Gosnold's visit to Massachusetts Bay, in 1602; and it hardly needs to be stated, that the expedition was undertaken with the consent of Raleigh, as coming within his jurisdiction; that the cost was chiefly defrayed by the Earl of Southampton; that the design of the voyage was to find a direct and shorter way across the ocean and a proper seat for a plantation; that the company consisted of thirty-two men, twenty of whom were to remain in the country ; that, in fact, they were the first to take a straight course across the Atlantic, instead of the usual passage to Virginia by the West Indies; that they reached land near Salem Harbor; that from them came the familiar names of Cape Cod, Martha's Vineyard, the Elizabeth Islands, &c.; and that they built a fort at Cuttyhunk in Buzzard's Bay. They were delighted with the country, but were compelled to return home for larger supplies. Before they could come back better provided for a permanent settlement, Queen Elizabeth died, Raleigh was thrown into prison by her successor, and all schemes for American colonization were of necessity to be abandoned, or organized upon a new basis under a new sovereign himself destitute of energy and enterprise. Fortunately, Gosnold and his companions were not merely men of action, but could write and speak as well; and to their glowing narratives and zealous exertions, aided by the famous Hakluyt, and men of influence at Court, historians ascribe the procurement of the charter of 1606, from which the ultimate settlement of the United States and the resulting heritage of territorial rights are to be dated.

The fact of Gosnold's selection of our own coast for an intended colony is sufficiently well known; but I am sure, that the characters and services of the leaders of that little company are not sufficiently understood and appreciated, or, instead of the farce which was enacted over the later and inconsequential landing and brief continuance of a body of outlaws on the coast of Maine, all New England would have united in measures to honor the memory of the

GRANTS UNDER THE GREAT COUNCIL FOR NEW ENGLAND

real founders of permanent habitation and indisputable title within our national bounds.

For some reason, the charter of 1606 did not embrace the whole of the British claim. It extended no farther south than the present limits of North Carolina, and no farther north than the present limits of the State of Vermont; that is, from the thirty-fourth to the forty-fifth degree of latitude. Within these bounds there were to be two colonies under separate administrations, subject to a paramount administration in the mother country. The southern colony could plant anywhere between the thirty-fourth and forty-first degrees, and the northern colony, anywhere between the thirty-eighth and forty-fifth degrees; leaving three degrees, or the space from the southern point of Maryland to the southern point of Connecticut, as common ground.

The northern company had need of hot haste in choosing a location; as, in the race for possession, the French had once more taken the lead, and renewed their plans of founding an American empire. Having before sent over a shipload of felons from the jails, who were left to take care of themselves at the Isle of Sables, a more formidable expedition was organized in 1603, the year succeeding Gosnold's memorable voyage. Henry the Great, being then King of France, a gentleman of his household, named De Monts, received from him a patent of the American territory from the fortieth to the forty-sixth degree of north latitude, with power, as lieutenant-general, to colonize and rule it. It will be noticed that this grant almost exactly covers the territory assigned to the northern colony of Virginia by the English charter of 1606. De Monts lost no time in entering upon his dominion; and he and his followers settled themselves in Nova Scotia, at Montsdésert (now called Mount Desert), and along the coast of Maine as far as the Penobscot. They looked into Boston Harbor in search of a more genial climate, but were repelled by the hostile attitude of the natives.

The company of outlaws which, in imitation of the French, Chief-Justice Popham sent to the mouth of the Sagadehoe or Kennebec River, in 1607, was undoubtedly intended and expected to check the advances of that nation. It not only failed, but its failure paralyzed the energies of the northern company of Virginia for many succeeding years.

That portion of the duplex contrivance of James I. accomplished nothing important of itself until, after much opposition, a separate organization and charter were obtained in 1620. In the mean time, its twin-brother, at Jamestown, flourished, after a fashion; it is doubtful whether most aided or hindered by the frequent interference of the English monarch, that " Dominie Sampson" spoilt into a king, who believed himself to be the fountain of wisdom, not less than the fountain of honor. It was able, in 1613, to fit out an armed vessel, commanded by Captain Argall, which broke up the French settlements at Port Royal, Mount Desert, &c., and compelled their inhabitants to retire towards Canada; protesting all the while, that whatever abstract rights Great Britain might possess, if any there were, the Virginia charter expressly excepted in its grants regions already occupied by any Christian prince or people; they (the French) being a Christian people, in occupation of the places from which they were driven two years before the Virginia charter was made; which was very true.

Upon the island of Manhattan at the mouth of Hudson's river, on the common ground of the two so-called Virginia companies, the Dutch had located themselves, claiming title from its discovery by Hudson, in their service. While returning from his expedition against the French, Captain Argall called on them also, and required submission. They were too feeble to resist; but the next year a new governor came from Amsterdam, with reinforcements, asserting the right of Holland to the country, and refusing the tribute which his predecessor had consented to pay to the English.

GRANTS UNDER THE GREAT COUNCIL FOR NEW ENGLAND

It was to this inheritance, of not undisputed possessions, to which the new corporation, styled " The Council established at Plymouth, in the County of Devon, for the Planting, Ruling, and Governing of New England in America," succeeded on the 3rd of November, 1620.

The charter, after referring to the previous charter of 1606, and the changes that had since been made for the benefit of the southern company, states that Sir Ferdinando Gorges, and other principal adventurers of the northern company, with divers per- sons of quality who now intend to be their associates, resolving to prosecute their designs more effectually, and intending to establish fishery, trade, and plantation, within the precincts of the said northern company; for that purpose, and to avoid all confusion and difference between themselves and the other company, have desired to be made a distant body.

It proceeds to grant to the persons named, the territory from the fortieth to the forty-eighth degree of north latitude and through the main land from sea to sea, to be called NEW ENGLAND; that is, from the latitude of Philadelphia to the middle of Newfoundland, and through all that width from the Atlantic to the Pacific; varying a few degrees of latitude from the bounds prescribed in the original patent.

They were to be one body politic and corporate, to consist of forty persons, and no more, with perpetual succession. Vacancies were to be filled by the members. They were empowered to establish laws not contrary to the laws of England; and to their " governors, officers, and ministers," according to the natural limits of their offices, was given authority to correct, punish, pardon, and rule all English subjects that should become colonists, according to the laws and instructions of the Council; and in defect thereof, in cases of necessity, according to their good discretions, in cases criminal and capital as well as civil, and both marine and others. Such proceedings to be, as near as conveniently may be, agreeable to the laws, statutes, government, and policy, of the realm of England. The continent, from the fortieth to the forty-eighth degree, from sea to sea, was absolutely given, granted, and confirmed to the said Council and their successors, to be holden, as of the manor of Kast Greenwich, in free and common socage, as distinguished from the feudal tenure of personal service; and all subjects were forbidden to trade or fish within their limits without a license from the Council under seal.[3]

The rank and personal standing of the grantees corresponded to the extent of territory and the magnitude of the powers be- stowed upon them. They consisted of many of the highest nobility of the kingdom, and knights and gentlemen of prominence and influence. Their aims and purposes were not less lofty and aristocratic. Upon the general ground, that kings did first lay the foundations of their monarchies, by reserving to them- selves the sovereign power (as fit it was), and dividing their kingdoms into counties, baronies, hundreds, and the like, they say, —

> *This foundation being so certain, there is no reason for us to vary from it; and therefore we resolve to build our edifices upon it. So as we purpose to commit the management of our whole affairs there in general unto a governor, to be assisted by the advice and counsel of so many of the patentees as shall be there resident, together with the officers of State.*

Among the *officers of State* were to be a treasurer, a marshal, an admiral, and a master of ordnance. 'Two parts of the whole territory were to be divided among the patentees, and the other third reserved for public uses; but the entire territory was to be formed into counties, baronies, hundreds, and the like. From every county and barony deputies were to be chosen to consult upon the laws to be framed, and to reform any notable abuses. Yet these are not to be assembled but by order of the President and Council in England, "

GRANTS UNDER THE GREAT COUNCIL FOR NEW ENGLAND

who are to give life to the laws so to be made, as those to whom of right it best belongs." The counties and baronies were to be governed by the chief, and the officers under him, with a power of high and low justice, subject to an appeal, in some cases, to the supreme courts. The lords of counties might also divide their counties into manors and lordships, with courts for determining petty matters. When great cities had grown up, they were to be made bodies politic to govern their own private affairs, with a right of representation by deputies or burgesses.[4] There was a provision in the charter for its renewal and amendment, if changes should be found expedient; and measures were taken for a new patent, omitting the requirement that their government should be as near the laws of England as may be, and inserting authority to create titles of honor, and establish feudal tenures. The chief managers of the affairs of the Council were Sir Ferdinando Gorges, a friend and fellow-soldier of Raleigh, who, ever since the failure of the Popham enterprise in Maine, had been striving to settle a plantation for trade and fishing there on his own account; Captain John Mason, who had been governor of Newfoundland; and the Earl of Warwick, the President. The patents issued to colonists, whether companies or single adventurers, were intended to conform to the political system they had adopted. The influence of Gorges is seen in the project, which was early started, of laying out a county, on the general behalf, forty miles square, on the Kennebec River, and building a great city at the junction of the rivers Kennebec and Androscoggin.

> *Two kinds of patents were provided for by the Council: one for private undertakers of petty plantations, who were to have a 'certain quantity of land allotted them at an annual rent, with conditions that they should not alienate without leave, and should settle a stated number of persons with cattle, &c., within a definite period; the other for such parties as proposed to build towns, with large numbers of people, having a government and magistrates, who were to have power to frame such laws and constitutions as the majority should*

think fit, subordinate to the State which was to be established, " until other order should be taken.

The grand schemes of the Council were not destined to experience even the promise of success. They began to fail from the very beginning of their operations. They had to con- tend not only against the active hostility of the Southern corporation, the remonstrances of the French, and the pertinacity the Hollanders, who said little, while they encroached upon the fisheries, and inclined to take possession of Connecticut River; but the fishermen and fur-traders of England itself, whose rights, become prescriptive by long enjoyment, were so summarily interfered with. The matter was taken up by Parliament, and Sir Ferdinando Gorges was summoned to their bar. His argument, that the enlargement of the King's dominions and the advancement of religion were of more consequence than a disorderly course of fishing, which, except for their plantation, would soon be given over, (as so goodly a coast could not long be left unpeopled by the French, Spanish, or Dutch), if it did not satisfy the Commons, had weight with the King, who continued his favor and protection.

Gorges was to be the Governor of the new State, and, in 1623, the attempt was made to transfer an operative government to American soil. The King had issued a proclamation enforcing their authority, and now Robert Gorges, son of Sir Ferdinando, was sent over as Lieutenant-General and Governor of New England, with a suite of officers, to establish his court at Massachusetts Bay, where a tract extending ten miles on the north-east side of the bay had been granted to him personally by patent.

This proved an unfortunate procedure. It increased the hostile feeling in England, so that, in a list of public grievances brought forward by Parliament, the first was the patent for New England. This public declaration of the House's dislike, Gorges tells us, *shook off all adventurers from the plantation and made many of the patentees quit their interest.* The Lieutenant-Governor and his military and ecclesiastical officers were advised to return home; and thus the plan of a State ruled by a Company, such as we have seen to succeed in India, failed in New England.

The other purpose of the Council, viz., to derive a profit from the fisheries and the fur-trade, with a view also to the ultimate advantages of territorial proprietorship, was continued in a feeble and desultory way. The great object was to get the country occupied at all events, and grants of land were made with a singular disregard of boundaries and of previous conveyance. Gorges and Mason were the only persons at all acquainted with localities here, and Gorges had become despondent and almost desperate. Many members of the corporation gave up their partnership rather than pay their shares of the expenses ; and it was difficult to find others to take their places. They tried the policy of dividing the whole territory among their members, in severalty, which came to nothing. Dissensions arose, and the Earl of Warwick withdrew from their meetings, but still kept the great seal, and evaded the calls that were made upon him to deliver it to the treasurer. They did not know what patents had been issued, and the President was *entreated to direct a course for finding out*. It was proposed to send over a surveyor to settle limits, and commissioners to hear and determine grievances. 'The company became reduced from forty to twenty-one, notwithstanding recruits had been diligently sought among the merchants. Their records from November 1632 to January 1634 are wanting. When they begin again, the only remaining objects aimed at seem to have been a renewal of the policy of assigning to members distinct portions of the region embraced in their charter, and a surrender of the charter to the King, who is besought to graciously ratify the division, and confirm it by his own decree. This he does not appear ever to have formally done; and the Great Council for planting, ruling, and governing New England, came to an end in 1635, leaving no other encumbrances upon the soil than such as arose from a few larger patents, which depended for their force and validity very much upon the royal sanction they ultimately received, and some grants whose proprietors were in the country engaged in actual occupancy or management.

Dr. Palfrey, in his history, gives a list of twenty-four grants made, or supposed to have been made, by the Council for New England before the final partition attempted among themselves. From these we must take the doubtful, or at any rate futile, division among the partners alleged to have been effected in 1622; also the Charter of Nova Scotia to Sir William Alexander, which came directly from the King with the assent of the Council, how signified does not appear; also the supposed grants to Thompson, Weston, and Wollaston, which, if ever formally executed, were soon forfeited or abandoned, like some others that might be added from the Records; also the patent of Connecticut, March 19, 1631, which proceeded from the Earl of Warwick personally, and was apparently founded on an actual or expected title passed, or to be passed, from the Council to himself. It is possible that, like the deed of Cape Ann to the Pilgrims, by Lord Sheffield in 1623, it was based on a contemplated division among the Council that was never perfected.[5] Grants were sometimes spoken of as made that were not drawn up, and sometimes the execution, long delayed, was not formally completed, so that the Council felt at liberty to confirm or reject them. To some patents, there were conditions attached, such as rent and the introduction of settlers within a certain time, to remain a certain time, which, if not complied with, might occasion a forfeiture.

Four in Dr. Palfrey's list are for the benefit of the Pilgrims at Plymouth; but the last and amplest absorbed or cancelled the others.

The first act of this nature for the benefit of the Pilgrims, was dated June 1, 1621. The other grants to them of 1622, 1627, and 1630, enlarged their property and powers at Plymouth, and gave them a large tract of land on the Kennebec, for trade with the Indians; by the special favor, it is said, of the Earl of Warwick, who seems to have been devoted to the interests of the Puritans.

GRANTS UNDER THE GREAT COUNCIL FOR NEW ENGLAND

There remain to be mentioned fourteen grants professedly emanating from the Council : —

1st, To Captain John Mason, March 9, 1622, of the coast and islands between Salem River and the Merrimack, called by him " Mariana." It is said to have been imperfectly executed; and was disregarded in sub- sequent conveyances.

2d, To Gorges and Mason jointly, Aug. 10, 1622, of the country between the Merrimack and Kennebec Rivers, and sixty miles inland from their mouths, "which they intend to name the Province of Maine."

3d, To Robert Gorges, of ten miles from Boston towards Salem, just before he came over as Lieutenant-Governor. The tenure was by the sword, or per gladium comitatus.

4th, To a grandson of Sir F. Gorges and his associates, of twenty-four thousand acres, on both sides of the York River in Maine, with the islands within three leagues of the coast. This patent, though referred by Gorges to 1623, was not executed till Dec. 2, 1631, and was reissued the following March, with a partial change of associates. The consideration was their engagement to build a town.

5th, To the Massachusetts Company, which, as confirmed by the royal charter, March 4, 1629, covered Mason's Mariana, the tract of Robert Gorges, and a part of the territory of Gorges and Mason; as it was to embrace the country from three miles north of every part of the Merri- mack River to three miles south of Charles River.

6th, To Captain John Mason, Nov. 7, 1629, from the middle of the Merrimack River to the middle of the Piscataqua, and sixty miles inland from their mouths, and all islands within five leagues of the coast; *which he intends to name New Hampshire.*

A series of grants succeeded, which are well known for being prolific of suits and legal questions to the inhabitants of Maine. These are —

1st, The joint patents of what are now the towns of Saco and Biddeford.

2d, The Muscongus, or Lincoln grant, between the Muscongus and the Penobscot Rivers, which became the famous Waldo patent.

3d, The Lygonia, or Plough patent, of forty miles square, between Cape Porpous and Cape Elizabeth, including the now City of Portland. The date and the grantees are both uncertain.[6]

4th, The Swamscot patent, covering the towns of Dover, Durham, and Stratham.

5th, The Black Point grant of fifteen hundred acres in Scarborough.

6th, To Gorges and Mason, and certain associates, of lands on the Piscataqua, where some of their people had settled.

7th, To Richard Bradshaw, fifteen hundred acres above the head of *Pashippscot*, where he had been living.[7]

8th, To Trelawney and Goodyear, a tract between the Black Point patent and the Casco River.

9th, The well-known Pemaquid patent of twelve thousand acres, Feb. 29, 1632, to be land *not lately granted, settled, and inhabited by any English.*

All writers, until recently, have called the grant of Aug. 10, 1622, the Laconia grant. It was not till a copy of the grant of August 1622 was obtained from England by the Maine Historical Society for publication in 1863 that the error became apparent. The real Laconia grant was dated Nov. 17, 1629, — and conveyed to Gorges and Mason "all those lands and countries bordering upon the great lake, or lakes and rivers known — by the name of the River and Lake, or Rivers and Lakes of the — Iroquois," meaning thereby Lake Champlain. The final and effective grant of the Province of Maine

GRANTS UNDER THE GREAT COUNCIL FOR NEW ENGLAND

was made directly to Gorges by the King on April 3, 1639, when the Council for New England had ceased to exist.

The heirs of Gorges and Mason, after making vain efforts to sustain their title to Maine and New Hampshire, ultimately surrendered their claims for a moderate consideration; while the minor tracts, over time, came to be defined and adjusted through legislative and judicial intervention.

It may be said, with probable truth, that, but for the success of Massachusetts, all other grants or patents from the Council would have come to nought; and that, on one side the French, and on the other the Daten, or else the original natives, would have become possessed of all New England. It was so ascertained when Massachusetts was summoned to show cause why its charter should not be revoked.

Yet the charter of the Massachusetts Company gave the detail five blows to the Council for New England. In connection with the litigious attacks of the Virginia Gianaes. who desired to break up the monopoly of the fisheries, and the protest of the French ambassador, it is assigned, by themselves, as the principal cause of the surrender of their charter. They complained that their own grant to this company had been unfairly obtained and unreasonably enlarged, absorbing the tract of Robert Gorges, and riding over the heads of all those lords who had portions assigned them in the King's presence; that its members wholly excluded themselves from the government of the Council, and made themselves a free people, *whereby they did rend in pieces the first foundation of the building.* On account of these troubles, and upon these considerations, they resolved to surrender their own patent to the King.

The political purpose of the founders of Massachusetts, and its friends in England, when clearly understood, will be seen to shed a new light upon many obscure points of our own and also of English history.

A TALE OF TWO BOSTONS

It is curious to observe, among the men who intended to come to New England, Pym, Hampden, Sir Arthur Hazierig, and Oliver Cromwell. It is instructive to notice, that it was the Earl of Warwick who managed to obtain the patent for the Massachusetts Company, as Gorges relates; that it was the same earl who, on his own responsibility, conveyed Connecticut to Lord Saye and Sele, Lord Rich, Charles Fiennes, John Pym, John Hampden, Herbert Pelham, and others; and then to re- mark that, in the revolution which soon took place in England, the Earl of Warwick, Lord Saye and Sele, and Lord Mandeville, _ the son-in-law of Warwick, are designated by Clarendon as chief managers among the Peers; while in the House of Commons, Pym, Hampden, Sir Harry Vane, and Nathaniel Fiennes, brother of Charles, were principal leaders. From these, and many other coincidences, it looks as if the revolution at home was only a carrying out and extending of the political experiment which it had first been their intention to try in New England. And the impression is strengthened when we learn that members of the original Massachusetts Company took a prominent part in all the public movements of the revolutionary party, in Parliament, in the Army, in the Assembly of Divines at Westminster, and among the Judges appointed for the trial of the King. It is not strange that the lesser purpose, and the more limited intention, should have been forgotten or obscured, amid the exciting _ events of the grander and more comprehensive undertaking.[8]

A more particular account of the grants made or proposed by the Council, which would have been tedious in a lecture before a general audience, is given in a supplement.

GRANTS UNDER THE GREAT COUNCIL FOR NEW ENGLAND

SUPPLEMENT

Every one at all familiar with the grants from the Council for New England must be aware that their history would properly fill the pages of a large volume. All that a single lecture can accomplish, even with the aid of : supplement, is to take the place of an introductory chapter, giving some account of the subject-matter, and an abstract of the most important facts and conclusions. It is believed that the list of grants here presented is more full an ad more correct than any before attempted; but in a case where our most careful historians have been led into remarkable errors, it would be unreasonable to demand absolute accuracy or completeness. The patience required for the selection and verification of the particulars now brought together, the reader will hardly be able to appreciate.

SUMMARY OF GRANTS FROM
THE GREAT COUNCIL FOR NEW ENGLAND

No. 1 The first grant from the Council, of which there is any record was taken out in the name of John Peirce, citizen and clothworker of London, and his associates, June 1, 1621, for the benefit of the Pilgrims at Plymouth. It allowed one hundred acres to each planter within seven years, free liberty to fish on the coast of New England, and fifteen hundred acres for public uses. After seven years, a rent of two shillings for every one hundred acres to be paid annually. The lands having been properly surveyed and set out by metes and bounds at the charge of the grantees, upon reasonable request within seven years they are to be confirmed by deed, and letters of incorporation granted, with liberty to make laws and constitutions of government. In the meantime, the undertakers and planters are authorized to establish such laws and ordinances, and appoint such officers, as they shall by most voices agree upon. This patent was first printed from the original manuscript, with an introduction and notes, by Charles Deane, Esq., in 1854. The land was to be taken anywhere not within ten miles of land already inhabited, or located by authority of the Council, unless it be on the opposite side of some river.

No. 2. —1622, March 9. Captain John Mason's "Mariana." The nes d- land "known by the name of Tragabigsenda, or Cape Anne, with the north, south, and east shores thereof," from Naumkeag River, to a river north-west- ward from the Cape (the Merrimack), then up that river to its head, thence across to the head of the other river; with all the islands within three miles of the shore. Hubbard, Hist. of N. E., pp. 614-16.,

No. 3. — 1622, April 20. To John Peirce. This was an attempt of Peirce to surrender the indenture of June 1, 1621, and take a deed of the lands himself, his heirs, associates, and assigns. When it was ascertained that his associates were not privy to this movement, he was compelled to agree to submit the matter to the authority and pleasure of the Council. (See Council Records, in Proceedings of American Antiquarian Society of April, 1867.)

No. 4.— 1622, May 31. In the Records of the Council of this date, it is stated that "order is given for patents to be drawn for the Earl of Warwick, and his associates, the Lord Gorges, Sir Robert Mansell, Sir Ferdinando Gorges." Dr. Palfrey regards this order as referring to a division of the country, from the Bay of Fundy to Narraganset Bay, among twenty associates, in which the region about Cape Ann fell to Lord Sheffield, who sold a patent for it to the New-Plymouth people. Captain John Smith, in his "Generall Historie," published in 1624, says that New England was "engrossed by twenty patentees who divided my map into twenty parts, and cast lots for their shares." Mr. Thornton, in his interesting work on Cape Ann, has a map from Purchas representing this division, and a facsimile of the patent from Lord Sheffield above mentioned. 'here may have been such a division suggested when Captain Smith wrote, and Purchas, writing at the same date, may have prepared the map to correspond with that expectation. 'The above order from the Records of the Council seems, however, to be limited in its application to the Earl of Warwick, and three associates; and there is no account of such a division as the map exhibits in the Records, as we have them, or in the "Relation of the President and Council," or in the " Briefe Narration" of Gorges, or in the act of the Resignation of the Charter, where it would naturally appear. The division referred to by Gorges in his " Briefe Narration," and which is described in the proceedings for the surrender of the charter, is a very different one, and quite inconsistent with that exhibited by the map. It is not improbable that the distribution mentioned by Smith, may be alluded to in the agreement for the division, Feb. 3, 1634-5, thus: " Forasmuch as... in the 8th (? 18th) year of the reign of King James, of blessed memory, in whose presence lots were drawn for settling of divers and sundry divisions of land, on the sea-coast of the said country, upon most of us, which hitherto have never been confirmed in the said lands so allotted, and to the intent that every one of us according to equity, and in some reasonable manner answerable to his adventures or other interest, may enjoy a proportion of the said country to be immediately holden of his Majesty, we therefore," &c. The deed from Lord Sheffield, dated Jan. 1, 1623—4, is in direct conflict with the grant from the Council to Mason, May 9, 1622. (See above, No. 2.) Lord Sheffield's conveyance of Cape Ann, like that of Connecticut by the Earl of Warwick, was probably based upon a proposed division that was never legally completed. See note at the end of this Supplement.

No. 5.—1622, Aug. 10: By indenture to Sir Ferdinando Gorges and Captain John Mason, " All that part of the mainland in New England lying upon the sea-coast, betwixt the rivers of Merrimack and Sagadahoc, and to the furthest heads of the said rivers, and so forwards up into the land westward, until threescore miles be finished from the first entrance of the aforesaid rivers, and half way over; that is to say, to the midst of the said two rivers," " together with all the islands and islets within five leagues' distance of the premises," which, it is stated, the grantees with the consent of the

President and Council intend to name " The Province of Maine." 28 History Of The Grants Under The The error of Dr. Belknap in supposing this-to be the Laconia grant, has — been repeated by historians to the present time. Mr. Deane, who saw the ~ true Laconia deed in the Record Office in London, two years ago, gives the correct statement in the Report of the Council of the American Antiquarian — Society, Oct. 21, 1868. The grant of Aug. 10, 1622, is given in full in the Provincial Papers of New Hampshire, edited by Dr. Bouton (Concord, 1867), who also makes the correction. Hutchinson, Hist., vol.i. p. 282, ed. of 1795, says this grant " did not appear to have been signed, sealed, or witnessed by any j order of the Council." See Provincial Papers of New Hampshire, p. 28, note. For an interesting opinion of Sir William Jones, the King's Attorney-General, in 1679, on the validity of the several grants to Mason, on the absence of any right in the Council for New England to confer powers of government, and on the requirement of their charter that their grants should appear to be the acts — of a majority of the Council present at a lawful meeting, see Hubbard's Hist. of N. E., pp. 616-621.

No. 6.— 1622, Nov. 16. The Council Records speak of Mr. Thompson's patent as " this day signed." In the Appendix to the memorial volume of the Maine Historical Society, is a copy of an ancient, but imperfect list of New- England patents, from the Record Office, London, in which the first named is "a patent to David Thompson, M. Jobe, M. Sherwood, of Plimouth, for a pt. of Piscattowa River." Whatever Thompson's grant may have been, it came to nothing. He was a Scotchman, apparently in the service of the Gorges' family, and lived at one time on the Piscataqua River; and at another, on "« Thompson's Island," in Boston Harbor. € No. 7. 1622. Thomas Weston was supposed to have a patent of land at Wessagusset (Weymouth, Mass.). Bradford, p. 122. '* Weston's patent is not extant, and little is known respecting it." Deane, in Bradford, p. 124, note.

GRANTS UNDER THE GREAT COUNCIL FOR NEW ENGLAND

No. 8. — 1622, Dec. 30. To Robert Gorges, son of Sir Ferdinando, " A that part of the mainland commonly called Messachusiac, on the north-east side of the Bay known by the name of Massachuset, together with all the shores along the sea for ten English miles in a strait line towards the north-east, an "*the sword," per Gladium Comitatus. When Robert Gorges came over, he located himself at Wessagusset, which was not within his grant. Among the manuscript records of Massachusetts is a memorandum to the effect that Robert Gorges, having died without issue, the land descended to his eldest brother, John, who conveyed it to Sir William Brereton, Jan. 10, 1628. Brereton died, leaving a son and a daughter. The son died, and the daughter married Edmund Lenthall ; and their only daughter and heir married Mr. Levett, of the Inner Temple, who claimed the land in right of his wife. See note to the "* Briefe Narration " of Gorges, in Coll. of Me. Hist. Soc., vol. ii. p. 46.

No. 9. — 1623. To Ferdinando Gorges, grandson of Sir Ferdinando, and his associates, among whom were Walter Norton, Lieutenant-Colonel Thomas Coppyn, Esq., Samuel Maverick, Esq., Thomas Graves, Gent. (an engineer), Raphe Glover, merchant, William Jeffryes, Gent., John Busley, Great Council For New England. 29 Gent., Joel Woolsey, Gent., all of New England." -The date of 1623 is derived from the " Briefe Narration," chap. xxv., where Gorges says his grandson, and some of his associates, hastened to take possession at the time, carrying with them their families; but according to the Council Records, the date of sealing the patent was Dec. 2, 1631. It was renewed March 2, 1632, with some change in the associates, and the former patent cancelled. The grant was first, of one hundred acres to each person transported within seven years, if he remained three years; second, of twelve thousand more, to the associates, on the east side of the river Agamenticus, on the coast three miles, and into the land so far as to contain twelve thousand acres, and one hundred acres more for each person; third, to F. Gorges himself, besides the above, twelve thousand acres on the opposite or western side of the river along the coast westerly to the land appropriated to the plantation at Pascataquack (Portsmouth), and so along the river Agamenticus, and the bounds of Pascataquack, into the mainland so far as to contain twelve thousand acres; with all the islands within three leagues into the ocean. In consideration that they have undertaken to build a town. 'Two shillings to be paid yearly for every one hundred acres of arable land after seven years. 'This description is from the Records of the Council, in Proceedings of the American Society of April, 1867. See also respecting this grant, Coll. of Me. Hist. Soc., vol. 11. pp. 49, 50, note. At a meeting of the Council, March 22, 1637 (after the surrender of their charter), it is stated that this grant was renewed to Edward Godfrey and others, and " this day the seal of the company was set thereunto."

No. 10.—1628. To the Plymouth people, of lands on the Kennebec. Renewed and enlarged the next year. Bradford, p. 232.

No. 11.—The Massachusetts patent of March 19, 1628, made into a Royal charter, March 4, 1629. Dr. Palfrey expresses an opinion that the patentees among whom the coast of New England had been partitioned six years before surrendered their claims, founded on the following record of the Massachusetts Company: " Sept. 29, 1629. — It is thought fit, and ordered, that the secretary shall write out a copy of the former grant to the Earl of Warwick and others, which was by them resigned to this company, to be presented to his lordship." The patent of the Massachusetts Company from the New-England Council is not extant; and there is some mystery attending the manner of its procure- ment, as well as about its original extent. Sir F. Gorges says, that, on the request of the Earl of Warwick, he consented to a grant that should not be prejudicial to the interests of his son Robert. In the act of resignation of their charter by the Council, they say, that the Massachusetts Company, " present- ing the names of honest and religious men, easily obtained their first desires ; but those being once gotten, they used other means to advance themselves a step beyond their first proportions to a second grant, surreptitiously gotten, of other lands also, justly passed unto Captain Robert Gorges long before." Robert Mason, petitioning the King, in 1676, for possession of the lands granted to his grandfather, declares that the Massachusetts Company " did surreptitiously, and unknown to the said Council, get the seal of the said Council affixed to a grant of certain lands;" and did, by their subtile practices, get a 30 History Of The Grants Under The confirmation under the great seal of England. In their answer to this petition, the Massachusetts authorities deny the charge, no doubt with sincerity ; but all circumstances leave an impression on the mind that, by the influence, perhaps. by the management, of the Earl of Warwick, advantages were gained, which — many, if not most, of the Council would have objected to. By the favor of Warwick, the Plymouth people obtained their lands on the Kennebec; and the : patent of Connecticut was made in his own name, by what authority does not sufficiently appear. These facts may explain the dissatisfaction which arose between the Council and Warwick, their president, and the efforts of the Council to get the seal out of his possession. He seems not to have eared for personal proprietorship, but to have desired to give his Puritan friends the advantage of his official position and influence.

No. 12.—1629, Nov. 7. By indenture, to Captain John Mason, part of the same territory which was conveyed by a similar deed to Gorges and Mason, jointly, Aug. 10, 1622. The difference being, that instead of extending from the middle of the Merrimack River to the middle of the Sagadahoc, on the coast, and back into the interior sixty miles between those limits, this grant extends no farther than the middle of the Piscataqua River, but the same distance into the interior between the Merrimack and the Piscataqua, including also islands within five leagues of the shore; " which the said Captain John Mason, with the consent of the President and Council, intends to name New Hampshire." In the deed to Gorges and Mason, it was proposed to call the whole territory the Province of Maine. The form and general phraseology of the two deeds are alike. If the first instrument was valid, this one, of necessity, could be of no effect. See above, No. 5; Provincial Papers of New Hampshire, pp. 21 and 28, note; Hazard, vol. i. p. 289.

No. 13.—1629, Nov.17. This is the true Laconia grant, which, by a mistake, originating doubtless in a misprint, has sometimes had the date Nov. 27, instead of Nov. 17, assigned to it. There is a copy of it in the office of the Secretary of State of Massachusetts. It embraces, in substance, the lands bordering upon the great lake (Champlain), or lakes and rivers commonly — known by the name of the river and lake, or rivers and lakes, of the Iroquois; together with those lakes and rivers, and the land within ten miles of any part of them on the south or east, and from the west end or sides so far to the west as shall extend half-way into the next great lake to the westward; thence northward into the north side of the main river running from the great western lakes into the river of Canada, including all islands within the precincts. The nullity of this grant is shown by the fact, that so many careful historians have confounded it with that of Aug, 10, 1622, another imperfect and ineffectual instrument. See N. H. Provincial Papers, vol. i. pp. 28 and 38. Hubbard, Hist. of N. E., chap. xxxi., says, that after three years of fruitless endeavors for the more full discovery of "an imaginary Province called Laconia," the agents of Gorges returned to England with a "non est inventa Provincia."

No. 14. — 1629, o.s., Jan.13. The last Plymouth patent, to William Bradford and his associates, in consideration that they have lived nine years in New England, and planted a town at their own cost, and are able to relieve new planters: All that part of New England between the middle of Cohasset River oS TD Great Council For New England. 31 and the middle of Narraganset River, and up from the mouths of those rivers in a strait line into the mainland as far as the utmost limits of the country called " Pokenacutt, alias Sowamsett;"' and bounded on the east by the ocean, without including islands on the coast. And as the grantees have no con- venient place for trading or fishing within their own precincts, there is also conveyed to them all that tract of land, between, or extending from, the utmost limits of Cobbisconte, which adjoins the river Kennebec, towards the western ocean, and a place called the Falls at Nequamkike; and the space of fifteen miles on each side of the river Kennebec, and all the said river Kennebec that lies within the said limits and bounds, eastward, westward, northward, or southward, last above mentioned. 'The patent gave a right of passage to and from the ocean, and the right of fishing on the neighboring shores, not inhabited or otherwise disposed of, and also privileges of administration. It appears to have no other signature than that of the Earl of Warwick. The Plymouth people tried in vain to procure a charter from the Crown with powers of government. They strengthened their rights in Maine by deeds from the Indians, and endeavored to establish settlements; but tired of the vexation which that property gave them, they sold their entire interest, in 1661, to four persons, for four hundred pounds. In 1753, the then owners became a corporation, by the name of " the Proprietors of the Kennebec Purchase," and, after much controversy and litigation, the obscure boundaries were ultimately adjusted. See Gardiner's " Hist. of the Kennebec Purchase," in Coll. of Maine Hist. Society, vol. ii. The patent is in Hazard, vol. 1. pp. 298-303.

No. 15.— 1630, Feb. 12. At this date, two deeds were issued of the land between Cape Elizabeth and Cape Porpoise in Maine, each of four miles along the coast, and eight miles into the mainland; one on the north side of the Saco River to Thomas Lewis and Richard Bonython, the other on the south side of the Saco River to John Oldham and Richard Vines. From these grants have sprung the two towns of Saco and Biddeford, retaining nearly the same limits. Hist. of Saco and Biddeford, by George Folsom.

No. 16. — 1630, March 13. The Muscongus grant, afterwards known as the Waldo patent. The abstract of this grant, in Hazard, Coll. vol. 1. pp. 304, 305, taken from the Maine Records, is unintelligible. Williamson, Hist. of Me. vol. i. p. 240, describes it as extending from the seaboard, between the rivers Penobscot and Muscongus, to an unsurveyed line running east and west so far north as would, without interfering with any other patent, embrace a territory equal to thirty miles square; and adds, in a note, that the north line, as since settled, is in the south line of Hampden, Newbury, and Dixmont. The grant was to John Beauchamp and Thomas Leverett, of England. Leverett is said to have succeeded to the property on the death of Beauchamp. John Leverett, President of Harvard College, as sole heir of his grandfather, became the owner in 1715. By the admission of partners, a company was formed, consisting of thirty proprietors, who first employed Brigadier-General Samuel Waldo as agent, and ultimately assigned to him the largest interest in the patent. Coll. of Me. Hist. Society, vol. vi. art. xv.

No. 17. —1630. The Lygonia, or Plough patent, considered to extend from Kennebunk River to Harpswell in Casco Bay, or, as usually stated, from Cape 32 History Of The Grants Under The Porpoise to Cape Elizabeth, and forty miles inland. Hubbard, Ind. Wars, 7 part ii. p. 9, says the patent was granted in the year 1630, and signed by the Earl of Warwick and Sir Ferdinando Gorges. Willis, Hist. of Portland, p. 29, says he has never " been able to discover this patent, nor ascertain its date, . nor who are the patentees."" Different names are given in different accounts, An unsuccessful attempt at settlement was made in 1631. In 1643 the patent was transferred to Alexander Rigby, a rich English lawyer, who appointed — George Cleaves as his deputy. The contest of conflicting jurisdictions between _ the representative of Rigby and the representatives of Gorges was only ended > when Massachusetts took possession of the whole territory in 1672. Sullivan, ' Hist. of Me., pp. 309-319, 'Land Titles," p. 44; Williamson, Hist. of Me. vol. i. p. 288; Folsom, Hist. of Saco and Biddeford, pp. 26-28. a

No. 18. — 1631, March 12. To Edward Hilton, 'all that part of the river — Piscataqua called Hilton's Point, with the S. side of the said river up to the falls — of Squamscot (or Swamscot), and three miles

GRANTS UNDER THE GREAT COUNCIL FOR NEW ENGLAND

into the mainland for breadth. " Following Dr. Belknap and Dr. Palfrey, I stated in the lecture that this grant covered the towns of Dover, Durham, and Stratham. But in the recently published Provincial Papers of New Hampshire, p. 29, Dr. Bouton, the editor, says, "No document relating to New Hampshire has been so grossly misrepresented as this. . . . It covered only Hilews Point; . . . and the whole did not — exceed a township five miles square." Its extent and its ownership, in 1656, — as shown in a record of partition, by authority of Massachusetts, may be seen in ., pp. 221-223. i

No. 19. — 1631, Nov. 4, by the Council Records (Willis, and others, say Nov. 1). To Thomas Cammock, fifteen hundred acres, lying upon the mainland along the sea-coast, on the east side of Black Point River. This is _ now a part of Scarborough, and included Stratton's islands. Possession given : in 1633; patent confirmed by Gorges in 1640. The tract is now held under — this title. Willis, Hist. of Portland, p. 31.

No. 20. —1631, Nov. 4. To Richard Bradshaw, " fifteen hundred acres, — to be allotted above the head of Pashippscot (Pejepscot), on the north side — thereof, not formerly granted to any other." Council Records. This, and the — grant to Cammock, were in consideration that the grantees had been living on { the premises for some years. a The Council Records of Dec. 2, 1631, say, that Lord Gorges and Sir Fendinando Gorges gave order for two patents, one for Walter Bagnall for a small — 4 island, called Richmond Island, and fifteen hundred acres on the mainland, to } be selected by Walter Neale and Richard Vines ; another for John Stratton, of two thousand acres, on the south side of Cape Porpoise, and "on the other — side northwards into the south side of the harbor's mouth of Cape Porpoise." — Sainsbury's Calendar, p. 137, has it " John Stratton of Shotley, co. Suffolk, i and his associates." Bagnall was at Richmond Island in 1628, where he was killed by the Indiana Oct. 8, 1631 (previous to the date above stated). Willis, Hist. of Portland. p. 25.

No. 21.— 1631, Nov. 4. To Sir Ferdinando Gorges and Captain John Mason, and their associates, a portion of land on the Piscataqua River, " along — the seashore westward five miles, and by an imaginary line into the mainland, oie diet Sa Wied Great Council For New England. 33 north to the bounds of a plantation belonging to Edward Hilton ; and the islands within the same river eastward, together with three miles along the shore to the eastward of said river, and opposite to the habitation and plantation where Captain Neale lives, and up into the mainland northerly, by all the breadth aforesaid, thirty miles; with the lakes at the head of said river." In consideration of service formerly done, and the settlement there by Captain Neale, the erection of salt-pans, &e. They were to pay to the Council forty shillings sterling, payable at the Assurance House, Royal Exchange, London, if demanded. First payment at the Feast of St. Michael, 1632, "and so for all service from year to year." Abstract in the Council Records. Hubbard, Hist. of N. E., chap. xxxi., says, that in his time, a copy of this indenture was extant at Portsmouth. He makes the date Nov. 3, 1631, and the instrument to be without signature or seal; but he says, "it seems to be of as much force as other instruments of like nature produced on such' like accounts at the present time." The Council Records state that the patent was sealed Nov. 4. Hubbard calls the sum to be paid forty-eight pounds per annum, instead of the forty shillings mentioned in the Records. The names of the associates are in Hubbard.

No. 22.— 1631, Dec. 1. To Robert Trelawny and Moses Goodyear, the tract lying between Cammock's patent " and the bay and river of Casco, and extending northwards into the mainland, so far as the limits and bounds of the lands granted to the said Thomas Cammock, do and ought to extend towards the north." It was claimed that this grant included Cape Elizabeth, and nearly all the ancient town of Falmouth, and part of Gorham and Richmond island. A contest was maintained, in reference to boundaries, for many years, extending beyond the lives of the first settlers. Willis, Hist. of Portland, pp. 32, 33; Council Records.

No. 23.— 1632, Feb. 29. To Robert Aldworth and Giles Elbridge: first. one hundred acres for every person transported by them within seven years, adjacent to twelve thousand acres, afterwards mentioned, and not lately granted, or settled and inhabited, by any English. Second, twelve thousand acres more to be laid out near the river Pemaquid, along the sea-coast as the coast lieth, and up the river as far as may contain the said twelve thousand acres and the hundred acres for each person transported, together with all the islands opposite their coast within three leagues into the ocean. In consideration that they have undertaken to build a town, &c. Powers of government, or ad- ministration, are also expressed in the deed, which was signed by the Earl of Warwick and Sir Ferdinando Gorges. Pemaquid, like other territories in Maine, has been a subject of much controversy, and has experienced many vicissitudes. It is said that one of its sons is preparing a history of its fortunes. "Ancient Pemaquid" has already been the subject of an Historical Review, by Mr. Thornton. A notarial copy on parchment of the original deed, and two volumes of the records of its proprietors, from 1743 to 1774, are in the library _ of the American Antiquarian Society.

No. 24. — 1632, June 16. Under this date, in Mr. Sainsbury's Calendar of Colonial Papers in the State Paper Office, London, is the following entry: "Grant of the Council for New England to George Way and Thomas Purchas, 34 History Of The Grants Under The of certain lands in New England, called the River Bishopscotte, and al bounds and limits the mainland adjoining the river to the extent of two By Bishopscotte is meant Pejepscot, now ew Brunswick. Purchas, it is took possession in 1628, and lived there many years. In 1639, he conve the title and jurisdiction to Massachusetts, reserving the interest and possession of such lands as he should use and improve within seven years. Hazard, vol p- 407. The country was depopulated during the Indian war of 1675; which, Richard

Wharton obtained the claims of both Purchas and Way, expecting a confirmation from the King, but died before his plans were comp See Willis, Hist. of Portland, p. 24; Coll. of Me. Hist. Society, vol. iii. artic. v. and vi. The original deed to Way and Purchas has long since been lost, only record of it remains. This grant was the subject of a long and bitter controversy between the Pejepscot proprietors and other claimants, not finally se till about 1814. Willis, Hist. of Portland, p. 64, note. The efforts of the Council to divide New England into provinces, or ships, and distribute these among themselves, remain to be noticed. — are indications that such a design was entertained at an early period; but charter was found to be defective, and arrangements were soon made for a one, from which all the patentees who had not paid their dues were to be included. To entitle a partner to the benefit of the lands and the privilege a patentee, a payment of £110 was required. It was voted that delinquent should forfeit all interest under the charter, and their rights and privileges transferred to persons willing to take their places and make the payment not more than half of the original patentees accepted the conditions of membership, and fewer still seem to have redeemed their pledges.

At various dates in the Records (May 31, 1622, July 24, 1622, June 32), an agreement was introduced having in view the assignment of territory, more or less particularly designated, to certain persons. But all these orders and agreements, whatever may have been the intentions of the Council at the time, were treated as of no validity when they surrendered the charter to the King. In preparation for that event, they met on the 3rd of February, 1634/35, and divided the coast of New England into eight parts; viz.:

- 1st From me, the Pinas limits in the fortieth degree of latitude to the Hud River.
- 2d, From Hudson's River to a river or creek (" near a place called Redunes or Reddownes") about sixty miles eastward.

GRANTS UNDER THE GREAT COUNCIL FOR NEW ENGLAND

- 3d, From that river eastward about forty-five miles, to a river or creek called Fresh River.
- 4th, From the Connecticut River to the Narragansett River, accounted for sixty miles.
- 5th, From Narragansett River around Cape Cod to Naumkeag (Salem).
- 6th, From Naumkeag to Piscataqua Harbor and River.
- 7th, From Piscataqua Harbor to the Kennebec River.
- 8th, From the Kennebec River to the St. Croix.

By comparing the Council Records, the " Briefe Narration" of Gorges, and Hubbard's History of New England, we find:

- the first portion was assigned to the Earl of Arundel (Gorges says Lord Mulgrave, who was originally Lord Sheffield);
- the Second to the Duke of Richmond (in place of the Duke of Lenox);
- the third to the Earl of Carlisle;
- the fourth to Lord Gorges;
- the fifth to the Marquis of Hamilton;
- the Sixth to Captain John Mason;
- the Seventh to Sir Ferdinando Gorges;
- the eighth to Lord Alexander.

Each of these divisions was to extend back into the interior sixty miles, except the last, which reached to *the river of Canada.*

Each division, except the last two, was to have, in addition, ten thousand acres on the " east part of Sagadahoc." The seventh division was to have with it the north half of the Isles of Shoals and the Isles of Capawock, Nautican, near Cape Cod; and the eighth division the Island called Mattawack, or the Long Island, west of Cape Cod. The southern half of the Isles of Shoals was to go with the division of Captain Mason.

There is apparently a space omitted between " Fresh River," wherever that was, and the Connecticut.

These divisions are described with particularity in the Records of the Council. It is stated that the grants were signed and delivered on the fourteenth day of April; that, on the eighteenth, leases, for three thousand years, of the several divisions, were made to the persons interested; and that on the twenty-second, deeds of feofoment were made to them.

To every one that had previously a lawful grant of lands was reserved the freehold with its rights, he *laying down his jura regalia (if he have any) and paying some small acknowledgement, for that he is now to hold his land anew of the proprietor of the division.*

It is to be inferred that this remnant of the Council included all who were then desirous, or qualified, to receive assignments of territory.

The account of this division by Hubbard, Hist. of N. E., chap. xxxi., differs from that in the Records in many important particulars, and is less likely to be correct.

On the 26th of April, 1635, the Council prepared a petition to the King that he would cause patents to be made for the several divisions, to be held immediately from himself; and on the 5th of May resolved that the deeds should be acknowledged before a Master in Chancery, and enrolled before the surrender of the charter, and the King be requested to confirm them under the Great Seal; also to prosecute a suit at law for the repeal of the Massachusetts patent. They also prepared a form of acceptance for the King to adopt upon their surrender of the charter, along with a declaration of the reasons for which the surrender was made. The formal resignation was dated June 7, 1635.

The acceptance of the surrender may have been held in abeyance for a time, as meetings of the Council are recorded, Nov. 26, 1635, March 22, 1637, and Nov 1, 1638, at which business was transacted.

GRANTS UNDER THE GREAT COUNCIL FOR NEW ENGLAND

The Earl of Lindsay. desired to have a proportion of land allotted to him, which was assented to, to be "on ye river where the Flemings are seated," above the Duke of Richmond. Lord Maltravers wished for "a degree more in longitude and latitude joining his limits (*had he taken the place of someone of the eight grantees ?*), which the Council were willing to assent to, if he would declare in what direction he wanted it. The Earl of Sterling's (Lord Alexander's) proportion was carried more distinctly to the Kennebec River; and Lord Gorges, and Sir Ferdinando Gorges, were each allowed sixty miles from up into the mainland.

Our supplement can afford no space for comments or inferences, but it is apparent that no such division as is referred to by Captain John Smith in 1624, and laid down on the map published by Purchas, was recognized by the Council as valid, and that no territorial rights were admitted as having belonged to the Earl of Warwick. The charter of Massachusetts was to be annulled, the entire coast of New England divided among the eight Proprietary's above named, and all remaining rights and powers belonging to the Grand Patent surrendered to the King, Sir Ferdinando Gorges to be made his Lieutenant or Governor over the whole country as a province of the Crown. Political events at home prevented the accomplishment of this design. Captain John Mason and Sir Ferdinando Gorges alone contrived to secure permanent advantages to themselves. No other executed deed of any of the proposed divisions has come down to us but that to Mason, April 22, 1635, without, however, a confirmation from the King. Gorges received his division, with the additional sixty miles into the interior, in the form of a charter from the Crown, dated April 3, 1639. Obscurity of description, the overlapping of boundaries in different deeds, the introduction of powers — which the Council could not legally confer (such as those of government and administration), and imperfect execution, seem to have rendered most of their early grants unsound in their own estimation; and perhaps all of them woulda have proved to be void or voidable if recieved to a strict legal test. It w simplify the subject, if we strike from the list of those which reach the final division the first eight and the thirteenth as of no subsequent con-— sequence, and rest to Mason and Gorges upon the deeds to Mason — of Nov. 7, 1629 and April 22, 1635, and the charter to Gorges of April 3, 1639, — as some of their representatives appear to have done (see Prov. Papers of N.H p- 28, note). Massachusetts ultimately took the place of these great proprietors and extended her jurisdiction over most of the territory covering the minor patents, whose adjustment among the parties interested was the work of much time and a great deal of law.

NOTE

In Hubbard's History of N.E., pp. 231-32, is what purports to be an attested copy of so much of the agreement for a division among themselves, by the Council, as relates to the portion assigned to Captain John Mason. It is signed by the other seven Council members. It also contains the paragraphs, which, in the Records of the Council, precede and follow the list and descriptions of the several divisions; _ and an error in copying the first paragraph has increased the confusion heretofore attending this subject. The agreement, as the Records show, was dated Feb. 8, 1634. The copyist of Hubbard's document introduced that date into the first paragraph, which alludes to an attempt in the lifetime of King James, and in his presence, to effect a similar division, making it appear as if the attempt occurred on that date. In the second edition of Hubbard, the editor, Mr. Harris, observing that there must be a mis, altered the figures from 1634 to 1624; a worse error, as it has led to the belief that a division was actually made on the 3rd of February, 1624. The Records mention no such date.

It is proper to state that the original Records of the Council for New England are not extant. The copy printed by the American Antiquarian Society in 1867 was obtained by me in London at the State Paper Office, where the parts so recovered exist in the form of a transcript, apparently made for official purposes. Our historians were already familiar with them there.

PETITION OF RIGHT

They doe therefore humblie pray your most Excellent Majestie, that no man hereafter be compelled to make or yeild any Guift Loane Benevolence Taxe or such like Charge without comon consent by Acte of Parliament, And that none be called to make aunswere or take such Oath or to give attendance or be confined or otherwise molested or disquieted concerning the same or for refusall thereof . . And that your Majestie would be pleased to remove the said Souldiers and Mariners and that your people may not be soe burthened in tyme to come. And that the aforesaid Comissions for proceeding by Martiall Lawe may be revoked and annulled. And that hereafter no Comissions of like nature may issue forth to any person or persons whatsoever to be executed as aforesaid, lest by colour of them any of your Majesties Subjects be destroyed or put to death contrary to the Lawes and Franchise of the Land.

All which they most humblie pray of your most Excellent Majestie as their Rightes and Liberties according to the Lawes and Statutes of this Realme, And that your Majestie would alsoe vouchsafe to declare that the Awards doings and proceedings to the prejudice of your people in any of the premisses shall not be drawen hereafter into consequence or example. And that your Majestie would be alsoe graciouslie pleased for the further comfort and safetie of your people to declare your Royall will and pleasure, That in the things aforesaid all your Officers and Ministers shall serve you according to the Lawes and Statutes of this Realme as they tender the Honor of your Majestie and the prosperitie of this Kingdome.

Quaquidem Petitione lecta & plenius intellecta per dictum Dominum Regem taliter est responsum in pleno Parliamento videlicet.

R. Soit droit fait come est desire.[1]

(*Which Petition having been read and more fully understood by the said Lord King, such response was given in full Parliament, namely. R[ex]. Let right be done as is desired.*)

The Petition of Right of 1628 stands as one of the most remarkable documents in English constitutional history—not because it innovated but because it remembered. It did not claim new liberties. It restored old ones. In an age when Charles I insisted that kings ruled by divine commission and not by consent, the Petition became the voice of a political nation pleading for the restoration of the ancient compact between ruler and subject. It was, in its deepest sense, an appeal for balance—one last attempt to persuade a king who had forgotten the limits of the crown he wore.

The Petition's significance cannot be understood apart from its authors, its circumstances, and the quiet yet profound way it shaped the men who would form the Massachusetts Bay Company. For those men—gentry, merchants, ministers—the Petition was not only a constitutional milestone. It was the last signpost before the road bent toward the Atlantic.

PETITION OF RIGHT

The Petition was not written by radicals. It was written by conservators—men who believed that England had already achieved the delicate equilibrium that Europe's other kingdoms still struggled to imagine. At the center stood Sir Edward Coke, once the greatest jurist of Elizabeth's reign, now a grizzled elder statesman whose memory stretched back to the peace and discipline of the Tudor settlement.[2]

Coke's entire career had been grounded in a single conviction:

> *that the common law was older than kings and that kings, therefore, must obey it.*

By 1628, Coke saw that this ancient understanding had come perilously close to collapse. Charles had dismissed Parliament twice, imprisoned subjects without cause, levied the Forced Loan, revived obsolete taxes, and billeted soldiers in private homes. To Coke, this was not misjudgment. It was disorder—an offense against the architecture of the English constitution.

Alongside Coke worked John Eliot, Denzil Holles, and a cohort of gentry MPs who represented counties already inflamed by the Forced Loan. Lincolnshire, Suffolk, Essex, and the eastern shires—all nurseries of the Puritan conscience—sent men to Westminster who carried the indignation of their neighbors into the chamber of the Commons.[3]

Together, they shaped a document that asked nothing novel and demanded nothing extravagant. They sought only that the king obey the law.

The Petition of Right contains four simple clauses. Each is a distillation of centuries of English experience with tyranny and restoration.

- No taxation without parliamentary consent. This was the heart of the matter. The Forced Loan had broken trust. Parliament insisted that money could not be extracted without the nation's voice.
- No imprisonment without cause shown. The detention of the Five Knights—ordinary gentlemen who refused the Forced Loan—had revealed how quickly liberty could vanish when a king claimed to act above the law.
- No billeting of soldiers in private homes. For families forced to house undisciplined troops, the line between military necessity and domestic invasion had blurred beyond recognition.
- No use of martial law against civilians in peacetime. Charles had used emergency powers to bypass courts; Parliament now insisted that such powers remain extraordinary, not habitual.

These demands were not innovations. They were reaffirmations. If Magna Carta was the fountainhead, the Petition of Right was its echo—eloquent, necessary, and weary.

Charles resisted. He knew that granting the Petition would shackle the absolutist theory he had inherited from his father and embraced without reservation. But he also needed money—desperately—for the failing wars against Spain and France.

So Charles assented to the Petition on June 7, 1628. He stood before Parliament, gave his approval, and allowed the document to become part of English law.[4] But Charles treated assent as expedience, not obligation. Within weeks, he resumed collecting customs without parliamentary grant.

He defended the Forced Loan. He protected Buckingham until the assassin's knife removed him. And he dissolved Parliament in 1629 with a finality that echoed across the kingdom.

PETITION OF RIGHT

The Petition had attempted to recall the king to the covenant between monarch and nation. Charles answered by severing the covenant altogether.

For the men of Boston, Lincolnshire—Cotton's parishioners, Johnson, Bellingham, Hough, Dudley—the Petition of Right was more than a parliamentary document. It was a moral threshold. They had resisted the Forced Loan. They had watched neighbors imprisoned for principles woven into the English soul. They had witnessed Charles accept the Petition and then break it. And they had drawn their conclusion:

If a king cannot remember his promises, then the kingdom is no longer whole.

The Petition became the line that divided hope from departure. Parliament had appealed to the king to restore the old constitutional balance. The Boston Men watched the appeal fail. When Charles entered his Personal Rule, governing without Parliament for eleven years, the men of Lincolnshire saw not stability but a kingdom drifting toward a kind of royal solitude that left no room for them—or for liberty.

Their decision to leave England was not an act of rebellion. It was an act of preservation—of the very liberties the Petition had sought to defend. The Petition of Right, in that sense, did not merely precede the founding of the Massachusetts Bay Colony. It shaped its imagination.

It taught the Boston Men that community must be governed by consent, covenant, and accountability—not by the prerogatives of a king who believed himself above the law.

England would remember the Petition, though not immediately. Its principles resurfaced in the Long Parliament.

They reappeared in the debates of the Civil Wars. They informed the execution of Charles I and the Glorious Revolution of 1688. And eventually they found new life in the constitutions of the American colonies and the United States.

But in 1630, when the Arbella set sail, the Petition of Right was not yet triumph. It was wound. It was disappointment. It was the realization that the monarchy had turned its face from the nation. And in that disappointment lay the seed of New England.

History often remembers the loud actors—the kings, the rebels, the orators whose voices filled the chambers of power. Yet constitutional liberty in England owes as much to its scholars as its soldiers.

Among those scholars, Sir Robert Cotton stands as one of the most influential and least celebrated. He was not a man of armies or street crowds; he fought with manuscripts, memory, and the deep conviction that the past contained England's best defenses against tyranny.

Without Robert Cotton, the Petition of Right would have lacked its intellectual backbone. He became the quiet architect behind Parliament's most important constitutional stand against Charles I.

He furnished precedents, unearthed forgotten statutes, guided medieval law from the shadows, and gave the opposition the one thing the king could not easily dismiss: the authority of English history itself.

In a reign where Charles believed himself the creator of law, Robert Cotton reminded England that law had always preceded kings and was the great antiquarian of his age. His library—later the foundation of the British Library—contained treasures unmatched in Europe:

PETITION OF RIGHT

- Magna Carta
- the Confirmation of the Charters
- the Mirror of Justices
- treatises of Bracton, ancient parliament rolls
- chronicles reaching back to the Anglo-Saxon heptarchy.[5]

Parliamentarians knew this. When disputes with Charles escalated, they turned not to pamphleteers but to Cotton. His library became the intellectual armory of constitutional resistance.

- Where Charles reached for divine right, Robert Cotton reached for precedent.
- Where Charles spoke of prerogative, Robert Cotton produced parchment showing its limits.
- Where Charles insisted that the king alone shaped law, Robert Cotton pointed to centuries in which kings themselves had sworn to uphold it.

Although the Petition of Right was formally drafted by Sir Edward Coke and other leading members of Parliament, Robert Cotton's influence lay behind nearly every clause.

He supplied Coke with historical citations and ancient statutes proving:

- That taxation required parliamentary consent (Magna Carta and the Confirmatio Cartarum)
- That imprisonment required cause shown (Articles of Edward I and III)
- That billeting of soldiers was unlawful without consent (Statutes from the reigns of Richard II and Henry IV)
- That martial law could not be used on civilians in peacetime (Parliamentary rolls from the 14th century)

Coke, though a formidable jurist, had not spent a lifetime collecting manuscripts. Cotton had. And it was Cotton who provided the historical ammunition that transformed the Petition from moral protest into constitutional doctrine.[6]

The Petition of Right was thus not merely a parliamentary act. It was a historical assertion, a return to first principles discovered by a man who believed that the memory of a nation is its greatest safeguard.

Robert Cotton believed kingship was ancient, dignified, and necessary—but lawful. In his view, kings were trustees of a constitutional inheritance rather than authors of it. This placed him squarely at odds with James I's theories of divine right and Charles I's attempts to rule without Parliament.

- When Charles imprisoned men without cause, Cotton produced precedents showing this violated the very essence of English liberty.
- When Charles levied the Forced Loan, Cotton demonstrated that forced finance had triggered rebellions in prior centuries.
- When Charles insisted he could dissolve Parliament indefinitely, Cotton unearthed medieval records showing Parliament's role as a necessary component of governance.[7]

Cotton's gift was not defiance but memory. He reminded England of what it had always been. Kings do not easily forgive those who constrain their power.

Charles grew increasingly wary of Cotton's influence. The antiquarian who armed Parliament with the past was, in the king's eyes, a greater threat than many who opposed him openly. In 1629—after Charles dissolved Parliament and began his Personal Rule—Cotton's library was sealed by royal order.

PETITION OF RIGHT

The official reason was that Cotton's manuscripts could *"kindle sedition."* The real reason was clearer:

Cotton's memory of England threatened the king's reinvention of it. The man who had preserved the realm's constitutional DNA was silenced because he made it difficult for Charles to rewrite the anatomy of power. Cotton never recovered from the humiliation. He died in 1631, just two years after his life's work was seized.

If the Petition of Right shaped the Boston Men intellectually, Cotton shaped them imaginatively. For them:

- The past was not archaic—it was binding.
- The law was not the king's will—it was the people's inheritance.
- Liberty was not innovation—it was restoration.

This vision resonated deeply with the Puritan conscience. Men like Isaac Johnson, Richard Bellingham, Thomas Dudley, and John Cotton (no relation) believed that England was betraying its own ancient equilibrium. The Petition of Right had affirmed their values; Charles's violation of it had confirmed their fears.

Robert Cotton never crossed the Atlantic, never imagined a colony in Massachusetts, never fought a battle, never held high political office. Yet his influence traveled farther than any ship in the Winthrop Fleet. He taught England—and through England, New England—that:

- A nation forgets its past at its peril.
- A king who severs himself from history severs himself from his people.
- And liberty, once recalled through memory, can be carried anywhere—even to the edges of the known world.

MASSACHUSETTS BAY COMPANY ROYAL CHARTER

CHARLES, BY THE, GRACE, OF GOD, Kinge of England, Scotland, Fraunce, and Ireland, Defendor of the Fayth, &c. To all to whome theis Presents shall come Greeting. WHEREAS, our most Deare and Royall Father, Kinge James, of blessed Memory, by his Highnes Letters-patents bearing Date at Westminster the third Day of November, in the eighteenth Yeare of His Raigne, HATH given and graunted vnto the Councell established at Plymouth, in the County of Devon, for the planting, ruling, ordering, and governing of Newe England in America, and to their Successors and Assignes for ever all that Parte of America, lyeing and being in Bredth, from Forty Degrees of Northerly Latitude from the Equinoctiall Lyne, to forty eight Degrees Of the saide Northerly Latitude inclusively, and in Length, of and within all the Breadth aforesaid, throughout the Maine Landes from Sea to Sea; together also with all the Firme Landes, Soyles, Groundes, Havens, Portes, Rivers, Waters, Fishing, Mynes, and Myneralls, as well Royall Mynes of Gould and Silver, as other Mynes ind Mvneralls, precious Stones, Quarries, and all and singular other Comodities, Jurisdiccons, Royalties, Priviledges,

Franchesies, and Prehemynences, both within the said Tract of Land vpon the Mayne, and also within the Islandes and Seas adjoining: PROVIDED alwayes, That the saide Islandes, or any the Premisses by the said Letters-patents intended and meant to be graunted, were not then actuallie possessed or inhabited, by any other Christian Prince or State, nor within the Boundes, Lymitts, or Territories of the Southerne Colony, then before graunted by our saide Deare Father, to be planted by divers of his loveing Subjects in the South Partes. TO HAVE and to houlde, possess, and enjoy all and singular the aforesaid Continent, Landes Territories, Islandes, Hereditaments, and Precincts, Seas, Waters, Fishings, with all, and all manner their Comodities, Royalties, Liberties, Prehemynences, and Proffits that should from thenceforth arise from thence, with all and singuler their Appurtenances, and every Parte and Parcell thereof, vnto the saide Councell and their Successors and Assignes for ever, to the sole and proper Vse, Benefitt, and Behoofe of them the saide Councell, and their Successors and Asignes for ever: To be houlden of our saide most Deare and Royall Father, his Heires and Successors, as of his Mannor of East Greenewich in the County of Kent, in free and comon Soccage, and not in Capite nor by Knight's Service: YEILDINGE and paying therefore to the saide late Kinge, his heires and Successors, the fifte Parte of the Oare of Gould and Silver, which should from tyme to tyme, and at all Tymes then after happen to be found, gotten, had, and obteyned in, att, or within any of the saide Landes, Lymitts, Territories, and Precincts, or in or within any Parte or Parcell thereof, for or in Respect of all and all Manner of Duties, Demaunds and Services whatsoever, to be don, made, or paide to our saide Dear Father the late Kinge his Heires and Successors, as in and by the saide Letters-patents (amongst sundrie and other Clauses, Powers, Priviledges, and Grauntes therein conteyned), more at large appeareth:

AND WHEREAS, the saide Councell established at Plymouth, in the County of Devon, for the plantinge, ruling, ordering, and

MASSACHUSETTS BAY COMPANY ROYAL CHARTER

governing of Newe England in America, have by their Deede, indented vnder their Comon Seale, bearing Date the nyneteenth Day of March last past, in the third Yeare of our Raigne, given, graunted, bargained, soulde, enfeofled, aliened, and confirmed to Sir Henry Rosewell, Sir John Young, Knightes, Thomas Southcott, John Humfrey, John Endecott, and Symon Whetcombe, their Heires and Assignes, and their Associats for ever, all that Parte of Newe England in America aforesaid, which lyes and extendes betweene a greate River there comonlie called Monomack alias Merriemack, and a certen other River there, called Charles River, being in the Bottome of a certayne Bay there, comonlie called Massachusetts, alias Mattachusetts, alias Massatusetts Bay, and also all and singuler those Landes and Hereditaments whatsoever, lyeing within the Space of three English Myles on the South Parte of the said Charles River, or of any, or everie Parte thereof; and also, all and singuler the Landes and Hereditaments whatsoever, lyeing and being within the Space of three English Myles to the Southward of the Southermost Parte of the saide Bay called Massachusetts, alias Mattachusetts, alias Massatusets Bay; and also, all those Landes and Hereditaments whatsoever, which lye, and be within the space of three English Myles to the Northward of the said River called Monomack, alias Merrymack, or to the Northward of any and every Parte thereof, and all Landes and Hereditaments whatsoever, lyeing within the Lymitts aforesaide, North and South in Latitude and breath, and in Length and Longitude, of and within all the Bredth aforesaide, throughout the Mayne Landes there, from the Atlantick and Westerne Sea and Ocean on the East Parte, to the South Sea on the West Parte; and all Landes and Groundes, Place and Places, Soyles, Woodes and Wood Groundes, Havens, Portes, Rivers, Waters, Fishings, and Hereditaments whatsoever, lyeing within the said Boundes and Lymitts, and everie Parte and Parcell thereof; and also, all Islandes lyeing in America aforesaide, in the saide Seas or either of them on the Westerne or Eastern Coastes or Partes of the said Tractes of Lande, by the saide Indenture mencoed to be given, graunted, bargained, sould, enfeofled, aliened, and confirmed, or any of them; and also, all Mynes and Myneralls, as well Royall Mynes of Gould and Silver, as other Mynes and Myneralls whatsoeuer, in the saide Lands and Premisses, or any Parte thereof; and all Jurisdiccons, Rights, Royalties, Liberties, Freedomes, Ymmunities, Priviledges, Franchises, Preheminences, and Comodities whatsoever, which they, the said Councell established at Plymouth, in the County of Devon, for the planting, ruling, ordering, and governing of Newe England in America, then had, or might vse, exercise, or enjoy, in or within the saide Landes and Premisses by the saide Indenture mencoed to be given, graunted, bargained, sould, enfeoffed, and confirmed, or in or within any Parte or Parcell thereof:

To HAVE and to hould, the saide Parte of Newe England in America, which lyes and extendes and is abutted as aforesaide, and every Parte and Parcell thereof; and all the saide Islandes, Rivers, Portes, Havens, Waters, Fishings, Mynes, and Myneralls, Jurisdiccons, Franchises, Royalties, Liberties, Priviledges, Comodities, Hereditaments, and Premisses whatsoever, with the Appurtenances vnto the saide Sir Henry Rosewell, Sir John Younge, Thomas Southcott, John , John Endecott, and Simon Whetcombe, their Heires and Assignes, and their Associatts, to the onlie proper and absolute vse and Behoofe of the said Sir Henry Rosawell, Sir John Younge, Thomas Southcott, John , John Endecott, and Simon Whettcombe, their Heires and Assignes, and their Associatts forevermore; TO BE HOULDEN of Vs. our Heires and Successors, as of our Mannor of Eastgreenwich, in the County of Kent, in free and comon Soccage, and not in Capite, nor by Knightes Service; YEILDING and payeing therefore vnto Vs. our Heires and Successors, the fifte Parte of the Oare of Goulde and Silver, which shall from Tyme to Tyme, and at all Tymes hereafter, happen to be founde, gotten, had, and obteyned in any of the saide Landes, within the saide Lymitts, or in or witllin any Parte thereof, for, and in

Satisfaccon of all manner Duties, Demaundes, and Services whatsoever to be done, made, or paid to Vs. our Heires or Successors, as in and by the said recited Indenture more at large maie appeare.

NOWE Knowe Yee, that Wee, at the humble Suite and Peticon of the saide Sir Henry Rosewell, Sir John Younge, Thomas Southcott, John , John Endecott, and Simon Whetcombe, and of others whome they have associated vnto them, HAVE, for divers good Causes and consideracons, vs moveing, graunted and confirmed, and by theis Presents of our especiall Grace, certen Knowledge, and meere mocon, doe graunt and confirme vnto the saide Sir Henry Rosewell, Sir John Younge, Thomas Southcott, John , John Endecott, and Simon Whetcombe, and to their Associatts hereafter named; (videlicet) Sir Richard Saltonstall, Knight, Isaack Johnson, Samuel Aldersey, John Ven, Mathew Cradock, George Harwood, Increase Nowell, Richard Perry, Richard Bellingham, Nathaniell Wright, Samuel Vassall, Theophilus Eaton, Thomas Goffe, Thomas Adams, John Browne, Samuell Browne, Thomas Hutchins, William Vassall, William Pinchion, and George Foxcrofte, their Heires and Assignes, all the saide Parte of Newe England in America, lyeing and extending betweene the Boundes and Lvmytts in the said recited Indenture expressed, and all Landes and Groundes, Place and Places, Soyles, Woods and Wood Groundes, Havens, Portes, Rivers, Waters, Mynes, Mineralls, Jurisdiccons, Rightes, Royalties, Liberties, Freedomes, Immunities, Priviledges, Franchises, Preheminences, Hereditaments, and Comodities whatsoever, to them the saide Sir Henry Rosewell, Sir John Younge, Thomas Southcott, John , John Endecott, and Simon Whetcombe, theire Heires and Assignes, and to their Associatts, by the saide recited Indenture, given, graunted, bargayned, solde, enfeoffed, aliened, and confirmed, or mencoed or intended thereby to be given, graunted, bargayned, sold, enfeoffed, aliened, and confirmed: To HAVE, and to hould, the saide Parte of Newe England in America, and other the Premisses hereby mencoed to be graunted and confirmed, and every Parte and Parcell thereof with the Appurtenuces, to the saide Sir Henry Rosewell, Sir John Younge, Sir Richard Saltonstall, Thomas Southcott, John , John Endecott, Simon Whetcombe, Isaack Johnson, Richard Pery, Richard Bellingham, Nathaniell Wright, Samuell Vassall, Theophilus Eaton, Thomas Gode, Thomas Adams, John Browne, Samuel Bromine, Thomas Hutchins, Samuel Aldersey, John Ven, Mathewe Cradock, George Harwood, Increase Nowell, William Vassall, William Pinchion, and George Foxcrofte, their Heires and Assignes forever, to their onlie proper and absolute Vse and Behoofe for evermore; To be holden of Vs. our Heires and Successors, as of our Mannor of Eastgreenewich aforesaid, in free and comon Socage, and not in Capite, nor by Knights Service; AND ALSO YEILDING and paying therefore to Vs. our Heires and Successors, the fifte parte onlie of all Oare of Gould and Silver, which from tyme to tyme, and aft all tymes hereafter shalbe there gotten, had, or obteyned for all Services, Exaccons and Demaundes whatsoever, according to the Tenure and Reservacon in the said recited Indenture expressed.

AND FURTHER, knowe yee, that of our more especiall Grace, certen Knowledg, and meere mocon, Wee have given and graunted, and by theis Presents, doe for Vs. our Heires and Successors, give and graunte onto the saide Sir Henry Rosewell, Sir John Younge. Sir Richard Saltonstall, Thomas Southcott, John , John Endecott, Symon Whetcombe, Isaack Johnson, Samuell Aldersey, John Ven, Mathewe Cradock, George Harwood, Increase Nowell, Richard Pery, Richard Bellingham, Nathaniel Wright, Samuell Vassall, Theophilus Eaton, Thomas Gode, Thomas Adams, John Browne, Samuell Browne, Thomas Hutchins, William Vassall, William Pinchion, and George Foxcrofte, their Heires and Assignes, all that Parte of Newe England in America, which lyes and extendes betweene a great River there, comonlie called Monomack River, alias Merrimack River, and a certen other River there, called Charles River, being in the Bottome of a certen Bay there, comonlie called Massachusetts, alias

MASSACHUSETTS BAY COMPANY ROYAL CHARTER

Mattachusetts, alias Massatusetts Bay; and also all and singuler those Landes and Hereditaments whatsoever, lying within the Space of Three Englishe Myles on the South Parte of the said River, called Charles River, or of any or every Parte thereof; and also all and singuler the Landes and Hereditaments whatsoever, lying and being within the Space of Three Englishe Miles to the southward of the southermost Parte of the said Baye, called Massachusetts, alias Mattachusetts, alias Massatusets Bay: And also all those Landes and Hereditaments whatsoever, which lye and be within the Space of Three English Myles to the Northward of the saide River, called Monomack, alias Merrymack, or to the Norward of any and every Parte thereof, and all Landes and Hereditaments whatsoever, lyeing within the Lymitts aforesaide, North and South, in Latitude and Bredth, and in Length and Longitude, of and within all the Bredth aforesaide, throughout the mayne Landes there, from the Atlantick and Westerne Sea and Ocean on the East Parte, to the South Sea on the West Parte; and all Landes and Groundes, Place and Places, Soyles, Woodes, and Wood Groundes, Havens, Portes, Rivers, Waters, and Hereditaments whatsoever, lyeing within the said Boundes and Lymytts, and every Parte and Parcell thereof; and also all Islandes in America aforesaide, in the saide Seas, or either of them, on the Westerne or Easterne Coastes, or Partes of the saide Tracts of Landes hereby mencoed to be given and graunted, or any of them; and all Mynes and Mynerals as well Royal mynes of Gold and Silver and other mynes and mynerals, whatsoever, in the said Landes and Premisses, or any parte thereof, and free Libertie of fishing in or within any the Rivers or Waters within the Boundes and Lymytts aforesaid, and the Seas therevnto adjoining; and all Fishes, Royal Fishes, Whales, Balan, Sturgions, and other Fishes of what Kinde or Nature soever, that shall at any time hereafter be taken in or within the saide Seas or Waters, or any of them, by the said Sir Henry Rosewell, Sir John Younge, Sir Richard Saltonstall, Thomas Southcott, John , John Endecott, Simon Whetcombe, Isaack Johnson, Samuell Aldersey, John Ven, Mathewe Cradock, Greorge Harwood,

Increase Noell, Richard Pery, Richard Bellingham, Nathaniell Wright, Samuell Vassell, Theophilus Eaton, Thomas Goffe, Thomas Adams, John Browne, Samuell Browner, Thomas Hutchins, William Vassall, William Pinchion, and George Foxcrofte, their Heires and Assignes, or by any other person or persons whatsoever there inhabiting, by them, or any of them, to be appointed to fishe therein.

PROVIDED alwayes, That yf the said Landes, Islandes, or any other the Prernisses herein before menconed, and by theis presents, intended and meant to be graunted, were at the tyme of the graunting of the saide former Letters patents, dated the Third Day of November, in the Eighteenth Yeare of our said deare Fathers Raigne aforesaide, actuallie possessed or inhabited by any other Christian Prince or State, or were within the Boundes, Lymytts or Territories of that Southerne Colony, then before graunted by our said late Father, to be planted by divers of his loveing Subiects in the south partes of America, That then this present Graunt shall not extend to any such partes or parcells thereof, soe formerly inhabited, or lyeing within the Boundes of the Southerne Plantacon as aforesaide, but as to those partes or parcells soe possessed or inhabited by such Christian Prince or State, or being within the Bounders aforesaide shal be vtterlie voyd, theis presents or any Thinge therein conteyned to the contrarie notwithstanding. To HAVE and hould, possesse and enioye the saide partes of New England in America, which lye, extend, and are abutted as aforesaide, and every parse and parcell thereof; and all the Islandes, Rivers, Portes, Havens, Waters, Fishings, Fishes, Mynes, Myneralls, Jurisdiccons, Franchises, Royalties, Liberties, Priviledges, Comodities, and Premisses whatsoever, with the Appurtenances, vnto the said Sir Henry Rosewell, Sir John Younge, Sir Richard Saltonstall, Thomas Southcott, John , John Endecott, Simon Whetcombe, Isaack Johnson, Samuell Aldersey, John Yen, Mathewe Cradock, George Harwood, Increase Noweil, Richard Perry, Richard Bellingham, Nathaniell Wright, Samuell Vassall, Theophilus Eaton, Thomas Gofle, Thomas Adams, John Browne, Samuell Browne,

Thomas Hutchins, William Vassall, William Pinchion, and George Foxeroft, their Heires and Assignes forever, to the onlie proper and absolute Vse and Behoufe of the said Sir Henry Rosewell, Sir John Younge, Sir Richard Saltonstall, Thomas Southcott, John , John Endecott, Simon Whetcombe, Isaac Johnson, Samuell Aldersey, John Ven, Mathewe Cradocke, George Harwood, Increase Noweil, Richard Pery, Richard Bellingham, Nathaniell Wright, Samuell Vassall, Theophilus Eaton, Thomas Goffe, Thomas Adams, John Browne, Samuell Browne, Thomas Hutchins, William Vassall, William Pinchion, and George Foxcroft, their Heires and Assignes forevermore: To BE HOLDEN of Vs. our Heires and Successors, as of our Manor of Eastgreenwich in our Countie of Kent, within our Realme of England, in free and comon Soccage, and not in Capite, nor by Knights Service; and also yeilding and paying therefore, to Vs. our Heires and Sucessors, the fifte Parte onlie of all Oare of Gould and Silver, which from tyme to tyme, and at all tymes hereafter, shal be there gotten, had, or obteyned, for all Services, Exaccons, and Demaundes whatsoever; PROVIDED alwaies, and our expresse Will and Meaninge is, that onlie one fifte Parte of the Gould and Silver Oare above mencoed, in the whole, and noe more be reserved or payeable vnto Vs. our Heires and Successors, by Collour or Vertue of theis Presents, the double Reservacons or rentals aforesaid or any Thing herein conteyned notwithstanding. AND FORASMUCH, as the good and prosperous Successe of the Plantacon of the saide Partes of Newe-England aforesaide intended by the said Sir Henry Rosewell, Sir John Younge, Sir Richard Saltonstall, Thomas Southcott, John , John Endecott, Simon Whetcombe, Isaack Johnson, Samuell Aldersey John Ven, Mathew Cradock, George Harwood, Increase Noell, Richard Pery, Richard Bellingham, Nathaniell Wright, Samuell Vassall, Theophilus Eaton, Thomas Goffe, Thomas Adams, John Browne, Samuell Browne, Thomas Hutchins, William Vassall, William Pinchion, and George Foxcrofte, to be speedily sett vpon, cannot but cheifly depend, next vnder the Blessing of Almightie God, and the support of our Royall Authoritie vpon the good Government of the same, To the Ende that the Affaires and Buyssinesses which from tyme to tyme shall happen and arise concerning the saide Landes, and the Plantation of the same maie be the better mannaged and ordered, WEE HAVE FURTHER hereby of our especial Grace, certain Knowledge and mere Mocon, Given, graunted and confirmed, and for Vs. our Heires and Successors, doe give, graunt, and confirme vnto our said trustie and welbeloved subjects Sir Henry Rosewell, Sir John Younge, Sir Richard Saltonstall, Thomas Southcott, John , John Endicott, Simon Whetcombe, Isaack Johnson, Samuell Aldersey, John Yen, Mathewe Cradock, George Harwood, Increase Nowell, Richard Pery, Richard Bellingham, Nathaniell Wright, Samuell Vassall, Theophilus Eaton, Thomas Goffe, Thomas Adams, John Browne, Samuell Browne, Thomas Hutchins, William Vassall, William Pinchion, and George Foxcrofte: AND for Vs. our Heires and Successors, Wee will and ordeyne, That the saide Sir Henry Rosewell, Sir John Young, Sir Richard Saltonstall, Thomas Southcott, John , John Endicott, Svmon Whetcombe, Isaack Johnson, Samuell Aldersey, John Ven, Mathewe Cradock, George Harwood, Increase Noell, Richard Pery, Richard Bellingham, Nathaniell Wright, Samuell Vassall, Theophilus Eaton, Thomas Goffe, Thomas Adams, John Browne, Samuell Browne, Thomas Hutchins, William Vassall, William Pinchion, and George Foxcrofte, and all such others as shall hereafter be admitted and made free of the Company and Society hereafter mencoed, shall from tyme to tyme, and att all tymes forever hereafter be, by Vertue of theis presents, one Body corporate and politique in Fact and Name, by the Name of the Governor and Company of the Mattachusetts Bay in Newe-England, and them by the Name of the Governour and Company of the Mattachusetts Bay in Newe-England, one Bodie politique and corporate, in Deede, Fact, and Name; Wee doe for vs. our Heires and Successors, make, ordoyne, constitute, and confirme by theis Presents, and that by that name they shall have perpetuall Succession, and that by the same Name they and their Successors shall and maie be capeable and enabled aswell to implead, and to be impleaded, and to prosecute, demaund, and aunswere, and be aunsweared veto, in all and singuler Suites, Causes, Quarrells, and Accons, of what kinde or nature soever. And also to have, take, possesse, acquire, and purchase any Landes, Tenements, or Hereditaments, or any Goodes or Chattells, and the same to lease, graunte, demise, alien, bargaine, sell, and dispose of, as other our liege People of this our Realme of England, or any other corporacon or Body politique of the same may lawfully doe.

AND FURTHER, That the said Governour and Companye, and their Successors, maie have forever one comon Seale, to be vsed in all Causes and Occasions of the said Company, and the same Seale may alter, chaunge, breake, and newe make, from tyme to tyme, at their pleasures. And our Will and Pleasure is, and Wee doe hereby for Vs. our Heires and Successors, ordeyne and graunte, That from henceforth for ever, there shalbe one Governor, one Deputy Governor, and eighteene Assistants of the same Company, to be from tyme to tyme constituted, elected and chosen out of the Freemen of the saide Company, for the tyme being, in such Manner and Forme as hereafter in theis Presents is expressed, which said Officers shall applie themselves to take Care for the best disposeing and ordering of the generall buysines and Affaires of, for, and concerning the said Landes and Premisses hereby mencoed, to be graunted, and the Plantacion thereof, and the Government of the People there. AND FOR the better Execucon of our Royall Pleasure and Graunte in this Behalf, WEE doe, by theis presents, for Vs. our Heires and Successors, nominate, ordeyne, make, & constitute; our welbeloved the saide Mathewe Cradocke, to be the first and present Governor of the said Company, and the saide Thomas Goffe, to be Deputy Governor of the saide Company, and the saide Sir Richard Saltonstall, Isaack Johnson, Samuell Aldersey, John Ven, John , John Endecott, Simon Whetcombe, Increase Nowell, Richard Pery,

Nathaniell Wright, Samuell Vassall, Theophilus Eaton, Thomas Adams, Thomas Hutchins, John Browne, George Foxcrofte, William Vassall, and William Pinchion, to be the present Assistants of the saide Company, to continue in the saide several Offices respectivelie for such tyme, and in such manner, as in and by theis Presents is hereafter declared and appointed.

AND FURTHER, Wee will, and by theis Presents, for Vs. our Heires and Successors, doe ordoyne and graunte, That the Governor of the saide Company for the tyme being, or in his Absence by Occasion of Sicknes or otherwise, the Deputie Governor for the tyme being, shall have Authoritie from tyme to tyme vpon all Occasions, to give order for the assembling of the saide Company, and calling them together to consult and advise of the Bussinesses and Affaires of the saide Company, and that the said Governor, Deputie Governor, and Assistants of the saide Company, for the tyme being, shall or maie once every Moneth, or oftener at their Pleasures, assemble and houlde and keepe a Courte or Assemblie of themselves, for the better ordering and directing of their Affaires, and that any seaven or more persons of the Assistants, togither with the Governor, or Deputie Governor soe assembled, shalbe saide, taken, held, and reputed to be, and shalbe a full and sufficient Courte or Assemblie of the said Company, for the handling, ordering, and dispatching of all such Buysinesses and Occurrents as shall from tyme to tyme happen, touching or concerning the said Company or Plantacon; and that there shall or maie be held and kept by the Governor, or Deputie Governor of the said Company, and seaven or more of the said Assistants for the tyme being, vpon every last Wednesday in Hillary, Easter, Trinity, and Michas Termes respectivelie forever, one grease generall and solempe assemblie, which foure generall assemblies shalbe stiled and called the foure grease and generall Courts of the saide Company; IN all and every, or any of which saide grease and generall Courts soe assembled, WEE DOE for Vs. our Heires and Successors, give and graunte to the said Governor and Company, and their Successors, That the Governor, or in his absence, the Deputie Governor of the saide Company for the tyme being, and such of the Assistants and Freeman of the saide Company as shalbe present, or the greater nomber of them so assembled, whereof the Governor or Deputie Governor and six of the Assistants at the least to be seaven shall have full Power and authoritie to choose, nominate, and appointe, such and soe many others as they shall thinke fitt, and that shall be willing to accept the same, to be free of the said Company and Body, and them into the same to admits; and to elect and constitute such Officers as they shall thinke fitt and requisite, for the ordering, mannaging, and dispatching of the Affaires of the saide Govenor and Company, and their Successors; And to make Lawes and Ordinnces for the Good and Welfare of the saide Company, and for the Government and ordering of the saide Landes and Plantacon, and the People inhabiting and to inhabite the same, as to them from tyme to tyme shalbe thought meete, soe as such Lawes and Ordinances be not contrarie or repugnant to the Lawes and Statuts of this our Reaime of England. AND, our Will and Pleasure is, and Wee doe hereby for Vs, our Heires and Successors, establish and ordeyne, That yearely once in the yeare, for ever hereafter, namely, the last Wednesdav in Easter Tearme, yearely, the Governor, Deputy-Governor, and Assistants of the saide Company and all other officers of the saide Company shalbe in the Generall Court or Assembly to be held for that Day or Tyme, newly chosen for the Yeare ensueing by such greater parse of the said Company, for the Tyme being, then and there present, as is aforesaide. AND, yf it shall happen the present governor, Deputy Governor, and assistants, by theis presents appointed, or such as shall hereafter be newly chosen into their Roomes, or any of them, or any other of the officers to be appointed for the said Companv, to dye, or to be removed from his or their severall Offices or Places before the saide generall Day of Eleccon (whome Wee doe hereby declare for any Misdemeanor or Defect to be removeable by the Governor, Deputie Governor, Assistants, and Company, or such greater Parte of them in any of the publique Courts to be assembled as is aforesaid) That then, and in every such Case, it shall and maie be lawfull, to and for the Governor, Deputie Governor, Assistants, and Company aforesaide, or such greater Parte of them soe to be assembled as is aforesaide, in any of their Assemblies, to proceade to a new Eleccon of one or more others of their Company in the Roome or Place, Roomes or Places of such Officer or Officers soe dyeing or removed according to their Discrecons, And, Mediately vpon and after such Eleccon and Eleccons made of such Governor, Deputie Governor, Assistant or Assistants, or any other officer of the saide Company, in Manner and Forme aforesaid, the Authoritie, Office, and Power, before given to the former Governor, Deputie Governor, or other Officer and Officers soe removed, in whose Steade and Place newe shabe soe chosen, shall as to him and them, and everie of them, cease and determine

PROVIDED alsoe, and our Will and Pleasure is, That aswell such as are by theis Presents appointed to be the present Governor, Deputie Governor, and Assistants of the said Company, as those that shall Succeed them, and all other Officers to be appointed and chosen as aforesaid, shall, before they undertake the Execucon of their saide Offices and Places respectivelie, take their Corporal Oathes for the due and faithfull Performance of their Duties in their severall Offices and Places, before such Person or Persons as are by theis Presents hereunder appointed to take and receive the same; That is to saie, the saide Mathewe Cradock, whoe is hereby nominated and appointed the present Governor of the saide Company, shall take the saide Oathes before one or more of the Masters of our Courte of Chauncery for the Tyme being, vnto which Master or Masters of the Chauncery, Wee doe by theis Presents give full Power and Authoritie to take and administer the said Oathe to the said Governor accordinglie: And after the saide Governor shalbe soe sworne, then the said Deputy Governor and Assistants, before by theis Presents nominated and appointed, shall take the said severall Oathes to their

MASSACHUSETTS BAY COMPANY ROYAL CHARTER

Offices and Places respectivelie belonging, before the said Mathew Cradock, the present Governor, soe formerlie sworne as aforesaide. And every such person as shall be at the Tyme of the annuall Eleccon, or otherwise, vpon Death or Removeall, be appointed to be the newe Governor of the said Company, shall take the Oathes to that Place belonging, before the Deputy Governor, or two of the Assistants of the said Company at the least, for the Tyme being: And the newe elected Deputie Governor and Assistants, and all other officers to be hereafter chosen as aforesaide from Tyme to Tyme, to take the Oathes to their places respectivelie belonging, before the Governor of the said Company for the Tyme being, vnto which said Governor, Deputie Governor, and assistants, Wee doe by theis Presents Give full Power and Authoritie to give and administer the said Oathes respectively, according to our true Meaning herein before declared, without any Comission or further Warrant to be had and obteyned of our Vs. our Heires or Successors, in that Behalf. AND, Wee doe further, of our especial Grace, certen Knowledge, and meere mocon, for Vs. our Heires and Successors, give and graunte to the said Governor and Company, and their Successors for ever by theis Presents, That it shalbe lawfull and free for them and their Assignes, at all and every Tyme and Tymes hereafter, out of any our Realmes or Domynions whatsoever, to take, leade, carry, and transport, for in and into their Voyages, and for and towardes the said Plantacon in Newe England, all such and soe many of our loving Subjects, or any other strangers that will become our loving Subjects, and live under our Allegiance, as shall willinglie accompany them in the same Voyages and Plantacon; and also Shippmg, Armour, Weapons, Ordinance, Municon, Powder, Shott, Come, Victualls, and all Manner of clothing, Implements, Furniture, Beastes, Cattle, Horses, Mares, Merchandizes, and all other Thinges necessarie for the saide Plantacon, and for their Vse and Defence, and for Trade with the People there, and in passing and returning to and fro, any Lawe or Statute to the contrarie hereof in any wise notwithstanding; and without payeing or yeilding any Custome or Subsidie, either inward or outward, to Vs. our Heires or Successors, for the same, by the Space of seauen Yeares from the Day of the Date of theis Presents. PROVIDED, that none of the saide Persons be such as shalbe hereafter by especiall Name restrayned by Vs. our Heires or Successors. AND, for their further Encouragement, of our especiall Grace and Favor, Wee doe by theis Presents, for Vs. our Heires and Successors, yeild and graunt to the saide Governor and Company, and their Successors, and every of them, their Factors and Assignes, That they and every of them shalbe free and quits from all Taxes, Subsidies, and Customes, in Newe England, for the like Space of seauen Yeares, and from all Taxes and Imposicons for the Space of twenty and one Yeares, vpon all Goodes and Merchandizes at any Tyme or Tymes hereafter, either vpon Importacon thither, or Exportacon from thence into our Realme of England, or into any other our Domynions by the said Governor and Company, and their Successors, their Deputies, Factors, and Assignes, or any of them; EXCEPT onlie the five Pounds per Centum due for Custome vpon all such Goodes and Merchandizes as after the saide seauen Yeares shalbe expired, shalbe brought or imported into our Realme of England, or any other of our Dominions, according to the auncient Trade of Merchants, which five Poundes per Centum onlie being paide, it shall be thenceforth lawfull and free for the said Adventurers, the same Goodes and Merchandizes to export and carry out of our said Domynions into forraine Partes, without any Custome, Tax or other Dutie to be paid to Vs. our Heires or Successors, or to any other Officers or Ministers of Vs. our Heires and Successors. PROVIDED, that the said Goodes and Merchandizes be shipped out within thirteene Monethes, after their first Landing within any Parte of the saide Domynions.

AND, Wee doe for Vs. our Heires and Successors, give and graunte vnto the saide Governor and Company, and their Successors, That whensoever, or soe often as any Custome or Subsedie shall growe due or payeable vnto Vs our Heires, or Successors, according to the

MASSACHUSETTS BAY COMPANY ROYAL CHARTER

Lymittacon and Appointment aforesaide, by Reason of any Goodes, Wares, or Merchandizes to be shipped out, or any Retorne to be made of any Goodes, Wares, or Merchandize vnto or from the said Partes of Newe England hereby moncoed to be graunted as aforesaid, or any the Landes or Territories aforesaide, That then, and soe often, and in such Case, the Farmors, Customers, and Officers of our Customes of England and Ireland, and everie of them for the Tyme being, vpon Request made to them by the saide Governor and Company, or their Successors, Factors or Assignes, and vpon convenient Security to be given in that Behalf, shall give and allowe vnto the said Governor and Company, and their Successors, and to all and everie Person and Persons free of that Company, as aforesaide, six Monethes Tyme for the Payement of the one halfe of all such Custome and Subsidy as shalbe due and payeable unto Vs. our Heires and Successors, for the same; for which theis our Letters patent, or the Duplicate, or the inrollemt thereof, shalbe vnto our saide Officers a sufficient Warrant and Discharge. NEVERTHELESS, our Will and Pleasure is, That yf any of the saide Goodes, Wares, and Merchandize, which be, or shalbe at any Tyme hereafter landed or exported out of any of our Realmes aforesaide, and shalbe shipped with a Purpose not to be carried to the Partes of Newe England aforesaide, but to some other place, That then such Payment, Dutie, Custome, Imposicon, or Forfeyfure, shalbe paid, or belonge to Vs. our Heires and Successors, for the said Goodes, Wares, and Merchandize, soe fraudulently sought to be transported, as yf this our Graunte had not been made nor graunted. AND, Wee doe further will, and by theis Presents, for Vs. our Heires and Successors, firmlie enioine and comaunde, as well the Treasorer, Chauncellor and Barons of the Exchequer, of Vs. our Heires and Successors, as also all and singuler the Customers, Farmors, and Collectors of the Customes, Subsidies, and Imposts and other the Officers and Ministers of Vs our Heires and Successors whatsoever, for the Tyme Being, That they and every of them, vpon the strewing forth vnto them of theis Letters patents, or the Duplicate or exemplificacon of the same, without any other Writt or Warrant whatsoever from Vs. our Heires or Successors, to be obteyned or sued forth, doe and shall make full, whole, entire, and due Allowance, and cleare Discharge vnto the saide Governor and Company, and their Successors, of all Customes, Subsidies, Imposicons, Taxes and Duties whatsoever, that shall or maie be claymed by Vs. our Heires and Successors, of or from the said Governor and Company, and their Successors, for or by Reason of the said Goodes, Chattels, Wares, Merchandizes, and Premises to be exported out of our saide Domynions, or any of them, into any Parte of the saide Landes or Premises hereby mencoed, to be given, graunted, and confirmed, or for, or by Reason of any of the saide Goodes, Chattells, Wares, or Merchandizes to be imported from the said Landes and Premises hereby mencoed, to be given, graunted, and confirmed into any of our saide Dominions, or any Parte thereof as aforesaide, excepting onlie the saide five Poundes per Centum hereby reserved and payeable after the Expiracon of the saide Terme of seaven Yeares as aforesaid, and not before: And theis our Letters-patents, or the Inrollment, Duplicate, or Exemplificacon of the same shalbe for ever hereafter, from time to tyme, as well to the Treasorer, Chauncellor and Barons of the Exchequer of Vs. our Heires and Successors, as to all and singuler the Customers, Farmors, and Collectors of the Customes, Subsidies, and Imposts of Vs. our Heires and Successors, and all Searchers, and other the Officers and Ministers whatsoever of Vs. our Heires and Successors, for the Time being, a sufficient Warrant and Discharge in this Behalf.

AND, further our Will and Pleasure is, and Wee doe hereby for Vs. our Heires and Successors, ordeyne and declare, and graunte to the saide Governor and Company, and their Successors, That all and every the Subiects of Vs. our Heires or Successors, which shall goe to and inhabite within the saide Landes and Premisses hereby mencoed to be graunted, and every of their Children which shall happen to be borne there, or on the Seas in goeing thither, or returning from thence, shall have and enjoy all liberties and Immunities of free and naturall Subiects within any of the Domynions of Vs. our Heires or Successors, to all Intents, Construccons, and Purposes whatsoever, as yf they and everie of them were borne within the Realme of England. And that the Governor and Deputie Governor of the said Company for the Tyme being, or either of them, and any two or more of such of the saide Assistants as shalbe therevnto appointed by the saide Governor and Companv at any of their Courts or Assemblies to be held as aforesaide, shall and maie at all Tymes, and from tyme to tyme hereafter, have full Power and Authoritie to minister and give the Oathe and Oathes of Supremacie and Allegiance, or either of them, to all and everie Person and Persons, which shall at any Tyme or Tymes hereafter goe or passe to the Landes and Premisses hereby mencoed to be graunted to inhabite in the same. AND, Wee doe of our further Grace, certen Knowledg and meere Mocon, give and graunte to the saide Governor and Companv, and their Successors, That it shall and male be lawfull, to and for the Governor or Deputie Governor, and such of the Assistants and Freemen of the said Company for the Tyme being as shalbe assembled in any of their generall Courts aforesaide, or in any other Courtes to be specially sumoned and assembled for that Purpose, or the greater Parte of them (whereof the Governor or Deputie Governor, and six of the Assistants to be alwaies seaven) from tyme to tyme, to make, ordeine, and establishe all Manner of wholesome and reasonable Orders, Lawes, Statutes, and Ordilmces, Direccons, and Instruccons, not contrairie to the Lawes of this our Realme of England, aswell for selling of the Formes and Ceremonies of Governmt and Magistracy fitt and necessary for the said Plantacon, and the Inhabitants there, and for nameing and setting of all sorts of Officers, both superior and inferior, which they shall finde needefull for that Governement and Plantacon, and the distinguishing and setting forth of the severall duties, Powers, and Lymytts of every such Office and Place, and the Formes of such Oathes warrantable by the Lawes and Statutes of this our Realme of England, as shalbe respectivelie ministred vnto them for the Execucon of the said severall Offices and Places; as also, for the disposing and ordering of the Eleccons of such of the said Officers as shalbe annuall, and of such others as shalbe to succeede in Case of Death or Remove all and ministering the said Oathes to the newe elected Officers, and for Imposicons of lawfull Fynes, Mulcts, Imprisonment, or other lawfull Correccon, according to the Course of other Corporacons in this our Realme of England, and for the directing, ruling, and disposeing of all other Matters and Thinges, whereby our said People, Inhabitants there, may be soe religiously, peaceablie, and civilly governed, as their good Life and orderlie Conversacon, maie wynn and incite the Natives of Country, to the Knowledg and Obedience of the onlie true God and Saulor of Mankinde, and the Christian Fayth, which in our Royall Intencon, and the Adventurers free Profession, is the principall Ende of this Plantacion. WILLING, comaunding, and requiring, and by theis Presents for Vs. our Heiress Successors, ordoyning and appointing, that all such Orders, Lawes, Statuts and Ordinnces, Instruccons and Direccons, as shalbe soe made by the Governor, or Deputie Governor of the said Company, and such of the Assistants and Freemen as aforesaide, and published in Writing, under their comon Seale, shalbe carefullie and duly observed, kept, performed, and putt in Execucon, according to the true Intent and Meaning of the same; and theis our Letters-patents, or the Duplicate or exemplificacon thereof, shalbe to all and everie such Officers,-superior and inferior, from Tyme to Tyme, for the putting of the same Orders, Lawes, Statutes, and Ordinuces, Instruccons, and Direccons, in due Execucon against Vs. our Heires and Successors, a sufficient Warrant and Discharge.

AND WEE DOE further, for Vs. our Heires and Successors, give and graunt to the said Governor and Company, and their Successors bv theis Presents, that all and everie such Chiefe Comaunders, Captaines, Governors, and other Officers and Ministers, as by the said Orders, Lawes, Statuts, Ordinnces, Instruccons, or Direccons of the said Governor and Company for the Tyme being, shalbe from

Tyme to Tyme hereafter vmploied either in the Government of the saide Inhabitants and Plantacon, or in the Waye by Sea thither, or from thence, according to the Natures and Lymitts of their Offices and Places respectively, shall from Tyme to Tyme hereafter for ever, within the Precincts and Partes of Newe England hereby mencoed to be graunted and confirmed, or in the Waye by Sea thither, or from thence, have full and Absolute Power and Authoritie to correct, punishe, pardon, governe, and rule all such the Subiects of Vs. our Heires and Successors, as shall from Tyme to Tyme adventure themselves in any Voyadge thither or from thence, or that shall at any Tyme hereafter, inhabite within the Precincts and Partes of Newe England aforesaid, according to the Orders, Lawes, Ordinnces, Instruccons, and Direccons aforesaid, not being repugnant to the Lawes and Statutes of our Realme of England as aforesaid. AND WEE DOE further, for Vs. our Heires and Successors, give and graunte to the said Governor and Company, and their Successors, by theis Presents, that it shall and maie be lawfull, to and for the Chiefe Comaunders, Governors, and officers of the said Company for the Time being, who shalbe resident in the said Parte of Newe England in America, by theis presents graunted, and others there inhabiting by their Appointment and Direccon, from Tyme to Tyme, and at all Tymes hereafter for their speciall Defence and Safety, to incounter, expulse, repell, and resist by Force of Armes, aswell by Sea as by Lande, and by all fitting Waies and Meanes whatsoever, all such Person and Persons, as shall at any Tyme hereafter, attempt or enterprise the Destruccon, Invasion, Detriment, or Annoyaunce to the said Plantation or Inhabitants, and to take and surprise by all Waies and Meanes whatsoever, all and every such Person and Persons, with their Shippes, Armour, Municons and other Goodes, as shall in hostile manner invade or attempt the defeating of the said Plantacon, or the Hurt of the said Company and Inhabitants: NEVERTHELESS, our Will and Pleasure is, and Wee doe hereby declare to all Christian Kinges, Princes and States, that yf any Person or Persons which shall hereafter be of the said Company or

Plantacon or any other by Lycense or Appointment of the said Governor and Company for the Tyme being, shall at any Tyme or Tymes hereafter, robb or spoyle, by Sea or by Land, or doe any Hurt, Violence, or vnlawful Hostilitie to any of the Subjects of Vs. our Heires or Successors, or any of the Subjects of any Prince or State, being then in League and Amytie with Vs. our Heires and Successors, and that upon such injury don and vpon iust Complaint of such Prince or State or their Subjects, WEE, our Heires and Successors shall make open Proclamacon within any of the Partes within our Realme of England, comodious for that purpose, that the Person or Persons haveing comitted any such Roberie or Spoyle, shall within the Terme lymytted by such a Proclamacon, make full Restitucon or Satisfaccon of all such Iniureis don, soe as the said Princes or others so complayning, maie hould themselves fullie satisfied and contented; and that yf the said Person or Persons, haveing comitted such Robbery or Spoile, shall not make, or cause to be made Satisfaccon accordinglie, within such Tyme soe to be lymytted, that then it shalbe lawfull for Vs. our Heires and Successors, to putt the said Person or Persons out of our Allegiance and Proteccon, and that it shalbe lawfull and free for all Princes to prosecute with Hostilitie, the said Offendors, and every of them, their and every of their Procurers, Ayders, Abettors, and Comforters in that Behalf: PROVIDED also, and our expresse Will and Pleasure is, And Wee doe by theis Presents for Vs. our Heires and Successors ordeyne and appoint That theis Presents shall not in any manner envre, or be taken to abridge, barr, or hinder any of our loving subjects whatsoever, to vse and exercise the Trade of Fishing vpon that Coast of New England in America, by theis Presents mencoed to be graunted. But that they, and every, or any of them shall have full and free Power and Liberty to continue and vse their said Trade of Fishing vpon the said Coast, in any the Seas therevnto adioyning, or any Armes of the Seas or Saltwater Rivers where they have byn wont to fishe, and to build and sett vp vpon the Landes by theis Presents graunted, such Wharfes, Stages, and Workehouses as shalbe necessarie for the salting, drying, keeping, and packing vp of their Fish, to be taken or gotten vpon that Coast; and to cutt down, and take such Trees and other Materialls there groweing, or being, or shalbe needefull for that Purpose, and for all other necessarie Easements, Helpes, and Advantage concerning their said Trade of Fishing there, in such Manner and Forme as they have byn heretofore at any tyme accustomed to doe, without making any wilfull Waste or Spoyle, any Thing in theis Presents conteyned to the contrarie notwithstanding. AND WEE DOE further, for Vs. our Heires and Successors, ordeyne and graunte to the said Governor and Company, and their Successors by theis Presents that theis our Letters-patents shalbe firme, good, effectuall, and availeable in all Thinges, and to all Intents and Construccons of Lawe, according to our true Meaning herein before declared, and shalbe construed, reputed, and adjudged in all Cases most favourablie on the Behalf, and for the Benefist and Behoofe of the saide Governor and Company and their Successors: ALTHOUGH express mencon of the true yearely Value or certenty of the Premisses or any of them; or of any other Guiftes or Grauntes, by Vs. or any of our Progenitors or Predecessors to the foresaid Governor or Company before this tyme made, in theis-Presents is not made; or any Statute, Acte, Ordinnce, Provision, Proclamacon, or Restrainte to the contrarie thereof, heretofore had, made, published, ordeyned, or provided, or any other Matter, Cause, or Thinge whatsoever to the contrarie thereof in any wise notwithstanding.

IN WITNES whereof, Wee have caused theis our Letters to be made Patents.

WITNES ourself, at Westminster, the fourth day of March, in the fourth Yeare of our Raigne.

Per Breve de Privato Sigillo,

Wolseley.

Praedictus Matthaeus Cradocke Juratus est de Fide et Obedientia Regi et Successoribus suis, et de Debita Executione Officii Guberatoris Juxta Tenorem Praesentium, 18 Martii, 1628. Coram me Carolo Casare Milite in Cancellaria Mro.

CHAR.CÆSAR.[1]

The Great Seal of England appendant by a parti-coloured silk string.

CAMBRIDGE AGREEMENT

UPON due consideration of the state of the Plantation now in hand for New England, wherein we (whose names are hereunto subscribed) have engaged ourselves, and having weighed the greatness of the work in regard of the consequence, God's glory and the Church's good: As also in regard of the difficulties and discouragements which in all probabilities must be forecast upon the prosecution of this business: Considering withal that this whole adventure grows upon the joint confidence we have in each others fidelity and resolution herein, so as no man of us would have adventured it without assurance of the rest: Now, for the better encouragement of ourselves and others that shall join with us in this action, and to the end that every man may without scruple dispose of his estate and affairs as may best fit his preparation for this voyage, It is fully and faithfully agreed amongst us, and every one of us doth hereby freely and sincerely promise and bind himself, in the word of a Christian, and in the presence of God, who is the searcher of all hearts, that we will so really endeavor the prosecution of this work, as by God's assistance, we will be ready in our persons, and with such of our several families as are to go with us, and such provision as we are able conveniently to furnish ourselves withal, to embark for the said Plantation by the first of March next, at such port or ports of this land as shall be agreed upon by the Company, to the end to pass the Seas (under God's protection) to inhabit and continue in new England. Provided always, that before the last of September next, the whole Government, together with the Patent for the said plantation, be first, by an order of Court, legally transferred and established to remain with us and others which shall inhabit upon the said plantation. And provided also that if any shall be hindered by such just and inevitable Let or other cause to be allowed by 3 parts of four of these whose names are hereunto subscribed, then such persons for such times and during such lets to be discharged of this bond. And we do further promise every one for himself that shall fail to be ready through his own default by the day appointed, to pay for every day's default the sum of $3^{li.}$ to the use of the rest of the Company who shall be ready by the same day and time.[1]

This was done by order of Court the 29th of August. 1629.[2]

- Richard Saltonstall
- Thomas Dudley
- William Vassall
- Nicholas West [3]
- Isaac Johnson
- John
- Thomas Sharpe
- Increase Nowell
- John Winthrop
- William Pinchon
- Kellam Browne
- William Colbron

THE HVMBLE REQVEST OF HIS MAIESTIES

loyall Subjects, the Governour
and the Company late gone for
NEW-ENGLAND;

To the rest of their Brethren, in and of the
Church of *ENGLAND*.

For the obtaining of their Prayers,
and the removall of suspitions, and mis-
constructions of their Intentions.

LONDON,
Printed for IOHN BELLAMIE. 1630

HUMBLE REQUEST

REVEREND FATHERS AND BRETHREN:[1]

The general rumor of this solemn enterprise, wherein ourselves with others, through the providence of the Almighty, are engaged, as it may spare us the labor of imparting our occasion unto you, so it gives us the more encouragement to strengthen ourselves by the procurement of the prayers and blessings of the Lord's faithful servants. For which end we are bold to have recourse unto you, as God hath placed nearest to his throne of mercy, which as it affords you the more opportunity, so it imposeth the greater bond upon you to intercede for his people in all their straits. We beseech you therefore, by the mercies of the Lord Jesus, to consider us as your brethren, standing in very great need of your help, and earnestly imploring it. And however your charity may have met with some occasion of discouragement through the misreport of our intentions, or through the disaffection or indiscretion of some of us, or rather amongst us (for we are not of those that dream of perfection in this world), yet we desire you would be pleased to take notice of the principals and body of our Company, as those who esteem it our honor to call the Church of England, from whence we rise, our dear mother, and cannot part from our native Country, where she specially resideth, without much sadness of heart and many tears in our eyes, ever acknowledging that such hope and part as we have obtained in the common salvation we have received in her bosom, and sucked it from her breasts.[2]

We leave it not therefore as loathing, that milk wherewith we were nourished there; but, blessing God for the parentage and education, as members of the same body, shall always rejoice in her good, and unfeignedly grieve for any sorrow that shall ever betide her, and while we have breath, sincerely desire and endeavor the continuance and abundance of her welfare, with the enlargement of her bounds in the Kingdom of Christ Jesus.

Be pleased, therefore, reverend fathers and brethren, to help forward this work now in hand; which if it prosper, you shall be the more glorious, howsoever your judgment is with the Lord, and your reward with your God. It is a usual and laudable exercise of your charity, to commend to the prayers of your congregations the necessities and straits of your private neighbors: do the like for a Church springing out of your own bowels. We conceive much hope that this remembrance of us, if it be frequent and fervent, will be a most prosperous gale in our sails, and provide such a passage and welcome for us from the God of the whole earth, as both we shall find, and yourselves, with the rest of our friends, who shall hear of it, shall be much enlarged to bring in such daily returns of thanksgivings, as the specialties of His providence and goodness may justly challenge at all our hands. You are not ignorant that the spirit of God stirred up the Apostle Paul to make continual mention of the Church of Philippi, which was a Colony from Rome; let the same spirit, we beseech you, put you in mind, that are the Lord's remembrancers, to pray for us without ceasing, who are a weak Colony from yourselves making continual request for us to God in all your prayers.

HUMBLE REQUEST

What we entreat of you that are the ministers of God, that we also crave at the hands of all the rest of our brethren, that they would at no time forget us in their private solicitations at the throne of grace.

If any there be who, through want of clear intelligence of our course, or tenderness of affection towards us, cannot conceive so well of our way as we could desire, we would entreat such not to despise us, nor to desert us in their prayers and affections, but to consider rather that they are so much the more bound to express the bowels of their compassion towards us, remembering always that both nature and grace doth ever bind us to relieve and rescue, with our utmost and speediest power, such as are dear unto us, when we conceive them to be running uncomfortable hazards.

What goodness you shall extend to us in this or any other Christian kindness, we, your brethren in Christ Jesus, shall labor to repay in what duty we are or shall be able to perform, promising, so far as God shall enable us, to give him no rest on your beliefs, wishing our heads and hearts may be as fountains of tears for your everlasting welfare when we shall be in our poor cottages in the wilderness, overshadowed with the spirit of supplication, through the manifold necessities and tribulations which may not altogether unexpectedly, nor, we hope, unprofitably, befall us. And so commending you to the grace of God in Christ, we shall ever rest

Your assured friends and brethren,

From *Yarmouth*, aboard the *Arbella April 7, 1630*

- Jo: Winthrope, Gov.
- Rich: Saltonstall
- Charles Fines
- Isaac Johnston
- Tho: Dudley
- George Phillipps
- William Coddington

JAMES I & WITCHCRAFT

Witchcraft, in the reign of James I, stood at the center of a king's imagination and became, through law and rhetoric, a structure of power.[1] To understand James's reign fully, one must understand that *Daemonologie* was not an eccentric digression. It was a declaration of how he understood threat, authority, and the invisible architecture of the world.

Medieval English law rarely prosecuted witchcraft as a distinct crime. The Church handled accusations under canon law, treating sorcery as sin rather than felony. The state intervened only when sorcery intersected with treason—forecasting the king's death, harming nobles, or engaging in conspiracies that touched the crown.[2] Witchcraft, before the Reformation, belonged to the realm of confession, not execution.

In 1563, Parliament passed the Act Against Conjurations, Enchantments, and Witchcrafts. Elizabeth I walked a narrow path between skepticism and public anxiety. Her statute punished witchcraft only when demonstrable harm—death or bodily injury—

could be proven.[3] Lesser acts carried lesser penalties, reflecting her instinct to restrain panic rather than inflame it.

James I arrived with a personal theology shaped by the North Berwick witch trials. Convinced that witches had raised storms to destroy him, he viewed witchcraft as a direct assault on the divinely appointed body of the king.[4] Parliament's 1604 Witchcraft Act, passed shortly after his accession, reflected his fears.

This act had profound consequences. Judges who had once hesitated now acted with confidence; clergy preached more urgently; ordinary villagers scrutinized one another with new suspicion. The cultural imagination quickened. Shakespeare's *Macbeth*, written for James, captured precisely the king's belief that treason and witchcraft shared the same soil.

English common law favored physical evidence, but witchcraft forced courts to stretch the boundaries of proof. Under the Stuart legal system:

- Confessions—often shaped by intimidation—became central.
- Searches for the "devil's mark" carried quasi-legal authority.
- Informal tests, such as the notorious "swimming" of suspects, appeared despite judicial discomfort.[5]

However, England never descended into the mass hysteria common in parts of continental Europe and by the late seventeenth century, England began to grow skeptical.

Judges demanded stricter evidence; ministers questioned the reliability of confessions; natural philosophy offered alternative explanations for misfortune. Witchcraft, once treated as a genuine threat to the social order, became increasingly seen as a relic of older fears.

Parliament repealed the witchcraft laws in 1736. The era of diabolic prosecution had ended, but not before shaping how English people understood danger—and how Puritans carried those fears to New England.

The Boston Men, and the Puritans who followed them across the Atlantic, carried with them not only English law but the memory of its contradictions. They believed in the spiritual reality of evil yet feared the misuse of authority.

But the legacy of English witchcraft law persisted. The trials at Salem, though born of local circumstances, owed something to these inherited anxieties: a belief that the invisible can—and must—be made visible by law.

The tragedy of Salem in 1692 was not simply the fevered imagination of a frontier town or the consequence of personal grievances finally unmasked. Salem was, in many ways, England's past carried into New England's present—a legal, theological, and cultural inheritance transplanted across an ocean.

Two laws in particular shaped their worldview:

- The Witchcraft Act of 1563, passed under Elizabeth I, punished witchcraft when it caused demonstrable harm.
- The Witchcraft Act of 1604, passed under James I, expanded the crime to include conjuration, covenanting with spirits, and mere attempts at magic.[6]

The Massachusetts capital law on witchcraft reads:

> *If any man or woman be a witch—that is, hath or consulteth with a familiar spirit—they shall be put to death.*[7]

This is almost verbatim from the Jacobean statute. Salem existed in a world James I had shaped without ever knowing it.

JAMES I - PUBLISHED WORKS

Monarchs leave behind monuments, coins, and proclamations—objects shaped by others and polished by the calculations of power. James I left behind books that shaped his reign and, indirectly, shaped the world that gave rise to the Boston Men and the settlement of New England.

Basilikon Doron

When James composed *Basilikon Doron* in 1599, he intended it as private counsel for his son Henry, a father's attempt to instruct a future king in virtue, governance, and piety. It is a tender book—surprisingly so—filled with the anxieties of a man shaped by the dangers of Scottish politics. Yet woven through its gentleness is a doctrine that would haunt England: the belief that a king rules by God's hand and stands above the reach of earthly restraint.[1]

- James meant to teach wisdom; he taught absolutism.
- He meant to steady his son; he planted rigidity.

When Charles inherited this book, he absorbed its lessons without the caution Elizabeth had once urged James to cultivate. In *Basilikon Doron*, kings do not negotiate—they instruct. They do not share authority—they embody it. What was written as a paternal gift became, in Charles's hands, a manual for a kind of kingship England could no longer bear.

The True Law of Free Monarchies

A year before *Basilikon Doron*, James published *The True Law of Free Monarchies*, stating that kings "make the laws and break them," that they are accountable only to God, and that resistance is a sin against the divine order.[2]

This book might have passed harmlessly in Scotland, where his authority had always been contested but rarely diluted by constitutional theory. In England, it landed like a flint against stone. The English political nation—gentry, judges, merchants, and ministers—had grown accustomed to the idea that liberty rested on the ancient rights of Parliament and the common law. James's book taught the opposite.

When Charles later imprisoned subjects without cause and levied taxes without consent, the English recognized the shape of the doctrine. They had read it in James's own hand. What James had written as philosophy became, under Charles, an engine of confrontation.

Daemonologie

Daemonologie (1597) reveals something more unsettling: a king driven by fear. James had survived the North Berwick witch trials as a young man; the experience scarred him. The book is not the work of a detached scholar but of a mind convinced that the devil stalked the northern kingdom and that witchcraft must be rooted out by law, confession, and—where deemed necessary—execution.[3]

After James's accession, suspicion spread more readily. Parliament's 1604 Witchcraft Act hardened punishments. Witch trials multiplied. Shakespeare, ever attuned to a monarch's private passions, wove James's obsessions into *Macbeth*, turning the stage into a mirror of the king's fears.

New England inherited this legacy. Though the Puritans who settled Massachusetts Bay would regard their own judicial rigor as protective, the shadow of *Daemonologie* lay in the background of a culture deeply attentive to invisible forces.

An Apologie for the Oath of Allegiance

After the Gunpowder Plot of 1605, James imposed an Oath of Allegiance requiring subjects to deny papal authority. When the Pope condemned the oath, James responded with *An Apologie for the Oath of Allegiance* (1608), a lengthy defense of his right to command the conscience of his subjects.[4]

It is the work of a king who felt misunderstood and maligned, desperate to assert both orthodoxy and authority. James cast himself as a Protestant patriarch, a defender of order, a monarch standing between England and Catholic chaos.

James I's insistence that loyalty to the crown must govern the soul as well as the body, he revealed again the flaw at the heart of early Stuart kingship: a belief that obedience must be total to be genuine. Taken together, James's books show a mind striving for coherence yet blind to the consequences of its own logic.

THOMAS KNYVETT & THE GUNPOWDER PLOT

A handful of men—frustrated, devout, and reckless—attempted to rewrite the kingdom by fire. Their intention was absolute: to shatter the political order with a single explosion, to unmake the Stuart monarchy at its root, and to seize from Parliament and Protestant England the future they believed rightfully theirs.

Yet this story, recited for centuries in sermons and civic ritual, is not solely a tale of treason. It is also a story of the monarchy's fear, its response, and the quiet steadiness of one man at the center of it—Sir Thomas Knyvett, whose diligence and sense of duty prevented the destruction of an entire government.

To understand the Gunpowder Plot is to understand the fragility of early Stuart England: a kingdom ruled by a foreign-born king still struggling to earn trust, a Parliament uneasy before rumors of Catholic intrigue, and a populace that believed the unseen world was never far from the visible one.

James I had ascended the throne with Catholic hopes clinging to him like a shadow.

A TALE OF TWO BOSTONS

English Catholics, long persecuted under Elizabeth, believed—wrongly—that James's marriage to Anne of Denmark and his habit of theological subtlety signaled a more tolerant reign. Early gestures seemed promising. James softened certain penal laws and hinted at leniency. But the optimism collapsed quickly.

Parliament demanded harsher measures. Gunpowder priests continued to challenge the crown's authority. The discovery of Catholic conspiracies in 1603 and 1604 hardened public opinion. The Oath of Allegiance—requiring subjects to deny the Pope's authority—made clear that James, for all his gentleness, would not permit divided loyalty within his kingdom.[1]

It was in this atmosphere of disappointment and frustration that the Gunpowder Plot was born: not merely as treason, but as an act of desperation from men who believed God required them to restore England to the Catholic fold.

Robert Catesby—charismatic, embittered, and convinced of divine sanction—became the architect of the plot. To him, the death of James, his councillors, and the assembled Parliament was not a crime but a sacrifice, a single violent act meant to cleanse England of heresy. Among his followers were Thomas Percy, Jack Wright, Robert Wintour, and the man whose image has come to dominate the popular memory of the plot: Guy Fawkes.

Fawkes, seasoned in war and known for his steadiness, was the ideal choice to oversee the barrels of gunpowder stored beneath the House of Lords. Yet the plot, for all its elaborate planning, had a flaw: it depended upon silence in a kingdom where confession, rumor, and conscience were inevitable forces.

It was a letter—anonymous, fearful, perhaps written by a conspirator who remembered mercy—that stirred suspicion at court. The letter urged Lord Monteagle to avoid the opening of Parliament, for *they shall receive a terrible blow, yet shall not see who hurt them.*[2]

Monteagle carried the warning to the authorities. And so attention turned toward the undercroft beneath Parliament. Knyvett (sometimes spelled Knyvet or Knevet) was not a man of bluster. He was a seasoned courtier, a Justice of the Peace, and Keeper of Whitehall Palace—trusted, discreet, and loyal without theatrics. When Monteagle's warning reached Robert Cecil, now Earl of Salisbury, it was Knyvett whom Cecil entrusted with the delicate task of searching the Parliament cellars.[3]

On the night of November 4, Knyvett and his men made their way into the undercroft. At first glance, nothing seemed amiss. Bundles of firewood and coal lay stacked neatly, as if awaiting transport. But Knyvett was a man trained to read signs. Something in the arrangement of the wood did not sit easily with him.

Sir Thomas Knyvett arresting Guy Fawkes

Behind the wood lay thirty-six barrels of gunpowder—enough to obliterate the Lords, the Commons, and James I himself.

Near the barrels stood Guy Fawkes, disguised, armed, and holding a watch. Knyvett seized him and within hours the plot unraveled. Knyvett's act was quiet, decisive, and without spectacle. He saved the monarchy not through ideology but through duty—the unadorned diligence that forms the backbone of any stable kingdom.

In later years, Parliament would honor the day with bonfires and sermons. But without Knyvett's composure, England might have awakened to ruins. The Gunpowder Plot did not lead James toward tolerance. It drove him deeper into suspicion. Penal laws against Catholics intensified. Jesuits were hunted more aggressively.

The Gunpowder Plot entered English memory not merely as history but as ritual. November 5th became a day of thanksgiving. Children chanted *"Remember, remember,"* and effigies of Fawkes burned in marketplaces.

A crime of faith became a cultural script, reenacted annually reinforcing Protestant identity.

Yet beneath the ritual lay a deeper lesson of how fragility of trust divided the kingdom.

James's reign, already strained by disputes over prerogative, union, and ecclesiastical order, carried forward a sense that danger might erupt from within.

The monarchy learned to see enemies in invisible places, and this habit of suspicion—already visible in James's writings on witchcraft—became one of the quiet engines of Stuart governance.

For those who would one day cross the Atlantic, the Gunpowder Plot was remembered as both a calamity and a parable that reinforced their conviction that societies built on fear collapse from within.

NOTES

PROLOGUE

1. Anderson, Robert Charles. *The Great Migration Directory: Immigrants to New England, 1620-1640*, Boston: The New England Historical and Genealogical Society, 2015. [*The Mayflower was the first ship in the* Great Migration *and left England on September 16th, 1620. England's Long Parliament opened on November 3rd, 1640, and was not dissolved for 20 years, during which Archbishop William Laud and Charles I were tried for treason and executed.*]
2. The first meeting of the Massachusetts Bay Company Court of Assistants in America took place at Charleston on August 23, 1630.
3. Anderson, R. C. *The Winthrop Fleet*. (New England Historical and Genealogical Society, 2012). P10 [*William Laud was named Archbishop of Canterbury at the age of 60 after the death of George Abbot on August 4, 1633. Laud was notorious for his persecution of Calvinists and Puritans in an effort to restore the Church of England to its preformation glory.*]
4. Cressy, D. *Coming Over*. (Cambridge University Press, 1987). p-vii
5. Thompson, P. *The History and Antiquities of Boston*. (Longman and Co.; Simpkin and Co., 1856).
6. The Electorate of the Palatinate (Kurfürstentum Pfalz in German) was a state that was part of the Holy Roman Empire. It was established in the Early Middle Ages (5th century) and continued for over 800 years until its dissolution in 1806 during the Napoleonic Wars.
7. The Thirty Years' War is arguably the most destructive in European history. It rivaled the Black Death in demographic damage and exceeded even World Wars I and II in local destructiveness when measured by mortality rates, agricultural devastation, and societal breakdown over time. The *Thirty Years' War*, which lasted from 1618 to 1648, was a conflict between the Catholic Habsburgs (represented by Spain, France, and Austria) and the Protestant states (including Sweden, Denmark, and the Dutch Republic).
8. The failure of James I and Charles I to provide sufficient aid to Protestant causes contributed to their loss of domestic credibility and set the stage for domestic unrest that led to the English Civil War.
9. An estimated 4.5 to 8 million soldiers and civilians died from battle, famine, and disease. Some areas of what is now modern Germany experienced a loss of over 50% of their population.
10. Lockhart, Paul Douglas (1996). *Denmark in the Thirty Years' War, 1618-1648: King Christian IV and the decline of the Oldenburg State*. Susquehanna University Press.

11. On August 27, 1626, four horses were shot out from under King Christian IV of Denmark, and he fled to Wolfenbüttel in Lower Saxony with what remained of his cavalry, leaving 3,000 dead or wounded on the battlefield. The Battle of Lutter (German: *Lutter am Barenberge*) occurred south of Salzgitter, in Lower Saxony.
12. Cust, Richard (1985). "Charles I, the Privy Council, and the Forced Loan". *Journal of British Studies.*
13. Cust, Richard. *Charles I*
14. Trevor-Roper, Hugh *Archbishop Laud*. Phoenix Press reissue 2000 pp. 317–324 [Edgar Lee Masters commented in the early 1900s, "In the Star Chamber, the council could inflict any punishment short of death, and frequently sentenced objects of its wrath to the pillory, whipping and the cutting off of ears. With each embarrassment to arbitrary power, the Star Chamber became emboldened to undertake further usurpation. The Star Chamber finally summoned juries before it for verdicts disagreeable to the government and fined and imprisoned them. It spread terrorism among those who were called to do constitutional acts. It imposed ruinous fines. It became the chief defense of Charles against assaults upon those usurpations which cost him his life."]
15. 1686 James II established the Dominion of New England and Edmond Andros as governor. Three years later, in 1689, the Glorious Revolution replaced the Stuarts with William III and Mary II. Simon Bradstreet replaced Edmond Andros and again served as governor until 1692 when the Massachusetts Bay Colony, the Plymouth Colony, and the territory of Maine were merged to form the Provence of Massachusetts Bay by William III, Sir William Phips was appointed governor.
16. Lincolnshire migration numbers have been extracted from the New England Historical and Genealogical Society's Great Migration Project database and *The Great Migration Directory: Immigrants to New England, 1620-1640* by R.C. Anderson.
17. Rose-Troup misused the term "Adventurers." The Records of the Massachusetts Bay Company use "Adventurer" to mean those who joined the company as investors who had no intention of settling in New England. Those who intended to settle in New England were called the "Planters."
18. Rose-Troup, F. *The Massachusetts Bay Company and Its Predecessors.* (The Grafton Press, 1930).
19. Mitchell, Stewart. *The New England Quarterly*, vol. 3, no. 4, New England Quarterly, Inc., 1930, pp. 758–62.
20. Winship, M. P. *Godly Republicanism: Puritans, Pilgrims, and a City on a Hill.* (Harvard University Press, 2012). Kindle Edition. p-190-191
21. My research indicates that the Earl of Lincoln, Theophilus Clinton, was not active in forming the Massachusetts Bay Company, though he encouraged its formation and influenced his father-in-law, Lord Saye & Sele, and the Earl of Warwick, to lobby for its formation.
22. Michael Winship mistakenly identified Isaac Johnson as Theophilus Clinton's son-in-law when, in fact, he was his brother-in-law.
23. Rose-Troup, *The Massachusetts Bay Company and Its Predecessors.*

NOTES

24. Haven, Samuel Foster. *History of Grants Under the Great Council for New England: A Lecture of a Course by Members of the Massachusetts Historical Society, Delivered Before the Lowell Institute, January 15, 1869.* (Press of John Wilson & Son, 1869). pp 3

BOSTON'S VICAR

1. Cotton, John, Sr. *A Practicall Commentary, or an Exposition with Observations, Reasons, and Vses Upon the First Epistle Generall of John,* London: Printed by R.I. and E.C. for Thomas Parkhurst to be sold at the Three Crownes at the lower end of Cheapside., 1656. pp 96
2. An advowson is the right of an avowee (patron) to nominate an appointee to the bishop of the diocese. Thus, an advowson has the right to appoint a person to parish priest - subject to episcopal approval. Most commonly, such rights were held by the lords of large aristocratic estates.
3. Lewin, Stephen. 1895. *A Concise Sketch of the History of St. Botolph's Church, Boston, in the County of Lincoln.* Horncastle: W.K.Morton. pp 16
4. In 1583, John Whitgift, the new Archbishop of Canterbury, introduced a document known as the *Three Articles*. This was an attempt to bring into line nonconformists who were unwilling to follow the Elizabethan Church. Whitgift had gained a reputation as a man who had no love of the Puritans even before his appointment by Elizabeth. He used his Three Articles to attack the Puritans, trapping them by their answers. They would be tied to the Church if they agreed to all three. If they disagreed with just one of the Three Articles, they were deprived of their living. To give added clout to his work, the Court of High Commission adjudicated on any answers given. The Three Articles read as follows: "That none be permitted to preach, read, catechize, minister the sacraments, or to execute any other ecclesiastical function unless he consents and subscribes to the Articles following: 1. That her Majesty, under God, hath, and ought to have, the sovereignty and rule over all manner of persons born within her realms....either ecclesiastical or temporal, soever they be. 2. That the Book of Common Prayer, and of ordering bishops, priests and deacons, containeth in it nothing contrary to the word of God....and that he himself will use the form of the said book prescribed in public prayer and administration of the sacraments, and none other. 3. That he alloweth the book of Articles, agreed upon by the archbishops and bishops of both provinces and the whole clergy in Convocation holden at London in the year of our Lord God 1562....and that he believeth all the Articles therein contained to be agreeable to the word of God."
5. *Transcription of Minutes of the Corporation of Boston: Vol II (1608-1638)* Bailey, J. F. (Ed.) (1981). History of Boston Project. pp 105 ["*At this assemblie Mr Benjamin Alexander the preacher within this Borough hath yealed upp his place of the maiors Champline and Mr Wooll hath likewise yealded up his place of a vicaridge and Mr Benjamin Alexander is chosen vicar in Mr Woolls Rome and he to have the same stpend and allowance the late Vicar hade and Mr.*

A TALE OF TWO BOSTONS

Alexander to pay his ffirst fruits himselfe without any Allowance of this house towards the same."]

6. Transcription of Minutes of the Corporation of Boston: Vol II. pp 106-107 [*"Allsoe at this assemblie Mr Benjamin Alexander being heartofore chosen Vicare of this Borough hath yealed upp the same and requested that this house would provide a new Vicar for this Borough which surrender this house is willing to accept accordingly. At this assemblie Mr Wooll, Mr Jankinson, Mr Dresby, Mr Doctor Baron & Mr John Camocke are requested to goe to Cambridge for to provide this Borough of a ne vicar and this comapany after such Choyce made to give allowance or disallowance of such as they shall soe commend."*]

7. Baron's father was a distinguished scholar from France who immigrated to England in 1573 and earned a Doctor of Divinity at Cambridge. Peter, entered Cambridge's Peterhouse as a sizar in 1576 and completed his Master's Degree in medicine in 1585. In 1606, he naturalized with his wife and moved to Boston where he served as town physician until his death in 1630. In addition to his Boston medical practice, Dr. Baron *leavened many of the chief men of the town with Arminianism*—the Lutheran doctrine advocated by his father.

8. Arminians belonged to a branch of Protestantism based on the theological ideas of the Dutch Reformed theologian Jacobus Arminius (1560–1609) and his historic supporters known as Remonstrants, who supported an attempt to moderate the doctrines of Calvinism related to its interpretation of predestination.

9. Lord Burghley, Thomas Cecil, 1st Earl of Exeter, was the son of William Cecil, Lord High Treasurer under Elizabeth I. He served as MP for Lincolnshire, first in the House of Commons and later in the House of Lords.

10. Transcription of Minutes of the Corporation of Boston: Vol II. pp 37

    [*"Coppie of the Letter sent ffrom my Lord Exeter tougheinge Mr Doctor Baron one of the Aldermen.*

    After my very harty Comendacons beinge given to understand that one Mr Peeter Baron Doctor n Phisicke is lately chosen one of the Aldermen of Your Towne of Boston beinge a man (as I am credably informed) of very good part both for his learneinge sufficyency and carriadege, and haveinge had (before his eleccon to that romme) his place at meeteings in your towne above any of the Aldermen next unto the Deputy Recorder Notwithstandeinge that the greater part of the sufficyentest Aldermen & Comon Councell of the Towne are contented to yeald it to him, Theare are (as I heare) some few of the Aldermen farre infoerior to the Said Doctor Baron whoe refuse to give him place I have there uppon thought good hereby to write and advise you, since it will much tend to the indignity of your Towne to seeke to bringe him to a lower rowme by beinge of your Company than hee formerly held amongst you Duputy Recorder & some of your bretheren the Aldermen would take such speedy order for avoydeinge all further inconveince & discontnetment that may arise as that he may quietly take & hold his place in your Towne next the Recorder oas afeoresaid, wherein if you shall finde any opposiscion to bee made by any of those persons that seeme to withstand him I pray you to cerifie mee theire names That such further course maybee taken for redresse of theire Copntention as shalbee requisite & epedient

NOTES

And so wisheing you all unity & mutuall love amongst you I leave you to Gods protection, Burghley this Xth of August 1609

To my very loveinge ffrends the Maior of Boston for the time beinge the Deputy Recorder & the rest of the Aldermen theire.

Youre loveinge ffrend

Exeter"}

11. Thompson, *The History and Antiquities of Boston*. pp 414
12. Thompson, *The History and Antiquities of Boston* pp 414-415
13. Transcription of Minutes of the Corporation of Boston: Vol II. pp108 ["*At this assembly Mr John Cotton Maister of Arts is now elected and Chosen Vicar of this Borrough in the Rome & place of Mr Wooll the late incombetn theare for that Mr Alexander uppon whom the vicaridge was purposed to have been bestowed hath yeilded up the same and he is to have his presentation forthwith sealed and to have the same stipend & allowance that Mr Wooll the late Vicar theare had at the same time he departed with the same.*"]
14. Thompson, *History and Antiquities of Boston*. pp- 414
15. Whiting, Samuel. "Concerning the Life of the Famous Mr. Cotton, Teacher to the Church of Christ at Boston in New England." In *Chronicles of the First Planters of the Colony of Massachusetts Bay, From 1623-1636*, Boston: Charles C. Little and James Brown, 1846. pp 422-423
16. It is interesting to note that Alexander Young's *Chronicles of the First Planters of the Colony of Massachusetts Bay from 1623 to 1636* footnotes that "*this same Simon Biby helped restore Richard Mather to his parish at Toxteth*" in November 1633 after he had been suspended for Nonconformity the preceding August.
17. Whiting, "Concerning the Life of the Famous Mr. Cotton." pp 423
18. *Transcription of Minutes of the Corporation of Boston: Vol II (1608-1638)*. pp 108
19. Mather, Cotton. 1855. *Magnalia Christi Americana*. Vol. I. Hartford: Silas Andrus and Son. pp 257
20. None of the controversy in Mather's account appears in the *Transcription of Minutes of the Corporation of Boston* (pages 98-118) for 1612 while Nicholas Smyth was mayor of Boston.
21. Cotton's father was a lawyer who desired his son, John, to study law. The head of the Derby Grammar School, Richard Johnson, was a fellow of Trinity College—England's primer legal studies site. As young Cotton neared the end of his studies at the Derby School, his father solicited Richard Johnson's help in finding John a place at Trinity College. In 1604, two years into Trinity's master's program, Cotton's father died and left him "*the somme of Twenty marks*". In seventeenth-century England, the mark did not exist as coinage. Rather it was an equity amount used in transactions like wills, land sales, and dowries. Twenty marks were roughly two-thirds of its equivalent in pound sterling or 13 pounds 6 shillings and 10 pence. £13 6s 10d in 1604 is the equivalent of £5,000 today.
22. The intention of Emmanuel College founder, Sir Walter Mildmay, was that the college be devoted to the sole purpose of sending preachers out to the parishes of England. The statutes founding Emmanuel College included a *De Mora* (delay)

Statute that essentially prohibited Emmanuel graduates from delaying entry to the priesthood by staying at University and required them to leave the college once they obtained their Bachelor of Divinity degree.

23. Mather, *Magnalia Christi Americana*. pp 258
24. *Transcription of Minutes of the Corporation of Boston: Vol II (1608-1638)*. pp 127
25. Venn, John. 2015. "Alumni Cantabrigienses." *Cambridge University Library*. Cambridge: Cambridge University Press.
26. The term sizar is thought to derive from *sizes* or the apportionment of food and drink at college tables which sizars were obliged to serve in return for the larger share of their college tuition. Sizars assigned to fellows or fellow-commoners as waiters and valets were termed *private* or *proper* sizars. They dined on leftovers from the high table and often shared beds in crowded conditions that necessitated taking turns sleeping. Put simply, sizars were the lowest level students at Cambridge University, and they paid the least to attend, which was five shillings tuition per term.
27. *Transcription of Minutes of the Corporation of Boston: Vol II (1608-1638)*. Vol. 2 .pp 131
28. Venn, J., *Alumni Cantabrigienses: A Biographical List of All Known Students, Graduates, and Holders of Office at the University of Cambridge, from the Earliest Times to 1900*
29. Hawkred- alternately appears in *The Parish Registers of Boston in the County of Lincoln* as Hawcred, Acroide, Akroid, Haucridge, Hawckred, Hawcrick, and Hawkrit. The surname appears repeatedly as Hawkred in the *Transcription of Minutes of the Corporation of Boston: Vol II (1608-1638)*. As a result, I have chosen to use "Hawkred" in this work, though publications of the New England Historic Genealogical Society render it Hawkred.
30. Whiting. "Concerning the Life of the Famous Mr. Cotton"
31. Cotton's Latin Thesis was *Vos estis sal terrae. Quod si sal evanuerit, in quo salietur? Ad nihilum valet ultra, nisi ut mittatur foras, et conculcetur ab hominibus.*
32. Whiting, "Concerning the Life of the Famous Mr. Cotton."
33. William Chappell served as John Milton's tutor at Christ's College from 1625-1626.
34. Norton, John. *Abel Being Dead Yet Speaketh: or the Life and Death of ... John Cotton, Late Teacher of the Church of Christ, at Boston, in New England*, London: Tho. Newcomb for Lodowick Lloyd, 1658. pp 33
35. Commencement at Cambridge is traditionally held on the first Tuesday of July.
36. *Records of the Parish of Holy Trinity, Balsham: Marriages 1558-1994*.
37. Lane, Belden C. 2011. *Ravished by Beauty: the Surprising Legacy of Reformed Spirituality*. New York: Oxford University Press. pp 114
38. Mather, C., *Magnalia Christi Americana*, pp 258
39. Rosenmeier, Jesper. 2012. *'Spirituall Concupiscence': John Cotton's English Years, 1584-1633*. Boston, Lincs.: Richard Kay Publications. [*The title of his work, Spiritual Concupiscence, denotes strong sexual desire or lust.*]
40. Lane, *Ravished by Beauty* pp 114

NOTES

41. Cotton, John, Sr. 1642. *A Brief Exposition of the Whole Book of Canticles, or Song of Solomon*. London: Philip Nevil. (Song of Songs 4:3)
42. Lane, *Ravished by Beauty* pp 114
43. Cotton, John, Sr. 1646. *Milk for Babes. Drawn Out of the Breasts of Both Testaments. Chiefly, for the Spirituall Nourishment of*. London: Henry Overton. [Although John Cotton evoked suckling breasts as a metaphor to illustrate God's grace, it is ironic to note that his first real experience with breastfeeding took place in the middle of the Atlantic Ocean on a ship bound for New England when his second wife, Sarah Hawkred, gave birth to his first child- a son they named Seaborn. At the time, Cotton was nearly fifty years old. Tragically, his beloved first wife, Elizabeth Horrocks, died childless after eighteen years of marriage and appears to have been infertile as Cotton's fertility was confirmed when he fathered six children with his second wife, Sarah.]
44. Avery, Gillian. 2000. *Origins and English Predecessors of the New England Primer*. American Antiquarian Society.
45. Bailey, J E. 1883. "Jeremiah Horrox." *The Observatory* 6 (November). pp 319
46. Adams, Oscar Fay. 1908. "Our English Parent Towns: Maldon." Edited by F. Apthrop Foster. *The New England Historical and Genealogical* ... 62 (245). Boston: pp 167 [Also see The Will of Alexander Horrocks in *The Palatine Notebook: For the Intercommunication of Antiquaries, Bibliophiles and Other Investigators Into the History and Literature of the Counties of Lancaster, Chester, Etc, Volume 3, pp 24 & 25*]
47. Horrocks, Alexander. *Will of Alexander Horrocks*, Last Will and Testament, 1650.
48. Clegg, *Annals of Bolton* pp 235
49. Venn, "Alumni Cantabrigienses."
50. The only two James Horrocks that I have been able to identify are a brother of Elizabeth's father, Christopher, who is named in her uncle Alexander Horrocks's Will; and a cousin of Elizabeth's father named James, who was a watchmaker and the father of Jeremiah Horrocks, the astronomer who first calculated the transit of Venus. For the period 1580 to 1640, I have been unable to locate any Rev. James Horrocks in Lancashire Church Records. A thorough search of the enrollment records of Oxford and Cambridge Universities failed to produce a James Horrocks, who graduated between 1580 and 1620.
51. Thomas Horrocks was born in Bolton in 1614. He attended school at Bolton and was admitted as a sizar to St. John's College, Cambridge April 9, 1631. He took his B.A. degree in 1634 and M.A. in 1638. He was master of the Free School, Rumford, rector of Stapleford Tawny, and in 1650 was presented with the living of All Saints, Maldon. This he held until the restoration of Charles II when he was ejected and cast in the dungeon of the town prison. In 1650, he was made executor of his uncle's (Alexander Horrocks) will. He was several times indicted for holding conventicles. Later, he became a preacher to the Anabaptists of Hertford. He died at Battersea in about 1687. *Abstracted from Our English Parent Towns- Maldon by Oscar Fay Adams, Esq., of Boston, April 1908, pp 167*

52. Bailey, J. E. *The Rev. Alexander Horrocks of Dean, Westhoughton and Turton. The Palatine Note-book* III, (1883).
53. *Registers of the Parish Church of Wigan in the County of Lancaster Christenings, Burials and Weddings 1580-1625.* (Printed for the Lancashire Parish Register Society by Strowger & Son at the Clarence Press, 1899).
54. Heywood, O. *A Narrative of the Life and Death of the Rev. John Angier, Minister of the Gospel at Denton.* in vol. I (1827).
55. *Parish Registers of Boston in the County of Lincoln*
56. Venn, "Alumni Cantabrigienses."
57. *The Great Migration Begins: Immigrants to New England 1620-1633, Volumes I-III.* 'William Aspinwall'
58. At Harvard College, John Angier earned a BA in 1653 and an MA in 1655
59. Cotton, J. "Rev. John Cotton 1652: Earliest Wills on Record in Suffolk County." *The New England Historical and Genealogical*, V, 1–2 (1851).

BOSTON'S CONGREGATION

1. Cotton's pastoral workload for the twenty years he served as parish vicar was compiled and analyzed by the author from *The Parish Registers of Boston in the County of Lincoln.* by Besant, Frank. 1915. Edited by C W Foster. Vol. II. Horncastle: Lincoln Record Society.
2. *Parish Registers of Boston in the County of Lincoln*, pp 51
3. *Parish Registers of Boston in the County of Lincoln*, pp 54
4. *Parish Registers of Boston in the County of Lincoln*, pp 54
5. It was not uncommon for burials to follow baptisms in seventeenth-century England, as infant mortality then averaged fourteen percent. See- Payne, Lynda. 2015. "Health in England (16th–18th Centuries.)." *Children & Youth in History.* http://chnm.gmu.edu/cyh/primary-sources 166
6. Thompson, *The History and Antiquities of Boston.* pp 429
7. *Parish Registers of Boston in the County of Lincoln.* pp 45
8. Leverett, Charles Edward. *A Memoir Biographical and Genealogical, of Sir John Leverett, Knt., Governor of Massachusetts, 1673-79,* Boston: Crosby, Nichols and Company, 1856.
9. An usher is an assistant teacher in archaic British usage
10. Thompson, *The History and Antiquities of Boston.* pp 284-285
11. *Transcription of Minutes of the Corporation of Boston: Vol II.* pp 137
12. *Parish Registers of Boston in the County of Lincoln.* pp 57
13. *Transcription of Minutes of the Corporation of Boston: Vol II (1608-1638).* Vol. 2. pp 121-122
14. Holman, Mary Lovering, and Harriet Grace Scott. *Ancestors and Descendants of John Coney of Boston, England, and Boston, Massachusetts,* Rumford Press, 1928.
15. Triber, Jayne E. *A True Republican,* Univ of Massachusetts Press, 2001. 6-8
16. Parish Registers of Boston in the County of Lincoln. pp 54

NOTES

17. Brayton, John A. 2007. "Additions to the Ancestry of Sarah (Hawkred) (Story) (Cotton) Mather of Boston, Lincolnshire." *The Genealogist* 21 (1). Rockland, ME: 108–28. pp 198
18. Isabel Hawkred was 44 years old when she died after giving birth to a son, John.
19. *Parish Registers of Boston in the County of Lincoln.* pp 61
20. Venn, *"Alumni Cantabrigienses."*
21. Thompson, *The History and Antiquities of Boston.* pp 413
22. Thompson, *The History and Antiquities of Boston.* pp 153
23. Tertian ague was a form of malaria prevalent in the coastal marshes of England during the 16th and 17th centuries according to Dobson, Mary J, and Richard Smith. 2003. *Contours of Death and Disease in Early Modern England.* Cambridge University Press.

PURITANISM & CALVINISM

1. Ziff, Larzer. *The Career of John Cotton*, Princeton, NJ: Princeton University Press, 1962. 46
2. Bagley, George S. *Boston: Its Story & People*, Boston, Lincs.: The History of Boston Project, 1986. 71
3. "Neile, Richard". Dictionary of National Biography. London: Smith, Elder & Co. 1885–1900. pp 71
4. Rosenmeier, *'Spirituall Concupiscence': John Cotton's English Years, 1584-1633.* pp. 151-152
5. "Neile, Richard". Dictionary of National Biography. pp 71
6. Durant, Will, and Ariel Durant. 2011. *The Story of Civilization VII: the Age of Reason Begins.* Simon and Schuster.
7. The Thirty-Nine Articles of Religion of 1563, following the Act of Uniformity, defined the doctrine of the Church of England in response to controversies during the English Reformation. Articles 19 through 39 are known as 'The Anglican Articles' that established the Episcopal Polity of the church.
8. Ziff, Larzer. *The Career of John Cotton.* pp 18-22
9. Collinson, Patrick. 1967. *The Elizabethan Puritan Movement.* Routledge. 125
10. Peterson, Randall J.; Beeke, Joel R. (2013-02-10). Meet the Puritans (Kindle Location 6539). Reformation Heritage Books. Kindle Edition.
11. Mather, *Magnalia Christi Americana.* pp 254
12. Norton, *Abel Being Dead Yet Speaketh.* pp 29
13. Calvin, John. 1816. *Institutes of the Christian Religion.* Vol. III. Philadelphia: Philip H. Nicklin and Hezakiah Howe. Chapter 21
14. The other four tenets of Calvinism are total depravity of the human condition, limited atonement, conversion by irresistible grace, and perseverance of the saints.
15. Durston, Christopher, and Jacqueline Eales. 1996. *The Culture of English Puritanism, 1560-1700.* Edited by Christopher Durston and Jacqueline Eales. Macmillan. 7
16. Dever, Mark. 2000. *Richard Sibbes.* Mercer University Press. 30

17. Clarke, Samuel. 1662. "The Life and Death of Mr. John Cotton, Who Died an Christi 1652." In *A Collection of the Lives of Ten Eminent Divines*, 55–84. London: William Miller at the Guilded Acorn. pp 58
18. Mather, *Magnalia Christi Americana*. pp 255
19. Mather, *Magnalia Christi Americana*. pp 256
20. Bremer, Francis J. 1994. *Congregational Communion*. Boston: Northeastern University Press. 256
21. Bendall, Sarah, Christopher Brooke, and Patrick Collinson. 1999. *A History of Emmanuel College, Cambridge*. Woodbridge, Suffolk: Boydell Press. pp 191-192
22. Bremer, *Congregational Communion*. pp 5
23. Moore, Jonathan D. 2007. *English Hypothetical Universalism: John Preston and the Softening of Reformed Theology*. Wm. B. Eerdmans Publishing. P 5
24. Ball, *The Life of the Renowned Doctor Preston*. P 7
25. Venn, "Alumni Cantabrigienses."
26. Mather, *Magnalia Christi Americana*. pp 261
27. Fuller, Thomas, D.D. *The History of the Worthies of England*. Edited by P Austin Nuttal LL.D. Second. Vol. III, London: Thomas Tegg, 73 Cheapside, 1840. P 51
28. Young, M. *King James VI and I and the History of Homosexuality*, Basingstoke: Springer, 1999.
29. "Preston, John (1587-1628)". *Dictionary of National Biography*. London: Smith, Elder & Co. 1885–1900. [Note: Sir Ralph Freeman was related to John Preston and married a relative of Buckingham.]
30. Lockyer, Roger. *Buckingham*, Routledge, 2014. 114. ["*Those they called puritans were growing, and in Parliament were thought considerable...such that the King's affection might cool, and he [Buckingham] needed friends.*"]
31. Ball, *The Life of the Renowned Doctor Preston*. P 94 & 167-176. [Note: Lincoln Inn is one of four institutions constituting the Inns of Court. The other three are the Inner Temple, the Middle Temple, and Grey's Inn. Preston continued as Master of Emmanuel College until his death from tuberculosis in July 1628 at forty.]
32. Moore, *English Hypothetical Universalism*.
33. Gonzalez, Justo L. (2014). *The Story of Christianity*. Volume 2: The Reformation to the Present Day. HarperOne. ISBN 978-0-06-236490-6. [*Arminianism is related to Calvinism historically. However, because of their differences over the doctrines of divine predestination and election, many people view these schools of thought as opposed to each other. The distinction is whether God allows His desire to save all to be resisted by an individual's will (in the Arminian doctrine) or if God only desires to save some people and that his grace is irresistible to those God chooses to save.*]
34. Kenneth Fincham, Nicholas Tyacke, *Altars Restored: The Changing Face of English Religious Worship, 1547-c.1700* (2007), P 130
35. Lockyer, Roger. *Buckingham*, Routledge, 2014. P306
36. Moore, *English Hypothetical Universalism: John Preston and the Softening of Reformed Theology*.

NOTES

37. Feoffees for impropriations (*act.* 1625–1633), were a London-based group formally associated as a committee to buy up and dispense patronage of parish livings and to create new preaching appointments in the Church of England. Frustrated by what they saw as a lack of progress since the Reformation in supplying cures with educated and godly ministers and pulpits with frequent and effective sermons, the feoffees tapped a longstanding tradition of fundraising for pious charitable causes and exploited the large-scale sixteenth-century transfer of monastic property onto the open market and hence into lay hands. Their activities bypassed the episcopal hierarchy and especially antagonized those bishops who were of the increasingly influential ceremonialist or Arminian persuasion. This eventually led to their prosecution and suppression.
38. Fuller, T. *The church-history of Britain from the birth of Jesus Christ until the year M.DC.XLVIII.* (1655).
39. Larminie, Vivienne. "Feofees for Impropriations." *Oxford Dictionary of National Biography*, Oxford, May 28, 2015.
40. This was possible due to an oversight in the East India Company's Charter that gave each investor one vote rather than allocating votes by the number of shares owned.
41. Brenner, Robert. *Merchants and Revolution: Commercial Change, Political Conflict, and London's Overseas Traders, 1550-1653*, New York: Verso first published by University of Princeton Press, 2003. P 262 & 684
42. Brenner, *Merchants and Revolution.* pp 273-274
43. Van Duinen, Jared. "Prosopography and the Providence Island Company: the Nature of Puritan Opposition in 1630s England." In *Prosopography Approaches and Applications*, edited by K S B Keats-Rohan, 527–40, Oxford: Occasional Publications UPR, 2007.
44. Van Duinen, "Prosopography and the Providence Island Company"
45. Brenner, *Merchants and Revolution.* P 100

THE 1626 FORCED LOAN

1. Cust, "Charles I, the Privy Council, and the Forced Loan"
2. Pauline Croft, *King Charles I*, Palgrave Macmillan, 2008.
3. Phrase attributed to a Lincolnshire dissenter in Winship, *Hot Protestants* (2019).
4. Winship, *Godly Republicanism* P 190-191
5. Winship, *Godly Republicanism* P 191
6. The Privy Council is formally known as His/Her Majesty's Most Honourable Privy Council. It is comprised of senior members of the House of Lords and the House of Commons and formally advises the sovereign on the exercise of the Royal Prerogative.
7. Coke, John. *The Manuscripts of the Coke Family, of Melbourne, Co. Derby, Belonging to the Earl of Cowper, K.G., Preserved at Melbourne Hall.* Vol. III,

London: Printed for Her Majesty"s Stationery Office, by Eyre and Spottiswoode, Printers to the Queen"s Most Excellent Majesty, 1889.
8. Brenner, *Merchants and Revolution:* P 261-262
9. "Banbury: Introduction," in *A History of the County of Oxford: Volume 10, Banbury Hundred*, ed. Alan Crossley (London: Victoria County History, 1972), 5-18. *British History Online*, accessed October 26, 2017, http://www.british-history.ac.uk/vch/oxon/vol10 P 5-18.
10. "The Original Lists of Persons of Quality, Emigrants, Religious Exiles, Political Rebels, Serving Men Sold for a Term of Years, Apprentices, Children Stolen, Maidens Pressed, and Others Who Went From Great Britain to the American Plantations, 1600-1700." Edited by John Camden Hotten, London: Chatto and Windus, 1874.
11. "Fleet Prison - British History Online." *British-history.ac.uk*. Retrieved 2 August 2021. [Note: The Fleet Prison was built in 1197 near what is now Farringdon Street on the eastern bank of the River Fleet and was a special prison for Star Chamber offenders, including many dogged Puritans. After the abolition of Archbishop Laud's detestable Star Chamber court in 1641, the Fleet Prison was reserved for debtors and contempt of the Courts of Chancery, Common Pleas, and Exchequer. The prison burnt down in London's Great Fire and was finally demolished in 1846.]
12. Forsythe, James Neild (2000). *State of the Prisons in England, Scotland, and Wales, Not for the Debtor Only, But for Felons Also, and Other Less Criminal Offenders.* London: Routledge. [Note: Built-in 1370 as the gatehouse of Westminster Abby, the Gatehouse Prison was first used as a prison by the Abbot of Westminster Abbey. While imprisoned in the Gatehouse for petitioning to have the Clergy Act of 1640 annulled, Richard Lovelace wrote "To Althea, from Prison"—with its famous line—"Stone walls do not a prison make, Nor iron bars a cage." The prison was demolished in 1776.]
13. Hill, F., *Tudor and Stuart Lincoln.* (Cambridge University Press, 1956).
14. King, David, M.D. of Newport R.I., William Coddington: Resistance by him and others in Lincolnshire to the Royal Loan, 1626-7, *The New England Historical and Genealogical Register.* Boston, MA: New England Historical and Genealogical Society, 1847. P 138-143
15. *Records of the Governor and Company of the Massachusetts Bay in New England, 1628-1641, Vol. I.* P 14
16. Hardy, S. T. D. *Syllabus (in English) of the documents relating to England and other kingdoms contained in the Collection known as "Rymers' Fœdera."* vol. II (Longman & Co. and Trübner & Co., Paternoster Row, 1873).
17. *The Original Lists of Persons of Quality, Emigrants, Religious Exiles, Political Rebels, Serving Men Sold for a Term of Years, Apprentices, Children Stolen, Maidens Pressed, and Others Who Went From Great Britain to the American Plantations, 1600-1700.*
18. Cust, Richard (1985). "Charles I, the Privy Council, and the Forced Loan". *Journal of British Studies.* 24 P 208–235 [Note: In March 1627, Sir Thomas Darnel and four other knights, Sir John Corbet, Sir Walter Earl, Sir Edmund Hampden, and Sir John Hevingham were arrested by the order of King Charles I

NOTES

for refusing to contribute to the Forced Loan. The knights demanded that the crown show cause for their imprisonment or that they be released on bail. In November 1627, their appeal for a writ of habeas corpus was argued before the King's Bench. Counsel for the knights appealed mostly to medieval precedents, including clause 39 of the Magna Carta, which stipulated that no man should lose his liberty without due process of law.]

19. Hostettler, John (1997). *Sir Edward Coke: A Force for Freedom*. Barry Rose Law Publishers.
20. *Petition of Right*, Acts of Parliament in the National Archives, retrieved from https://www.legislation.gov.uk/aep/Cha1/3/1
21. *Petition of Right*, Acts of Parliament in the National Archives.
22. Hostettler, *Sir Edward Coke: A Force for Freedom*.

CLINTON EARLS OF LINCOLN

1. *The Complete Peerage*, vol. 7 (London, 1896), 671.
2. Norton, E. (2011). *Bessie Blount: The King's Mistress*. Amberley.
3. J. A. Froude, *History of England* (London, 1856), 219.
4. Norton, *Bessie Blount*.
5. Duffin, "Clinton, Edward Fiennes de, first earl of Lincoln (1512–1585)," *Oxford Dictionary of National Biography* (2004)
6. *Letters and Papers, Foreign and Domestic, Henry VIII*, vol. 11 (1536), ed. James Gairdner, nos. 778, 825, 892.
7. Fuller, *Worthies of England*, 1662.
8. Hall, John, *An Elizabethan Assassin: Theodore Paleologus: Seducer, Spy and Killer*. The History Press. (2015)
9. Gorges, Raymond, and Frederick Brown. *The Story of a Family Through Eleven Centuries, Illustrated by Portraits and Pedigrees*. Grace Gorges (private printing). Boston: D.P. Updike, The Merrymount Press, 1944. P 64 [Note: This quote is from Sir Arthur Gorges' comments to Robert Cecile regarding a letter sent to him by Henry Clinton, 2nd Earl of Lincoln. Arthur Gorges married Elizabeth Clinton, Henry Clinton's daughter, in 1597.]
10. Thrush, Andrew, and John P Ferris. *The House of Commons Members Database (1604-1629)*. Vol. 1, London: The Institute of Historical Research, 2010. Clinton, Sir Henry (d.1616) of Tattershall, Lincs. by N.M. Fuidge
11. Gould, J D. "The Inquisition of Depopulation of 1607 in Lincolnshire." *The English Historical Review* LXVII, no. CCLXIV (1952)
12. "Tattershall Castle, Lincolnshire; a Historical & Descriptive Survey by the Late Marquis Curzon of Kedleston, K. G., and H. Avray Tipping.," 1929. P 136
13. Sometime after 21 September 1584, the Earl of Huntington wrote that he hoped the match between Clinton and Knyvett would soon be settled. So Elizabeth Knyvett must have been born around 1570 and was fourteen when betrothed to Thomas Clinton. From- Travitsky, Betty S. *"Clinton [Née Knevitt], Elizabeth, Countess of Lincoln (1574?–1630?)*, Oxford Dictionary of National Biography

14. Parkinson, C N. *Gunpowder, Treason and Plot*, London: Weidenfeld & Nicholson, 1976. [*Note: On the evening of the 26th of October 1605, the Catholic Lord Monteagle received an anonymous letter warning him to stay away from Parliament during the opening, and to "retyre youre self into yowre contee whence yow maye expect the event in safti for ... they shall receyve a terrible blowe this parleament". Monteagle's letter was shown to King James. The King ordered Knyvet to conduct a search of the cellars underneath Parliament, which he carried out with Edmund Doubleday in the early hours of November 5th. Guy Fawkes was found by Knyvett leaving the cellar, shortly after midnight, and arrested. Inside, the barrels of gunpowder were discovered hidden under piles of firewood and coal.*]
15. Katherine Manners was selected by the formidably ambitious Mary Villers to marry her son, George Villiers. However, Manners was Roman Catholic, and the King refused to allow Villiers to marry her. In addition, the Earl of Rutland refused to accept the Countess of Buckingham's demands for a dowry. Manners converted to Protestantism to satisfy the Villiers family. Invited to visit the Countess of Buckingham, Katherine was forced to spend the night due to an attack of illness. Believing his daughter's honor to be compromised, the Earl of Rutland refused to receive her back and demanded that George Villiers marry her immediately. At this, Villiers refused to marry her, but did a few weeks later, on 16 May 1620. from *Katherine Villiers, Duchess of Buckingham*, Wikipedia
16. A 'marriage portion' is property (usually money) given to a woman at her marriage. Also called a Vide Dowry.
17. Travitsky, 'Clinton, Elizabeth, Countess of Lincoln'
18. Thrush, Andrew, and John P. Ferris. *The House of Commons Members Database (1604-1629)*. Vol. 1, London: The Institute of Historical Research, 2010. (Clinton, alias Fiennes, Thomas, Lord Clinton (c1568-1619) of Tattershall, Lincs. by Paula Watson & Rosemary Sgroi)
19. $5.7 million in today's dollars. In order to convert British currency of former generations to present-day American dollars; L. E. Davis and J. R. T. Hughes, "A Dollar-Sterling Exchange, 1803-1895," *Economic History Review*, 2nd ser. 13:1 (August 1960): 52-78; Douglas Jay, *Sterling: Its Use and Misuse, a Plea for Moderation* (London: Sidgwick & Jackson, 1985), esp. "Appendix: The Purchasing Power of the Pound Sterling 1264-1983."; John J. McCusker, *How Much is that in Real Money?: A Historical Price Index for Use as a Deflator of Money Values in the Economy of the United States*, reprinted from *Proceedings of the American Antiquarian Society* (101:2 [Oct. 1991]), Worcester, MA: American Antiquarian Society, 1992.
20. N. H. Keeble, 'Bradstreet, Anne (1612/13–1672)', *Oxford Dictionary of National Biography*, Oxford University Press, 2004; online edition, May 2014. [*Note: Keeble said, "On the recommendation of William Fiennes, first Viscount Saye, and Sele, in 1619, he (Dudley) became steward to Fiennes's future son-in-law Theophilus Clinton, fourth earl of Lincoln (c.1600–1667) at Sempringham, Lincolnshire."*]
21. A demensne is land attached to a manor and retained for the owner's use. The lands of an estate.

NOTES

22. Mather, Cotton. *The Life of Mr. T. Dudley, Several Times Governor of the Colony of Massachusetts*. Edited by Charles Deane, Cambridge: John Wilson and Son, 1870.
23. Jones, Augustine. *The Life and Work of Thomas Dudley the Second Governor of Massachusetts*, Cambridge, MA: Houghton, Mifflin and Co., 1900. P 40-41
24. Mather, C., *The Life of Mr. T. Dudley*.
25. Note: Dudley moved to Boston five years after becoming steward to the Earl of Lincoln and not nine or ten as stated by Mather.
26. Gray's Inn is one of the Inns of Court that functioned as a '3rd university' (after Oxford and Cambridge) to provide legal education to nobles and aspiring barristers. According to Wilfred Prest in *The Rise of the Barristers*, roughly twenty percent of barristers followed in the footsteps of their fathers in the 17th century. The Inns of Court had a monopoly on legal training up until the 19th century as until then the only law taught in English universities was ecclesiastical canon law. The four institutions comprising the Inns of Court are the Inner Temple, the Middle Temple, Lincoln's Inn, and Gray's Inn.
27. Fredrick V, Elector Palatine, married Elizabeth Stuart, sister of James I. Fredrick led the Protestant Union at the outbreak of the Thirty Years' War.
28. Jones, *The Life and Work of Thomas Dudley the Second Governor of Massachusetts*.
29. It is obvious that Cotton Mather had little understanding of the geography of England as Boston is north of London, so Dudley would not have "resolved himself, in his passing up to London" but rather in passing down to London. Cambridge is approximately halfway between Boston and London to the south.
30. Mather, *The Life of Mr. T. Dudley, Several Times Governor of the Colony of Massachusetts*. P 214-215
31. Under the influence of her companion, Marie de Rohan-Montbazon, the queen let herself be drawn into political opposition to Richelieu and became embroiled in several intrigues against his policies.
32. In: Van Strien, C D. *British Travellers in Holland During the Stuart Period*, Brill, 1993, page 30 states: "At eighteen leagues from Antwerp we came to the isle of Walcheren and pass by a block-house called Ramekins and then entered a strait channel which Brough us to Middleburg.
33. The lesser share or part, which in this case means "less than half"
34. Wilson, Arthur. "The Life and Reign of James, the First King of Great Britain." In *A Complete History of England*, London, 1706. P 789
35. Brenner, *Merchants and Revolution*. P 255
36. Frederick V, Elector Palatine, was a German Calvinist who married Elizabeth Stuart—sister to Charles I and daughter of James I of England. He is known as the "Winter King" because he reigned as King of Bohemia from the 4th of November 1619 until the Battle of White Mountain, where forces of the Holy Roman Empire defeated him on the 8th of November 1620. He fled with his family to the Dutch Republic, where he lived in exile at The Hague until his death.
37. Dudley, Joseph. "The Life of Mr. Thomas Dudley." *Proceedings of the Massachusetts Historical Society* XI (n.d.). (Note: Joseph Dudley incorrectly

assumed that the Earl of Lincoln was living at Sempringham when, in fact, his mother, the Dowager Countess, Lady Elizabeth, occupied Sempringham. The Earl and his wife moved to Tattershall soon after their marriage in 1623.)

38. The Palsgraves (during the Middle Ages) referred to the lord of a palatinate who exercised sovereign powers over his lands.
39. Cust, Richard. *Charles I: a Political Life,* London: Routledge, 2014.
40. "May 1649: An Act Declaring and Constituting the People of England to be a Commonwealth and Free-State." Firth, C.H & Rait, R.S., eds. (1911), P 122
41. The Massachusetts Bay Company's Royal Charter was issued on the 3rd of March 1628 in the Old Style Calendar in use at the time Thomas Dudley wrote to Lady Bridge, the Countess of Lincoln. The Old Style Calendar began the New Year on Lady Day, March 25th, and did not change to January 1st until the New Style Calendar was implemented in 1752. Dudley's reference to some *"in London and the West Country"* refers to two sets of stakeholders in what became the Massachusetts Bay Company: a group of London merchants under Matthew Craddock's leadership and what remained of the Dorchester Company under the leadership of Rev. John White and John Humfrey, who at the time was living in Boston and became friends with Thomas Dudley and Isaac Johnson, husband of Lady Arbella, sister of the Earl of Lincoln.
42. F. Hill, F., *Tudor and Stuart Lincoln.* (Cambridge University Press, 1956).
43. *Burke's Peerage, Baronetage & Knightage,* 107th edition, 3 volumes C. Mosley, editor, (Wilmington, Delaware, Genealogical Books Ltd, (2003)
44. *Burke's Peerage, Baronetage & Knightage,* 107th edition, 3 volumes.
45. Allen, T. *The History of the County of Lincoln.* vol. I (John Saunders, Jr., 1833).
46. Mather, *Magnalia Christi Americana.* p 126
47. Jones, A., *The Life and Work of Thomas Dudley* p-47

CLINTON MARRIAGES

1. Christy, Miller. "Attempts Toward Colonization: the Council for New England and the Merchant Venturers of Bristol, 1621-1623." Edited by J Franklin Jameson. *The American Historical Review* IV (1899). P 678–702.
2. The Gorges family were originally from Normandy. In the early 11th century, Henry III knighted Thomas de Gorges and appointed him warden of the Royal manor of Powerstock in Dorset. Gorges, Raymond, and Frederick Brown. *The Story of a Family Through Eleven Centuries, Illustrated by Portraits and Pedigrees.* Grace Gorges (private printing). Boston: D.P. Updike, The Merrymount Press, 1944. P 6-9
3. Like his uncle, Nicholas Gorges, Arthur served in the Navy and commanded the *War-Sprite* against the Spanish Armada.
4. Hasler, P W. "Gorges, Arthur (1557-1625), of Chelsea, Mdx.." Edited by Sir Lewis Namier. *The History of Parliament,* London. Accessed June 11, 2020.
5. The Virginia Company of London, also known as "The London Company," was formally established by James I's royal charter, granted April 10, 1606. The Second Virginia Charter of May 23, 1609, created a joint stock company—a

NOTES

group-invested business enterprise. Apparently, the buy-in price in May 1609 was £12 10s per share.

6. Stephenson, N W, and Lyon G Tyler. "Some Inner History of the Virginia Company." *The William and Mary Quarterly* 22 (1914). http://www.jstor.org/stable/1915253.
7. Bradford, William. *Of Plimoth Plantation*. Edited by Francis Bremer, Kenneth Minkema, and Jeremy Dupertuis Bangs. First. Boston: Colonial Society of Massachusetts and the New England Historical and Genealogical Society, 2020. P 139
8. Warwick & Gorges worked together to monopolize the colonization of New England. In 1606, James I established *The Virginia Company of London* and *The Virginia Company of Plymouth*. The London Company founded Jamestown and was primarily controlled by London merchants. The Plymouth Colony established the Popham Colony in 1607, and in 1620, was reorganized into the *Council of New England* under the control of Warwick and Gorges.
9. Ames, Azel. *The May-Flower and Her Log, July 15, 1620 - May 6, 1621*. Second. Boston: Houghton, Mifflin and Company; The Riverside Press, 1901.
10. Bradford, *Of Plimoth Plantation*. P 103-104
11. Dudley, Joseph. "The Life of Mr. Thomas Dudley." *Proceedings of the Massachusetts Historical Society XI*, 1869-1870, Boston. p 212
12. Jones, *The Life and Work of Thomas Dudley*. P 42 [*Note: William Fiennes, 8th Baron Saye, and Sele was created Viscount Saye and Sele. in 1624. The current Lord Saye is over 100 years old and lives at Broughton Castle, which was originally built in the 14th century. English actors Joseph and Ralph Fiennes are descendants of Frederick Twisleton-Wykeham-Fiennes, 16th Baron Saye, and Sele.*]
13. Theophilus Clinton was a 7th cousin twice removed to Bridget Fiennes.
14. Theophilus Clinton and his siblings were 7th cousins once removed to William Fiennes, Lord Saye & Sele (as was Lady Elizabeth Gorges, daughter of Sir Arthur Gorges). After Bridget Fiennes's death, Theophilus Clinton married Lady Elizabeth Gorges, who was his 1st cousin—being the daughter of his father's sister, Elizabeth (Clinton) Gorges.
15. Clinton, Elizabeth. *The Countesse of Lincolnes Nurserie*, Oxford: John Lichfield and James Short, Printers to the famous Universitie, 1622.
16. Curzon, George Nathaniel, and Tipping, Henry Avray. *Tattershall Castle, Lincolnshire; a Historical & Descriptive Survey*, London: Jonathan Cape, 1929.
17. Travitsky, "Clinton [Née Knevitt], Elizabeth, Countess of Lincoln (1574?–1630?), Noblewoman and Writer."
18. Following a series of disputes with Parliament over granting taxes, Charles I imposed *the forced loan* in 1626 and imprisoned those who refused to pay without trial. This was followed in 1628 by martial law, forcing private citizens to feed, clothe, and accommodate soldiers and sailors. This action implied the king could deprive any individual of property or freedom without justification. It united opposition at all levels of society, particularly those elements the monarchy depended on for financial support, collecting taxes, administering justice, etc., since wealth simply increased vulnerability. A committee in the

House of Commons prepared four resolutions declaring such actions illegal by re-affirming the Magna Carta and *habeas corpus*. Charles depended on the House of Lords for support against the Commons, but the House of Lords' willingness to work with the House of Commons forced him to accept the Petition. The Petition of Right passed on 7 June 1628, was part of a wider conflict between Parliament and the Stuart monarchy that led to the English Civil Wars (1638 to 1651) and was ultimately resolved by the Glorious Revolution in 1688.

19. Smith, David L., *'Fiennes, William, first Viscount Saye and Sele (1582–1662)',* Oxford Dictionary of National Biography, Oxford University Press, 2004.
20. Irons, E A. "Isaac Johnson: a Memoir." Edited by G Phillips. *The Rutland Magazine and County Historical Record,* Oakham, 1908. P 162
21. Thompson, Roger., 'Johnson, Isaac (bap. 1601, d. 1630)', Oxford Dictionary of National Biography, Oxford University Press, 2004; online edition, May 2006
22. *Lincoln Marriage Licenses: an Abstract of the Allegation Books Preserved in the Registry of the Bishop of Lincoln- 1598 -1628.* Edited by A Gibbons, London: Mitchell and Hughes, 1888.
23. Felton, E C. "Samuel Skelton, M.a., First Minister of the First Church at Salem, Mass.." *The New England Historical and Genealogical Register,* 53 (July 25, 2020. P 1–8.
24. Thompson, Pishey. "The Johnson Family." The New England Historical and Genealogical ... VIII (1854): 359–62—"*Extracts from a paper written by Abraham Johnson,*" *Gentleman and Esquire,*" *1638, and identified as his writing by a relative. The paper in possession of Wm Hopkinson, Esq., of Stamford, Lincolnshire."*
25. Venn, "Alumni Cantabrigienses."
26. Haven, *History of Grants Under the Great Council for New England.* P 28
27. Chartier, Craig S. "An Investigation Into Weston's Colony at Wessagusett." *Plymouth Archeology,* Weymouth, MA, March 2011. www.plymoutharch.com.
28. *History of Weymouth, Massachusetts,* Weymouth Historical Society Weymouth, Mass., 1923.
29. Thompson, 'Johnson, Isaac"
30. *Letter from John Humfrey to Isaac Johnson, 09 & 23 December 1630,* Papers of the Winthrop Family, Vol. 2: An Electronic Archive, Massachusetts Historical Society. In these letters, Humfrey refers to Isaac Johnson as "brother". [*Note:* Lady Susan's older sister, Arbella, married Isaac Johnson in 1623, and Humfrey became Johnson's brother-in-law after he married Lady Susan.]
31. *Records of the Council for New England.* (Press of John Wilson and Son, 1867) P 59
32. Winthrop, J. *Winthrop's Journal, "History of New England,"* 1630-1649. vol. I (Charles Scribner's Sons, 1908). *Page 127 (Note by editor James Kendall Hosmer)*
33. Calendar of State Papers, Domestic Series, of the Reign of Charles I, Her Majesty's Public Record Office, John Bruce 1858
34. Winthrop, *Winthrop's Journal,* P 333

NOTES

35. Lewis, Alonzo. *History of Lynn*. Press of J.H. Eastburn, 60 Congress Street, 1829.
36. Winthrop, *Winthrop's Journal*.
37. *Records of the Governor and Company of the Massachusetts Bay in New England: Vol. II, 1642-1649*. (William White, Printer to the Commonwealth, 1853). P 12-13
38. *Records of the Governor and Company of the Massachusetts Bay in New England: Vol. II, 1642-1649*. P 13
39. *Records of the Governor and Company of the Massachusetts Bay in New England: Vol. II, 1642-1649*. P 13
40. *Records of the Governor and Company of the Massachusetts Bay in New England: Vol. II, 1642-1649*. P 13
41. Gov. John Winthrop Papers P 216

PLANTERS & ADVENTURERS

1. Dudley, Thomas. "To the Right Honourable, My Very Good Lady, the Lady Bridget, Countess of Lincoln, March 28, 1630." In *First Planters of New-England, the End and Manner of Their Coming Thither, and Abode There: in Several Epistles*, edited by Joshua Scottow and Paul Royster, Lincoln, NB: Joshua Scottow Papers, Libraries at University of Nebraska-Lincoln, 2007.
2. Francis Bridges, a salter from Surrey; Richard Davis, a wine merchant from London; and George Harwood, a haberdasher from London. (See- Larminie, Vivienne. "Feofees for Impropriations." *Oxford Dictionary of National Biography*, Oxford, May 28, 2015.
3. Brenner, *Merchants and Revolution*. P 118
4. *Parish Registers of Boston in the County of Lincoln*. vol. II
5. Chester, J. L. Herbert Pelham, his ancestors and descendants. *The New England Historical and Genealogical Review*, (1879).
6. Oxford Dictionary of National Biography - Saltonstall, Sir Richard (1521?–1601). (2018) See The Pelham & West Families, page 153.
7. Register of admission to Gray's Inn, 1521-1889, together with the register of Marriages in Gray's Inn Chapel, 1695-1754. *Notes Queries* s7-VIII, 299–299 (1889).
8. *The Records of the Honorable Society of Lincoln's Inn, Vol. 1, Admissions 1420 - 1799*. vol. I (Society of Lincoln's Inn, 1896).
9. Watson, P. & Sgroi, R. Bellingham, Richard II, (c.1592-1672). in (The Institute of Historical Research, 2010).
10. Gorges, *The Story of a Family Through Eleven Centuries, Illustrated by Portraits and Pedigrees*. P 130
11. Samuel Haven notes that Edward Johnson, the colonial Massachusetts chronicler, reported Bellingham's role in drafting the Rosewell Grant.
12. Although Sir Henry Rosewell was not an original member of the Dorchester Company, he had purchased a knighthood from James I in February 1618 and, therefore, was listed foremost among patentees. Likewise, John Younge was not

429

a Dorchester Company member but was the son of the original member, Sir Walter Younge. Thomas Southcote was the only patentee who was an original member of the Dorchester Company.

13. Andrews, C. M., *The Colonial Period of American History*. vol. I P 357
14. Rose-Troup, *The Massachusetts Bay Company and Its Predecessors*.
15. Ball, *The Life of the Renowned Doctor Preston*. [Note: "So dear was Preston to Lord Saye, that Saye was at his side when Preston died of tuberculosis in 1628 and was named executor of Preston's Will."]
16. *Records of the Governor and Company of the Massachusetts Bay in New England, 1628-1641, Vol. I*. P 3
17. "Also, it beeing propounded by Mr. Coney, in behalfe of the Boston men, (whereof dyvers had pmised, though not in our booke underwritten, to adventure 400£ for the joint stock) that now there desire was that 10 psons of them might underwrite 25£ a man in the joint stock, they wthall pmisinge wth theise ships to adventure in there pticuler about 250£ more, and to puide abell men to send ouer for manadging the busissines; wch though it bee preiudiciall to the general stock, by the abatement of so much money thereout, yeet appearing realley to conduce more to the good of the plantation, wch is most desired, it was condiscended unto". - From original fragment of Massachusetts Bay Company Records dated March 2, 1629
18. *Transcription of Minutes of the Corporation of Boston: Vol II (1608-1638)* P 555
19. *Records of the Governor and Company of the Massachusetts Bay in New England, 1628-1641, Vol. I.* P 28
20. Aylmer, *The King's Servants: The Civil Service of Charles I, 1625-42*. p 304
21. Haven, *History of Grants Under the Great Council for New England*. p 29-30
22. For a joint stock company to be officially incorporated, receive a royal patent, and be given a monopoly to develop ventures in a particular geographic area required an ambassador to the crown (patents were not easy or inexpensive to obtain). In the case of the Massachusetts Bay Company, Lord Saye & Sele and the Earl of Warwick were called upon for support. This was the most powerful form of company and could raise the considerable capital needed for colonization - money for ships and supplies to support a settlement in its early years.
23. Winthrop Papers, Vol. 2, 1557-1649. P 329
24. Register of admission to Gray's Inn.
25. Winthrop Papers. P 29-30
26. Winthrop Journal, P 14
27. Rutman, *John Winthrop's Decision for America, 1629*. P 31
28. *Records of the Governor and Company of the Massachusetts Bay in New England, 1628-1641, Vol. I.* P 49
29. *Agreement of Cambridge, August 26, 1629*. Library of the Massachusetts Historical Society; Thomas Hutchinson, *Collection of Original Papers* (Boston, 1769) See the Cambridge Agreement in Original Documents.
30. *Records of the Governor and Company of the Massachusetts Bay in New England, 1628-1641, Vol. I.* P 48/49

NOTES

31. Robbins, W. G. The Massachusetts Bay Company: An Analysis of Motives. *Historian* 32, 83–98 (1969).
32. *Records of the Governor and Company of the Massachusetts Bay in New England, 1628-1641, Vol. I.* P 58
33. *Records of the Governor and Company of the Massachusetts Bay in New England, 1628-1641, Vol. I.* P 56
34. In 1606, James I established *The Virginia Company of London* and *The Virginia Company of Plymouth*. The London Company founded Jamestown and was primarily controlled by London merchants. The Plymouth Colony established the Popham Colony in 1607. In 1620, both companies were reorganized to form the *Council of New England* under the control of the Earl of Warwick and Sir Ferdinando Gorges.
35. *Records of the Governor and Company of the Massachusetts Bay in New England, 1628-1641, Vol. I.* P 59
36. Thompson, 'Johnson, Isaac (bap. 1601, d. 1630)', *Oxford Dictionary of National Biography*.
37. Letter from John Humfrey to Isaac Johnson, 09 & 23 December 1630, Papers of the Winthrop Family, Vol. 2: An Electronic Archive, Massachusetts Historical Society. In these letters, Humfrey refers to Isaac Johnson as "brother." [Note: Lady Susan's older sister, Arbella, had married Isaac Johnson in 1623, and Humfrey became Johnson's brother-*in-law after he married Lady Susan*.]

CITY ON A HILL

1. It is said that Cotton's sermon, *God's Promise to His Plantation*, gave birth to what became known as "American Exceptionalism". For a rather humorous treatment of this subject, see *The Wordy Shipmates* by Sarah Vowell.
2. Cotton, *God's Promise to His Plantation*.
3. Winthrop, *Journal of John Winthrop, 1630-1649*.
4. William Pelham's siblings (John, Elizabeth & Penelope Pelham) later migrated to Massachusetts on the *Susan & Ellen* in 1635. In 1641, Penelope married Richard Bellingham, Governor of Massachusetts, at age twenty-two.
5. Mather, *Magnalia Christi Americana*, P 262
6. *Transcription of Minutes of the Corporation of Boston: Vol II (1608-1638)*.
7. Bush, S. *The Correspondence of John Cotton*. (University of North Carolina Press, 2001). P180
8. *Transcription of Minutes of the Corporation of Boston: Vol II (1608-1638)*. P 630
9. Dudley, *To the Right Honorable, My very good Lady, The Lady Bridget, Countess of Lincoln*.
10. The Arabella, Jewell, Ambrose, and Talbot. The Arabella was the Flagship of the Fleet and was named after Arabella Clinton-Johnson, sister to the Earl of Lincoln, Theophilus Clinton, and wife of Isaac Johnson, the primary investor in the Massachusetts Bay Company.

11. The eight were: the *May-Flower*, the *Whale*, the *Hopewell*, the *William and Francis*, the *Trial*, the *Charles*, the *Success*, and the *Gift*.
12. The Lyon and Mary-John
13. One of the two was the Handmaid. The other of the two and the merchant ship names are unknown.
14. Meaning that they were provided for out of the new provisions.
15. Mather says the first settlers "called it *Salem* for the peace they had hoped in it." The Planter's Plea (page 14) seems to be a better authority and says its original name, *Naumkeag*, was changed to *Salem* "*though upon a faire ground in remembrance of a peace settled upon a conference at a general meeting between them and their neighbours, after expectancy of some dangerous jarre.*"
16. Dudley, *To the Right Honorable, My very good Lady, The Lady Bridget, Countess of Lincoln*.
17. Thompson, 'Johnson, Isaac'
18. *Records of the Governor and Company of the Massachusetts Bay in New England, 1628-1641, Vol. I.* P 75
19. Dudley, *To the Right Honorable, My very good Lady, The Lady Bridget, Countess of Lincoln*.
20. Winthrop, *Journal of John Winthrop, 1630-1649*.
21. Anderson, *The Winthrop Fleet*. P 10
22. Winthrop, *Winthrop's Journal, 1630-1649*
23. *Records of the First Church in Boston 1630-1868* (I). The Colonial Society of Massachusetts. (1961)
24. Winthrop, *Winthrop's Journal, 1630-1649*
25. *History of Boston Latin School – oldest public school in America*, Boston Latin School. Archived from the original on 2007-05-02. Retrieved 2022/9/18.
26. Hosmer, James K., *The Life of Young Sir Henry Vane: Governor of Massachusetts*, Houghton, Mifflin and Co., Boston & New York, 1889
27. Quincy, Josiah, *The History of Harvard University*, Crosby, Nichols, Lee, & Co., Boston, 1860
28. *Records of the Governor and Company of the Massachusetts Bay in New England, 1628-1641, Vol. I.* p 217
29. *Records of the Governor and Company of the Massachusetts Bay in New England, 1628-1641, Vol. I.* p 228
30. *Records of the Governor and Company of the Massachusetts Bay in New England, 1628-1641, Vol. I.* p 217
31. *Records of the Governor and Company of the Massachusetts Bay in New England, 1628-1641, Vol. I.* p 253
32. Morison, S. E. *Founding of Harvard College*. (Harvard University Press, 1935). p 232/233
33. *Records of the Governor and Company of the Massachusetts Bay in New England, 1642-1649, Vol. II.* p 275
34. Quincy, *The History of Harvard University*
35. *Records of the Governor and Company of the Massachusetts Bay in New England, 1642-1649, Vol. II.* p 217 Harvard College Record, Part I, 1636-1750,

NOTES

The University Press: John Wilson and Son, Cambridge, 1925: from Publications of the Colonial Society of Massachusetts, Vol XV, p 174

36. Winthrop, *Winthrop's Journal, 1630-1649*
37. Winthrop, *Winthrop's Journal, 1630-1649*
38. Winthrop, *Winthrop's Journal, 1630-1649*
39. Winthrop, *Winthrop's Journal, 1630-1649*
40. Britannica, T. Editors of Encyclopaedia. "Short Parliament." *Encyclopedia Britannica*, June 23, 2019. https://www.britannica.com/topic/Short-Parliament.
41. Charles I of England summoned what is now termed the Short Parliament (April 13–May 5, 1640) (the first to be summoned for 11 years, since 1629). Determined to impose the Anglican liturgy on the Scots, Charles sent an army northward in the first of the so-called Bishops' Wars. The campaign was abortive, and Charles then called a new parliament to grant the subsidies he desperately needed for a second campaign.
42. The Fifth Vial - Revelations (16:10-11) And the fifth angel poured out his vial upon the seat of the beast...
43. Thorton, John Wingate, *The Historical Relation of New England to the English Commonwealth*, Press of A. Mudge, Boston, 1874
44. Bremer, *Congregational Communion*.
45. Ziff, Larzer. *The Career of John Cotton*. pp 253
46. Note: rendered by the author in Biblical Greek known as Koine Greek (Greek: ἡ κοινὴ διάλεκτος), which literally means "the common dialect" or "the common language."
47. *The Gist of Carlye's Cromwell, being an abridgment with extracts of "Olivers Cromwell's Letters and Speeches, with elucidations by Thomas Carlyle"*, compiled by W.T. Stead, Mowbray House, London, 1899 p 68
48. Rogers, *Mary Dyer of Rhode Island, the Quaker Martyr*, p 61

POLITICAL STRIFE

1. *Love Letters: 2,000 Years of Romance*, edited by Andrea Clarke, published by the British Library in 2012, Note: "As both King James VI of Scotland and later as King of England, James I's sexuality and choice of male partners were the subject of gossip from the taverns to the Privy Council. When James inherited the English throne from Queen Elizabeth I in 1603, it openly joked that '*Rex fuit Elizabeth: nunc est regina Jacobus*' ('Elizabeth was King: now James is Queen')."
2. Tracy Borman, *The Stolen Crown* (2024).
3. William Camden, *Annales Rerum Anglicarum et Hibernicarum Regnante Elizabetha* (1615).
4. McElwee, *The Wisest Fool in Christendom: The Reign of King James I and VI*.
5. King James I, *The True Law of Free Monarchies*, 1598.
6. Stone, L. *The Crisis of the Aristocracy, 1558-1641*. (Oxford University Press, 1965).

7. Tracy Borman, *The Stolen Crown*, 2024.
8. Geoffrey Smith, "Sir Walter Raleigh and the Politics of Execution," *Journal of Early Modern England*, 2010.
9. Paulina Kewes, *The Oxford Handbook of Holinshed's Chronicles*, 2013.
10. Bergeron, D. M. *King James and Letters of Homoerotic Desire*. (University of Iowa Press, 2002). P 32-143
11. Hallam, H. (1827). *The Constitutional History of England from the Accession of Henry VII to the Death of George II*. Ward, Lock & Company.
12. Michael Winship, *Hot Protestants: A History of Puritanism in England and America*, Yale University Press, 2019.
13. Mark Kishlansky, *Parliamentary Selection: Social and Political Choice in Early Modern England*, Cambridge University Press, 1986.
14. Pauline Croft, *King Charles I*, Palgrave Macmillan, 2008.
15. Morrill, J. (2011, February 17). *Oliver Cromwell*. BBC History. https://www.bbc.co.uk/history/british/civil_war_revolution/cromwell_01.shtml
16. Adamson, J. (1990). Oliver Cromwell and the Long Parliament. In J. Morrill (Ed.), *Oliver Cromwell and the English Revolution*. Longman Publishing Group.
17. "The full proceedings of the High Court of Iustice against King Charles in Westminster Hall, on Saturday the 20 of January, 1648 together with the Kings reasons and speeches and his deportment on the scaffold before his execution / translated out of the Latine by J.C. ; hereunto is added a parallel of the late wars, being a relation of the five years Civill Wars of King Henry the 3d. with the event of that unnatural war, and by what means the kingdome was settled again." In the digital collection *Early English Books Online*. https://name.umdl.umich.edu/A40615.0001.001. University of Michigan Library Digital Collections. Accessed November 18, 2023.
18. DeLisle, L. *The White King: Charles I, Traitor, Murderer, Martyr*. (Public Affairs, Hachette Book Group, 2017).
19. Hobbes, T. *Leviathan or the Matter, Forme and Power of a Commonwealth, Ecclesiasticall and Civil*. printed by Andrew Crooke, London, 1651

RELIGIOUS STRIFE

1. Shown in today's dollars, equivalent to approximately £391 million in today's pounds sterling.
2. The Thirty-Nine Articles of Religion of 1563 following the Act of Uniformity defined the doctrine of the Church of England in response to controversies that during the English Reformation. Articles 19 through 39 are known as 'The Anglican Articles' that established the Episcopal Polity of the church.
3. Arminianism is a movement that took its name from Jacob Arminius (1560-1609), a Dutch theologian who challenged the Calvinist doctrine of predestination and instead focuses on the belief that salvation can be achieved through free will.

NOTES

4. The Star Chamber was notorious for judgments favorable to the Crown. For example, Archbishop Laud had William Prynne branded on both cheeks through its agency in 1637 for seditious libel. Early in the 1900s, Edgar Lee Masters commented: *"In the Star Chamber, the council could inflict any punishment short of death, and frequently sentenced objects of its wrath to the pillory, whipping and the cutting off of ears. ... With each embarrassment to arbitrary power the Star Chamber became emboldened to undertake further usurpation. ... The Star Chamber finally summoned juries before it for verdicts disagreeable to the government and fined and imprisoned them. It spread terrorism among those who were called to do constitutional acts. It imposed ruinous fines. It became the chief defense of Charles against assaults upon those usurpations which cost him his life."*
5. Prynne, William". *Dictionary of National Biography*. London: Smith, Elder & Co. 1885–1900. (Being pilloried was to be placed in stocks made of a wooden frame with holes for the head and hands that imprisoned an offender to public ridicule and abuse.)
6. An *ordinance of attainder* is a law that punishes a specific person or group without a judicial trial. The term comes from English law and was used to punish those who attempted to overthrow the government.
7. Pennington, D.H.. "William Laud". *Encyclopedia Britannica*, 21 Mar. 2024, https://www.britannica.com/biography/William-Laud. Accessed 13 August 2024.
8. Prynne, W. *Canterburies Doome, or the First Part of a Compleat History of the Commitment, Charge, Tryall, Condemnation, Execution of William Laud, Late Arch-bishop of Canterbury.* (printed by John Macock for Michael Spark, Sr. at the sign of the Blue Bible in Green Arbour, 1646) by Order of the House of Commons (4 Martii 1644)
9. George, D.M., *Catalogue of Political and Personal Satires; Preserved in the Department of Prints and Drawings in the British Museum.* Vols. 1–11 (British Museum).
10. a pillory is more commonly known as 'the stocks' and were wooden frames with holes for the head and hands in which prisoners were placed for public abuse.
11. Weale is archaic for commonwealth.
12. Massie, Allan. The Royal Stuarts. St. Martin's Publishing Group. Kindle Edition. P 187
13. Waterman, L. Wm. Laud, Archbishop of Canterbury and Martyr. *Notes Queries* s4-VI, 93–94 (1914).
14. Collinson, Patrick (1984). *The Religion of Protestants: The Church in English Society 1559–1625*. Oxford University Press. p. 90.
15. Laud, W. *The works of the Most Reverend Father in God, William Laud, sometime Lord Archbishop of Canterbury.* vol. III (John Henry Parker, 1853) p170

FAMILY TIES

1. Smith, David L., *'Fiennes, William, first Viscount Saye and Sele (1582–1662)'*, Oxford Dictionary of National Biography, Oxford University Press, 2004.
2. March 18th, 1628, Old Style (O.S.) equates to March 4th, 1629, in New Style (N.S.) In the 17th century, the new year started on the 25th of March (Lady Day), and dates were recorded in Old Style (O.S.) according to the Julian calendar. In this work, however, dates are rendered New Style (N.S.) to conform to the Gregorian calendar in modern use
3. Aylmer, G. E. (1961). *The King's Servants: The Civil Service of Charles I, 1625-42*. Columbia University Press. p 304
4. Gorges, *The Story of a Family Through Eleven Centuries, Illustrated by Portraits and Pedigrees*. P 6-9 [Note: The Gorges family were originally from Normandy and in the early 11th century. Henry III knighted Thomas de Gorges and appointed him warden of the Royal manor of Powerstock in Dorset.]
5. Van Duinen, "Prosopography and the Providence Island Company"
6. Kenyon, J. P. *The Stuarts: A study in English kingship*. (Fontana, 1970). P 50 & 55
7. Lee, Sidney, ed. (1893). "Manners, Francis." *Dictionary of National Biography*. Vol. 36. London: Smith, Elder & Co. P 49–50.
8. Villiers, George & Kathrine *Letters of the Duke and Duchess of Buckingham*. (Andesite Press, 2017).
9. Felton believed that his personal grievances against Buckingham were part of a larger picture of treacherous and wicked governance of England by the Duke. He resolved to kill Buckingham, and after saying goodbye to his family, he traveled to Portsmouth, where Buckingham was staying while planning to liberate La Rochelle. After being tried and found guilty, Felton was hanged at Tyburn on November 29, 1628.
10. Universal Review: XVII. *Original Letters illustrative of English History, including numerous Royal Letters from Autographs in the British Museum with notes by Henry Ellis, Esq.*, September 1824, P 132
11. Anderson, R. C. *Puritan Pedigrees*. (New England Historical and Genealogical Society, 2018).
12. Braddick, M. (2008). *God's Fury, England's Fire: A New History of the English Civil Wars* (1st ed.). Penguin Books Ltd.
13. Palmer, W. (2004). St John, Oliver. In *Oxford Dictionary of National Biography*. Oxford University Press. https://doi.org/10.1093/ref:odnb/24504
14. Whiting, W. (1873). Memoir of Rev. Samuel Whiting, D.D., and of His Wife, Elizabeth St. John, with References to Some of Their English Ancestors and American Descendants.(2nd ed.). Rand, Avery, & Company. p 36
15. Tyler, M. C. (1883). *A History of American Literature 1607-1676* (Vol. 1). G.P. Putnam's Sons.
16. Latin for *"From table and bed"*, but more commonly translated as *"from bed and board."* This phrase designates a divorce which is akin to a separation granted by a court whereby a husband and a wife are not legally obligated to live together,

NOTES

but their marriage has not been dissolved. Neither spouse has the right to remarry where there is a divorce *a mensa et thoro;* only parties who have been awarded a divorce *a vinculo matrimonii,* the more common type of divorce, can do so.

17. Watson, P. & Sgroi, R., *Irby, Sir Anthony* (1605-1682), *of Whaplode, Lincs. and Westminster. The History of Parliament: the House of Commons 1604-1629,* ed. Andrew Thrush and John P. Ferris, University of Cambridge Press, 2010
18. Hosmer, James K., *The Life of Young Sir Henry Vane: Governor of Massachusetts,* Houghton, Mifflin and Co., Boston & New York, 1889
19. Pepys, S. *The Diary of Samuel Pepys.* (1899).

SCHOOL TIES

1. Chart based on: 1) Venn, J. *Alumni Cantabrigienses: A Biographical List of All Known Students, Graduates and Holders of Office at the University of Cambridge, from the Earliest Times to 1900.* vol. 1 (2011). 2) Foster, J. *The Register of Admissions to Gray's Inn, 1521-1889.* (The Hansard Publishing Union, Ltd., 1889). and 3) *The Records of the Honorable Society of Lincoln's Inn, Vol. 1, Admissions 1420 - 1799.* vol. I (Society of Lincoln's Inn, 1896)
2. Prest, W. R. *The Rise of the Barristers.* (Clarendon Press, 1986).

COLONIAL MASTERMINDS

1. Brenner, *Merchants and Revolution.* P 684
2. Brenner, *Merchants and Revolution.* P 267
3. *Warwick Patent,* copied by John Talcott in 1631, Connecticut State Library, State Archives, Towns and Lands, Series 1, Vol. 1, Doc 5.

GODLY ALLIES

1. Donagan, B. The Clerical Patronage of Robert Rich, Second Earl of Warwick, 1619-1642. *Proceedings of the American Philosophical Society* (1976).
2. Brenner, *Merchants and Revolution.* P 263-264
3. Ball, Thomas. *The Life of the Renowned Doctor Preston (Authored 1628).* Edited by E W Harcourt, London: Parker and Co, 1885.

DORCHESTER REMNANTS

1. Lepionka, M. E. (2018). *The Settlement of Cape Ann: What is the Real Story?* Enduring Gloucester. https://enduringgloucester.com/2018/02/14/the-settlement-of-cape-ann-what-is-the-real-story/
2. Dudley, *To the Right Honourable, My Very Good Lady, the Lady Bridget, Countess of Lincoln.*

A TALE OF TWO BOSTONS

3. The important distinction between *adventures* and *planters* split the New England Company and later the Massachusetts Bay Company. The *adventurers* were investors that had no desire to leave England and settle in New England; whereas, the *planters* were primarily made up of men from Boston, Lincolnshire, whose sole purpose for joining in the venture was to migrate to New England.

LONDON TRADESMEN

1. Brenner, *Merchants and Revolution*. P 77
2. Brenner, *Merchants and Revolution:* P 135-36
3. Dudley, Thomas. "To the Right Honourable, My Very Good Lady, the Lady Bridget, Countess of Lincoln, March 28, 1630." In *First Planters of New-England, the End and Manner of Their Coming Thither, and Abode There: in Several Epistles*, edited by Joshua Scottow and Paul Royster, Lincoln, NB: Joshua Scottow Papers, Libraries at University of Nebraska-Lincoln, 2007.

TIMELINE

1. Winship, M. P. *Godly Republicanism: Puritans, Pilgrims, and a City on a Hill.* (Harvard University Press, 2012). Kindle Edition. p-190-191

MEMBERSHIP

1. The eleventh man from Boston was Rev. Samuel Skelton, who was recruited by the company to head the Salem church.
2. Brenner, *Merchants and Revolution.* P 118
3. *The Federal and State Constitutions, Colonial Charters, and Other Organic Laws of the State, Territories, and Colonies Now or Heretofore Forming the United States of America.* Edited by Francis Newton Thorpe. Vol. III (Kentucky - Massachusetts), Washington D.C.: Government Printing Office, 1909.
4. The charter of the Massachusetts Bay Company (1629) was unusual in that it failed to specify where the company would hold its annual meetings. The early stockholders used the loophole to hold the meetings not in England but in Boston, thus distancing themselves from supervision by the English government. The officers of the company who actually moved to Massachusetts decided in 1631 to expand the membership of the company by 116; later expansions had the effect of turning the company charter into a constitution. Massachusetts existed under this charter until 1683.
5. *The Federal and State Constitutions, Colonial Charters.*
6. Edward Johnson, the colonial Massachusetts chronicler, reported Bellingham's role in drafting the Rosewell Grant.
7. Haven 1869 xlviii
8. Haven 1869 xlix

NOTES

9. Haven1869 xlix
10. Haven1869 l
11. Haven1869 li
12. Haven1869 4
13. Haven1869 lxvi
14. See Isaac Johnson #7 in the section titled, THE BOSTON MEN.
15. Haven1869 lix
16. Haven1869 lv
17. Haven1869 lvi
18. Haven1869 lvi
19. Haven1869
20. Haven1869 lvii
21. Haven1869 lxviii-lxix (also see Bellingham #1 in the section titled, THE BOSTON MEN).
22. Haven1869 ix-xx
23. Haven1869 lxx-lxxi
24. Haven1869 lxxi-lxxii
25. Haven1869 lxxii-lxxiii
26. Haven1869 lxxiii-lxxiv
27. Haven1869 lxxiv-lxxvi
28. Haven1869 lxxvii
29. Haven1869 lxxviii
30. Haven1869 lxxix
31. Rose-Troup1930
32. Hughes-Penny, Robert, 2020, *Alderman Hughes-Penny,* City of London, 1/20/2022, <https://hughespenney.uk>
33. *Winthrop Papers, Vol. 1-5, 1557-1649.* (Online database. AmericanAncestors.org. New England Historic Genealogical Society, 2016.) *Originally published as: Winthrop Papers.* Boston: Massachusetts Historical Society, 1929.
34. Hughes-Penny2020
35. Brown, David, *Empire and enterprise: Money, power and the Adventurers for Irish land during the British Civil Wars.* Manchester University Press, 2020.
36. Rose-Troup1930-Chapter 16
37. Ibid.
38. Ibid.
39. Ibid.
40. Ibid.
41. Ibid.
42. Ibid.
43. See Simon Bradstreet #2 in the section titled, THE BOSTON MEN.
44. Haven1869 lxxiii-lxxiv
45. Rose-Troup1930-Chapter 16
46. Haven1869 lxxxvii-lxxxviii
47. Rose-Troup1930-Chapter 16
48. Ibid.

49. Russell, Michael. "Members of the Dorchester Company 1624-1626", Dorset Online Parish Clerks, Dec. 2021, https://www.opcdorset.org/fordingtondorset/
50. Rose-Troup1930- Chapter 16
51. Ibid.
52. See Family & School Ties, Pelham and West Families.
53. See William Coddington #3 in the section titled, THE BOSTON MEN.
54. Haven1869 xcvi
55. Rose-Troup1930- Chapter 16
56. Ibid.
57. Haven1869 lxxxii-lxxxiii
58. Haven1869 xc-xci
59. Haven1869 lxxxi
60. Bishop, K. and Healy, S., "Darley, Henry (1595/6-1671) of Scryingham, Yorks. and Gray's Inn Lane, London." The History of Parliament, London, (online), Accessed September 16, 2022
61. Bremer, F.J., "Davenport, John (bap. 1597, d/ 1670) minister in America", Oxford Dictionary of National Biography, Oxford University Press, 2004; online edition, May 2014
62. Rose-Troup1930-Chapter 16
63. Russell, Michael. "Members of the Dorchester Company 1624-1626", Dorset Online Parish Clerks, Dec. 2021, https://www.opcdorset.org/fordingtondorset/
64. Haven1869 cv
65. See Thomas Dudley #4 in the section titled, THE BOSTON MEN.
66. Rose-Troup1930-Chapter 16
67. See Charles Fiennes #5 in the section titled, THE BOSTON MEN.
68. Rose-Troup1930-Chapter 16
69. Haven1869 cii-ciii
70. Rose-Troup1930-Chapter 16
71. Haven1869 lxxxix
72. Rose-Troup1930-Chapter 16
73. Haven1869 lxxxix
74. Ibid.
75. Ibid.
76. Rose-Troup1930-Chapter 16
77. Ibid.
78. See Atherton Hough #6 in the section titled, THE BOSTON MEN.
79. "The Hubbard Family." FreePages.RootsWeb, https://freepages.rootsweb.com/~nyterry/genealogy/hubbard/hubbard.html, accessed April 20, 2023
80. Rose-Troup1930-Chapter 16
81. Ibid.
82. Ibid.
83. Ibid.
84. See Thomas Leverett #8 in the section titled, THE BOSTON MEN.
85. Haven1869 cxiii-cxiv
86. *Records of the Governor and Company of the Massachusetts Bay in New England, 1628-1641, Vol. I.* P 28

NOTES

87. Rose-Troup1930-Chapter 16
88. Ibid.
89. See Abraham Mellows #9 in the section titled, THE BOSTON MEN.
90. Rose-Troup1930-Chapter 16
91. Russell. "Members of the Dorchester Company 1624-1626", Dorset Online Parish Clerks, Dec. 2021, https://www.opcdorset.org/fordingtondorset/
92. Haven1869 cxi-cxii
93. Rose-Troup1930-Chapter 16
94. Haven1869 lxv-lxvi
95. *Records of the Governor and Company of the Massachusetts Bay in New England, 1628-1641, Vol. I.* P 78 & 128
96. See Herbert Pelham #10 in the section titled, THE BOSTON MEN.
97. *Records of the Governor and Company of the Massachusetts Bay in New England, 1628-1641, Vol. I* P 226
98. *Records of the Governor and Company of the Massachusetts Bay in New England, 1628-1641, Vol. I* P 333
99. *Records of the Governor and Company of the Massachusetts Bay in New England, 1628-1641, Vol. I* P 204, 262 & 371
100. Pestana, Carla Gardina, 'Peter, Hugh (bap. 1598, d. 1660)', Oxford Dictionary of National Biography, Oxford University Press, 2004
101. *Records of the Governor and Company of the Massachusetts Bay in New England, 1628-1641, Vol. I* P 80 & 366
102. Haven1869 cxx
103. Rose-Troup1930-Chapter 16
104. Ibid.
105. Ibid.
106. Hoadly, C. J., *The Warwick Patent.* (Hartford Press, 1902).
107. Haven1869 cix
108. Haven1869 xcvii-xcviii
109. Rose-Troup1930-Chapter 16
110. Haven1869 cix & cx
111. Anderson2015
112. Rose-Troup1930-Chapter 16
113. Ibid.
114. Ibid.
115. Haven1869 lix
116. Anderson2015
117. Rose-Troup1930-Chapter 16
118. Ibid.
119. Haven1869 lxxxix
120. Rose-Troup1930-Chapter 16
121. Harris, Charles Alexander, "Ward, Nathaniel (1578-1652). Dictionary of National Biography, 1885-1900, Volume 59
122. Rose-Troup1930-Chapter 16
123. Russell, "Members of the Dorchester Company 1624-1626"
124. Rose-Troup1930-Chapter 16

125. Ibid.
126. Ibid.
127. Haven1869 cvi-cviii
128. *Records of the Governor and Company of the Massachusetts Bay in New England, 1628-1641, Vol. I.* P 46
129. Rose-Troup1930-Chapter 16
130. Ibid.
131. Ibid.
132. Ibid.
133. Ibid.

ROYAL CHARTER

1. This four-point synthesis is a new interpretive contribution, developed through comparative reading of the 1620 charter, Council minutes, Gorges's *America Painted to the Life*, and Warwick's colonial papers. Earlier historians have noted these contradictions, but they have rarely integrated them into a single explanatory framework.
2. Council charter of 1620, in Deane, *Documentary History of Massachusetts*.
3. Ferdinando Gorges, *America Painted to the Life*, (London, 1658).
4. Haven, *History of Grants Under the Great Council for New England.* P 29
5. Haven, *History of Grants Under the Great Council for New England.* P 29
6. Andrews, C. M., *The Colonial Period of American History.* vol. I P 357
7. Rose-Troup, *The Massachusetts Bay Company and Its Predecessors.*
8. Chisholm, Hugh, ed. (1911). "Thomas Coventry". *Encyclopædia Britannica.* Vol. 7 (11th ed.). Cambridge University Press. pp. 340–341.
9. Clerk of the Petty Bag was a clerk in the Petty Bag office of the English Court of Chancery. The Petty Bag office dealt with common-law issues in the Court of Chancery and dated from as early as the 14th century, declining in importance towards the end of the 17th century. Its responsibilities were various, including dealing with suits against solicitors or attorneys and officers of the court itself, issuing writs for Parliamentary elections and the elections of bishops, summonses to Parliament, and enrolling solicitors of the court itself. It also concerned itself with patents for inventions. The name of the office stemmed from the practice of keeping records in small paper bags. (Source Wikipedia)
10. Aylmer, G. E. (1961). *The King's Servants: The Civil Service of Charles I, 1625-42.* Columbia University Press. p 303-305
11. *Records of the Governor and Company of the Massachusetts Bay in New England, 1628-1641, Vol. I.* P 39
12. *Records of the Governor and Company of the Massachusetts Bay in New England, 1628-1641, Vol. I.* P 52
13. *Records of the Governor and Company of the Massachusetts Bay in New England, 1628-1641, Vol. I.* P 56
14. In 1606, James I established *The Virginia Company of London* and *The Virginia Company of Plymouth.* The London Company founded Jamestown and was

NOTES

primarily controlled by London merchants. The Plymouth Colony established the Popham Colony in 1607. In 1620, both companies were reorganized to form the *Council of New England* under the control of the Earl of Warwick and Sir Ferdinando Gorges.

BOSTON MEN'S MOTIVES

1. John Guy, *Tudor England*, Oxford University Press, 1988.
2. James I, *The True Law of Free Monarchies*, 1598.
3. Colin Tite, *The Manuscript Library of Sir Robert Cotton*, 1994.
4. Mark Kishlansky, *Parliamentary Selection*, 1986.
5. J.H. Baker, *The Reinvention of Magna Carta*, 2000.

TUDOR ORIGINS OF MASSACHUSETTS

1. Elizabeth Norton, *Bessie Blount: The King's Mistress* (Stroud: Amberley Publishing, 2011).
2. Ibid.
3. *Letters and Papers, Henry VIII*, Vol. IV, Part I, ed. J.S. Brewer (London, 1875), entry 2373 (1525); *Calendar of Patent Rolls*, 17 Henry VIII.
4. G.R. Elton, *England Under the Tudors* (London: Methuen, 1955), 128–131; also Brewer, *Letters and Papers*, vol. 4.
5. Ibid.
6. Norton, *Bessie Blount*.
7. *Inquisitions Post Mortem*, Henry VIII period, Lincolnshire (Tailboys estates; Kyme holdings).
8. S.J. Duffin, "Clinton, Edward Fiennes de, first earl of Lincoln (1512–1585)," *Oxford Dictionary of National Biography* (Oxford, 2004).
9.
10. J.H. Baker, *An Introduction to English Legal History*, 4th ed. (London, 2002), 257–259.
11. *Letters and Papers*, Henry VIII, vol. 11, ed. James Gairdner (London, 1888), nos. 778, 825, 892.
12. *Letters and Papers*, Henry VIII, vol. 14, pt. 1, ed. James Gairdner (London, 1894), no. 364 (1539).
13. F. Hill, *Tudor and Stuart Lincoln* (Cambridge: Cambridge University Press, 1956).
14. Duffin, ODNB.
15. Idbid.
16. Thomas Fuller, *The Worthies of England* (London, 1662).
17. Hill, *Tudor and Stuart Lincoln*.
18. Duffin, ODNB.
19. Fuller, *Worthies*.
20. Hall, John, *An Elizabethan Assassin: Theodore Paleologus: Seducer, Spy and Killer*. The History Press. (2015)

21. John J. McCusker, *How Much is That in Real Money?* (Worcester, MA: American Antiquarian Society, 1992).
22. Cotton Mather, *The Life of Thomas Dudley*, ed. Charles Deane (Cambridge, 1870).
23. N.H. Keeble, "Bradstreet, Anne," *Oxford Dictionary of National Biography*.
24. *Oxford Dictionary of National Biography*, "Isaac Johnson."
25. *Oxford Dictionary of National Biography*, "John Humphrey."
26. *Records of the Governor and Company of the Massachusetts Bay in New England, 1628–1641*, Vol. I (Boston, 1853), pp. 3, 28, 49.
27. Dudley, Thomas. "To the Right Honourable, My Very Good Lady, the Lady Bridget, Countess of Lincoln, March 28, 1630." In *First Planters of New-England, the End and Manner of Their Coming Thither, and Abode There: in Several Epistles*, edited by Joshua Scottow and Paul Royster, Lincoln, NB: Joshua Scottow Papers, Libraries at University of Nebraska-Lincoln, 2007.

DUDLEY'S LETTER TO THE COUNTESS OF LINCOLN

1. Dudley, *To the Right Honourable, My Very Good Lady, the Lady Bridget, Countess of Lincoln, March 28, 1631.*

    Note: This copy of the Letter of Thomas Dudley to the Countess of Lincoln, written in March 1631, is the earliest complete printing of the text. It appeared in the New Hampshire Historical Collections, volume 4 (1834), pages 224-249. It was also issued separately in Concord, N.H., by Marsh, Capen, and Lyon that same year. Approximately three-quarters of the letter had previously appeared in 1696 in the volume published in Boston titled Massachusetts, or The First Planters, possibly compiled and edited by Joshua Scottow. This present text was printed from a manuscript discovered "by one of the Publishing Committee" bound in a copy of Edward Johnson's Wonder-Working Providence and Edward Winslow's New England Salamander Discovered. The editor of this text, John Farmer, suggests that this manuscript was the printer's copy for the text printed in 1696, relating that the excerpts are marked for the printer and correspond to the printed 1696 version.
2. 1631 in the Julian calendar. The convention of the double date (1630/31) omitted.
3. His name in Narragansets is Wonohasquaham.
4. His name in Narragansets is Montowampate. He died three years after the date of this letter. (Lewis, History of Lynn, p- 16 & 17)
5. Thomas Weston who established the settlement of Weymouth in May 1622. He eventually returned to England and died at Bristol.
6. Edward Winslow
7. Richard Wollaston
8. meaning what remained of the Dorchester Company
9. The Massachusetts Bay Company's Royal Charter was issued on 3rd of March 1628 in the Old Style Calendar in use at the time Thomas Dudley wrote to

NOTES

    Lady Bridge, the Countess of Lincoln. The Old Style Calendar began the New Year on Lady Day, March 25th and did not change to January 1st until the the New Style Calendar was implemented in 1752.

10. Charles I
11. The Planters Plea printed in London by William Jones in 1630 give the following account of Endicott's endeavor: "Master Endecott was sent over Governor assisted with a few men, and arriving in safety there, in September 1628, and uniting his own men with those which were formerly planted in the country, into one body; they made up in all not much above fiftie or sixtie persons. His prosperous Journey and safe arrival of himselfe and all his Company, and good report he sent backe of the Country, gave such encouragement to the worke, that more Adventurers joining with the first Undertakers, and all engaging themselves more deeply for the prosecution of the designe; they sent over the next yeare about three hundred persons more, most Servants, etc."
12. The Arabella, Jewell, Ambrose and Talbot. The Arabella was the Flagship of the Fleet and named after Arabella Clinton-Johnson, sister to the Earl of Lincoln, Theopilus Clinton and wife of Isaac Johnson, the primary investor in the Massachusetts Bay Company.
13. The May-Flower, Whale, Hopewell, William and Francis, Trial, Charles, Success and Gift.
14. The Lyon and Mary-John
15. One of the two was the Handmaid. The other of the two and the merchant ship names are unknown.
16. meaning that they were provided for out of the new provisions.
17. Cotton Mather (Magnalia Vol. I p62) says the first settlers "called it *Salem* for the peace they had hoped in it" but the Planter's Plea (page 14) seems to be a better authority and says its original name, *Naumkeag*, was changed to *Salem* "*though upon a faire ground in remembrance of a peace settled upon a conference at a general meeting between them and their neighbours, after expectancy of some dangerous jarre.*"
18. from the Mary & John
19. William Pierce, Master of the Lyon out of Bristol.
20. later called the New Towne and afterwards, Cambridge.
21. For 1,000 years, until recent times, there were 12 pennies or pence to a shilling and 20 shillings to a Pound Sterling, the monetary denomination of the time. A Pound Sterling, £1, meaning then about a pound of silver, was worth about the equivalent purchasing power of the modern US$1,000.
22. Value of the stock in the London exchange.
23. Samuel Maverick, who resided on Noddle's Island. He came over several years before Dudley did and was very useful to th early emigrants. According to Joselyn, he was "the only hospitable man in all the country, giving entertainment to all comers gratis." Maverick died March 10, 1664.
24. a small boat, with sails or oars, forming part of the equipment of a warship or other large vessel.
25. trade

445

26. Martha's Vineyard
27. a heavy stone used by small craft as an anchor.
28. This rendering of Bristol was common among the first settlers of Massachusetts and the spelling conforms somewhat closely with the Saxon pronunciation, which was *Brightstow*.
29. the English Channel
30. enemy Spanish vessels from the Flemish coast
31. "far from his thunderbolt" from the Latin proverb: Procul a Jove, procul a fulmine or "Far from Jupiter, far from his thunderbolt". Construction is similar to procul ex coulis, procul ex meant or "out of sight, out of mind".
32. soldiers
33. musket
34. secretive
35. passenger pigeons, a species that is now extinct
36. turtle doves
37. expense of shipping & handling

CHARTER OF THE GREAT COUNCIL FOR NEW ENGLAND

1. *The Federal and State Constitutions Colonial Charters, and Other Organic Laws of the States, Territories, and Colonies Now or Heretofore Forming the United States of America* Compiled and Edited Under the Act of Congress of June 30, 1906, by Francis Newton Thorpe, Washington, DC: Government Printing Office, 1909.

GRANTS UNDER THE GREAT COUNCIL FOR NEW ENGLAND

1. When Captain John Smith visited the Susquehanna Indians, in 1608, they had utensils of iron and brass, which, by their own account, originally came from the French of Canada.
2. The superior naval advancement of Italy at that period is illustrated by the fact that the leaders of discovery in the western hemisphere — Columbus in the service of Spain, Cabot in the service of England, Vespucius in the service of Portugal, and Verrazano in the service of France — were Italians.
3. An estate of the highest nature that a subject under any government can receive and hold." — Sullivan, Land Titles in Massachusetts, p. 36.
4. Brief Relation of the President and Council. In Mass. Hist. Soc. Col., vol. xix
5. Historians have stated, without giving any authority, that the Connecticut territory was granted by the Council to Warwick in 1630 and even that it was confirmed to him by the King. But the Council Records show that "a rough draft" of a patent for the Earl of Warwick, relating to the same territory, was under consideration three months after his conveyance to Lord Say and Sele.
6. Willis, in Hist. of Portland.

NOTES

7. This is added from the Council Records.
8. Dr. Palfrey (Hist. of N. E., vol. i. p. 808) refers to the probable purpose of a renovated England in America entertained by the Puritan leaders, in view of the clouds that were gathering over the political prospects at home; and quotes a remark of Chg, of Burke, to whom the same reflection had occurred. See also Hist. of N. E., vol. i. p. 390, n.

PETITION OF RIGHT

1. Coke, J. (1627). *The Petition of Right*. Legislation of Parliament. https://www.legislation.gov.uk/aep/Cha1/3/1
2. J.H. Baker, *The Reinvention of Magna Carta*, Cambridge University Press, 2000.
3. Michael Winship, *Hot Protestants*, Yale University Press, 2019.
4. Mark Kishlansky, *Parliamentary Selection*, Cambridge University Press, 1986.
5. Colin Tite, *The Manuscript Library of Sir Robert Cotton*, British Library, 1994.
6. J.H. Baker, *The Reinvention of Magna Carta*, Cambridge University Press, 2000
7. Glenn Burgess, *British Political Thought, 1500–1660*, Macmillan, 1999.

MASSACHUSETTS BAY COMPANY ROYAL CHARTER

1. *The Federal and State Constitutions Colonial Charters, and Other Organic Laws of the States, Territories, and Colonies Now or Heretofore Forming the United States of America* Compiled and Edited Under the Act of Congress of June 30, 1906, by Francis Newton Thorpe, Washington, DC: Government Printing Office, 1909

CAMBRIDGE AGREEMENT

1. *Agreement of Cambridge, August 26, 1629*. Library of the Massachusetts Historical Society; Thomas Hutchinson, *Collection of Original Papers* (Boston, 1769)
2. Archaic spelling has been rendered into modern English for ease of reading.
3. Nicholas West and Kellam Browne are the only two signers of the Cambridge Agreement that did not migrate to New England and little is known about them.

HUMBLE REQUEST

1. Humble Request. In. Joshua Scottow Papers, Libraries at University of Nebraska-Lincoln. (1696).
2. Text has been rendered into modern English to facilitate reading.

A TALE OF TWO BOSTONS

JAMES I & WITCHCRAFT

1. James Sharpe, *Instruments of Darkness: Witchcraft in Early Modern England*, 1996.
2. Norman Cohn, *Europe's Inner Demons*, 1975.
3. Parliament of England, Witchcraft Act of 1563.
4. Lawrence Normand and Gareth Roberts, *Witchcraft in Early Modern Scotland*, 2000.
5. Marion Gibson, *Reading Witchcraft*, 1999.
6. Parliament of England, Witchcraft Acts of 1563 and 1604.
7. Massachusetts Body of Liberties, 1641.

JAMES I - PUBLISHED WORKS

1. James I, *Basilikon Doron*, 1599.
2. James I, *The True Law of Free Monarchies*, 1598.
3. James I, *Daemonologie*, 1597.
4. James I, *An Apologie for the Oath of Allegiance*, 1608.

THOMAS KNYVETT & THE GUNPOWDER PLOT

1. John Guy, *The Reign of James I*, Oxford University Press, 2014.
2. David Cressy, *Dangerous Talk: Scandalous, Seditious, and Treasonable Speech in Pre-Modern England*, Oxford University Press, 2010.
3. Pauline Croft, "The State Papers and the Gunpowder Plot," *Historical Journal*, 1997.

BIBLIOGRAPHY

PRIMARY SOURCES

Agreement of Cambridge, August 26, 1629. Library of the Massachusetts Historical Society; Thomas Hutchinson, *Collection of Original Papers* (Boston, 1769)

Angier, J. (1896). John Angier Will in Genealogical Gleanings In England. *The New England Historical and Genealogical Register*, 50

Barnfield, Richard. *Dedication to The Affectionate Shepherd.* London, 1594.

Baynes, Paul. *A Counterbane against Earthly Carefulnes.* London, 1619.

Baynes, Paul. *Holy Helper in God's Building.* London, 1618.

Baynes, Paul. *A Discourse on the Lord's Prayer.* London, 1619.

Baynes, Paul. *The Diocesans Tryall.* London, 1621.

Baynes, Paul. *Help to True Happiness.* London, 1635.

Baynes, Paul. *Commentary on Colossians.* London, 1635.

Boston Births, Baptisms, Marriages and Deaths, 1630-1699. City of Boston. (1883)

Bradford, William. *Of Plimoth Plantation.* Edited by Francis Bremer, Kenneth Minkema, and Jeremy Dupertuis

Bradstreet, A. (1867). *The Works of Anne Bradstreet in Prose and Verse.* Abram E. Cutter.

Calendar of State Papers, Domestic Series, of the Reign of Charles I, Her Majesty's Public Record Office, John Bruce, 1858

Calvin, John. 1816. *Institutes of the Christian Religion.* Vol. III. Philadelphia: Philip H. Nicklin and Hezekiah Howe.

Camden, William. *Annales Rerum Anglicarum et Hibernicarum Regnante Elizabetha.* London, 1615.

"Cicely Chaderton to Isaac Johnson." (Aug. 24, 1625), Winthrop Papers, Vol. 1-5, 1557-1649. Winthrop Papers Digital Collection, Massachusetts Historical Society

Clinton, Elizabeth. "The Countess of Lincoln's Nursery." In C. F. Otten (Ed.). University Press of Florida. Retrieved from http://www.worldcat.org/title/english-womens-voices-1540-1700/oclc/7161084510 (1992)

Coke, John, *The Manuscripts of the Coke Family, of Melbourne, Co. Derby, Belonging to the Earl of Cowper, K.G., Preserved at Melbourne Hall. Vol. III,* London: Printed for Her Majesty's Stationery Office, by Eyre and Spottiswoode, Printers to the Queen's Most Excellent Majesty, 1889

Coke, J. (1627). *The Petition of Right*. Legislation of Parliament. https://www.legislation.gov.uk/aep/Cha1/3/1

Cotton, J., *A Brief Exposition of the Whole Book of Canticles, or Song of Solomon*. (1642)

Cotton, J., *God's Promise to His Plantation. As it was delivered in a Sermon by John Cotton, B.D., and preacher of God's word in Boston*. (1630)

Cotton, J., *Milk for Babes. Drawn Out of the Breasts of Both Testaments. Chiefly, for the Spirituall Nourishment of Boston Babes in Either England: But May Be of Like Use for Any Children*. (1646)

Cotton, J. *The Bloudy Tenent, Washed and Made White in the Bloud of the Lambe*. (1647)

Cotton, J., "John Cotton to Sarah Hawkred Story Cotton, October 3, 1632." S. B. Jr. (Ed.), (P.173 - 175). University of North Carolina Press. 2001

Cotton, J. "Rev. John Cotton 1652: Earliest Wills on Record in Suffolk County." *The New England Historical and Genealogical,* **V**, 1–2 (1851).

Court Records at the Rhode Island State Archives: https://www.sos.ri.gov/divisions/state-archives

Declaration of Sports (1633), authorized by Charles I, promoted by Laud.

Federal and State Constitutions, Colonial Charters, and Other Organic Laws of the States, Territories, and Colonies Now or Heretofore Forming the United States of America Compiled and Edited Under the Act of Congress of June 30, 1906, by Francis Newton Thorpe, Washington, DC: Government Printing Office, 1909.

Foster, J., *The Register of Admissions to Gray's Inn, 1521-1889*. The Hansard Publishing Union, Ltd. 1889

Goodwin, Thomas. Testimony in Works of Thomas Goodwin. London, 1681.

Harvard College Record, Part I, 1636-1750, The University Press: John Wilson and Son, Cambridge, 1925: from Publications of the Colonial Society of Massachusetts, Vol XV

Hawthorne, Nathaniel. *Grandfather's Chair: A History for Youth.* Boston: E.P. Peabody. New York: Wiley & Putnam, 1841.

Hawthorne, Nathaniel. *The Scarlet Letter: A Romance.* Ticknor, Reed, and Fields, Boston, 1850.

HMC Reports on various manuscripts: William Cleverly Alexander, vol. 3 (London, 1904)

Hobbes, T. *Leviathan or the Matter, Forme, and Power of a Commonwealth, Ecclesiasticall, and Civil.* printed by Andrew Crooke, London, 1651

Horrocks, A. *Will of Alexander Horrocks.*

Humble Request. In. Joshua Scottow Papers, Libraries at the University of Nebraska-Lincoln. (1696)

BIBLIOGRAPHY

Journal of the House of Lords: Volume 3, 1620-1628 (III). His Majesty's Stationery Office. Retrieved from http://www.british-history.ac.uk/ (1767)

Laud, W. (1853). *The works of the Most Reverend Father in God, William Laud, sometime Lord Archbishop of Canterbury* (III). Oxford: John Henry Parker.

"Letter from John to Isaac Johnson, 09 & 23 December 1630", Papers of the Winthrop Family, Vol. 2: An Electronic Archive, Massachusetts Historical Society.

Letters and Papers, Foreign and Domestic, of the Reign of Henry VIII, vols. 10–12.

Lincoln Marriage Licenses: an Abstract of the Allegation Books Preserved in the Registry of the Bishop of Lincoln- 1598 -1628. Edited by A. Gibbons, London: Mitchell and Hughes, 1888.

Longfellow, H.W., The New-England Tradgies, Ticknor and Fields, Boston. (1868

Mather, C., *Magnalia Christi Americana* (I). Silus Andrus and Son. (1820)

Mather, C., *The Life of Mr. T. Dudley, Several Times Governor of the Colony of Massachusetts*. John Wilson and Son. (1870)

Mather, C., *Diary of Cotton Mather, 1681-1724: 1681-1708*. Massachusetts Historical Society. (1911)

Massachusetts General Court. *The Body of Liberties*, 1641.

Original Lists of Persons of Quality, Emigrants, Religious Exiles, Political Rebels, Serving Men Sold for a Term of Years, Apprentices, Children Stolen, Maidens Pressed, and Others Who Went From Great Britain to the American Plantations, 1600-1700. Edited by John Camden Hotten, London: Chatto and Windus, 1874

Parliament of England. Witchcraft Acts of 1563 and 1604.

Parish Registers of Boston in the County of Lincoln (Vol. I). edited by Besant, F. (1914). Lincoln Record Society.

Parish Registers of Boston in the County of Lincoln (Vol. II). edited by Besant, F. (1915). Lincoln Record Society.

Pepys, S., *The Diary of Samuel Pepys*. (1899)

Perkins, William. *The Arte of Prophesying*. London, 1592; reprint, Banner of Truth Trust, 1996.

Perkins, William. *A Reformed Catholike*. London, 1597.

Perkins, William. *A Golden Chaine*. London, 1591.

Perkins, William. *The Works of William Perkins*. 3 vols. Cambridge, 1603–1618.

Peter, Hugh. *God's Doings and Man's Duty*. London, 1646.

Peter, Hugh. A Word for the Army. London, 1647.

Peter, Hugh. Good Work for a Good Magistrate. London, 1651.

Peter, Hugh. *Dying Father's Last Legacy*. London, 1660.

Petition of Right, Acts of Parliament in the National Archives, retrieved from https://www.legislation.gov.uk/aep/Cha1/3/1

Prynne, W. (1646). *Canterburies Doome, or the First Part of a Compleat History of the Commitment, Charge, Tryall, Condemnation, Execution of William Laud, Late Archbishop of Canterbury.* printed by John Macock for Michael Spark, Sr., at the sign of the Blue Bible in Green Arbour.

Prynne, William. *Histriomastix.* (London, 1632); State Trials, vol. 3, 1637 proceedings.

Records of the First Church in Boston 1630-1868 (I). The Colonial Society of Massachusetts. (1961)

Records of the 1st Church in Salem, Massachusetts, 1629-1736. (1974)

Records of the Court of Assistants of the Colony of the Massachusetts Bay, 1630- 1692 - Vol I (I). Suffolk County

Records of the Court of Assistants of the Colony of the Massachusetts Bay, 1630-1692 - Vol II (II). Suffolk County

Records of the Governor and Company of the Massachusetts Bay in New England, 1628-1641, Vol. I. (Shurtleff, Nathaniel Bradstreet, 1810-1874. ed; Massachusetts. General Court), Boston, W. White, printer to the Commonwealth.

Records of the Governor and Company of the Massachusetts Bay in New England, 1642-1649, Vol. II. (Shurtleff, Nathaniel Bradstreet, 1810-1874. ed; Massachusetts. General Court), Boston, W. White, printer to the Commonwealth.

Records of the Governor and Company of the Massachusetts Bay in New England, 1644-1657, Vol. III. (Shurtleff, Nathaniel Bradstreet, 1810-1874. ed; Massachusetts. General Court), Boston, W. White, printer to the Commonwealth.

Records of the Governor and Company of the Massachusetts Bay in New England, 1644-1657, Vol. IV-Part I. (Shurtleff, Nathaniel Bradstreet, 1810-1874. ed; Massachusetts. General Court), Boston, W. White, printer to the Commonwealth.

Records of the Honorable Society of Lincoln's Inn, Vol. 1, Admissions 1420 - 1799 (I). Society of Lincoln's Inn. (1896)

Records of the Island of Rhode Island, March 7, 1638-March 12, 1644

Records of the Parish of Holy Trinity, Balsham: Marriages 1558-1994. Cambridgeshire Archives.

Register of admission to Gray's Inn, 1521-1889, together with Marriages in Gray's Inn Chapel, 1695-1754. *Notes Queries* s7-VIII, 299–299 (1889)

Registers of the Parish of Wigan in the County of Lancaster: Christenings, burials, and weddings, 1580-1625. Stowger & Son. (1899)

"Rev. Alexander Horrocks of Dean, Westhoughton & Turton." *The Palatine Notebook for 1883, III,* (1883)

BIBLIOGRAPHY

Sibbes, Richard. *The Bruised Reed and Smoking Flax.* London, 1630.
Sibbes, Richard. *The Soules Conflict.* London, 1635.
Sibbes, Richard. *The Saint's Cordial.* London, 1629.
Sibbes, Richard. *Works.* 7 vols. Edinburgh, 1862–64.
Sigourney, L.H., "Lady Arbella Johnson." *The Religious Souvenir*, Schofield & Voorhies, New York, (1839)
State Trials. Vols. 3–4. London, 1730.
Stuart, J. *An Apologie for the Oath of Allegiance.* London, 1608.
Stuart, J. *Basilikon Doron* (Βασιλικὸν Δῶρον), Imprinted in London by Felix Kyngston, for John Norton, according to the copy printed at Edinburgh. 1603
Stuart, J. *Daemonologie.* Edinburgh, 1597.
Stuart, J., *The True Lawe of Free Monarchies*, printed by Robert Waldegrave, printer to the King's Majestie, Anno Dom. 1598, cum Piviegio Regio, Edingurgh
Sidney, Philip. *Astrophel and Stella.* London, 1591.
The full proceedings of the High Court of Justice against King Charles in Westminster Hall, on Saturday the 20 of January 1648 together with the King's reasons and speeches and his deportment on the scaffold before his execution / translated out of the Latine by J.C.; hereunto is added a parallel of the late wars, being a relation of the five years Civill Wars of King Henry the 3d. with the event of that unnatural war, and by what means the kingdome was settled again. In the digital collection *Early English Books Online.* https://name.umdl.umich.edu/A40615.0001.001. University of Michigan Library Digital Collections. Accessed November 18, 2024.
The Gist of Carlye's Cromwell, being an abridgment with extracts of "Oliver Cromwell's Letters and Speeches, with elucidations by Thomas Carlyle", compiled by W.T. Stead, Mowbray House, London, 1899
Transcription of Minutes of the Corporation of Boston: Vol II (1608-1638) Bailey, J. F. (Ed.) (1981). History of Boston Project.
Tuckney, Anthony. *Balm of Gilead for the Wounds of England.* London, 1643.
Tuckney, Anthony. *Catechism.* London, 1628.
Tuckney, Anthony. *Death Disarmed.* London, 1653.
Tuckney, Anthony. *Eight Letters to Benjamin Whichcote.* London, 1753.
Tuckney, Anthony. *Forty Sermons.* London, 1676.
Tuckney, Anthony. *Praelectiones Theologicae.* Amsterdam, 1679.
Universal Review: *XVII. Original Letters illustrative of English History, including numerous Royal Letters from Autographs in the British Museum with notes by Henry Ellis, Esq.*, September 1824, p. 132
Vane, H. (1642). "Speech by Sir Henry Vane." In C. O. T. K. Bench, Thomas (Ed.).

Venn, J., *Alumni Cantabrigienses: A Biographical List of All Known Students, Graduates, and Holders of Office at the University of Cambridge, from the Earliest Times to 1900*

Villiers, G., & Kathrine, *Letters of the Duke and Duchess of Buckingham*. Andesite Press. (2017)

Warwick Patent, copied by John Talcott in 1631, Connecticut State Library, State Archives, Towns and Lands, Series 1, Vol. 1, Doc 5.

Winthrop, J. (1908). *Winthrop's Journal, "History of New England," 1630-1649*

Winthrop Papers, Vol. 1-5, 1557-1649. *(Online database. AmericanAncestors.org. New England Historic Genealogical Society, 2016.)* Published initially as Winthrop Papers. Boston: Massachusetts Historical Society, 1929.

BIBLIOGRAPHY

SECONDARY SOURCES

Abernethy, Susan. *"Elizabeth Blount, Royal Mistress."* The Freelance History Writer (online).

Adams, Oscar Fay. 1908. "Our English Parent Towns: Maldon." Edited by F. Apthrop Foster. The New England Historical and Genealogical Register.

Adamson, J. (1990). Oliver Cromwell and the Long Parliament. In J. Morrill (Ed.), *Oliver Cromwell and the English Revolution*. Longman Publishing Group.

Ames, Azel. *The May-Flower and Her Log, July 15, 1620 - May 6, 1621*. Second. Boston: Houghton, Mifflin and Company; The Riverside Press, 1901

Anderson, R. C., *Charles Fiennes.* (Great Migration Newsletter, V.1-25, 2015)

Anderson, R. C., *Puritan Pedigrees.* (New England Historical and Genealogical Society, 2018)

Anderson, R. C., *The Great Migration Directory: Immigrants to New England, 1620-1640*, Boston: The New England Historical and Genealogical Society, 2015

Anderson, R. C., *The Winthrop Fleet.* (New England Historical and Genealogical Society, 2012)

Archer, I., "Saltonstall, Sir Richard (1521?–1601)" *Oxford Dictionary of National Biography.* (2018)

Arnold, S. G. History of the State of Rhode Island and Providence Plantations. (D. Appleton & Company, 1859)

Andrews, C. M., *The Colonial Period of American History*. vol. I (Yale University Press, 1934)

Avery, Gillian, *Origins and English Predecessors of the New England Primer*. 2000. American Antiquarian Society.

Aylmer, G. E. (1961). *The King's Servants: The Civil Service of Charles I, 1625-42*. Columbia University Press.

Bagley, George S., *Boston: Its Story & People, Boston*, Lincs.: The History of Boston Project, 1986

Bailey, J. E. 1883. "Jeremiah Horrox." The Observatory, Vol. 6, P 318-328 (1883)

Bailey, J. E., "The Rev. Alexander Horrocks of Dean, Westhoughton, and Turton." The Palatine Note-book III, (1883)

Baker, J.H. *The Reinvention of Magna Carta*. Cambridge University Press, 2000.

Ball, Thomas, *The Life of the Renowned Doctor Preston* (Authored 1628). Edited by E W Harcourt, London: Parker and Co, 1885

"Banbury: Introduction," in *A History of the County of Oxford: Volume 10, Banbury Hundred*, ed. Alan Crossley (London: Victoria County History, 1972). British History Online, accessed October 26, 2017, http://www.british-history.ac.uk/

Bangs, J. D. *Pilgrim Edward Winslow*. (New England Historic Genealogy Society, 2004).

Barnes, Viola Florence. *The Dominion of New England: A Study in British Colonial Policy*. New York: Frederick Ungar. (1960) [1923]. ISBN 978-0-8044-1065-6

Beeke, Joel, and Randall Pederson. *Meet the Puritans*. Grand Rapids: Reformation Heritage Books, 2006.

Bendall, Sarah, Christopher Brooke, and Patrick Collinson. *A History of Emmanuel College, Cambridge*. Woodbridge, Suffolk: Boydell Press, 1999

Bergeron, D. M., *King James and Letters of Homoerotic Desire*. (University of Iowa Press, 2002)

"Billingborough and Horbling station (498482)". Historic England Research records retrieved 14 December 2022

Bishop, K. and Healy, S., "Darley, Henry (1595/6-1671) of Scryingham, Yorks. and Gray's Inn Lane, London." The History of Parliament, London, (online), Accessed September 16, 2022

Borman, Tracy. *The Stolen Crown: Treachery, Deceit and the Death of the Tudor Dynasty*. London: Hodder & Stoughton, 2024.

Braddick, M. (2008). *God's Fury, England's Fire: A New History of the English Civil Wars* (1st ed.). Penguin Books Ltd.

Brayton, John A. 2007. "Additions to the Ancestry of Sarah (Hawkred) (Story) (Cotton) Mather of Boston, Lincolnshire." The Genealogist 21. Rockland ME

Bremer, Francis J., *Congregational Communion*. Boston: Northeastern University Press. 1994

Bremer, Francis J., "Davenport, John (bap. 1597, d/ 1670) minister in America", Oxford Dictionary of National Biography, Oxford University Press, 2004; online edition, May 2014

Bremer, Francis J. *First Founders: American Puritans and Puritanism in an Atlantic World*. Durham, 2012.

Brenner, Robert, *Merchants and Revolution: Commercial Change, Political Conflict, and London's Overseas Traders*, 1550-1653, New York: Verso, first published by University of Princeton Press, 2003

Brown, David, *Empire and enterprise: Money, power and the Adventurers for Irish land during the British Civil Wars*. Manchester University Press, 2020.

Bruce, J. (2008). *Documents Relating to the Proceedings Against William Prynne*. Biblio Bazaar, LLC.

Burgess, Glenn. *British Political Thought, 1500–1660*. Macmillan, 1999.

BIBLIOGRAPHY

Burke's Peerage, Baronetage & Knightage, 107th edition, three volumes, C. Mosley, editor, (Wilmington, Delaware, Genealogical Books Ltd, 2003)

Burnet, Gilbert. *History of His Own Time.* London, 1724.

Bush, S., *The Correspondence of John Cotton.* (University of North Carolina Press, 2001)

Byrne, Conor. "*A Portrait of Bessie Blount (c.1500–1539?).*" (online essay).

Calamy, Edmund. *The Ejected Ministers of 1662.* London, 1713.

Calder, I. M. *Richard Sibbes.* London, 1979.

Chartier, Craig, "An Investigation Into Weston's Colony at Wessagusett." Plymouth Archeology, Weymouth, MA, March 2011.

Carpenter, E.J., *A Woman of Shawmut: A Romance of Colonial Times,* Little, Brown and Company, Boston, 1891. Chester, J. L., "Herbert Pelham, his ancestors and descendants." The New England Historical and Genealogical Review (1879).

Chisholm, Hugh, ed. (1911). "Thomas Coventry". *Encyclopædia Britannica*. Vol. 7 (11th ed.). Cambridge University Press.

Christy, Miller. "Attempts Toward Colonization: the Council for New England and the Merchant Venturers of Bristol, 1621-1623." Edited by J Franklin Jameson. The American Historical Review IV (1899)

Cohn, Norman. *Europe's Inner Demons: An Enquiry Inspired by the Great Witch-Hunt.* Sussex University Press, 1975.

Clarke, Samuel, "The Life and Death of Mr. John Cotton, Who Died an. Christi 1652." In A Collection of the Lives of Ten Eminent Divines, London: William Miller at the Guilded Acorn. 1662

Clegg, James. "Annals of Bolton", Bolton Chronicle, 1888

Cliffe, J. T. *The Puritan Gentry: The Politics of a Social Class.* London, 1984.

Collinson, Patrick. *The Elizabethan Puritan Movement.* Routledge. 1967

Collinson, Patrick, *The Religion of Protestants: The Church in English Society 1559–1625.* Oxford University Press. 1984

Conley, Patrick T., *Rhode Island's Founders: From Settlement to Statehood.* Charlestown, SC: The History Press, 2010

Connolly, Sharon Bennett. *"Bessie, Mother of the King's Son"*; *"BESSIE BLOUNT – Tudor Society in Lincolnshire."* (online essays).

Cressy, D., *Coming Over.* (Cambridge University Press, 1987)

Curzon, George Nathaniel, and Tipping, Henry Avray. *Tattershall Castle, Lincolnshire: A Historical & Descriptive Survey.* London: Jonathan Cape, 1929

Cust, Richard, *Charles I: A Political Life.* London: Routledge, 2014 (Kindle Edition)

Cust, Richard. "Charles I, the Privy Council, and the Forced Loan." *Journal of British Studies*, vol. 24, no. 2, 1985, pp. 208–35. JSTOR, http://www.jstor.org/stable/175703. Accessed 21 May 2020.

De Lisle, L., *The White King: Charles I, Traitor, Murderer, Martyr.* (Public A#airs, Hachette Book Group, 2017)

Dever, Mark. 2000. *Richard Sibbes*. Mercer University Press.

Dobson, Mary J., and Richard Smith, *Contours of Death and Disease in Early Modern England.* Cambridge University Press. 2003

Donagan, B., "The Clerical Patronage of Robert Rich, Second Earl of Warwick, 1619-1642." *Proceedings of the American Philosophical Society* (1976)

Dudley, Dean, *History of the Dudley Family*. Dean Dudley, Publisher, Wakefield, MA, 1886

Dudley, Joseph, "The Life of Mr. Thomas Dudley." *Proceedings of the Massachusetts Historical Society XI*, 1869-1870, Boston.

Duffin, A. (2004). Clinton, Edward Fiennes de, first earl of Lincoln (1512–1585). In the *Oxford Dictionary of National Biography*. Oxford University Press.

Durant, Will, and Ariel Durant. *The Story of Civilization VII: The Age of Reason Begins.* Simon & Schuster. 2011

Felton, E C. "Samuel Skelton, M.A., First Minister of the First Church at Salem, Mass." The New England Historical and Genealogical Register, 53.

Fincham, Kenneth and Tyacke, Nicholas, *Altars Restored: The Changing Face of English Religious Worship, 1547-c.1700*, (2007)

Firth, C. H. "Peter, Hugh" *Dictionary of National Biography.* London: Smith, Elder & Co. 1885–1900

Firth, C.H., "Prynne, William". *Dictionary of National Biography.* London: Smith, Elder & Co. 1885–1900

"Fleet Prison - British History Online." British-history.ac.uk. Retrieved 2 August 2021

Forsythe, James Neild, *State of the Prisons in England, Scotland, and Wales, Not for the Debtor Only, But for Felons Also, and Other Less Criminal Offenders.* London: Routledge. (2000)

Froude, James, *History of England from the fall of Wolsey to the Death of Elizabeth,* Vols. I-III, London: J.W. Parker and Sons, 1863

Fuidge, N.M., "Clinton, Sir Henry (d.1616) of Tattershall, Lincs." *The Institute of Historical Research House of Commons Members Database* http://www.historyofparliamentonline.org

Fuller, Thomas. The Church History of Britain from the Birth of Jesus Christ until the *Year M.DC.XLVIII*. (1655)

Fuller, Thomas. *The History of the Worthies of England*. Edited by P. Austin Nuttall, LL.D. 2ND. Vol. III, London: Thomas Tegg, 73 Cheapside, 1840

BIBLIOGRAPHY

Gardiner, S. R., "Constitutional Documents of the Puritan Revolution," p. xxv; in 2nd Edition, p. XXvi

George, D.M., *Catalogue of Political and Personal Satires; Preserved in the Department of Prints and Drawings in the British Museum.* Vols. 1–11 (British Museum).

Gibson, Marion. *Reading Witchcraft: Stories of Early English Witches.* Routledge, 1999.

Gonzalez, Justo L., *The Story of Christianity. Volume 2: The Reformation to the Present Day.* HarperOne. ISBN 978-0-06-236490-6. (2014)

Gordon, C., *Mistress Bradstreet.* (Little, Brown, 2007)

Gorges, Raymond, and Frederick Brown. *The Story of a Family Through Eleven Centuries, Illustrated by Portraits and Pedigrees.* Grace Gorges (private printing). Boston: D.P. Updike, The Merrymount Press, 1944

Gould, J D. "The Inquisition of Depopulation of 1607 in Lincolnshire." The English Historical Review LXVII, no. CCLXIV (1952)

Grosart, A. B. (ed.). *The Works of Richard Sibbes.* Edinburgh, 1862–64.

Guy, John. *The Rights and Liberties of the English People.* Oxford University Press, 2005.

Guy, John. *Tudor England.* Oxford: Oxford University Press, 1988.

Hall, David D. *The Antinomian Controversy, 1636–1638, A Documentary History.* Durham [NC] and London: Duke University Press. (1990). ISBN 0822310910.

Hall, Robert A. *Place-Names of Lancashire*, (Cambridge: Cambridge University Press, 1951).

Haller, William. *The Rise of Puritanism.* New York: Columbia University Press, 1938.

Harris, Charles Alexander, "Ward, Nathaniel (1578-1652). Dictionary of National Biography, 1885-1900, Volume 59

Hardy, S. T. D. *Syllabus (in English) of the documents relating to England and other kingdoms contained in the Collection known as "Rymers' Foeedera."* vol. II (Longman & Co. and Trübner & Co., Paternoster Row, 1873)

Hasler, P W., "Gorges, Arthur (1557-1625), of Chelsea, Mdx." Edited by Sir Lewis Namier. The History of Parliament, London. (online), Accessed June 11, 2020

Haven, Samuel Foster, *"History of Grants Under the Great Council for New England: A Lecture of a Course by Members of the Massachusetts Historical Society,"* Delivered Before the Lowell Institute, January 15, 1869. (Press of John Wilson & Son, 1869)

Helms, M.W. & Mimadiére, A.M., "Wolseley, Sir Charles, 2nd Bt. (c.1630-1714) of Wolseley, Staffs." *The House of Commons Members Database* http://www.historyofparliamentonline.org.

Heywood, O., *A Narrative of the Life and Death of the Rev. John Angier, Minister of the Gospel at Denton.* London: Printed for Tho. Parkhurst, 1683

Hill, Christopher. *Society and Puritanism in Pre-Revolutionary England.* London, 1964.

Hill, F., *Tudor, and Stuart Lincoln.* (Cambridge University Press, 1956)

History of Boston Latin School – the oldest public school in America, Boston Latin School. Archived from the original on 2007-05-02. Retrieved 2022/9/18.

History of Weymouth, Massachusetts. Weymouth Historical Society Weymouth, Mass. 1923

Hoadly, C. J., *The Warwick Patent.* (Hartford Press, 1902).

Holman, M.L., & Scott, H.G., *Ancestors and Descendants of John Coney of Boston, England, and Boston, Massachusetts*, Rumford Press, 1928

Hosmer, James K., *The Life of Young Sir Henry Vane: Governor of Massachusetts*, Houghton, Mifflin and Co., Boston & New York, 1889

Hostettler, John (1997). *Sir Edward Coke: A Force for Freedom.* Barry Rose Law Publishers.

Hughes-Penny, Robert, 2020, *Alderman Hughes-Penny*, City of London, Accessed 1/20/2022, https://hughespenney.uk

Hutton, W.H., "Neile, Richard". *Dictionary of National Biography.* London: Smith, Elder & Co. 1885–1900

Irons, E A. "Isaac Johnson: a Memoir." Edited by G Phillips. The Rutland Magazine and County Historical Record, Oakham, 1908

Jardine, Lisa. *Still Harping on Daughters: Women and Drama in the Age of Shakespeare.* New York: Columbia University Press, 1983.

Jewett, Clarence F., *The memorial history of Boston: including Suffolk County, Massachusetts. 1630–1880.* Ticknor and Company, 1881

Jinkins, Michael. *Perkins, William (1558–1602).* Oxford Dictionary of National Biography. Oxford: OUP, 2004.

Jones, Augustine, *The Life and Work of Thomas Dudley, the Second Governor of Massachusetts, Cambridge, MA.* Houghton, Mifflin and Co., 1900

Jordan, Constance. "Penelope Rich and the Politics of Female Counsel." Renaissance Quarterly 44, no. 2 (1991): 210–32.

Keeble, N. H., "Bradstreet, Anne (1612/13–1672)", *Oxford Dictionary of National Biography*, Oxford University Press, 2004; online edition, May 2014

Kenyon, J. P., *The Stuarts: A study in English kingship.* (Fontana, 1970)

Kewes, Paulina (ed.). *The Oxford Handbook of Holinshed's Chronicles.* Oxford University Press, 2013.

King, David, "William Coddington: Resistance by Him and Others in Lincolnshire to the Royal Loan, 1626-7," New England Historical and Genealogical Register 6, 1882

BIBLIOGRAPHY

Kishlansky, Mark. *Parliamentary Selection: Social and Political Choice in Early Modern England*. Cambridge University Press, 1986.

Knowles, J. D., *Memoir of Roger Williams, Founder of the State of Rhode Island*. (Lincoln, Edmands and Co., 1834).

Lake, Peter. *Laudian and Royalist Polemic*. Oxford, 2001.

Lake, Peter. *Moderate Puritans and the Elizabethan Church*. Cambridge: Cambridge University Press, 1982.

Lane, Belden C., *Ravished by Beauty: The Surprising Legacy of Reformed Spirituality*. New York: Oxford University Press. 2011.

LaPlante, Eve, *American Jezebel*. (HarperCollins e-books, 2010).

Larminie, Vivienne. "Feofees for Impropriations." Oxford Dictionary of National Biography, Oxford, May 28, 2015.

Lepionka, M. E. (2018). *The Settlement of Cape Ann: What is the Real Story?* Enduring Gloucester. https://enduringgloucester.com/2018/02/14/the-settlement-of-cape-ann-what-is-the-real-story/

Leverett, Charles Edward, *A Memoir Biographical and Genealogical of Sir John Leverett, Knt., Governor of Massachusetts, 1673-79*, Boston: Crosby, Nichols and Company, 1856

Lewin, Stephen, *A Concise Sketch of the History of St. Botolph's Church, Boston, in the County of Lincoln*. Horncastle: W.K.Morton. 1895

Lewis, Alonzo, *History of Lynn*. Press of J.H. Eastburn, 60 Congress Street, 1829

Lockhart, Paul D. (1996). *Denmark in the Thirty Years' War, 1618-1648: King Christian IV and the decline of the Oldenburg State*. Susquehanna University Press.

Lockyer, Roger. *Buckingham: The Life and Political Career of George Villiers*. London, 1981.

Lockyer, Roger, *Buckingham*, Routledge, 2014

Love Letters: 2,000 Years of Romance, edited by Andrea Clarke, published by the British Library in 2012.

"Massachusetts Bay Company." Encyclopedia Britannica, 16 Jan. 2021

Massie, Allan, *The Royal Stuarts*. St. Martin's Publishing Group. Kindle Edition.

'May 1649: An Act Declaring and Constituting the People of England to be a Commonwealth and Free-State.', in *Acts and Ordinances of the Interregnum, 1642-1660*, ed. C H Firth and R S Rait (London, 1911), p. 122. *British History Online* http://www.british-history.ac.uk/no-series/acts-ordinances-interregnum/p122 [accessed 29 October 2021].

Mayers, R.E., 'Vane, Sir Henry, the younger (1613–1662)', *Oxford Dictionary of National Biography,* Oxford University Press, 2004

McElwee, W., *The Wisest Fool in Christendom: The Reign of King James I and VI*. (Harcourt, 1958)

McKern, B. Find A Grave. www.findagrave.com/memorial/1723/simon bradstreet

McLaughlin, John D. *Vikings in the Irish Sea Region: Settlement and Identity, 800–1200* (Dublin: Four Courts Press, 2005).

Mitchell, S. "Review of *The Massachusetts Bay Company and Its Predecessors by Frances Rose-Troup*", The New England Quarterly, vol. 3, no. 4, New England Quarterly, Inc., 1930

Milton, Anthony. 'Anthony Tuckney,' in *Oxford Dictionary of National Biography*.

Milton, Anthony. 'Laud, William,' in *Oxford Dictionary of National Biography*.

Moore, J. B., *Lives of the Governors of New Plymouth and Massachusetts Bay*. Boston: C. D. Strong. OCLC 11362972 (1851)

Moore, J., *English Hypothetical Universalism: John Preston and the Softening of Reformed Theology*. Wm. B. Eerdmans Publishing. 2007

Moore, J., "Preston, John (1587-1628)". *Dictionary of National Biography*. London: Smith, Elder & Co. 1885–1900

Morison, S. E., *Founding of Harvard College*. (Harvard University Press, 1935)

Morrill, J. *The Religious Context of Early Stuart England*. Cambridge University Press, 1991.

Morrill, J. (2011, February 17). *Oliver Cromwell*. BBC History. https://www.bbc.co.uk/history/british/civil_war_revolution/cromwell_01.shtml

Neal, D., Toulmin, J. (editor), *The History of the Puritans: or, Protestant nonconformists: from the Reformation in 1517, to the Revolution in 1688,* vol. 2, printed for Thomas Tegg and Son, London (1837)

New England Historical and Genealogical Register. Boston, MA: New England Historical and Genealogical Society, 1847-. Volume: 54

Normand, Lawrence, and Gareth Roberts, eds. *Witchcraft in Early Modern Scotland: James VI's Demonology and the North Berwick Witches.* Exeter University Press, 2000.

Norton, E. (2011). *Bessie Blount: The King's Mistress*. Amberley.

Norton, John, *Abel Being Dead Yet Speaketh: or the Life and Death of John Cotton, Late Teacher of the Church of Christ, at Boston, in New England,* London: Tho. Newcomb for Lodowick Lloyd, 1658

Parkinson, C.N., *Gunpowder, Treason and Plot,* London: Weidenfeld & Nicholson, 1976

Payne, Lynda, "Health in England (16th–18th C.)." *Children & Youth in History* 2015

Pennington, D.H.. "William Laud". *Encyclopedia Britannica*, 21 Mar. 2024, https://www.britannica.com/biography/William-Laud.

Pestana, Carla Gardina, 'Peter, Hugh (bap. 1598, d. 1660)', *Oxford Dictionary of National Biography*, Oxford University Press, 2004

Peterson, R. J. & Beeke, J.R., *Meet the Puritans,* Reformation Heritage Books. Kindle Edition. (2013-02-10)

Prest, W. R., *The Rise of the Barristers*. (Clarendon Press, 1986)

BIBLIOGRAPHY

Quincy, Josiah, *The History of Harvard University,* Crosby, Nichols, Lee, & Co., Boston, 1860

Richardson, D., Everingham, K. & Faris, D., *Plantagenet Ancestry: A Study in Colonial and Medieval Families.* Baltimore, MD: Genealogical Publishing Company. (2004). ISBN 978-0-8063-1750-2

Riches, Tony. *Penelope: Tudor Baroness.* Amazon, 2018.

Rigg, J. M. (1894). *Sir Henry Montagu.* Dictionary of National Biography. Retrieved from https://en.wikisource.org/wiki/Dictionary_of_National_Biography,_1885-1900/Montagu,_Henry

Robbins, W. G., "The Massachusetts Bay Company: An Analysis of Motives." Historian 32, 83–98 (1969)

Rogers, Horatio (1896). *Mary Dyer of Rhode Island, the Quaker Martyr That Was Hanged on Boston Common, June 1, 1660.* Providence, RI: Preston and Rounds.

Roper, L. H., *Advancing Empire.* (Cambridge University Press, 2017)

Rosenmeier, Jesper, *'Spirituall Concupiscence': John Cotton's English Years, 1584-1633.* Boston, Lincs. Richard Kay Publications. 2012

Rose-Troup, F., *The Massachusetts Bay Company and Its Predecessors.* (The Grafton Press, 1930)

Russell, Michael. "Members of the Dorchester Company 1624-1626", Dorset Online Parish Clerks, Dec. 2021, https://www.opcdorset.org/fordingtondorset/

Rutman, Darett, *John Winthrop's Decision for America, 1629,* (J.B. Lippincott, 1975)

Simkin, John. "Bessie Blount (Elizabeth Tailboys)." Spartacus Educational (online).

Sharpe, James. *Instruments of Darkness: Witchcraft in Early Modern England.* University of Pennsylvania Press, 1996.

Sharpe, Kevin. *The Personal Rule of Charles I.* New Haven, 1992.

Smith, David L., 'Fiennes, William, #rst Viscount Saye and Sele (1582–1662)', *Oxford Dictionary of National Biography*, Oxford University Press, 2004; online edition, Jan 2008

Smith, David. *The Stuart Parliaments, 1603–1689.* Pearson, 1999.

Smith, Geoffrey. "Sir Walter Raleigh and the Politics of Execution." *Journal of Early Modern England*, 2010.

Stearns, Raymond. *Hugh Peter, 1598–1660: Religious and Political Radical.* Harvard, 1954.

Stephenson, N W, & Lyon, G Tyler. "Some Inner History of the Virginia Company." The William and Mary Quarterly 22 (1914). http://www.jstor.org/stable/1915253.

Stewart, Alan. *Philip Sidney: A Double Life.* London: Chatto & Windus, 2000.

Stone, L., *The Crisis of the Aristocracy, 1558-1641.* (Oxford University Press, 1965)

The American Genealogist. New Haven, CT: D. L. Jacobus, 1 937. (Online database AmericanAncestors.org, New England Historic Genealogical Society, 2009)

The Culture of English Puritanism, 1560-1700. Edited by Christopher Durston and Jacqueline Eales. Macmillan. 1996

"The Hubbard Family." FreePages.RootsWeb, https://freepages.rootsweb.com/~nyterry/genealogy/hubbard/hubbard.html, accessed April 20, 2023

The Tudor Enthusiast. *"Henry VIII's and Elizabeth Blount's Daughter: A New Discovery"* (online).

Thomas, Keith. *Religion and the Decline of Magic.* Penguin, 1971.

Thompson, Pishey, *The History and Antiquities of Boston.* (Longman and Co.; Simpkin and Co., 1856)

Thompson, Pishey. "The Johnson Family." The New England Historical and Genealogical Register, VIII (1854): "Extracts from a paper written by Abraham Johnson, Gentleman & Esquire," 1638, and identified as his writing by a relative. The paper in possession of Wm Hopkinson, Esq., of Stamford, Lincolnshire."

Thompson, Roger, 'Johnson, Isaac (bap. 1601, d. 1630)', *Oxford Dictionary of National Biography*, Oxford University Press, 2004; online edition, May 2006

Thorton, John Wingate, *The Historical Relation of New England to the English Commonwealth*, Press of A. Mudge, Boston, 1874

Tite, Colin. *The Manuscript Library of Sir Robert Cotton.* The British Library, 1994.

Townsend, C. H. (1882). Bellingham Sketch. *New-England Historical and Genealogical Register*, XXXVI, 381–386.

Travitsky, Betty S. "Clinton [Née Knevitt], Elizabeth, Countess of Lincoln (1574?–1630?), Noblewoman and Writer." Oxford Dictionary of National Biography, Oxford: Oxford University Press, January 28, 2015

Trevor-Roper, Hugh, *Archbishop Laud,* Phoenix Press reissue 2000

Triber, Jayne E. A., *True Republican*, Univ of Massachusetts Press, 2001

Tucker, Edward L., *Longfellow's Play John Endicott*, Papers Presented at the Longfellow Commemorative Conference, April 1-3, 1982

Tyacke, Nicholas. 'Paul Baynes,' in Oxford Dictionary of National Biography, vol. 3 (1885–1900).

Tyler, M. C. (1883). *A History of American Literature 1607-1676* (Vol. 1). G.P. Putnam's Sons.

Van Duinen, Jared. "Prosopography and the Providence Island Company: the Nature of Puritan Opposition in 1630s England." In *Prosopography Approaches and Applications*, edited by K S B Keats-Rohan, 527–40, Oxford: Occasional Publications UPR, 2007

Waterman, L., "Wm. Laud, Archbishop of Canterbury and Martyr." Notes Queries s4-VI, 93–94 (1914)

BIBLIOGRAPHY

Watson, P. & Sgroi, R., "Bellingham, Richard II, (c.1592-1672), of Manton and Boston, Lincs.; later Boston, Mass." *The House of Commons Members Database* http://www.historyofparliamentonline.org.

Watson, P. & Sgroi, R., "Irby, Sir Anthony (1605-1682), of Whaplode, Lincs. and Westminster." *The House of Commons Members Database* http://www.historyofparliamentonline.org.

Watson, P., & Sgroi, R., "Clinton, alias Fiennes, Thomas, Lord Clinton (c1568-1619) of Tattershall, Lincs." *The House of Commons Members Database* http://www.historyofparliamentonline.org.

Watts, J.C.& Cutter, W.R., *A Documentary History of Chelsea*. Boston: Massachusetts Historical Society. (1908)

West, Randy A., "Samuel Bellingham, Son of Gov. Richard1 Bellingham of Massachusetts," The American Genealogist Vol. 91(Dec, 2021)

Whiting, Samuel. "Concerning the Life of the Famous Mr. Cotton, Teacher to the Church of Christ at Boston in New England." In *Chronicles of the First Planters of the Colony of Massachusetts Bay, From 1623-1636*, Boston: Charles C. Little and James Brown, 1846

Whiting, William. (1873). Memoir of Rev. Samuel Whiting, D.D., and of His Wife, Elizabeth St. John, with References to Some of Their English Ancestors and American Descendants. (2nd ed.). Rand, Avery, & Company.

"William Aspinwall", *The Great Migration Begins: Immigrants to New England 1620-1633*, Volumes I-III. (Online database: AmericanAncestors.org, New England Historical and Genealogical Society, 2010)

Wilson, Arthur. "The Life and Reign of James, the First King of Great Britain." In *A Complete History of England*, London, 1706

Winship, Michael. *Hot Protestants: A History of Puritanism in England and America*. Yale University Press, 2019.

Winship, Michael. *Godly Republicanism: Puritans, Pilgrims, and a City on a Hill*. (Harvard University Press, 2012). Kindle Edition

Winthrop, R. C., Jr. (1890). "Thomas Lyon, his family, and connections." *Proceedings of the Massachusetts Historical Society*. Second Series. VI: 1–20. JSTOR

Young, M. *King James VI and I and the History of Homosexuality*, Basingstoke: Springer, 1999

Ziff, Larzer. *The Career of John Cotton*. Princeton, NJ: Princeton University Press, 1962

INDEX

FAMILY GROUPS

BRADSTREET FAMILY

- Anne Bradstreet, 115, 496
- Dorothy Bradstreet, 115, 495
- Simon Bradstreet Sr., 32
- Simon Bradstreet, , 8, 32, 46, 54, 58, 75, 79, 88, 91, 105, 115, 170, 200, 202, 204, 206, 208, 218

CLINTON FAMILY— *see also* Earls of Lincoln

- Edward Clinton, 49–50, 61, 155
- Henry Clinton, 50
- Thomas Clinton, 51–52, 61, 157
- Theophilus Clinton, 10, 32, 41, 52-53, 59, 62, 65–66, 155, 199–200, 218

COTTON FAMILY— *see also* Boston (Lincolnshire); St. Botolph's Church; Massachusetts Bay Company

- John Cotton, 3, 7, 9–10, 13, 15, 17, 20, 22, 25–26, 31, 38–39, 44, 54, 54, 83, 91, 93, 95, 97, 99–101, 105, 107, 110–116, 134, 165–167, 185, 187, 200, 202, 206, 222, 225–226
- John Cotton Jr., 110, 115
- Seaborn Cotton, 110, 113, 115

DUDLEY FAMILY— *see also* Bradstreet Family; Winthrop Family

- Thomas Dudley, 10, 39, 44, 46, 53, 58, 65, 79, 83–85, 87–88, 91, 94, 101, 133, 194, 197, 200, 202–206, 208, 222, 226
- Dorothy Dudley, 115
- Anne Dudley (Anne Bradstreet), 91

GORGES FAMILY— *see also* Council for New England; Popham Colony

- Arthur Gorges, 59, 61, 155
- Elizabeth Gorges, 59, 62, 155–156
- Ferdinando Gorges, 11, 61–62, 68, 77, 80, 87, 155–156, 239–240, 246–247
- John Gorges, 61–62, 68, 155–156, 202, 218
- Nicholas Gorges, 61, 155
- Robert Gorges, 68, 156, 202

HAWKRED FAMILY— *see also* Bulkeley Family; Mayor of Boston, Lincs.

- Anthony Hawkred, 25
- Elizabeth Hawkred, 25, 165, 167
- Isabel Hawkred, 26
- Mary Hawkred, 25
- Sarah Hawkred, 19, 165–167

INDEX

HORROCKS FAMILY

- Christopher Horrocks, 22
- Elizabeth Horrocks, 18, 20–22
- James Horrocks, 18, 22

HUTCHINSON FAMILY— *see also* Antinomian Controversy

- Anne Hutchinson, 8, 99, 107–109
- Susanna Hutchinson, 167

JOHNSON FAMILY *see also* Massachusetts Bay Company

- Isaac Johnson, 10, 39, 44, 58, 67–69, 75–76, 78, 80–85, 87–88, 91, 95–97, 105, 113,
- 133, 156, 187, 192, 197, 202, 204, 206, 208, 211–213, 241
-
- Robert Johnson, 67

MATHER FAMILY

- Increase Mather, 110, 115
- Richard Mather, 111, 115–116, 167
- Sarah Mather, 116

PELHAM FAMILY

- Herbert Pelham (Sr), 76–77, 93, 162–164, 183, 187, 208, 220, 228
- Herbert Pelham II, 76, 162–163
- Herbert Pelham III, 76–77, 93, 162–164
- William Pelham, 93

RICH FAMILY *see also* Earl of Warwick; Warwick Patent

- Robert Rich, 157, 169–170, 182, 230
- Richard Rich, 157

STUART KINGS

- James I, 3, 5–6, 32–33, 54–55, 57, 125–126, 170, 201–202, 239–240, 243, 247
- Charles I, 3, 5–6, 33, 37, 42, 47, 73, 99, 110–112, 123–125, 137–140, 144, 159–161,
- 192, 202, 234, 240, 242, 247
- Charles II, 113, 115, 172, 230

WINSTANLEY FAMILY

- Ellen Winstanley, 22
- Gilbert Winstanley, 22

WINTHROP FAMILY — *see also* Arbella; Massachusetts Bay Company; Winthrop Fleet

- John Winthrop, 39, 70, 73, 82, 84–85, 92, 98–99, 101, 107, 133, 187, 205, 217, 222–223, 225–226, 232, 235
- John Winthrop Jr., 99

WRAY FAMILY — *see also* Fiennes Family (through intermarriage)

- Christopher Wray, 169, 171
- Frances Wray, 58, 169–171

INDEX

INDIVIDUALS

A

- Adams, Thomas, — see also Cambridge Agreement. 85, 212, 215
- Aldersey, Samuel, 212–213, 219, 234
- Alexander, Benjamin, 14
- Anderson, William, 42
- Andrews, Thomas, 217
- Angier, John, 22
- Angier, John Jr., 22
- Archer, John, 217
- Aspinwall, Hannah, 22
- Aspinwall, William, 22

B

- Baron, Peter, 14–16
- Bastwick, John, 146, 148, 150
- Baynes, Paul, — see also Calvinism. 14, 16, 18, 22, 31
- Bellingham, Richard, — see also Massachusetts Bay Colony; Antinomian Controversy. 8, 10, 39, 58, 77–78, 99, 164, 197, 202, 204, 208, 211–212, 214, 241
- Bellingham, Susanna, 99
- Blackhouse, William, 217
- Blount, Elizabeth, 49
- Blaxton, William, 67–68, 96, 105, 156, 202, 206
- Bowles, John, 218
- Bradford, William, — see also Plymouth. 64
- Brandon, Gregory, 148
- Brereton, William, 218
- Bridges, Francis, 35, 218
- Browne, John, 212

- Browne, Samuel, 35, 212, 215, 219
- Bulkeley, Elizabeth, 166–167
- Bulkeley, Peter, 167
- Burnell, Thomas, 219

C

- Chetwood, Grace, 168
- Coddington, William, — see also Hutchinson Family. 10, 44, 75, 88, 91, 93, 206, 208, 221
- Colbron, William, 221
- Cole, Samuel, 221
- Coney, Mary, 26
- Coney, Thomas, 25–26, 79–80
- Craddock, Matthew, — see also Massachusetts Bay Company. 76–78, 81, 162, 193–194, 211, 213–214, 231, 241–242
- Cromwell, Oliver, — see also English Civil Wars. 112, 115, 135, 165, 171, 229
- Crowther, William, 221

D

- Davenport, John, — see also New Haven. 35, 85, 214, 222
- Devereux, Penelope, 169
- Diconson, Benjamin, 44
- Dove, Barjonas, 19, 24
- Dunster, Henry, 104, 113
- Dyer, Mary, — see also Hutchinson Family; Antinomian Controversy. 107–108, 116

INDEX

E

- Eaton, Nathaniel, 102–103
- Eggington, Jeremiah, 115
- Endecott, John, — see also Salem; Massachusetts Bay Company. 77, 211–212, 241

F & G

- Fitzroy, Henry, 49
- Foord, Edward, 223
- Glover, John, 223
- Glover, Josse, 223, 227

H

- Harvard, John, — see also Harvard College. 101, 103, 105–106
- Harwood, George, 35, 212, 214
- Higginson, Francis, 215, 224
- Hodson, Daniel, 225
- Hooker, Thomas, — see also Connecticut Plantation (Saybrook). 83, 181, 185–186
- Humfrey, John, — see also Massachusetts Bay Company; Winthrop Family. 8, 10, 58, 69–70, 75–77, 81, 84–85, 87–88, 162, 183, 192, 194, 197, 203–204, 208, 211–213, 220

I-J-K

Ironside, Edward, 225

Jackson, Edmond, 44

Keane, Robert, 225–226

A TALE OF TWO BOSTONS

L

Laud, William, — see also Star Chamber; Arminianism. 4, 7, 33–34, 97, 111, 143, 146, 148, 229, 233

Leighton, Alexander, 150

Leverett, Jane, 23

Leverett, John, — see also Massachusetts General Court. 23–24, 112, 116–117

Leverett, Thomas, 23, 28, 44, 75, 97–98, 167, 208, 226

Lord Saye & Sele, — see also Saybrook Colony. 3, 42, 65–66, 153, 181–183, 185, 200–201, 209, 212, 230, 241, 244

Lowe, Thomas, 44

M

- Makepeace, Thomas, 167
- Malbon, John, 226
- Manesty, Nathaniel, 226
- Manners, Francis, 157
- Manners, Katherine, 157–159
- Mansfeldt, Ernst von, 55
- Marsh, Thomas, 226
- Mellows, Oliver, 165, 167
- Montagu, Richard, 33

N & O

- Nowell, Increase, — see also Massachusetts General Court. 73, 212, 214
- Nye, Philip, 227
- Oakeley, Richard, 170

INDEX

P

- Partridge, Ralph, 111
- Perkins, William, 28, 31, 228–229
- Perry, Richard, 85, 212, 214
- Peter, Hugh, 73, 181, 185–186, 229
- Phillips, George, 229
- Pormort, Philemon, 99
- Prynne, William, — see also Laud, William; Star Chamber. 146, 148, 150

R

- Raleigh, Walter, 36, 129
- Rogers, Katherine, 103
- Rossiter, Edward, 224, 228
- Rossiter, Joanna, 113

S

- Shepard, Thomas, 31
- Skelton, Samuel, 10, 67, 75, 81, 205, 209, 213, 218, 224, 231
- Smart, Peter, 150
- Smyth, John, 231
- Spenser, John, 231
- Spurstowe, William, 231
- St. John, Oliver, — see also Petition of Right. 135, 165
- Stevenson, Anne, 93
- Stileman, Elias, 231
- Storre, Augustine, 167
- Story, Elizabeth, 166

T

- Tilson, Edward, 42
- Tuckney, Anthony, 19, 25

V

- Vane, Henry, — see also Antinomian Controversy. 73, 99, 101, 107–110, 115, 171–172, 174, 229
- Vassall, William, 194, 212, 215
- Venn, John, 78, 85, 214, 241
- Villers, Mary, 158–159
- Villiers, George, 129–130, 158

W

Wade, Thomas, 233

Waller, Henry, 85, 233

Ward, Nathaniel, 232–233

Whiting, Samuel, 19–20, 166

Williams, Roger, — see also Providence; Puritanism. 73, 83, 229

Winslow, Josiah, 163

Woodbridge, Benjamin, 104

INDEX

PLACES

A

- Alford — see also Lincolnshire. 8–9, 99
- America, 4–5, 21, 24, 53, 61–62, 72, 81, 99, 105, 168, 182, 204, 209–213, 215, 223, 239
- Arbella Street, 95
- All Hallows Church, 217

B

- Banbury, 42
- Barlings Abbey, 50
- Bolton, 21–22
- Boston (Lincolnshire), — see also St. Botolph's Church; Cotton Family. 3, 5, 8, 58, 64, 93, 99, 155, 162, 166, 192, 197, 203–204, 207
- Boston (Massachusetts), — see also Shawmut; Winthrop Family. 22, 24, 107, 163, 165–166, 168, 202, 221, 223, 225
- Boston Common, 116
- Boston Grammar School, 19, 24, 99
- Boston Latin School, 99–100
- Broughton Manor, 42

C

- Cadiz, 134
- Cambridge (England), — see also Emmanuel College; Harvard, John. 225
- Carisbrooke Castle, 137
- Charlestown (Massachusetts), — see also Boston (Massachusetts). 101
- Chelsea, 51

- Colwich, 243
- Concord, 168

D

- Deane Parish, 22
- Dorchester — see also Dorchester Company. 10, 58, 76–78, 115, 162, 179, 189–192, 194, 197, 202–204, 213, 215–216, 222–223, 226–227, 232, 234, 241
- Downing Street, 51
- Dublin, 150

E - F - G

- Edinburgh, 113
- Emmanuel College — see also Cambridge (England); Harvard, John. 18–20, 22–24, 32–33, 53, 67, 99–100, 105–106, 156, 166, 170, 177, 187, 201, 224, 232–233
- Exeter, 15
- Fleet Prison — see also London. 41–43
- Guilford, 115

H

- Hague (the), — see also Palatinate. 57, 128
- Haverholme, 50
- Holy Trinity Church, 20
- House of Commons — see also Parliament. 33, 41, 137, 145, 170, 204, 218, 234
- House of Lords — see also Parliament. 3, 41, 50, 59, 137, 145, 153–154, 157, 165, 181–182, 193, 200–201

INDEX

I & K

- Ipswich, 234
- King's Chapel Burying Ground — see also Boston (Massachusetts). 97, 114, 116–117
- Kirton, 39
- Kyme, 49

L

- La Rochelle, 159–160
- Lincoln — see also Clinton Family; Earl of Lincoln. 8–10, 14–16, 27–28, 32–33, 35–37, 44–46, 49–55, 57–59, 61–62, 65, 67, 75–76, 81–82, 93–94, 153–155, 157–158, 165, 171, 177, 187, 199–200, 202–204, 208–209, 213, 225, 231, 234
- Lincolnshire — see also Boston Men; Boston (Lincolnshire). 3, 5, 7–10, 13, 15, 37–39, 46–48, 55, 58–59, 64, 75, 82, 99, 125, 131–132, 134, 155, 162, 166, 169, 192, 194, 197, 203–204, 207
- Lincoln's Inn, 33, 35, 76, 165, 177, 187, 208, 225, 234
- London — see also Tower Hill; Fleet Prison; Westminster. 7, 10, 35–36, 41–44, 51, 54–55, 62–63, 75–78, 80–81, 86–87, 97, 105, 110, 130, 144–145, 148, 162, 172, 181, 186, 190–191, 202–205, 211–212, 214–223, 225–235, 240–241, 243–247
- London Bridge, 229
- Lynn, 70–71

M & N

- Maldon, 225
- Musketaquid, 168
- Naumkeag, 191
- New England — see also Great Migration; Massachusetts Bay Company. 4, 7–9, 11, 19, 21, 39–40, 59–63, 68–71, 73, 75–79, 83–85, 87, 91–93, 97, 100–101, 105, 108, 111, 131, 134–135,

156–157, 162–164, 173, 179, 189, 194, 196–197, 199, 202–206, 211–215, 219, 221–222, 225–232, 234, 239–241, 244–247
- New Haven — see also Davenport, John. 214, 222
- New Towne — see also Cambridge (England). 101–103
- Norfolk, 132
- North Forty-Foot Drain, 38

O & P

- Oxford, 24, 65, 99, 144, 227
- Palatinate — see also La Rochelle; Hague (the). 55, 57, 159
- Peterborough, 68
- Plymouth — see also Bradford, William. 39, 68, 77, 87, 162–163, 189–190, 211, 215, 225, 227, 230–231, 239–240, 246–247
- Portsmouth — see also Naval activity. 160
- Providence Island — see also Providence Island Company. 70–71, 165, 221

Q & R

- Queen's College, 31–32, 200, 205
- Rotterdam, 229

S

- Salem — see also Endecott, John; Winthrop Fleet. 4, 7–8, 72–73, 78, 81–82, 95, 97, 115, 191, 204–206, 209, 218, 222, 229, 231
- Saugus, 70
- Saybrook — see also Lord Saye & Sele; Connecticut settlements. 69, 99, 135
- Scituate, 215
- Sempringham — see also Clinton Family; Pelham Family; Earl of

INDEX

Lincoln. 32, 38, 50, 52–53, 57–58, 66–67, 75, 81–83, 93, 204–205, 209

- Shawmut — see also Boston (Massachusetts). 68, 96, 156, 202, 206
- Skirbeck, 14
- Snarford, 170
- Southampton — see also Arbella; Winthrop Fleet. 7, 91, 134, 225
- Southwark, 232, 234
- St. Andrew's Church, 32, 209
- St. Botolph's Church, 27, 39, 92
- St. John's College, 22, 167
- St. Michael's, 227
- Stratford-Upon-Avon, 105

T

- Tattershall — see also Tattershall Castle. 49, 51–52, 59, 66
- Tattershall Castle, 49, 51
- Tower Hill, 111, 146, 150, 160, 172
- Tower of London, 41, 44, 58–59, 145, 172, 203–204
- Trimountaine, 96, 206

V & W

- Vienna, 99
- Weymouth, 70, 222, 235
- Whitehall, 58, 73, 137
- Wigan, 21–22
- Windsor Castle, 137, 234
- Winstanley — see also Winstanley Family. 21–22

A TALE OF TWO BOSTONS

COMPANIES - COLONIES - INSTITUTIONS - ORGANIZATIONS

- Ancient & Honorable Artillery Company of Massachusetts, 225
- Boston Borough Council, 26, 44, 171, 203
- Boston Men, — see also Lincolnshire; Council for New England; Massachusetts Bay Company. 3, 7, 9–11, 26, 39, 45, 76–77, 79–80, 91, 133–134, 162, 177, 179, 192, 194, 199, 204–205, 207–209, 211, 218, 222, 226, 228, 232, 235
- Cambridge Agreement, 83–85, 194, 205, 219, 234
- Cambridge Platform, 111
- Council for New England, — see also Gorges Family; Warwick Patent. 11, 62–63, 68, 77, 87, 156–157, 182, 189, 197, 219, 230, 239–241, 246–247
- Dorchester Company, — see also Massachusetts Bay Company. 58, 76–77, 162, 189–192, 194, 202–204, 213, 215–216, 219–220, 227, 232, 234, 241
- East India Company, 35–36, 193
- General Court of Massachusetts, 111
- Great Council for New England, 11, 240, 247
- Massachusetts General Court, 112
- Massachusetts Bay Company, — see also Winthrop Family; Cotton Family; Boston Men; Council for New England. 3–4, 7–11, 23, 26, 35, 44, 58, 66, 68–70, 72, 75–80, 82–85, 91, 97, 110, 121, 133, 153, 162–163, 166, 177, 179, 182, 192–193, 197, 199, 203–215, 217–218, 220–221, 227, 230, 234, 239–242, 244
- New England Company, 7, 77–79, 162, 192–193, 197, 199, 203–204, 213–214, 217, 220, 227, 229–232, 234, 240–241
- Popham Colony, — see also Gorges Family. 240, 247
- Providence Island Company, — see also Vane, Henry. 165
- Saybrook Colony, 69, 99, 135
- Sempringham Meeting, — see also Clinton Family; Pelham Family. 83, 205
- Virginia Company of London, 87, 246
- Virginia Company of Plymouth, 87, 246

INDEX

EDUCATIONAL INSTITUTIONS

- Boston Grammar School, 19, 24, 99
- Boston Latin School, 99–100
- Christ's College, Cambridge, 22
- Emmanuel College, Cambridge, — see also Cambridge (England). 22, 25–26, 32–33, 67, 99–100, 105, 166, 170, 177, 201, 224, 232–233
- King's College, Cambridge, 32, 98
- St. John's College, Cambridge, 22, 167
- Trinity College, Cambridge, 102

KEY BOOKS & RELIGIOUS TEXTS

- Basilikon Doron, — see also James I. 126
- Leviathan, — see also Hobbes; English Civil Wars. 140
- Magna Carta, 132
- Song of Songs, 21
- True Law of Free Monarchies, — see also James I. 126–127

LEGAL SYSTEM & COURTS

- Inns of Court, 54, 67, 76, 82, 177, 187, 200, 234, 243
- King's Bench, 46–47, 169
- Privy Council, 38, 41, 46, 51–52, 242, 247
- Star Chamber, — see also Laud, William; Prynne, William. 7, 41, 144, 148, 151

MILITARY EVENTS & WARFARE

- Battle of Lutter, 6, 37, 58
- Battle of Naseby, 135–136
- Defense, 20, 28, 129, 225

- English Civil Wars, — see also Cromwell, Oliver; Charles I. 59, 110, 112, 135, 218
- Gunpowder Plot, 51, 130, 132
- Gunpowder Plot of 1605, 130
- New Model Army, — see also Cromwell, Oliver. 137
- Thirty Years' War, — see also Palatinate; James I. 5–6, 33, 37, 47, 54–55, 57, 128, 133, 192

OFFICES, ROLES & TITLES

- Advowson, 14
- Archbishop of Canterbury, — see also Church of England. 144
- Bishop of Lincoln, — see also Lincoln; Lincolnshire. 14–16, 27, 67, 171
- Bishop of London, — see also Laud, William. 7, 97, 144, 229, 233
- Chaplain, 14, 33–34, 67, 81, 144, 201, 205, 209, 229, 231
- Curate, 209, 227
- Deacon, 97, 221
- Elder, 71, 98, 104, 108, 162, 221
- Governor of Massachusetts, — see also Massachusetts Bay Company. 8, 116–117
- Mayor, — see also Boston Borough Council. 14–15, 17, 25, 44, 80, 94, 204
- Member of Parliament, — see also House of Commons; House of Lords. 58, 232–233
- Patentee, — see also Massachusetts Bay Company. 69, 77, 183, 210–213, 239, 241
- Planter, — see also Dorchester Company; Great Migration. 68, 75, 79, 81, 83–87, 168, 205, 209, 235, 244–246
- Preacher, — see also Puritanism. 20, 26, 33, 35, 41, 97–98, 150, 187, 201, 233
- President of Harvard College — see also Harvard, John. 24, 115
- Rector, 32, 217, 223, 233

INDEX

- Steward, 10, 25, 46, 53, 58, 170, 200, 203–204, 208, 218
- Teacher, 98, 166
- Vicar, — see also Parish life; Church of England. 13–19, 21, 30, 93, 98–99

POLITICAL EVENTS & GOVERNMENT ACTIONS

- Forced Loan, — see also Petition of Right. 3, 5–7, 10–11, 37–47, 58, 66, 132–134, 153, 192, 199, 201–204
- Petition of Right, — see also St. John, Oliver. 41, 47, 66, 133, 154, 204
- Ordinance of Attainder, 146
- Long Parliament, 4, 110, 137, 171, 214
- Dissolution of the Monasteries, 50
- Lincolnshire Rising, 50
- Rosewell Grant, — see also Massachusetts Bay Company. 7, 77–78, 192, 194, 197, 211–214, 230, 241
- Royal Charter of the Massachusetts Bay Company, — see also Massachusetts Bay Company. 213, 242
- Warwick Patent, — see also Earl of Warwick; Rich Family. 182–183, 230
- Execution of Charles I, 112, 138, 140
- Trial of Charles I, 111
- Habeas Corpus, — see also King's Bench. 46, 132
- High Church Reforms, 3
- Laudian Migration, 97

RELIGIOUS MOVEMENTS & DOCTRINES

- Antinomian Controversy, — see also Hutchinson Family; Vane, Henry. 107, 109
- Arminianism, — see also Laud, William; Church of England. 15, 34, 144, 201

A TALE OF TWO BOSTONS

- Calvinism, — see also Puritanism. 15, 20, 27, 29, 33, 179, 185, 201
- Church of England, 14, 28–29, 33, 129, 132, 143–144, 232
- Congregational Way, 111
- Divine Right of Kings, 127
- Predestination, 29–30, 33
- Puritanism, — see also Massachusetts Bay Company; Williams, Roger. 27–29, 33, 99, 144
- Revelation 16, 110

SHIPS & MARINE EXPEDITIONS

- Abigail — see also Ships (general). 78, 99
- Arbella — see also Winthrop Fleet; Winthrop Family. 58, 67–68, 70–71, 83, 88, 91, 95–96, 124, 156, 202–203, 206, 213–215, 222, 224, 227
- Eagle, 88, 213
- Katherine — see also Winthrop Fleet. 52, 68, 105, 157–160
- Susan and Ellen — see also Ships (general). 168, 225
- Winthrop Fleet — see also Arbella; Massachusetts Bay Company. 87, 91, 93–94, 97–98, 164, 206, 213–215, 218, 221–222, 229–231
- Privateering, 36, 70, 158, 182

Success, 57, 78, 207 ??????

Timeline
1610 - 1692

1610s

- 610 July – John Cotton ordained deacon and priest at Lincoln
- 1610- John Wilson graduated Emmanuel College, Cambridge
- 1610 Oct – Thomas Leverett married Ann Fitch, Boston Lincs.
- *1611 – King James Bible published, shaping English language*
- 1612 Jan – John Preston converted by Cotton
- 1612 Jan– Birth of Anne Dudley Bradstreet
- 1612 June – Boston Town began search for new vicar
- 1612 July – John Cotton elected vicar of Boston Lincs
- 1612 July – Vicarage turned over to Cotton
- 1612 Aug – Anne Marbury married William Hutchinson
- 1612 Dec – Death of Sarah Hawkred's brother William.
- 1613 Feb – James I's daughter Elizabeth married Frederick V
- *1613 Apr – William Shakespeare died*
- 1613 May – Birth of Henry Vane
- 1613 May – Cotton repaid for repairs to vicarage
- 1613 May –Anthony Tuckney matriculated Emmanuel College
- 1613 July – John Cotton received Divinity Degree
- 1613 July – John Cotton married Elizabeth Horrocks
- 1613 July – Cotton's recommendation for schoolmaster of Boston Grammar School accepted
- 1613 Oct – Marriage of Thomas Coney and Mary Hawkrerd
- 1614 May 26 – William Blaxton enters Emmanuel College
- 1614 May – Isaac Johnson entered Emmanuel College
- 1614 June – Burial of Isabel Hawkrerd
- 1614 – George Villiers meets James I - became his favorite.
- *1614 – Addled Parliament breakdowns under James I.*

- *1614 – John Napier publishes logarithms, revolutionizing mathematics and navigation.*
- *1614-19 – 2nd Earl of Warwick made a fortune plundering Spanish ships laden with gold/silver return from South America*
- 1616 Mar – Anthony Hawkrerd elected Alderman
- 1616 Sept – Death of Henry Clinton, 2nd Earl of Lincoln
- *1616 – Death of William Shakespeare.*
- 1617 May – Isaac Johnson BA from Emmanuel College
- 1617 May – William Blaxton BA from Emmanuel College
- 1618 Jan – Marriage of Atherton Hough to Elizabeth Bulkeley
- 1618 Feb – William Story becomes freeman
- 1618 Apr– Theophilus Clinton admitted to Queen's College
- 1618 July – Theophilus Clinton granted MA Queen's College
- 1618 July – Simon Bradstreet a sizar at Emmanuel College
- 1618 – George Villiers was created viscount, earl, marquess in succession beginning 1616
- *1618 – Thirty Years' War begins; deep impact on Protestant politics in England and New England.*
- 1619 Jan– Thomas Clinton dies & Theophilus Clinton becomes 4th Earl of Lincoln
- 1619 May- Sarah Hawkred married her father's apprentice, William Story
- 1619 May – Elizabeth, Dowager Countess of Lincoln, facilitates Patent for the Mayflower
- 1619 – Thomas Dudley became steward to 4th Earl of Lincoln
- 1619 – George Villers appointed Lord High Admiral by James I

TIMELINE

1620s

- 1620 Feb – 4th Earl of Lincoln admitted to Inns of Court at Gray's Inn
- 1620 July – Frances Clinton married John Gorges
- 1620 Nov – Charter granted to Great Council for New England by James I
- 1620 – Earl of Lincoln's peerage acknowledged by the House of Lords
- *1620 – Francis Bacon's Novum Organum outlines empirical scientific method*
- 1620 – John Billington, Boston, Lincs. sailed on Mayflower and signed Mayflower Compact
- *1620 – Mayflower sails; Plymouth Colony founded.*
- 1620 - George Villers married Katherine Manners, heiress to the Earl of Rutland and 2nd wealthiest lady in England after his mother created a scandal to force the match.
- 1621 Jan – 4th Earl of Lincoln attended his first session of Parliament
- 1621 Jan – Isaac Johnson admitted to the Inns of Court at Gray's Inn
- 1621 July – John Preston made chaplain to Prince Charles
- 1621 July– Simon Bradstreet awarded BA from Emmanuel College, Cambridge
- 1621 – John Humfrey married Elizabeth Pelham, sister of Herbert Pelham Jr.
- 1621 – Simon Bradstreet hired to assist Thomas Dudley
- 1622 Apr – Theophilus Clinton 4th Earl of Lincoln married Lady Bridget Fiennes
- 1622 May – John Preston becomes preacher at Lincoln's Inn
- 1622 July – Theophilus' mother dedicated her book on breastfeeding Lady Bridget
- 1622 Aug – (disgusted) Theophilus & Bridget Clinton relocated to Tattershall Castle

- 1622 Sept – Lord Saye & Sele imprisoned for 6 months
- 1622 Oct – John Preston made the Master of Emmanuel College, Cambridge
- 1623 Apr – Isaac Johnson and Lady Arbella Clinton married
- 1623 May 3 – Herbet Pelham's son, Anthony baptized - Boston, Lincs.
- 1623 Aug 7 – William Blaxton sailed with Robert Gorges to New England
- 1623 – George Villiers created Duke of Buckingham by James I
- 1623 – Dorchester Company obtained license for the Great Council for New England
- *1623 – First Folio of Shakespeare published.*
- 1624 Apr– Robert Gorges returned to England
- 1624 July – Herbert Pelham Sr. buried - Boston, Lincs.
- 1624 Aug – Thomas Dudley and family moved into Boston
- 1624 Aug – Simon Bradstreet became the steward for the Earl of Lincoln
- 1624 Nov – Earl of Lincoln asked to raise horse troops for Elector Palatine by James I
- *1625 Mar –James died and Charles I became the king (renewed conflict with Parliament)*
- 1625 July – Isaac Johnson inherited £2.5 million from his grandfather
- 1625 Sept – Theophilus Clinton sued his mother for custody of his siblings
- 1625 Sept – William Coddingham became *freeman* of Boston, Lincs
- 1625 Nov – Richard Bellingham elected *Recorder* of Boston, Lincs.
- 1625 – William Blaxton settled Shawmut Peninsula
- 1626 Jan – Isaac Johnson became a *freeman* of Boston, Lincs.
- 1626 Feb – York House Conference took place at Buckingham's house

TIMELINE

- 1626 Mar – John Davenport co-founded the *Feoffees for Impropriations*
- 1626 – Thomas Leverett elected alderman and served until 1632
- *1626 June – Charles I suspended Parliament*
- *1626 Sept – Charles I imposed Forced Loan*
- 1626 Oct – Earl of Lincoln & Boston Men refused to pay the Forced Loan
- 1626 Nov – Earl of Lincoln imprisoned in Tower of London
- 1626 Dec – Lady Bridget petitioned the crown to visit her husband in the Tower of London
- 1626 Dec – Dorchester Company declared bankruptcy
- 1627– Earl of Lincoln remained imprisoned in the Tower of London
- 1627 – Arrest warrants issued for the Boston Men
- 1627 Apr – John Humfrey witnessed the signing of Isaac Johnson's will in Boston, Lincs.
- 1627 May - John Humfrey's son, Jonathan, baptized in Boston, Lincs.
- 1627 fall – Simon Bradstreet hired as Dowager Countess of Warwick's steward
- 1627 fall – Thomas Dudley returned to Sempringham as steward for Earl of Lincoln
- 1628 Feb – Richard Bellingham elected to represent Boston, Lincs. in Parliament
- 1628 Mar – Earl of Warwick granted land to Dorchester Company remnants
- 1628 Mar – Earl of Lincoln released from Tower
- 1628 Mar – King's troops caused fire at Banbury - the Estate of Lord Saye & Sele
- 1628 Mar – Atherton Hough elected Mayor of Boston
- 1628 Apr – Richard Bellingham helped draft New England Company Charter
- 1628 Apr – New England Company established with 41 members & Matthew Craddock elected president

A TALE OF TWO BOSTONS

- 1628 May – Sarah Hawkred's 1st husband, William Story died leaving her widowed with daughter
- 1628 June – John Endecott led first MBC expedition to Salem MA
- *1628 June – Petition of Right affirms parliamentary liberties against royal prerogative.*
- 1628 July – John Preston died of tuberculosis
- 1628 Sept – Anne Dudley contracted smallpox
- 1628 Nov – Elizabeth (Pelham) Humfrey died in Dorchester
- 1628 Dec – Simon Bradstreet married Anne Dudley
- 1628 – George Villiers, Duke of Buckingham assassinated by John Felton at Portsmouth
- 1629 Mar– Boston Men invested in MBC (as recorded in MBC records)
- 1629 – Lord Saye & Sele, William Fiennes solicited the help of Robert Wolseley for approval of a Royal Charter for the Massachusetts Bay Company (*perhaps by the engagement of their children*).
- 1629 Mar – Massachusetts Bay Company granted a Royal Charter
- 1629 Mar – Charles I dissolved Parliament
- 1629 May – Samuel Skelton sailed to Salem MA
- 1629 July – John Winthrop attended Cambridge commencement to hear John White speak
- 1629 July – *Sempringham Meeting* takes place to discuss plans for New England
- 1629 Aug– The *Cambridge Agreement* signed
- 1629 Oct – Dudley & Winthrop attend their first MBC meeting
- 1629 Oct– Winthrop elected Governor of MBC
- 1629 Oct – Dudley & Isaac Johnson elected *Assistants*
- 1629 – Robert Gorges died in England.
- *1629 – Charles I dissolved Parliament; established his "Personal Rule".*

TIMELINE

1630s

- 1630 Mar – MBC relocated to Southampton
- 1630 Mar – Coddington & Bradstreet elected *Assistants* of MBC
- 1630 Mar – Dudley replaced Humfrey as Deputy Governor of MBC
- 1630 Mar – John Cotton preached a farewell sermon to Winthrop Fleet
- 1630 Apr – MBC ships departed Southampton for New England
- 1630 June – Arbella landed at Salem MA
- 1630 Jul - Lady Arbella Clinton died of scurvy in Salem
- 1630 Aug – MBC moved from Salem to Charlestown seeking fresh supply of water
- 1630 Sept – Blaxton invited MBC to Shawmut Peninsula where fresh water is plentiful
- 1630 Sept – John Wilson elected paster of the the 1st Church in Boston
- 1630 Sept - Isaac Johnson died in Boston
- 1630 Dec– John Humfrey likely married Lady Susan Clinton
- 1630 – John Billington tried and executed for the murder of John Newcomen, the colony's first execution.
- 1631 Jan- John Cotton and his beloved wife, Elizabeth, contract Fen Fever and convalesce at the Earl of Lincoln's Sempringham resilience.
- 1631 Apr – Cotton's wife, Elizabeth, succumbs and dies of the fever.
- 1631 – Roger Williams migrated to New England
- 1631- Coddingham's wife Mary died and he returnd to England and married Mary Moseley
- 1632 Apr – John Cotton married Sarah (Hawkred) Story
- 1633 Aug - William Laud named Archbishop of Canterbury
- *1633 – Galileo condemned by Inquisition; controversy closely followed in England.*

- 1633 May – Coddington returned from England with new wife and four servants.
- 1633 July – John Cotton flees prosecution and sails to Massachusetts with 52 parishioners on the Griffin
- 1633 – Anthony Tuckney succeeded John Cotton as vicar of Boston Lincs.
- 1633 Aug – Birth of Seaborn Cotton at sea on the Griffin
- 1634 – William Blaxton sold his land in Boston and established Providence Rhode Island
- 1634 – Anne Hutchinson sailed to Boston with 32 family and follower from Alford.
- 1634 - Richard Bellingham sailed to Boston and is elected a magistrate.
- 1634 – Atherton Hough became a freeman of MBC & elected ruling elder of Boston's church.
- 1634-49 – Thomas Leverett served as *Recorder* for MBC Boston MA
- 1635 – John Winthrop Jr. founded Sayebrook Colony in Connecticut
- 1635 – Roger Williams banished from the MBC
- 1635 Oct– Sir Henry Vane arrived in Boston MA
- 1636 – Sir Henry Vane elected governor of MBC
- 1636 Oct – with Vane as governor the General Court funded £400 for a New College
- 1636 – Hugh Peter became head of Salem Church
- 1636 – Roger Williams founded Providence Plantations (later Rhode Island)
- 1636 – John Harvard married Anne Sadler
- 1636 -Richard Mather migrated to MBC & supported Anne Hutchinson
- 1636 – Thomas Hooker headed the congregation that founded Hartford, Connecticut.
- 1637 – John Harvard emigrates to Massachusetts
- 1637 Nov – The new college ordered to be at the New Towne

TIMELINE

- 1637 Nov– Court appoints governors of the New College; Nathaniel Eaton appointed first master
- 1637– John Davenport arrived in Boston MA & participated in Antinomian Controversy
- 1637 – John Winthrop presided over the trial of Anne Hutchinson
- 1637 – Anne Hutchinson tried over Antinomian
- 1637 – Coddington leaves MBC for Rhode Island
- 1637 – Sir Henry Vane returns to England, heads Long Parliament
- 1637 – Prynne, Burton, Bastwick pilloried and branded as Laudian crackdown peaks.
- 1638– John Davenport established the New Haven Colony in Connecticut with Theophilus Eton
- 1638 – William Coddington signs the Portsmouth Compact and elected judge
- 1638 – Anne Hutchinson was subjected to a church trial, excommunicated and banished from Massachusetts.
- 1638 - Mary Dyer banished from MBC
- 1638 - Anne Hutchinson moved to Rhode Island and helped found Portsmouth,
- 1638 – Richard Mather banished from Boston & founded Exeter, New Hampshire
- 1638 May – MBC Court orders the New Towne renamed Cambridge and grants three acres for the New School.
- 1638 Sept – John Harvard died, wills half estate and library to the New College
- *1638 – Scottish National Covenant signed; Bishops' Wars imminent.*
- 1639 Mar – the New College was renamed Harvard College after John Harvard's bequest
- 1638 – Nathaniel Eaton begins teaching at the New School
- 1639 May – Coddington founded Newport, Rhode Island

A TALE OF TWO BOSTONS

- 1639 July – John Leverett admitted to 1st Church in Boston and married Hannah Hudson
- 1639 – John Leverett joined the Artillery Company MBC
- 1639 – Elizabeth Glover began the Cambridge Press and first printed *Oath of a Freeman*
- 1639 Sept – Nathaniel Eaton was censured for beating Nathaniel Briscoe with a cudgel by striking him over two hundred blows. Mrs. Eaton confessed to the ill and scant diet she served students, including skimpy portions of bad food. However, she denied any knowledge of *goat dung being added to their hasty pudding*

TIMELINE

1640s

- *1640 – William Laud imprisoned in the Tower by the Long Parliament.*
- 1640 - *Bay Psalm Book* was the first book printed in America
- 1640 –John Cotton Jr. born to John Cotton at age 55
- *1640 – Long Parliament convened in a major constitutional confrontation.*
- *1641 – Grand Remonstrance challenges royal authority*
- 1641 – Hugh Peter returned to England as an agent of MBC and became Parliament's preacher and army chaplain.
- 1641 Richard Bellingham elected governor and marries Penelope Pelham amid controversy.
- 1641 – Elzabeth Glover married Henry Dunster, 1st president of Harvard College
- 1642 Sept – First commencement at Harvard College, nine graduates
- 1642 Sept – Cotton delivers First Harvard commencement address
- 1642 – Maria Cotton born
- 1642 – Simon Bradsreet elected overseer of Harvard College
- *1642 – Civil War begins; Charles I raises standard at Nottingham*
- 1642 – 2nd Earl of Warwick, Robert Rich appointed Lord High Admiral by Parliament.
- 1643 – Anne Hutchinson and family massacred near Pelham Bay in New York
- 1643 – Atherton Hough died in Boston MA
- 1643 – Herbert Pelham appointed the first Treasurer of Harvard College
- 1643 Dec – John Cotton elected a governor of Harvard College
- *1644 – John Milton published Areopagitica; classic defense of free speech.*
- 1644 – 2nd Earl of Warwick granted Providence Plantations charter to Roger Williams.

A TALE OF TWO BOSTONS

- 1644 – John Endicott appointed Major Geneal of the Boston Militia
- 1644 Dec – Roland Cotton born
- 1644 – Bridget (Fiennes) Clinton, died
- 1644-45 John Leverett joined in the English Civil Wars with Parliamentarian Forces
- 1645 Jan– William Laud tried and beheaded by Parliament
- *1645 – New Model Army created; professional revolutionary army.*
- 1645 – Anthony Tuckney elected Master of Emmanuel College
- 1646 – Congregational ministers petition for a Synod that led to the Cambridge Platform
- *1647 – Levellers' movement emerged with radical democratic ideas.*
- 1647 – Ferdinando Gorges died in England
- 1647-49 – Coddington served as president of the United Colony of Providence Plantation, RI
- 1648 & 53 – Anthony Tuckney elected Vice-Chancellor of Cambridge University
- 1648 – Anne, youngest daughter of William Fiennes, Lord Saye & Sele) married Charles Wolsely, son of Robert Wolseley, who sealed the Massachusetts Bay Company's Royal Charter
- 1648 –Charles I surrendered his crown
- 1649 – John Winthrop died in Boston MA
- 1649 – John Winthrop Jr. elected governor of Connecticut
- *1649 –Charles I tried and executed by Parliament and the Commonwealth established*

1650s

- 1650 – Smallpox epidemic took Cotton's children, Sarah and Roland
- 1650 – Thomas Leverett died Boston MA
- 1650 – Thomas Dudley signed the Harvard College Charter

TIMELINE

- 1650 – Anne (Dudley) Bradstreet's *The Tenth Muse Lately Sprung Up in America* published in London
- 1651 – John Humfrey died in England
- 1651 – Seaborn Cotton graduated Harvard College
- 1651 – Coddington lost governorship when Parliament annulled Rhode Island charter
- *1651 – Navigation Acts establish mercantilist control over colonies.*
- 1652 Nov – John Cotton preached at Harvard and took ill
- *1652 – First Anglo-Dutch War begins; naval empire competition.*
- 1652 Dec – Death of John Cotton in Boston, MA
- 1653 Apr – Sir Henry Vane defied Cromwell's dissolution of Parliament
- *1653 – Cromwell's Protectorate established*
- 1653 – Thomas Dudley died in Roxbury, Massachusetts
- *1653 – Anthony Tuckney elected Master of* of St John's College, Cambridge University
- 1654 June– Seaborn Cotton married Dorothy Bradstreet
- 1654 – Anne Hibbins widowed and began dispute with neighbors
- 1654-57 – John Leverett was the Military Governor of Acadia & Nova Scotia
- *1655 – Jamaica seized from Spain; key imperial pivot*
- 1656 – Sarah (Hawkred/Story) Cotton remarried Richard Mather, daughter Maria's father-in-law
- *1656 – Quakers spread into Massachusetts; Mary Dyer becomes symbol of conscience.*
- 1656 – Anne Hibbins tried as a witch and hanged in Boston Common
- 1656 – Coddington agreed to reunited Colony of Rhode Island & Providence Plantations
- 1657 – Oliver Cromwell declined crown
- 1657 – John Cotton Jr. graduated Harvard
- 1658 – Hugh Peter delivered sermon at Cromwell's funeral.

- 1658 –Seaborn's wife Dorothy gave birth to son John
- 1658 – Death of 2nd Earl of Warwick at Felsted, Essex
- *1658 – Death of Cromwell; instability set the stage for the Restoration.*
- 1659 – Richard Cromwell resigned as Protector

1660s

- 1660 – Davenport sheltered regicides Whalley and Goffe in New Haven
- 1660 – John Cotton Jr. married Joanna Rossiter
- *1660 – Restoration of Charles II; monarchy and Church of England reinstated.*
- *1660 – Royal Society founded in London, institutionalizing modern science.*
- 1660 May – Mary Dyer executed on Boston Common
- 1660 Oct – Hugh Peter executed at Charing Cross, London
- 1662 Mar- Maria. John Cotton's daughter, married Increase Mather, son of Richard Mather
- 1662 June – Sir Henry Vane executed by beheading on Tower Hill, London.
- *1662 – Act of Uniformity; thousands of ministers ejected (Great Ejection).*
- 1662 – William Fiennes, Lord Saye & Sele died at Broughton Castle at age 79
- 1663 – John Leverett became the Major General of the Massachusetts Militia
- 1665 – John Endicott died Boston MA
- *1665 – Great Plague of London.*
- 1666 – Loss of house in Andover inspired Anne Bradstreet's poem *Upon the Burning of Our House*
- *1666 – Great Fire of London; major urban rebuilding under Wren.*

TIMELINE

- 1667 – Theophilus Clinton, 4th Earl of Lincoln, died at Charing Cross, London
- 1667 – John Wilson, pastor of the 1st Church of Boston, died
- 1667 – John Davenport elected pastor of the 1st Church of Boston
- 1667 – *Milton's Paradise Lost published.*

1670s

- *1670 – Treaty of Dover secretly aligns Charles II with Catholic France.*
- 1671 – John Leverett elected Deputy Governor of MBC
- 1672 – Coddington hosted George Fox at Newport and became a Quaker
- 1672 – Richard Bellingam died.
- *1672 – Stop of the Exchequer; financial crisis undermined the monarchy.*
- *1673 – Test Act; excluded Catholics from office.*
- 1673 – Death of Herbert Pelham, Cambridge MA
- 1674-78 – Coddington served as Governor of Rhode Island and Providence Plantations
- 1675 – William Blaxton died at Cumberland, Rhode Island
- *1675–76 – King Philip's War devastated New England.*
- 1675–78 – John Leverett fought led forces in King Philip's War
- 1676 – John Winthrop Jr. died in Boston, MA
- 1676 May – Death of Sarah (Hawkred/Storey/ Cotton) Mather at age 75
- 1677 – John Leverett purchased the Gorges claims in Maine
- 1678 – Death of Anne (Dudley) Bradstreet, Andover MA
- 1678 – William Coddington died at New Port RI at age 78
- 1679 – John Leverett died in office as governor & buried in King's Chapel Burying Ground
- 1679 – Simon Bradstreet elected governor.
- *1679–81 – Exclusion Crisis; Whigs and Tories form as parties.*

A TALE OF TWO BOSTONS

1680s

- 1683 – Roger Williams died in Providence, Rhode Island.
- *1685 – James II became king; Catholic monarch amid Protestant anxieties.*
- 1685 – Increase Mather became president of Harvard College
- *1686- Dominion of New England established.*
- *1687 – Newton's Principia Mathematica published & became foundation of modern science.*
- *1688/89 – Glorious Revolution; James II deposed, William & Mary crowned.*
- 1689 – Simon Bradstreet restored as governor
- 1689 – Increase Mather led a delegation to England to secure a new charter
- *1689 – Bill of Rights defines constitutional monarchy.*

1690s

- *1690 – Massachusetts issued first paper money in the Western world.*
- *1691 – Massachusetts Bay Company charter dissolved; Province of Massachusetts Bay established, and Simon Bradstreet's governorship ended.*
- 1692 – Salem Witch Trials; climax of New England religious anxiety.
- 1692 – Increase Mather put an end to the madness of the Salem Witch Trials

ABOUT THE AUTHOR

Barry Arthur Cotton is the 7th great-grandson of John Cotton and self-publishes his work to make it available in eBook, paperback, and hardcover formats, doing business as *Scéalta Sinsear*. (Irish for *Ancestors Stories*). He served as Winthrop Society Trustee for eight years, four of which he was president and national chairperson, and was named *President Emeritus* by the Winthrop Society in 2012. Barry's commitment to historical and genealogical writing extends beyond writing and publishing. He has been a trustee for the Partnership of the Historic Bostons. He is a member of several lineage and historical organizations, including the Colonial Society of Massachusetts, the Society of the Cincinnati, and the General Society of the Mayflower. In addition, Barry maintains two websites, which serve as a platform for sharing his knowledge and engaging with a broader audience. He contributed to *Boston: The Small Town with the Big Story* in 2019 and 2023 and has written for the *Winthrop Journal* and *Mayflower Quarterly*. In 2017, Barry was awarded First Place for Nonfiction in the 2017 Writers League of Texas Manuscript Contest.

A Tale of Two Bostons is the first book published by Barry and is Book One in the series titled: *New England Origins*.

THE NEW ENGLAND ORIGINS SERIES

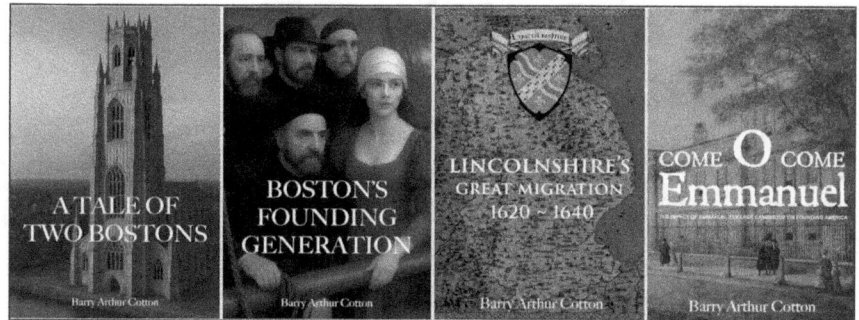

A series by Barry Arthur Cotton, founder of and publisher, under the imprint Scéalta Sinsear Heritage Press

The New England Origins investigates the English roots—geographic, intellectual, genealogical, religious, and political—that reshaped the Atlantic world in the first half of the seventeenth century. Through archival research, demographic reconstruction, and trans-Atlantic analysis, the series follows individuals whose decisions carried the Puritan project from England to New England. By integrating passenger lists, parish registers, kinship maps, wills, land records, and ship manifests, the series restores the human, institutional, and spiritual forces that defined New England for centuries and traces New England's formation back to:

- the market towns and manors of Lincolnshire, birthplace of a disproportionate share of New England's clergy, merchants, and founders;
- the dissenting ministries, grammar schools, and colleges of Cambridge, especially Emmanuel College;
- the corporate machinery of the Massachusetts Bay Company; and
- the families—gentry, artisans, merchants, servants—whose

migration transformed a small port town into the nucleus of a new Atlantic community.

VOLUME 1 — A TALE OF TWO BOSTONS: The Emergence of the Boston Men

This volume reconstructs the trans-Atlantic origins of Boston, Massachusetts by grounding the story in its English namesake: Boston, Lincolnshire. Drawing on the legal charters, parish registers, town records, and migration data represented throughout your Lincolnshire materials (e.g., Boston parish registers cited in *Lincolnshire's Great Migration*), the book identifies the individuals, families, and networks that developed into the governing elite known as the Boston Men.

It examines:

The corporate structuring behind the Massachusetts Bay Company, including the London merchants, Lincolnshire gentry, and Puritan clergy who shaped its political and financial framework.

The ministerial networks linking St. Botolph's and Boston's clerical culture to the religious vision carried into Massachusetts.

The early trans-Atlantic migration pipeline visible in the ship rosters and family movements (1620–1640) later expanded in Volume 3.

The emergence of a shared civic identity between English Boston and New England Boston — including naming, governance, and religious aspirations that defined the community from the start.

By following the men who bridged both Bostons—through sermons, charters, manuscripts, and town records — this volume reveals how a small Lincolnshire port gave birth to the ideological, religious, and political nucleus of New England.

THE NEW ENGLAND ORIGINS SERIES

VOLUME 2 — BOSTON'S FOUNDING GENERATION: Men & Women Who Built Boston MA

This volume profiles the first generation of New England's leadership, correlating their arrival records, ship rosters, and parish origins with the migration evidence contained in your demographic reconstructions (e.g., the appearances of Cotton, Hough, Leverett, Mellows, Bellingham, etc., in 1633–1634 datasets).

It offers a collective biography of the magistrates, ministers, clerics, gentry families, and dissenters who gave Massachusetts Bay its governing structure and religious character by weaving together personal narratives, institutional developments, and the demographic roots revealed in Volume 3, this volume shows how the Founding Generation translated English experience into American institutions. Core components include:

- John Cotton's arrival (Griffin, 1633) with his extended kin network, as documented across the multi-parish family tables.
- The Winthrop–Dudley axis, the political and theological tensions reflected in colony records and later summarized in *Come O Come Emmanuel*'s institutional chapters (MBC, Harvard).
- The social architecture formed by leading families: Bradstreet, Johnson, Saltonstall, Coddington, and others whose names thread through early church records and civic proceedings.
- The foundation and early governance of Harvard College, as outlined in Volume 4's educational chapters and tied back to Emmanuel-trained clergy.
- The construction of Puritan civic order — church covenants, discipline, magistracy, town governance, and norms of communal life.

A TALE OF TWO BOSTONS

VOLUME 3 — LINCOLNSHIRE'S GREAT MIGRATION, 1620–1640

This volume reconstructs the largest county-based migration stream into early Massachusetts, revealing why Lincolnshire—more than any other English county—supplied the clergy, merchants, magistrates, and family networks who defined Boston's early character.

Drawing on parish registers, wills, court papers, shipping manifests, and reconstructed migration tables (e.g., your year-by-year Boston-origin roster of the 1623 Gorges Expedition, the Bonaventura migrants of 1629, the Winthrop Fleet of 1630, the Griffin of 1633, Susan & Ellen of 1634, and later vessels), this volume establishes the demographic backbone of the New England Origins project.

Using reconstructed demographic tables, Volume 3 identifies more than a hundred individuals and families originating in the Boston–Wainfleet–Sempringham corridor whose migration shaped New England's population base. These include:

- Clergy networks: Cotton, Whiting, Wheelwright, Story
- Magistrate lines: Bellingham, Leverett, Pelham
- Merchant-adventurer families: Bradstreet, Johnson, Downing
- Farm and artisan households from Boston, Frampton, Horbling, Sempringham
- Servant migration patterns, such as Edward Doty and Edward Thomson
- Kin clusters visible on ships like the *Griffin*, *William and Francis*, and *Susan & Ellen*

A total 122 Boston-area migrants across these voyages, including 22 freemen, 28 families, 22 wives, 32 single women, 39 children, 16–19 servants.

Volume 3 documents the first complete Lincolnshire→Boston migration chronology spanning 1620–1641.

- the Mayflower (1620) precedents,
- the Gorges Expedition (1623) as the first formal Boston-area recruitment,
- the Bonaventura (1629) families (Skelton, Story),
- the transformative Winthrop Fleet (1630) — Bradstreet, Dudley, Coddington, Cheesborough, Woodward, Johnson, Fiennes, etc.,
- the Griffin (1633) — Cotton, Hough, Leverett, Mellows, Story, Chappell, Trewsdale, Pell, Ward, etc.,
- the Susan & Ellen (1634) — Bellingham-adjacent cluster, Cogswell, Dixon, Gunnison, etc.,
- the 1636 and 1638 Lincolnshire waves — Wheelwright, Bilsby, Whiting, Storre, Whittingham, Coye, Smith.

Volume 3 synthesizes:

- religious dissent (Puritan strongholds around Boston, Gainsborough, and Wainfleet),
- economic instability in fenland agriculture,
- patronage networks (Clinton, Fiennes, Rich, Gorges, Winthrop),
- common grammar school pathways (Boston Grammar School, Alford Free School),
- marriage and kinship strategies visible in your genealogical tables, and
- Emmanuel College ministerial recruitment (prefiguring Volume 4).

The result: Lincolnshire did not just participate in the migration — it helped engineer it.

VOLUME 4 — COME O COME EMMANUEL: The Impact of Emmanuel College, Cambridge on Founding America

Come O Come Emmanuel provides clear structural themes: Emmanuel's alumni networks, the migration statistics linking Lincolnshire to Massachusetts and the institutional chapters on the MBC and Harvard and documents how Emmanuel College, Cambridge became the intellectual and spiritual engine of early New England. Founded as a Puritan seminary, Emmanuel produced an extraordinary concentration of ministers, magistrates, administrators, and colonial architects whose influence shaped the Massachusetts Bay Colony more than any other institution in England. This volume traces:

- Emmanuel's theological program (Chaderton, Preston, Ward, Hooker), which trained clergy who later dominated Massachusetts pulpits.
- The Emmanuel-to-Massachusetts migration stream, visible in the passenger lists of the *Griffin* (Cotton, Hough, Leverett clusters), *Winthrop Fleet*, and associated ships.
- Cotton Mather's claim — "If New England hath been Immanuel's land, it is because Emmanuel College contributed more than a little to make it so" (p. 5) — grounding the volume's guiding thesis.
- Emmanuel's role in the founding of Harvard College, with many early tutors, presidents, and Fellows drawn from Emmanuel's ranks.
- The intellectual architecture of church polity, education, and governance that Emmanuel-trained leaders transplanted to New England.

www.ingramcontent.com/pod-product-compliance
Lightning Source LLC
Chambersburg PA
CBHW050157240426
43671CB00013B/2159